Becoming Noise Music

Becoming Noise Music

Style, Aesthetics and History

Stephen Graham

BLOOMSBURY ACADEMIC
Bloomsbury Publishing Inc
1385 Broadway, New York, NY 10018, USA
50 Bedford Square, London, WC1B 3DP, UK
29 Earlsfort Terrace, Dublin 2, Ireland

BLOOMSBURY, BLOOMSBURY ACADEMIC and the Diana logo are
trademarks of Bloomsbury Publishing Plc

First published in the United States of America 2023
This paperback edition published 2024

Copyright © Stephen Graham, 2023

For legal purposes the Acknowledgements on p. vi constitute an extension
of this copyright page.

Cover design: Louise Dugdale
Cover image © Oxygen/Getty Images.

All rights reserved. No part of this publication may be reproduced or
transmitted in any form or by any means, electronic or mechanical,
including photocopying, recording, or any information storage or retrieval
system, without prior permission in writing from the publishers.

Bloomsbury Publishing Inc does not have any control over, or responsibility for,
any third-party websites referred to or in this book. All internet addresses given in
this book were correct at the time of going to press. The author and publisher
regret any inconvenience caused if addresses have changed or sites have ceased
to exist, but can accept no responsibility for any such changes.

Whilst every effort has been made to locate copyright holders the publishers would be
grateful to hear from any person(s) not here acknowledged.

Library of Congress Cataloging-in-Publication Data
Names: Graham, Stephen (Musicologist) author.
Title: Becoming noise music : style, aesthetics, and history / Stephen Graham.
Description: New York : Bloomsbury Academic, 2023. | Includes bibliographical
references and index. | Summary: "The first book to focus exclusively and
comprehensively on the music of noise music, as opposed to contextual questions of politics,
history or sociology"– Provided by publisher.
Identifiers: LCCN 2022031370 (print) | LCCN 2022031371 (ebook) | ISBN 9781501378669
(hardback) | ISBN 9781501378706 (paperback) | ISBN 9781501378676
(epub) | ISBN 9781501378683 (pdf) | ISBN 9781501378690 (ebook other)
Subjects: LCSH: Noise music–History and criticism. | Noise rock
(Music)–History and criticism.
Classification: LCC ML3528.7 .G73 2023 (print) | LCC ML3528.7
(ebook) | DDC 781.6409–dc23/eng/20220831
LC record available at https://lccn.loc.gov/2022031370
LC ebook record available at https://lccn.loc.gov/2022031371

	ISBN:	
	HB:	978-1-5013-7866-9
	PB:	978-1-5013-7870-6
	ePDF:	978-1-5013-7868-3
	eBook:	978-1-5013-7867-6

Typeset by Integra Software Services Pvt. Ltd.

To find out more about our authors and books visit www.bloomsbury.com
and sign up for our newsletters.

Contents

Acknowledgements	vi
Preface	vii
Chapter Chronology	x
Noise Music Timeline	xi
Introduction: Becoming noise music?	1
Part 1 Noise music then	
1 Shouty and clangy credos: Power electronics and industrial music	23
2 Anti-music?	49
3 Global harsh power	69
4 Harsh noise in Japan	89
5 Harsh noise in the United States and Europe	107
Interlude: The story so far and to come	125
Part 2 Noise music now	
6 Harsh noise in the twenty-first century	129
7 Noise walls and atmospheric chambers	149
8 Noise erotics: Traumatic bodies and desires	167
9 Hybrid noisebloom Part One: Noise and …	189
10 Hybrid noisebloom Part Two: Noise music now	207
Conclusion	221
Bibliography	223
Index	232

Acknowledgements

Thanks first and foremost to the countless noise musicians, fans, critics, promoters, label heads, and many others whose boundless enthusiasm for noise music makes the scene what it is. Many, most, give a lot of their energy to noise without any financial reward or recognition. It's a cliché but noise is a labour of love; and there's a lot of love, as can be seen in the amount of information, criticism, and appreciation that's out there in zines, forums, databases, label pages, and so on. And in the overwhelming amount of noise that gets made. Kudos to all.

Particular thanks from me are due to the folks at *Noisextra* and Roman Leyva at *Harsh Truths*, to Richard Stevenson at *Noise Receptor*, to Jennifer Wallis and everyone involved with *Fight Your Own War*, to Seymour Glass and *Bananafish*, to *The Wire*, to *Discogs* (!), to *Special Interests*, to everyone who has ever uploaded a rare noise album to YouTube, and finally to all the noise musicians written about in the pages that follow. I don't know many of you personally, but this book would simply not have been possible without you and what you do. I also don't know the blind reviewers of my book, but much thanks to them, too, for their helpful comments and feedback, which (hopefully) deepened my arguments and sharpened my structures.

Thanks above all to my family, for everything.

Preface

I wrote this book because of an invitation to a podcast, and a hunch. In May 2020, my friend Deb Grant asked me to record a piece for her podcast, *What Goes Around*, describing why I liked noise music. Intended for a general audience of non-noise listeners, the piece required me to find a simple and direct way to talk about noise music. When Deb made her request, I'd recently been inspired by another podcast, *Noisextra*, to reengage with noise after a little lull. So, I had a hunch I'd have a lot to say. But I wasn't quite sure what that would be.

I thought about Deb's request as I prepared to record. I listened to favourite noise albums by Richard Ramirez and Merzbow and, in addition to inevitable surface impressions of loudness and intensity, words like 'unfinished', 'flow', 'emerging', 'process', 'conflict', and 'unresolved' came to my mind. Thinking both on this and also of favourite texts on noise by writers like Paul Hegarty (2007) and Greg Hainge (2013), I realized that what kept me coming back to noise was its emphasis on a kind of unresolved, relational, quasi-dialectical ('quasi' because of the fundamental irresolution of the process) *movement* and *tension*; on what I came to describe summarily as 'becoming'.

'Becoming' is a term of my own that nevertheless builds on similar inflections in Hainge and, in turn, the 'becoming', 'flow' and 'deterritorialization' of Deleuze and Guattari (2013; Rockefeller 2011). Hainge, for his part, uses 'becoming' in passing to describe noise's embodiment and even expression of what he describes as a universal 'relational ontology', an ontology that is based on an omnipresent, vibratory interaction of material and/or conceptual bodies, and that 'according to which the world comes to pass' (14, and 1). 'Becoming', in my usage, builds on Hainge's sense of noise's vibratory interactionism (and vice versa) but narrows focus from ontology (which includes aesthetics, in Hainge's understanding) to aesthetics (not quite including ontology, in mine). 'Becoming', in this sense, gestures at the noisiness of cosmic interactions and relations but transmutes these into an artistic and, as we'll see, psychological register.

'Becoming' therefore describes noise music's perennial sonic movement, tussle, and drift: its seeming, or (crucially, for me) partial resistance towards what Hainge describes as the sense of 'transcendental order' and 'internal necessity' that tends to be created by normative codes of western 'musicality' tied to things like standardized tonal, formal and rhythmic principles (262). Where such musicality deploys generic conventions to signify internal order, noise seems actively to resist such ordering conventions; at least it does according to Hainge, Hegarty and many others, from Jiří Kubíček (2020, 39) to Pauline Nadrigny and Catherine Guesde (2018, 9). As suggested by my 'partial' qualification just now, this is a view that I both partly endorse and also want to complicate. After all, unlike Hainge and the others, for me noise music clearly holds in tension and even reconciles apparent poles of musicality and 'noise'.

'Becoming', for me, therefore describes a suspended dialectical tension between musicality and noise resistance, not an antimony between them. And here we're close to Deleuze's Nietzschean notion of becoming, where becoming is, according to Rosi Braidotti, 'neither the dynamic confrontation of opposites, nor the unfolding of an essence in a teleologically ordained process leading to a synthesizing of identity'. It is, instead, an 'affirmation of the positivity of difference, meant as a multiple and constant process of transformation'; 'a flux of multiple becoming' (1993, 44).

To expand on the point of supposed noise becoming for a moment, and to give authors such as Hainge their due, it's true that noise artists from Merzbow and Ramirez to Ramleh, Moonbeam Terror, and many others do indeed largely play in the movement and instability that many other western musics leverage towards climactic, cathartic resolution. This lines up with typical characterizations of noise as an essentially aformal, amusical style; with its supposed 'irreducibility to identifiable forms', to quote Nadrigny and Guesde quoting Hegarty (2018, 8). And yet, it's also true that brief or sustained loops or regular pulsing, passing allusions to established styles, legible shapes and structures, and distinct 'musical' gestures and sound sources all regularly appear in noise. Quite a bit of noise music even works with stable rhythmic grids and discrete melodic motifs. As we'll see throughout the book, form, shape, and sign abound! Whether it's my own biases as a meaning- and structure-finding musicologist or not, I therefore can't help but hear 'music', and, in Hainge's sense, 'musicality', almost everywhere in noise. This is not, of course, to collapse noise completely into other forms. There *is* a difference between noise and other musics; noise never quite fully settles, stabilizes, or resolves, preferring to hunker down in mid-process or flow or simply to explode processes before they resolve. Moreover, noise certainly operates across a spectrum: for every steady, churning industrial beat in power electronics we can find seemingly aperiodic, amelodic, frequency saturation and textural chaos in harsh noise. But the difference between noise and other musics, I suggest, is simply one of degree, not necessarily of kind.

Noise music, then, holds musicality and noise resistance in productive tension, rather than abjuring the former in favour of the latter. This perennial and productive dialectical tension (not opposition) is music-stylistically and aesthetically compelling. But, just as importantly – even if perhaps less straightforwardly – it is also compelling on a personal, psychological level. As I listen to noise *becoming* I sometimes find my sense of self loosening, my conscious experience sliding into something that is not quite verbally and cognitively clear cut. In these situations, I enter a kind of psychedelic, transpersonal experience, merging into something larger and less bounded; many others, as we'll see, have said similar things about the meditative, immersive aspect of listening to noise. This psychological 'becoming' is harder to parse than music-stylistic becoming. But both are important aspects of how noise operates and, ultimately, how it can affect its listeners.

I ended up saying as much on *What Goes Around*: I like noise music because it offers listeners a chance to immerse into a particularly vivid form of musical and – if you're lucky and/or in the right frame of mind – psychological becoming. Other musics offer similar experiences to their listeners but, I argued, the particularly loud volumes, fractured and somewhat unpredictable shapes and sounds, and intense emotions of noise mean that it may well have a special claim on these different registers of becoming.

These ideas stayed with me. I started to think in a more structured way about how other authors had said similar things about noise, had attempted to grapple with its complex relation to musical norms and codes. We've already heard about Hainge's sense of noise's relation to 'musicality', but we'll also, for example, hear Hegarty in Chapter 4 commenting on the 'seaming of layers' in Merzbow and the 'permanent suspense' of Hijokaidan (2007, 159; 2012, 20), and from authors such as S. Alexander Reed (2013) and the aforementioned Pauline Nadrigny and Catherine Guesde on related subjects. But I realized that none of those authors had articulated the stylistic and subjective angles in the same way I had, particularly in terms of what I saw as noise's distinctive dialectic of musical norms and idiosyncrasies. More to the point, as my interpretation was so focused on noise aesthetics rather than on the more common contemplation of its politics, or its scene dynamics, or its import for philosophy or cosmology, I realized that a certain stylistic or aesthetic depth had sometimes been neglected in those sources. Finally, for related reasons, I saw that the particular range of noise I was interested in had not received the dedicated scholarly or critical attention it might have. Noise music, then, had been somewhat neglected as both aesthetic style and genre story (where 'genre' refers to a socially grounded, rule-defined 'unit of meaning' or 'cultural unit': 'something which a culture has defined as a distinctive unit, different from others'; Eco 1977, 74; Fabbri 1982, 134).

I started to plan a book – this book – that would answer that double neglect with an in-depth focus on noise style and aesthetic interpretation on the one hand, and a dedicated concentration on the genre of noise music on the other. By virtue of this dual focus on noise style and genre, the book would describe the (hi)story of noise music's development over the past fifty or so years. This would therefore add a second layer of 'becoming' to the musical and psychological becoming already discussed. That is, the story of how the genre of noise itself 'became'; how it developed from its origins in the late 1970s and 1980s, through its 'classic' 1990s period, and into hybrid twenty-first-century fringe music contexts. *Becoming Noise Music* therefore doubles up on becoming: it is about both the becoming it identifies *in* and the larger, genre-making process of the becoming *of*, noise music. It says a lot about the sound and the style of noise, and, in so doing, arrives at a version of the story of noise that, whilst not definitive, is wide-ranging and deep in the set of sounds, cast of characters, and range of ideas with which it engages.

Chapter Chronology

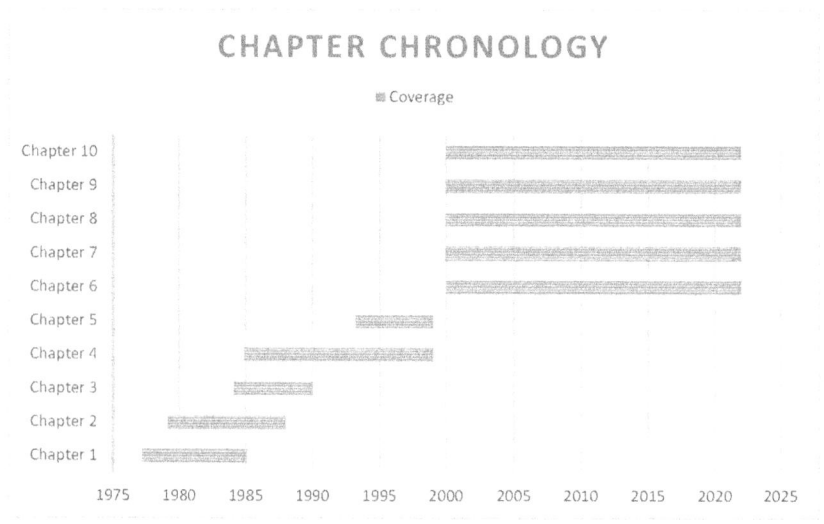

Figure p.1 Chapter chronology summarizing the main chronological focus of each chapter.

Noise Music Timeline

**Pre-History
1960s**
⬇

Free jazz and free improv, electronic music and post-war composition, experimental rock

**Emergent Noise
1970s**
⬇

Los Angeles Free Music Society, punk and post-punk, industrial music, early power electronics

**Early Noise
1980s**
⬇

Power electronics, industrial, Japanese noise, noise rock
guitar and synth-based

**Classic Noise
1990s**
⬇

Harsh noise, death industrial and dark ambient, power electronics
Feedback loops, pedals and filters, synths, contact mics, junk metal

**Contemporary Noise
2000s–present**

Harsh noise, harsh noise wall, hybrids
DAWs, and 1990s tools

Introduction: Becoming noise music?

I'll start by deconstructing my title, *Becoming Noise Music: Style, Aesthetics and History*. 'Becoming' is meant in two distinct senses, as I unpacked in the Preface. One, the book is based on a stylistic and aesthetic idea of 'becoming', where noise music hovers at the border between 'musical' order and 'noise' disorder, legible language and illegible speech, treating these different elements as coextensive dialectical antagonists rather than mutually opposing or cancelling opposites. This stylistic and aesthetic flickering into and out of stable sound can, in turn, create a corresponding sense of psychological flickering into and out of stable self. Two, the book tells the story of how noise music – a wide and varied genre whose roots stretch back through styles like power electronics, industrial, and free jazz and through cultures defined in part by a general late century, post-industrial malaise – grew from these roots to become noise music proper in the late 1980s and 1990s. And then, later, evolved and integrated into the broader twenty-first-century fringe music scene. How noise music 'became' noise music. Taken together, these two senses of 'becoming' account for the 'style, aesthetics and history' subtitle. After all, questions of style and aesthetic – where 'style' refers to repeated patterns of artistic 'language' (see Meyer 1989), and 'aesthetic', a complicated term at the best of times, to artistic content and form and theories of the same – underlie the first sense of becoming, whilst history underlies the second, the 'story' of the noise genre. 'Noise music', the only remaining phrase from the title, similarly unlocks foundational aspects of the book. There are two layers to 'noise music', the first related to genre and the second to dialectics. First, genre; and, by way of which, a brief literature review.

Only a small number of previous publications focus entirely on the genre of noise in the manner of this book. Some provide rich, interdisciplinary ethnographies of different social, musical, and cultural aspects of noise or of different noise scenes, as for example with Sarah Benhaïm's work on the DIY social practices and musical aesthetics of noise (2018 and 2019) and David Novak's study of the Japanese scene (2013). Many others mix the genre of noise with other forms of music, and/or with broader concepts or contexts. I have done this (2016). Writers such as Douglas Kahn (1999), (as we've seen) Greg Hainge (2013), and Marie Thompson (2017) have, for their part, weighted the scales somewhat towards concept over genre or style. And even specialists like Paul Hegarty tend to approach noise as both genre/aesthetic *and* theoretical proposition (e.g. 2007 and 2020).

Some sources, by contrast, have focused fairly exclusively on noise sound and style. Aarons Cassidy and Einbond's *Noise in and as Music* (2013), for example, comes close to my own concentration on noise style, gathering a variety of perspectives on noise as musical material and ultimately building these into a valuable extended study on the aesthetics of noise writ large. And yet, the book's genre scope is broad and wide: its chapters extend across a range of different musics, straying relatively far from what noise fans would recognize as 'noise'. *Noise in and as Music* indeed betrays a particular orientation towards contemporary composition; a point that's perhaps unsurprising, given the fact that its editors and many of its contributors are experimental composers. As Cassidy and Einbond state, 'our aim was to engage current practitioners, to expose a cross-section of the current motivations, activities, thoughts, and reflections of composers, performers, and artists who work with noise in all of its many forms' (2013, xv). Moreover, to underline another difference, the methods employed in *Noise in and as Music* tend to be generalist and descriptive rather than technical and analytical; the artist interviews that supplement each chapter are a useful illustration of this tendency.

A similar methodological approach is found in the book that is perhaps closest in spirit to the current one, Pauline Nadrigny and Catherine Guesde's *The Most Beautiful Ugly Sound in the World: À l'écoute de la noise* (2018). Focusing, as indicated by its subtitle, on the process of *listening* to noise, the book's stylistic purview aligns largely with my own, with artists such as The Haters' GX Jupiter-Larsen, Merzbow, C.C.C.C, Vomir, and many others mentioned in passing, or in depth, or interviewed. Where a contrast arises is in that focus on listening: though *The Most Beautiful Ugly Sound in the World* includes much reflection on the sound and style, and indeed on the generic limits, of noise, at its heart it provides a philosophically driven, ethnographically informed phenomenology of noise listening and, through this, noise aesthetics. As the authors themselves state in their Preface, referring back to the anecdote with which they started the book of a frustrated noise fan complaining about what they saw as the limited frequency range and timbral span of a baroque flute performance,

> our anecdote invited us to explore another way of accessing noise: that of listening. So, the question is not only 'how do we listen to noise?', but, 'is there a noise listening?' And, if so, how does it listen not only to what we would call noise but also … baroque flutes? Is it then possible that, in this listening, something original plays out in the connection of planes that theories and artistic currents have always expressed: planes of the acoustic, physiological and aesthetic?
>
> (2018, 8–9, translation my own)

Nadrigny and Guesde therefore focus on noise aesthetics via a physically grounded conception of listening. This focus is enriched by critical reflections grounded in questionnaires shared with attendees at Sonic Protest and with listeners and fans by the Angström records label and the artist Matthieu Saladin, and in interviews with artists such as Jupiter-Larsen. In all these ways – the music-analytical depth, the narrative range, and the methodological approach – *The Most Beautiful Ugly Sound in the World* contrasts with the current book. As we'll see at various points, Nadrigny and Guesde's approach yields much insight into both the aesthetics of noise and the listening body and mind that experience that noise, insights germane to my analysis. But, as with the other sources mentioned in this brief review, the spirit and scope of their book are ultimately very different to my own.

Second, the 'noise music' points about dialectics. Headlining *noise music* in my title, as opposed to the more widely applicable and manipulable 'noise' (a term I do use as shorthand for the genre – a distinction that should be clear in context), clearly signals my focus on noise music as distinct genre, style, and aesthetic. 'Noise music', in this way, seeds some of the central arguments of the book. It brings together noise, understood as a metaphor for disorder, and music, understood as a metaphor for ordered language, arguing that the genre of noise music is built on a deliberate, almost-nuclear-like unresolved, multiply dynamic and quasi-dialectical fusion of what might appear to be noise/music polarities. In reality, my argument is that no such polarity exists, at least in the wilds of sound and experience (the opposition obviously holds in culture and history): noise is always musical, always expresses conventional form, structure, and sense, even as it charges these with uncertainty and instability. Noise is music is noise.

This is something of a polemical point, as we've already started to see. Some authors have sought to delineate clearly between 'noise' and 'music', either directly or, in the manner of Hainge's 'musicality', indirectly. Paul Hegarty, for example, suggests that 'noise' is what 'occurs in the place of music' (2020, 73). Elsewhere, Hegarty describes noise as a loud, overwhelming, and seemingly spontaneous 'erotic' space of conceptual flickers and border conditions, where there is a kind of 'shutting down of structuring musicality in the form of a more unconscious expression' (2013, 139). Speaking about Japanese noise music in particular, Hegarty suggests that its variegated styles can be seen to ask what he calls the 'question of genre – what does it mean to be categorized, categorizable, definable?' (2007, 133). Picking on that same point of categorization, Sarah Benhaïm considers the widespread resistance both to categorization itself and to the category of music amongst noise musicians, commentators, and others:

> Leaning into noise as a genre already reminds the researcher to expose themself to a multitude of resistances. On the one hand, a resistance towards describing the musical material, to delimiting its stylistic contours and to analysing it, a resistance that aims in short to delimit the object itself, to attach a definition to it and to understand it as category … Noise embodies what is neither melodic nor harmonious. It is by its own properties, by its own action, if not simply by its own presence that it disturbs conventional rules and codes of music and even categorizations.
>
> (2018, 11 and 67, translation my own)

Meanwhile, speaking about the clear value of analysing noise in the manner of 'traditional' music analysis, Kubíček nevertheless asks whether it is 'desirable to try to "settle" noise music, to attempt to grasp it as music', in this kind of way (2020, 36).

For him, noise resists and eludes such ordering, 'musicalizing' analysis, whereas I don't think 'we' – those of us more or less schooled in western musical conventions, and perhaps in modes of 'structural' listening – have a choice in grasping noise as music. How could it not, itself, settle into (often conventional) hierarchies of pattern, shape, and tone?

S. Alexander Reed, for his part and finally, decries the idea of noise-as-music, at least viewed from the traditional perspective of assimilation and 'selling out':

> If industrial music's goal is to stake out extremes, then it's important that noise remain noise, both as metaphor and as a perceived sound, resisting assimilation into order, beauty and 'music'. *Noise as music* gains access to cultural and economic legitimacy, fosters traditions and tropes, and can aspire to pleasure as a primary aim, but in exchange it forswears a certain absoluteness of autonomy and a positive to critique music from the outside.
>
> (2013, 306)

However, even Reed himself ultimately goes against this point, arguing that assimilation is a necessary goal: 'The potency of the pan-revolutionary against the control machines depends on contact between the two; noise can only redefine music when the two touch' (313–14). (The two are always touching!) Though Reed is speaking in political terms here, his point – that noise and music must and indeed do 'touch' in their passage to meaning – resonates. The tension between the two is the power source. Hence, again, *noise music*.

My title, as a whole, therefore provides a compact picture of the book's subject, arguments, and approach. The rest of the Introduction fleshes these out in more detail. The next two sections develop each layer of the book's primary interpretative argument of 'becoming': style/language and then psychology. The third section offers more detail on the other aspect of the titular becoming, the 'story' of noise. The final two sections discuss the book's method and structure, respectively.

Becoming style (and language)

> With AMK's stuff, it gives you an 'in' because you have that pattern building that you can do, and it sort of retrains you and puts new grooves in your head … You know, I can hear structures being built; I always say noise is like a new language being built every night.
>
> (Chris Sienko in Connelly et al. 2020b)

The emphasis on stylistic becoming I've been exploring, where noise movement and irresolution hold in tension apparent poles of musicality and 'noise', plays out in different ways in different examples. Whilst the rest of the book is taken up with exploring this point, I offer here an initial series of brief but illustrative musical examples as a way of getting closer to the *feel* of noise music's stylistic becoming. I close this section by comparing noise music 'becoming' to other forms of musical becoming, through this describing noise style in more detail.

A lot of harsh noise – a central category in noise that I explore across three chapters later in the book – tends towards the kind of dense, manic, and unpredictable sound that might seem to align more with the kind of noise 'resistance' discussed by Benhaïm than the hybrid noise/music dialectic at the core of my interpretation. To wit, the immersive sound mayhem of C.C.C.C.'s *Chaos Is the Cosmos* (Cold Spring, 2007), or of Hijokaidan and Borbetomagus' live collaboration *Both Noises End Burning* (Les Disques Victo, 2007), may appear at first listen to be without order, form or syntax. But on closer examination, these albums reveal nuances of language and flow that pull the listener into a kind of drama of dialectical becoming. Though much of *Chaos Is the Cosmos* consists of dense sheets of messy synth noise slowly modulating in profile and interrelation, for example, distinct gestures emerge from the tumult at various points. A distorted, high-register bass guitar line, to cite just one notable moment, coils out intermittently from 2'18", like a strangled snake gasping for air. The individuated nature of the bass in this example – at least as compared to the relatively undifferentiated sounds around it – suggests defined action and individualistic intent within a dense storm of sound. This pulls me into the action as a kind of unfolding drama, articulating distinction, idiomatic contrast, and therefore narrative flow where otherwise we might only hear undifferentiated noise.

And yet, 'only' here isn't quite right, since 'undifferentiated' noise yields a powerful impression of becoming too. To take an apropos example, French artist Vomir's music, which is based on apparently 'unchanging' walls of static noise – 'no ideas, no changes, no development, no entertainment, and no remorse', goes his noise wall manifesto (Vomir 2017) – expresses musical order and form the more you listen. An album like *Proanomie* (At War with False Noise, 2009), for instance, can be heard as a 76-minute unspooling web of subtle psychoacoustic patterns of rise and fall, and revolving figure and ground, where small pockets of defined textural change or distinct motifs or gestures emerge to the listening. The album's bulldozing, largely mid-range static and white noise therefore yields order and form: as we'll see especially in Chapter 7, even single-minded harsh noise wall aligns closely with the imperatives of musical and psychological narrative. How could it not? Vomir himself acknowledges as much:

> I understand that people can hear very different sounds and effects in my work, but that depends on the ear and the brain of each individual listener as to what they get out of it. The human body finds continuous noises difficult to process so repeatedly looks for 'hooks' or familiar noises in noise walls. Also, our own pre-existing ideas also create images that are responsible for such ghost or phantom noises – that's where these things come from, not me.
>
> (Williams 2014)

The same tarrying of the familiar and unfamiliar, order and disorder, is found in other examples and forms of noise. For example, shifting idiomatic registers in artists like Facialmess and Merzbow invite the listener to find their way within a dramatic, varied musical discourse. The latter artist's 'Woodpecker No. 1', from the aptly titled *Pulse Demon* (Release, 1996), is a good illustration of this, with both sequential and simultaneous contrasts between a pile-driving industrial techno pulse and fuzzed-out, high-pitched static creating exciting but unresolved stylistic and dialectical tension. Indeed, as we'll see later in the book, Merzbow's coruscating harsh noise often shades into propulsive, broken-beat patterns in this kind of way. The group Sonar's music does something similar, with its admixtures of jagged, torn beats and various noise and industrial tropes, whilst Whitehouse's William Bennett's later project, Cut Hands, has been built around a techno-noise adaptation of African and Haitian vaudou rhythms.

As we can see even in these quick initial examples, noise music's stylistic becoming is therefore varied, mostly pivoting on different versions of a meta-stylistic dialectic of order and disorder but at other times exploring what we might call a more applied dialectic of style or idiom. However, it's important to acknowledge a wider point; that is, that all musics express some sense of 'becoming', some dialectical conflict between the appearance of order and disorder, the familiar and the unfamiliar, language and chaos. This section closes by comparing other forms of musical becoming to noise, ultimately establishing in more detail the way in which noise becomes, and how noise styles, as a result.

Even the most formulaic, repetitious music evokes becoming – either in the Deleuzian or in a more general sense – simply by virtue of existing and unfolding in time. However, some musical traditions elevate a kind of becoming to the level of credo. The organicist principle of western art music and its later derivation, 'developing variation' (Frisch 1982), are good illustrations of this: the motivic interrelatedness and variability of works like Beethoven's fifth symphony, Schubert's Wanderer Fantasy, and Brahms' F-major Cello Sonata Op. 99 indeed create a sense of progressive, even teleological momentum that we could understand as a form of becoming (albeit not in the Deleuzian sense, with its anti-Hegelian rejection of teleology). In comparison to this art-musical organicist becoming, noise can be said to radicalize 'becoming', shifting it from an internal idiomatic concern or a teleological evocation of destination into a situation in which the ordered status of the music itself is in question, and the destination almost never arrives. Where common-practice western art music deals in a grammar of becoming and become, noise music instead bases itself on a kind of deferred becoming of grammar (or language). Common-practice art music, for the most part, speaks in a stable language where conflict and disagreement serve a higher synthesis and order, whereas dynamic, unresolved conflict and disagreement are the higher order in noise.

This kind of approach is idiosyncratic but not entirely unique to noise; other stylistically 'radical' musics can be seen to be doing something similar. For example, modernist composers like Debussy and Schoenberg built some of their more challenging music on a similar mix of order and disorder, on a disruption of conventional musical language. Such music, particularly when we get later into the twentieth century with composers like Boulez and Stockhausen, could even be said to be organized around a search for an organizing principle or language structure.

Seth Brodsky has indeed written about musical modernism's neurotic search for 'a new musical language', which 'would be founded out of the failed attempt to find or re-find music's language'. This new musical language 'would stage repeatedly music's inability to secure the grounds of its own language' (2018, 181). Modernist music, in this understanding, neurotically but productively represses what its repeated failure to generate a stable ground of language reveals: that normative musical languages are always already fantasies made temporarily stable through habit (and here's the other side of my noise/music suspended dialectic: noise isn't just always musical, but music is always noisy). Modernism makes great hay out of this failure.

Noise music reflects modernist neurosis in its continual questioning of the ground of stable musical language. Both noise and modernist composition indeed exist in a kind of shared interstice between stable and unstable language, perhaps aspiring to the former but, in their refusal to accept the fantasy of a mastering language, necessarily lapsing into the latter. Nadrigny and Guesde draw a similar parallel in *The Most Beautiful Ugly Sound in the World*, discussing how in both noise and avant-garde music from the likes of John Cage it is mostly 'impossible' for listeners to settle into the work 'in a linear fashion', for example rejoicing when expectations may be met and being surprised when they are not (2018, 9).

And yet, for both myself and Nadrigny and Guesde, noise pushes these tendencies towards surprise and novelty to an unprecedented extreme. This is such that, for Nadrigny and Guesde, noise music seems to 'do everything' it can – ranging from active interference to chance and accident – 'to disconcert [its listener] or even divert them from the work and the possibility of its structure', ultimately forcing them 'to rethink [their] listening strategies' (10). Noise and modernist composition share a lot of common ground, then, but ultimately diverge in their approach and orientation. Modernism leans towards the neurotic whereas noise is probably closer to the psychotic, given its continual rejection of any stable ground of language and its active resistance towards structure.

An even more germane – and final – comparator is free improv, the 'spontaneous', fringe style of music derived from free jazz, experimental composition, and other forms that emerged in Europe, Japan, and elsewhere in the late 1950s and 1960s (Graham 2016 provides a more detailed history of the style). Ben Watson suggests that free improv is based on what he calls an 'intensely subjectivist' rendering of sounds, which are 'worked on by the musicians in real time' (2004, 374). For Watson, this focus on moment-to-moment 'concrete utterances', which, theoretically at least, emerge from a shared and communal non-hierarchical praxis, represents 'life lived as a dialectical contribution to human history'. Improv is, in this sense, 'as exhilarating and cold-to-breathe as the revolutionary idea itself' (2004, 377). Though the socialist, Marxist frame Watson hangs around free improv won't be to everyone's taste, his contention that the best examples of improv are based on a constantly worked, forming and reforming dialectic has obvious resonance and rightness. After all, across many famous examples and musicians, from Derek Bailey with Han Bennink and Evan Parker on *Topography of the Lungs* (Incus, 1970) to any number of more recent performances, the expressive power of the music seems clearly to reside in its search for, and in some case distance from, language. Bailey's much cited (and much misunderstood and/or criticized) 'non-idiomatic' label for free improv has stuck because it captures something important about how the music tends to float free of clear idiomatic signification, even if he and others recognized the music's potential for stylization (see Graham 2016, 22).

We can therefore identify a clear alliance between noise and improv. Both are foundationally concerned with the real-time emergence of what we can call language. However, I would argue that there is ultimately a clear difference between the two. In free improv I invariably hear a search for order and stability, for example, a search that often culminates in some form of agreement between the players (where it is not a solo performance), whether in the form of rhythmic alignment, or dynamic collusion or clear divisions and even hierarchies of labour within the musical texture. Not in all improv, and not even for the bulk of most improv performances; the search is, admittedly, often the thing. I also hasten to add that, since a lot of noise, at least in a live setting, is based on some level of improvisation, drawing a clear line between the two is dangerous. Nevertheless, I would ultimately argue that most noise simply doesn't aim for or achieve the same level of harmony, control, and order – the same language agreement, and to some extent the same notion of rise-and-fall and climax or destination – that is often arrived at in free improv. Noise so emphasizes both disorder itself, and the holding in tension of order and disorder more generally, that it is marked out even from improv.

These various comparisons between noise and other musics have underlined noise's particularly intense relationship to order, structure, and style. In closing, it's worth thinking further about both this relationship and noise's particular stylistic character. Noise's style and its relationship to order and structure are expressed most directly in its typical sound and shape, that is, its inveterate amelodicism, aperiodicism, inharmonicity, and aformalism. (Hainge makes a similar point at the start of his attempts to define 'noise': 'for the physicist', he points out, 'noise can be defined as a non-periodic complex sound, in other words, a sound that can be decomposed into a large number of sound waves all of different frequencies that [according to Fourier's theorem] are not multiples of one basic frequency and which do not therefore enter into harmonic relations with each other'; 2014, 3.) This is key; it's in the prevalence of these 'a' and 'in' qualities that any becoming-noise-exceptionalism is finally justified. After all, no other music so resolutely avoids or defers melody, periodic rhythm, regular harmony (and harmonic spectra), and clear or conventional form and texture. In largely avoiding such features, or drawing on them only in passing, unconventionally or in a complex way, noise suspends resolution, rest, stability, and other similar qualities that are invariably expressed in other musics. Like those other musics, noise suggests movement and conflict – suggests a process of becoming – but unlike most of them, it almost never resolves that becoming, preferring to sit with a kind of dynamic uncertainty, instability, and irresolution, in which moments of musicality and form emerge only to move continuously into other significations or sounds. Hence, becoming noise music.

Becoming self (or self-less)

The second layer of the book's interpretative argument relates closely to the first. As explored in the Preface and as mentioned at the outset of this chapter, it suggests that music-stylistic becoming can inspire listeners' own psychological experiences of 'becoming', where becoming is once again being used summarily; to account, in this case, for either heavy or light feelings of self-in-process, or 'emerging' self or self-loss. Listeners can, in this way, be moved beyond the rational in listening to noise music, flickering between and across ego and non-ego states, 'becoming' a different version of themselves or losing a familiar sense of themselves completely (if temporarily). I should note here that, primarily due to my disciplinary leanings as a musicologist focused around cultural theory and music analysis rather than psychology (though this is an area of interest), but also due to space pressures, methodological approach, and the overriding narrative focus of the book, this secondary layer of 'becoming' is less important for my interpretation than either the first layer, stylistic becoming, or the third layer, genre becoming/history. Like others, I find the psychological impact of noise to be too compelling to exclude from my analytical frame. But, due to space restrictions and due to my typically music-analytical focus on my own personal experiences and interpretations (as opposed to informants or experimental participants), I give this psychological aspect of the book less weight than the others.

We can, in any case, describe the psychological becoming I see in noise in terms derived from cognitive psychology. Noise generates cognitive overload in listeners through its phasing in and out of recognizable language and pattern, its emphasis on hard-to-parse inharmonic and irregular sounds. We can draw three complementary, closely related scenarios or categories of experience out of this. All three of these categories derive from, draw on, and play with the well-known dissociative 'depersonalization-derealization' disorder. People who experience this disorder have been described as 'experiencing a sense of unreality and detachment from their sense of themselves or their perception of the world' (Hunter, Charlton, David 2017, 1). In drawing on this psychological disorder for my three categories I do not mean to suggest that noise listeners are experiencing or suffering from a form of psychological illness when they listen to noise: instead, I am trying to harness the sense of unreality, of feeling 'wrong' or 'otherworldly' (Swain 2015), and apply it to an aesthetic experience with clear psychological dimensions. I am not attempting to diagnose but instead to play with this category as a way of exploring and explaining different reactions to noise music.

In the first category or scenario, the cognitive 'busyness' that often attends noise listening – that extreme novelty and challenge to convention discussed earlier and alluded to by Nadrigny and Guesde in their emphasis on noise forcing us to rethink our listening strategies – leads to a kind of ego *repletion* in the sense that Daniel Kahneman speaks of ego 'depletion' as a loss of motivation (2011, 43). Listeners, in this respect, are energized and motivated by the puzzle of noise, by its unresolving dialectic of order and disorder. In this example, the density and dialectics of noise music are experienced as a pleasurable form of *personalization*; a relatively light pleasure, a tickling of listeners' innate desire to unpack and unpuzzle, that affirms and secures their sense of rational self.

In the second scenario, the dense, unresolved dialectics of noise become so overwhelming for listeners that these are experienced more as a consuming mystery, an ecstatic infinity, than they are a puzzle to be solved. So, whether through loudness, density of information, disordering force or whatever, noise would take over and push people out of their puzzling, rational minds in this example. Here, then, noise overwhelm and overload leads to a form of (usually) pleasurable, even ecstatic *depersonalization* and self-loss (more on the latter below). Again, though this category clearly draws on the depersonalization-derealization disorder mentioned above – deliberately so, for how noise can estrange us from our sense of ourselves, can push us out of wordly ego security – it is not intended as a direct parallel to that disorder, but instead a creative playing with it.

In the third scenario, the mystery and puzzle of noise music become so bewildering that listeners experience a form of *hyperpersonalization*; a frantic, hyper-alert, triggered feeling of fight/flight/freeze where we enter a kind of 'conflict psychology' (Kalsched 2020). Hyperpersonalization in this sense is directly comparable to hypervigilance, the well-known psychological state in which sensitivity and awareness are neurotically heightened, often because of an encounter with triggers related to trauma or other external stimuli (Weymar, Keil, Hamm 2014). I prefer 'hyperpersonalization', however, as it more directly aligns with music's role in self-formation, and, especially, with noise music's particular activation of anxieties and fears related to personal boundaries and safety.

Personalization, depersonalization, and hyperpersonalization are useful overarching frames under which to gather the different kinds of psychological impact noise can have on listeners. But they are not being treated as fixed or rigid theories. Instead, they fold together several related but disparate possible psychological reactions to noise, setting up a somewhat impressionistic frame to enhance the music-stylistic discussions previous to that. These three categories do not exhaust the wider psychological context around that music-stylistic discussion. The rest of this section briefly explores that wider context, again to set up concepts and ideas for the rest of the book. It discusses Transpersonal and Jungian psychology, and then broader concepts of musical trancing and self-loss. The analyses in each chapter draw from these sources loosely but accordingly.

Transpersonal psychology, as understood particularly through the work of Stanislav and Christina Grof, focuses on transcendent, super-subjective dimensions of the psyche. For example, the psychic realms accessed in contemplating very early, peri-natal memories, or the capaciousness of so-called 'nonordinary', 'holotropic' experiences of self-transcendence or self-loss. Just as with the controlled breathwork of holotropic transpersonal practice, immersion in noise can sensitize us to transpersonal experiences of nonordinary consciousness. Its volume, intensity, and dialectical relentlessness and irresolution would open us, in this sense, to a deeper reality. Noise musician Dave Philips makes a similar point when he talks about noise and similar musics activating 'primordial shared emotions otherwise hidden under the debris of civilisation, [inviting] rumination, [endorsing] catharses' (Connelly et al. 2022). For some psychologists, such experiences can prove healing: 'Healing begins when the individual finds some way to reach across the divide between ego and non-ego and acknowledges some of the material as his/her own' (Boroson, Duffy, and Egan 1993).

In its focus on super-subjective aspects of the psyche, transpersonal psychology can be directly connected to the concepts of personalization, hyperpersonalization, and depersonalization discussed above; like those concepts, transpersonal psychology encompasses super-egoic states of being. It can also be understood as an extension of more familiar theories of the unconscious from Freud, Jung, Klein, and others. Jung's statement in *Memories, Dreams, Reflections* that 'Everything in the unconscious seeks outward manifestation, and the personality too desires to evolve out of its unconscious conditions and to experience itself as a whole' (1995, 13), indeed sums up nicely one of the ways we might think about noise-induced transcendence as a positive, healing experience. And whilst Jung typically worked within a language of images in describing the different layers and characters of the psyche, both Jung and later Jungian therapists have also emphasized the positive role that music and sound can play in therapeutic processes (Adler and Jaffé 1992; Attinello 2019).

These transpersonal and Jungian frames of healing nonordinary (un)consciousness chime with more general, non-noise-centred writing on music's role in different settings as an accompaniment to, or psychedelic driver of, unconventional and potentially healing psychological experiences. Judith Becker's work on 'music, emotion and trancing' in *Deep Listeners* is an obvious touchstone here (2004). As Becker suggests, 'the interpenetration of music with trancing is ancient and universal'; though often associated with non-western ritual practices, Becker shows how trancing as an emotional, communal, and active experience runs through all cultures. For Becker, trancing can be 'empowering for all concerned, attesting to the divine presence in one's midst … and often bestowing deep satisfaction on the individual listener' (1–2). Owen Coggins draws similar connection between music, mysticism, and trance, though in his case in the context of drone metal. Coggins quotes an audience member at a show by drone metal group Om: 'Another Om listener … described how Om's constant level of sonic intensity was meditative and calming, also mentioning connections with yoga, mantras and Gregorian chant' (2018, 2). Trance and mysticism, as covered here by Becker and Coggins, could be seen to relate to what is an almost universal property of human experience: collective joy/ecstasy. Barbara Ehrenreich points to the importance of such collective joy in *Dancing in the Streets* (2006). Ehrenreich describes social experiences of 'self-loss' where ego boundaries are transcended and individuals merge into the collective, often through activities such as communal dancing, singing, and music making (see 11–16). This parallels Thomas Turino's 'participatory' (as opposed to presentational) music performance cultures, where the focus is on 'sonic and kinesic interactions among participants', which lead to 'diminished self-consciousness' (2008, 28–9). Such collective, participatory experiences as described by both Ehrenreich and Turino channel the seemingly natural human capacity for synchronization or 'entrainment', where we unconsciously align with and groove into the movements of those around us, almost seeming to merge as a result. Ehrenreich makes a case for the unparalleled human, social value of collective experiences of this kind. Collective joy and its attendant self-loss, argues Ehrenreich, have been central both to our wellbeing and to our very survival as a species.

Noise music does not provide a straightforward example either of mystic trancing or participatory collective joy. For starters, listening to noise is often a solitary activity. Moreover, though one of my favourite features of noise music is when an unexpected, wonky groove emerges from the melee for a brief or extended passage of beat-driven intensity, on the whole most noise music tends to avoid periodic rhythm to which it might be easy to entrain (subgenres or substyles like death industrial excepted). Noise music therefore doesn't seem especially aligned with qualities we usually associate with experiences of trancing and collective joy. And yet, noise music *does* possess other crucial qualities that align it closely with the kinds of trancing and self-loss just described. As we saw with Dave Philips above, noise musicians and writers have indeed regularly picked up on noise's capacity to trance and transcend in this way; see for example C. Spencer Yeh's discussion of trancing in a *Sound Projector* interview (2011) and his description in *Bananafish* of 'going somewhere else in his mind' when performing (2004, 25). Or, on the other hand, see the discussion of Pharmakon's capacity to help listeners transcend self and trance into empathy in a *Tiny Mix Tapes* review of her 2017 album, *Contact* (Falisi 2017). Most obvious of such trancing and self-losing musical qualities in noise, as I've already explored, would be its intense volumes, its extreme subject matter, and its formal and stylistic 'becoming', the latter of which is secured above all through its 'a' and 'in' musical ingredients. These qualities jangle our normal psychological coordinates, leaving us unmoored as we try to orientate in the noise and the form. This can get us out of our heads, moving temporarily beyond our imprisoning neuroses and our conscious mind, perhaps to a position of depersonalised erotic abjection (more on this in Chapter 7) or perhaps to something that is more generous, more collective.

Of course, as we saw with stylistic becoming above, we can't treat noise as fully exceptional in any regard. Lots of music provides listeners with opportunities to transcend, whether through similarly loud volumes or other features, like a particularly powerful moment of musical synchronicity or an unexpected genre reference or turn in the style. To take just one obvious example, techno, house, and other club music have often been sites of ecstatic, blissful, communal self-loss; writing about techno and echoing similar sentiments in writers like Simon Reynolds (1998), Liam Cagney suggests that 'at its best, it is synthetic electronic music without any familiar features – no melody, no harmony, no song structure – relayed in dark featureless spaces. This means it can give a momentary release from history and identity, including race, gender, and sexual constructs' (2021). But the sonic and structural qualities of noise music create their own affordances around self-loss and transcendence; the febrile quality of noise, with its shifting intensities, its complex and unpredictable sounds, its tottering sense of order and disorder, and the becoming that emerges from all that, is especially conducive to nonordinary consciousness.

In summary, then, in its emphasis on overwhelming sound and complex cognitive overload, noise music makes possible experiences of personalization, and of nonordinary hyperpersonalization and depersonalization. These latter two experiences can be read as manifestations of the transpersonal or the collective in the manner discussed by Becker, Coggins, and Ehrenreich. Even if we don't want to get as grand and cosmic as this, though, it's still reasonable to suggest that noise music nevertheless offers a theatre of becoming in which order and disorder, self and nonself, play out a kind of dual *pas de deux*. The latter pair is less of a focus in the book than the former, as I've said. But *Becoming Noise Music* nevertheless aims to build a richer understanding of all this, the style and the psychology. As we've heard, the book also aims to tell the 'story' of noise music; to explore not just the becoming 'in' noise music but also the becoming 'of' noise music. The next section starts to add more detail to this story.

Becoming noise music

Noise music is both wide and deep; it spreads across the world and, though its history is relatively recent, it reaches back through other musical styles and cultural contexts (no wholistic, detailed history of the noise genre currently exists, though Hegarty's 2007 *Noise/Music: A History* comes closest; Kato David Hopkins' 2020 *Rumors of Noizu: Hijokaidan and the Road to 2nd Damascus,* meanwhile, offers a valuable historical account of the origins of noise in Japan). Noise music's *musical* roots reach back through late 1970s and 1980s Japanese proto- and early noise bands, and European and American power electronics and industrial artists, to genres such as punk, free jazz, free improv, and avant-garde and/or electronic composition (Hegarty traces this history in some detail). To wit, and for example, noise unites the freewheeling aggression and rough-and-ready experimentation of industrial and punk music with an emphasis on aesthetic and expressive extremes sympathetic with assorted experimentalist composers and free musicians. It is also, to step more into noise's *cultural* roots for a moment, sympathetic with art movements like anti-art, Futurism, Dadaism, and Art Brut, especially their varying taste for destruction, noise, and roughness. Noise therefore draws influence from a wide range of musical and cultural traditions. Moreover, it exists in quasi-popular contexts and largely outside established high-cultural institutions – Nadrigny and Guesde describe noise's sympathy with 'popular practices', pointing out that the vast majority of its practitioners have avoided traditional musical training: 2018, 24, and see 27 – whilst nevertheless exhibiting broad inaccessibility in its emphasis on challenging, aggressive sounds and themes. In all these respects, noise music is curiously positioned across art and popular culture, with complex musical, social, and cultural roots and affiliations.

Like other musics, these complex roots and affiliations reflect and emerge from the intercultural circuits of exchange that connected countries across the world by the 1970s and 1980s – especially those in the Global North – through shared media, markets, and culture. Globalizing technologies, political economies, and cultures across the twentieth century indeed facilitated a whole range of activity; transnationally shared touring networks, snail mail chains, media ecologies, and so on, for example, were pivotal in the development of musics like noise. Noise and similar forms, in this respect, developed in the first instance as 'transcultural' practices, where local geographical markers and distinctions were present but generally far outweighed by the generalist, global codes that tended to shape the style. We'll look at the transcultural dimension of noise in more detail in Chapter 4.

In both these senses of popular and art/elite confluences on the one hand and transcultural, global practice on the other, noise exemplifies a wider trend: the 1970s emergence of non-'high', non-prestigious, and often 'popular' and non-institutionally located culture that yet aspires to aesthetic complexity and rejects commercial imperatives. For various reasons, not least what seems to be a general move away from state-supported elite practices towards market-driven forms of culture – even with an obscure example like noise, models and media derived from the market are central – such culture had become more and more common in the late-twentieth-century period in which this book starts. I have argued previously that genres such as noise in this way embody an emerging cultural practice that exists outside or on the fringes of mainstream institutions and culture. This cultural fringe or underground takes up a key role in a shared project of minority artistic creation alongside subsidized high art, whose former vanguard role is being challenged (Graham 2016, 243–4 in particular). In all this, we can see routes to the musically and culturally new and strange being transformed and expanded (Graham 2019).

We'll encounter these themes of cultural history, exchange, and change at various points in the book, as we expand on the 'story' of noise music that we just started to tell. Each chapter situates the music and musicians it examines in context and, though my focus is often style and aesthetics, the book pays attention to such cultural (and, needless to say, political and social) dynamics throughout. After all, in telling the 'story' of noise it would make no sense to treat the music as if it emerged and existed in a cultural, social, political or historical vacuum.

Methodology

The book's methods are varied. They include music analysis – or, rather, what I'll call 'analytical criticism' – that is built on description and visualizations; auto-ethnographic interpretation; and general aesthetic and historical criticism. This section starts by outlining my approach to research, before describing the methodological focus and the methods employed throughout to develop that research.

As the May 2020 date mentioned in the Preface suggests, I wrote this book during a global pandemic. This suited my approach, which is largely based on 'desk' research; I spent most of my time on my laptop and speakers, or phone, listening to noise and absorbing every bit of noise discussion I could get my hands on. Any work in the 'field' that informs my arguments therefore largely comes from my fifteen or so years of pre-Covid noise fandom; mail order, streaming, and online sources dominated my research. This style of digital, web-based research may be sacrilegious to some readers. Noise is nothing if not traditional in its investment in supposedly 'authentic', artefact-based fan engagement. I would argue, nevertheless, that my web-anchored, listening-driven approach is both valid and more common amongst noise audiences than might be suspected. A different sensory and aesthetic experience arises when you mostly listen via physical rather than digital artefacts, no question (though I do listen via physical releases too). But I am still able to get to what, for me, is at the heart of the matter: the sonic and affective texture of the music as they appear to me, and the story of the evolution of these sonics and affects over time.

As I've made clear, *Becoming Noise Music* tells the story of noise over the past fifty years or so, with a particular focus on sound and aesthetics as interpreted from my own particular vantage point. The book is therefore not an ethnography in the mould of David Novak's aforementioned *Japanoise: Music at The Edge of Circulation* (2013), where musicians' voices and the author's experiences with those musicians and on the scene are foregrounded. Nor is it the kind of hybrid ethnography/analysis/criticism of the likewise aforementioned Sarah Benhaïm, where interviews and quotes, field work, topographies, aesthetic discussion, and other elements come together in a rich interdisciplinary mix (2018 and 2019). Nor, again, is it social research in the vein of my own *Sounds of the Underground* (2016), where questions of money, work, and social position were all central. The book includes but doesn't focus on such contexts. *Becoming Noise Music* instead structures its story around musical works or 'texts', even as it situates these texts in material and cultural contexts. This focus shouldn't be interpreted as a rejection of culturally and sociologically grounded accounts of music. As noted, social and cultural contexts lay important groundwork across the book as key interpretative vectors; musical texts are after all meaningful in both internal and external directions, in terms of musical *and* cultural logics. It is just that external contexts are not treated as ends in themselves, instead being treated as means that get us closer to the sound and to the people making and listening to that sound.

I use a 'monological' analytical-critical approach where insight and observation are derived from my own personal listening and contemplation; these are intersubjectively framed and formed, no doubt (as evidenced by, amongst other things, the amount of quotation and citation included here), but nevertheless foreground my own interpretative reaction. I describe my approach as 'monological' deliberately but playfully, attempting as I do to face up to and perhaps reclaim a term from the music sociologist Tia De Nora. In her book *Music and Everyday Life*, De Nora criticized the 'epistemological premise' underlying music analysis; that is, that the focus in working out questions of musical meaning should be on unilaterally interpreted musical works rather than audiences' reflexive, contextual experience of music. De Nora focused criticism on Susan McClary for supposedly treating music in this kind of way as a discrete, bounded object with only one signification, which would be uncoverable by her as a master interpreter (2000, 26–30 and see Kennet 2008 for a development of this monologist critical line). Whilst De Nora's emphasis on collective negotiations over meaning and value is clearly important and right, as I tried to suggest with my allusion to the 'intersubjectivity' of any one critical response above, it is impossible to interpret in a vacuum. We all analyse, we all interpret, in response to others' interpretations of that same, and similar, and not similar, music and art. Moreover, any one person's response does not need to be taken as the ultimate authority on what that music might mean and how it might work; it is most likely offered, instead, as one possible response amongst many, one that is hopelessly conditioned by the particular social and cultural background of the analyst. This is certainly how my own analyses should be taken: they are attempts to convey my heavily conditioned understanding and response to the music. They are not offered as some skeleton key to what the music 'actually' means for all and sundry, regardless of cultural origin and personality (and indeed we'll nuance our view of noise in different cultural contexts at various points, for example in Japan in Chapter 4). Instead, they are offered as an account of a meaningful, engaged response to the music from a particular vantage point, which hopefully conveys something valuable about how that music might be heard and about how we could think about how it works.

My analysis marries technical musical language with both non-technical, descriptive language and visualizations. The non-technical language generally takes two paths: straightforward, non-technical descriptions of what is happening in the music on the one hand, and more exploratory, 'auto-ethnographic' reflection on the other. 'Auto-ethnography' here refers to an approach in which 'personal experience' – in this case, personal experience of listening to noise – is described and analysed 'in order to understand cultural experience' (Ellis et al. 2010). Essentially, writing about yourself to explore something shared with others. These auto-ethnographic sections are presented in the present tense and in italics, and are used sparingly, given how jarring they can be (indeed they don't appear until Chapter 4, when the noise becomes overwhelming in its density). They offer detailed narrative descriptions of what is happening in the music through a mixture of technical and non-technical language as appropriate, pairing this with my own experiences in response. As such, they contain moments of looser, more poetic, feeling-driven language. This echoes previous writers on music. Hainge is a clear forebear, given the fact that he uses italics and present-tense description in key sections of *Noise Matters,* as for example in the Manifesto at the beginning or in later analytical sections, as with the opening to the chapter on David Lynch, where Hainge describes *Eraserhead* and *Inland Empire* in tandem (1–2 and 177–8). But the most obvious forebear, given both the specificities of the approach and the music being written about, is the aforementioned S. Alexander Reed, whose 'Suture: From the Author's Diary' section of the industrial-music-focused *Assimilate* (2013, unpaginated) mirrors my own approach both in language, in presentation (the words being italicized and present tense), and even in tone and emphasis. Reed's description of 'the possibility of ecstasy – being out of [himself]', of 'letting go', of 'submitting', and of being 'an electrified thing, gnashing in spasm but not self-destructive, because there is in this moment no self to destroy' – resonates closely with my own responses to noise.

Spectrograms, imperfect but helpful as they are, are by far the most common form of visualization used in the book. Spectrograms provide a visual illustration through time of the frequencies and volume/dynamics of a passage of music (and here I should acknowledge that another imperfection may creep in, depending on the fidelity of the sound file used as the basis of the spectrogram; the image is a means to an end, a translation, not a 'true' picture of the music). Frequencies are represented on the y-axis and time on the x-axis. The intensity of the white against the black background indicates volume of signal; sharper white equates to louder sound. In this sense, spectrograms can be understood as a kind of 'heat map', where, in my examples, increasing sharpness of the white shapes represent ascending volume and intensity. For example, Figure 0.1 visualizes C.C.C.C's *Chaos Is the Cosmos*. It uses the 'melodic range spectrogram' format preferred throughout the book; this format uses linear colour and logarithmic frequency scales, as opposed to the dbv colour scale of the generally less defined 'plain' spectrogram format, to bring out distinct sonic events more clearly. Though the image below is high-level, depicting all forty-five minutes of the album, it does at least give a sense of the frequency and dynamic range, and the gestural and formal shape, of the sound.

Spectrograms have become an increasingly important tool for music writers working especially with non-notated music over the last few decades (see Blake 2012). They allow potentially elusive music to be represented and therefore analysed in a meaningful way. It's of course important to acknowledge that spectrograms leave out, underplay or obscure key elements of musical sound, from psychoacoustic patterns to distinct features like metres and rhythm, and higher-level emergent features such as form. This can't be avoided but it can be mitigated; for example, it's very easy to adjust the parameters and scale of spectrograms and also to annotate the image. Figure 0.2 below zooms in on *Chaos* accordingly, depicting only its first 2'50" and using a downward arrow to highlight the bass guitar gesture at 2'18" that was mentioned above.

Spectrographic images can't hope to replace sophisticated, listening-led analysis and other forms of representation (notably, of course, literary representation). But, used sensitively, they can supplement and perhaps even enhance traditional approaches.

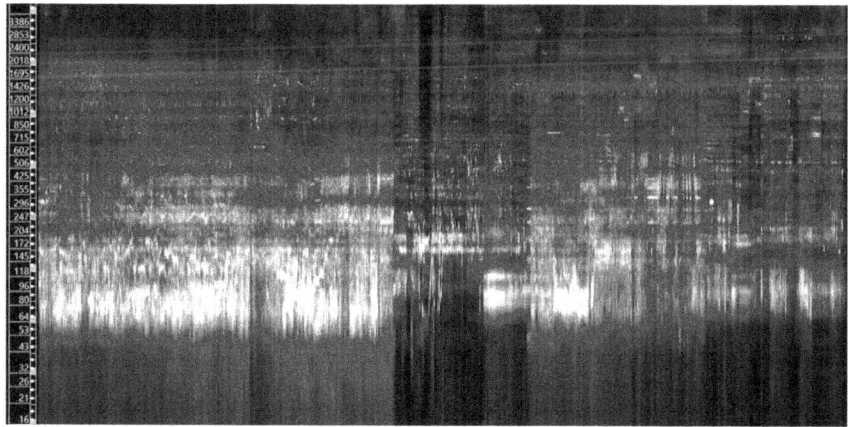

Figure 0.1 Melodic range spectrogram of C.C.C.C.'s *Chaos Is the Cosmos* (2007).

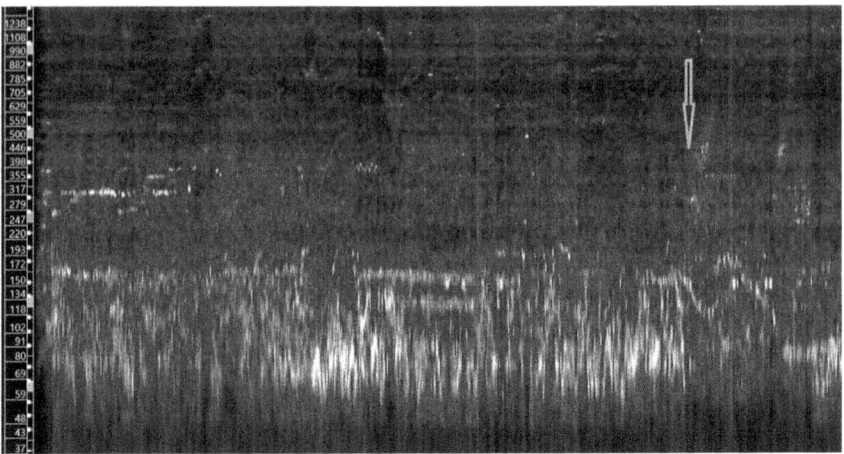

Figure 0.2 Melodic range spectrogram of *Chaos Is the Cosmos*, 0'00" – 2'50", with bass guitar figure at 2'18" highlighted.

The visualizations and the technical and non-technical descriptions I've been discussing allow me to demonstrate what I described as the 'musical' features, logics, and details of noise tracks in what is intended – contra Kubíček's point about 'settling' noise through analysis earlier – as a reasonable, clear, apropos, and non-forbidding way. Meanwhile, the auto-ethnographic sections allow me to flesh out the psychological argument in more detail. Each element of my approach is deployed according to the music under discussion; so, where the dense, unpredictable harsh or harsh-adjacent examples across the middle chapters are responded to with illustrative spectrograms and with loose, non-technical, auto-ethnographic description, later, 'hybrid' forms of noise in which conventional forms and sounds are prominent are instead met with more traditional forms of analytical-critical language. In short, where traditional technical language is helpful it is used, but when it is less suitable, non-technical, perhaps auto-ethnographic and/or spectrographic tools are used.

Given the emphasis on generalist descriptive language mentioned above and the complementary, stylistic and psychological interpretative focus of the book, in the end it probably makes more sense to describe my core method more as a kind of 'analytical criticism' than as traditional music analysis per se. 'Analytical criticism' tries to express the analysis-like centring of musical language and style that runs through the book but acknowledges the looser language and interpretative emphasis of the approach. The tone and style being used here, then, sit somewhere between the abstractions and scientism of traditional formal analysis and the more accessible, non-specialist language of musical criticism (Kerman 1980 offers a famous development of this analysis versus criticism theme).

Structure

The book is in two parts, with an Interlude between them. Part One covers a host of pre-, proto-, early, and 'classic' (where 'classic' simply reflects a common scene framing of the 1990s period) noise artists and albums from the late 1970s–90s. It takes a loosely chronological approach; its chapters are organized as a sort of 'feather' covering the late 1970s to the late 1990s, each one moving the story on even as it may overlap in time somewhat with the window covered in the previous chapter (although each chapter is somewhat internally static, with artists stacked up alongside each other rather than necessarily telling a further internal story of change in the manner of the chapters as wholes). The Chapter Chronology visualizes how this feathering works.

The chapters of Part One are also divided up thematically, either in terms of distinct subgenres or substyles of noise and/or in terms of geographical location. So, Chapter 1 looks at largely British power electronics and industrial music in the late 1970s and early 1980s. Chapter 2 looks at 'anti-music' in Britain and the United States in the early-to-mid 1980s. Chapter 3 looks at power electronics and post-power-electronics 'harsh power' music in Europe and the United States in the mid-to-late 1980s. Chapter 4 looks at Japanese harsh noise primarily in the 'classic' 1990s period. Chapter 5 looks at European and American harsh noise in that same period. Part One therefore tells the musical and cultural story of noise from the late 1970s to 1990s, using musical, geographical, and temporal lenses to do so. The Interlude, which follows, summarizes the story so far and sets the stage for the story to come.

Part Two brings the story up to date in looking at twenty-first-century noise music. Part Two largely loses the chronological structure of Part One, in that each of its five chapters ranges loosely across the 2000s, 2010s, 2020s. These chapters are organized around the themes of harsh noise in Chapters 6 and 7 (in the twenty-first century, and then in subgenres or substyles harsh wall noise and dark ambient and death industrial); noise erotics in Chapter 8; and then genre hybridity across Chapters 9 and 10. So, where Part One was organized, in temporal terms, as a kind of feathered chronology, Part Two is organized as five parallel thematic slices that collectively add up to a five-part overview of noise in the twenty-first century. Again, the Chapter Chronology visualizes how this works.

Taken as a whole, the book ultimately provides a detailed picture of noise music as a set of related but divergent musical practices. It tells local stories about noise's evolution and a meta-story about the development of noise music since the 1970s. And in its sustained focus on noise music as sound, the book paints a fine-grained picture of noise music as style and aesthetic.

Part One

Noise music then

1

Shouty and clangy credos: Power electronics and industrial music

We start our story in the UK in the late 1970s, where a rich cultural heritage and relative economic prosperity barely hid the social unrest and the hunger for new, modern forms of art, music, and life that broiled across the country's young population. Industrial music and – the primary focus of this chapter – power electronics emerged into this late 1970s and early 1980s moment filled with the same mandate for change, the same desire to challenge and even upset the polite surfaces of (primarily) British society, that had defined punk just a few years earlier. As with some forms of American post-punk at this time – no wave chief amongst them – industrial and power electronics adopted this mantle of change but went to an aesthetic and social extreme in realizing it. Made using popular tools such as guitars, synthesizers, and untutored voices but motivated by an avant-garde desire to radically remake and renew art and society, power electronics and industrial blended intense and blunt sonic palettes, aggressive performance styles, and provocative themes to create music whose messages were challenging but also rarely straightforward. The musical and political character of this work laid a template for emerging pre- and early noise artists in Japan and America in the later 1980s, as we'll see across Part One.

The chapter is orientated around 'classic' artists such as Whitehouse, Throbbing Gristle, Con-Dom, and Ramleh. It concentrates on the late 1970s and, especially, 1980s period that saw such an unprecedented flowering of these musics. Later power electronics and industrial-aligned artists will be considered in subsequent chapters, where the focus opens out to a broader array of voices than the largely white-male-dominated (and, potentially, politically highly problematic) period covered here. Finally, the chapter's binding theme is 'credo', given how much of the music was driven by polemical, strongly voiced views that invariably expressed an opposition to mainstream manners and mores. The first section explores the history, contexts, and primary aesthetic features of power electronics. The second builds on that in widening scope to look at the many musical, social, and cultural parallels between power electronics, industrial, and anti-music. The following three sections turn back to power electronics with a series of case studies of key British artists Whitehouse, Ramleh, and Con-Dom. The Conclusion prepares the ground for both the anti-musical and the post-power electronics of the next two chapters with its overarching interpretation of the aesthetics and style of power electronics.

What is power electronics?

Power electronics is a style of music – as we'll see, the noise/music dyad leans to the latter throughout this chapter – that emerged in the early 1980s out of various strands of music, culture, and society. These included Dada and Viennese Actionism, punk and post-punk, Thatcherite social unrest, and an emerging, global infrastructure of underground cassette culture and mail art. Industrial music, a genre that emerged in parallel to punk in the mid-to-late 1970s and focused on transgressive themes and harsh electronic sounds, is the most obvious forebear of power electronics, sharing an aesthetic, social milieu, and cultural context with it. Power electronics was given its name by William Bennett, leader of the British group Whitehouse, in the liner notes to the group's 1982 album *Psychopathia Sexualis* (Come Organisation). Its activity was concentrated initially in England and to some extent also in Italy and Germany, but later expanded to the United States, Australia, and Japan. We'll explore this expansion in Chapter 3.

Both power electronics and industrial music are relatively well-covered by published literature. Resources on power electronics include scholarly or journalistic books such as *Fight Your Own War: Power Electronics and Noise Culture* (Wallis 2016), *Grudge for Life: A Book about Ramleh* (Johnson 2020), and *Noise/Music: A History* (Hegarty 2007), as well as zines, fora, and magazines like *Special Interests, Bananafish, Re/Search*, and *Noise Receptor*. Given this rich array, it's unsurprising that many have attempted to define power electronics. For example, Philip Taylor describes the approach of 1960s Viennese Actionism as a key precedent for power electronics artists a couple of decades later, who similarly trucked in shock and taboo.

> Audiences could expect to be challenged and provoked, the 'art' often proving an unpleasant or uncomfortable experience ... Its deliberately shocking performances were intended to highlight the endemic violence of humanity. They wanted to trigger a reaction from the audience. Their actions, usually filmed and photographed, involved such things as self-mutilation, dead animals, blood, organs, public defecation, and masturbation, posing the question: What was taboo?
>
> (2016, Locations 221 and 230)

The next three quotes, from David Keenan, Scott Candey, and Richard Johnson respectively, pick up this same idea of transgressive, taboo-baiting performance and art but now in the context of power electronics. As they say, power electronics mirrors such extreme subject matter with an extreme approach to sound and, in many cases, political content – though it's important also to acknowledge Candey's point that the presence of lyrics in power electronics lends it musical definition and structure as compared to later, more 'free-form' noise.

> [Power electronics] has become a generic term for anyone making use of non-structured noise, aggressive vocals and transgressive subject matter.
>
> (Keenan 2009, 32)

The lyrical component of power electronics makes it a bridge between structured music and more free-form noise and dark ambient. There is something concrete to hang on to, it has an anchor that steers the response. When you take the vocal element out of it, defining power electronics against other experimental genres becomes cloudy. Stephen Petrus of Murderous Vision suggests how those elements of structure make power electronics what it is: 'To me, it is the combination of noise, rhythm and vocals. PE differs from standard harsh noise in the fact that there are traces of a traditional song structure. That structure sets it apart for me even more than the subject matter.'

(Candey 2016, Location 848)

Utilising what sometimes sounds like static or a swarm of bees alongside vocals that seem like they've shouted from deep within a mineshaft, the album [Whitehouse's 1980 *Total Sex*] represents a wholly new form of music that, alongside subject matter which suited it perfectly – drawn from the very darkest sides of human nature most prefer to ignore – Whitehouse took even further over the course of the group's lifespan.

(Johnson 2020, 157)

The next two quotes, from Drew Daniel and Jennifer Wallis, further unpick the transgressive themes and subject matter of power electronics mentioned above, alluding to the controversy and political and personal upset it has often generated:

I see power electronics as inherently dramaturgical, a self-theatricalizing attempt to summon, document and savor [sic] extreme states of mind across the entire affective spectrum: hatred, desire, mockery, longing, and despair. That extremity includes opening the Pandora's box of the unconscious and, with it, an array of energies and scenarios that one would call 'antisocial' were their protocols not so wearily familiar in their mainstream forms as the murderous engines of countless narrative entertainments. 'Warning: extreme electronics – acquire with due caution' says the ad copy on the Whitehouse release.

(Daniel 2020)

Hence, the widespread view of power electronics as a group of (mostly male) socially unaware, jackbooted fascists with an unhealthy interest in death, murder, and sexual sadism.

(Wallis 2016, Location 99)

My final quote, from Richard Stevenson, complicates the mainstream dismissal of power electronics as music made by and for Nazis, white supremacists, and similar groups, which Wallis' quote alludes to. I'll return to this point below.

Despite its apparent 'extremity', power electronics is a style of music that leans towards being a more complex art form, which requires thought and analysis to be properly appreciated. Simply put, power electronics does not offer easy answers, positions or views on anything. It demands thought and intellectual effort on the part of the listener, representing a sort of musical Rorschach test.

(Stevenson 2016, Location 3536)

These quotes collectively paint a picture of power electronics as a genre in which upsetting, extreme themes; a deliberately, provocatively ambiguous (ambiguous, at least, to fans of the style) approach to politics; and aggressive sounds, a melding of structured song forms with looser, unstructured noise, and the anchoring presence of vocals, all come together to create a potently noisy aesthetic approach.

My extended case studies later go into much more detail on how all this works on the level of power electronics music. Ahead of those, I'll survey some important examples of albums, artists, and tracks now as a way of extending the generalist picture of power electronics painted so far. Whitehouse's fourth album, *Dedicated to Peter Kürten* (Come Organisation, 1981), is a good place to start, given its characteristic sound and subject matter and given the group's prominence within the scene. *Dedicated to Peter Kürten* foregrounded upsetting subject matter in what was by then a typical manner for the group – Kurten was an early-twentieth-century German serial killer, whilst the album contains several deliberately provocative track titles, from 'Prosexist' to 'Rapeday' and 'Ripper Territory'. It was also characteristic in its use of abrasive verbal or electronic sound, with sampled speeches from news reports and fragmented screams and wails being surrounded by abstracted feedback and whirring noise from a Wasp synthesizer. Sticking with Whitehouse, the album *Buchenwald* (Come Organisation, also 1984) resembles the spirit and sound of *Kürten* closely: songs are dedicated to mass murderers or named for Nazi concentration camps, whilst crunchy beating, scratchy and shouty vocals, and piercing high tones and feedback dominate the music. *Psychopathia Sexualis*, from 1982, features seven tracks named after a famous serial killer or killers, with the sound world going from the flanging beats of 'Peter Kürten' (the song, not the album) to the abstract, clanging, chaotic noise of the twenty-minute-long 'Live Action 4'. The latter's length and lack of verbal content is an exception that proves the rule of Whitehouse tracks, which tend to feature some form of verbal content as anchor (whether shouting or screaming, or sampled news reports) and run to only a few minutes in length.

In a similar topical vein, but stepping away from Whitehouse, Italian artist Maurizio Bianchi (commonly known as M.B. or MB) released *Symphony for a Genocide* on Broken Flag in 1981. The album features seven tracks each named after Nazi concentration or extermination camps. The album also features graphic imagery of a mass grave on its sleeve, along with the words 'The moral of this work: the past punishment is the inevitable blindness of the present'. It's important to note, however, that the lack of verbal content and the relatively refined, timbrally varied sonic palette on *Symphony*, where rudimentary, delayed drum loops and stereo-separated, gloopy, and distressed synth motifs revolve darkly in ramshackle but powerful arrangements, places its affect and politics into quite a different place to those of Whitehouse. But, as with something like Krzysztof Penderecki's *Threnody to The Victims of Hiroshima*

(1960), the extra-musical picture-painting is very much dependent on verbal and visual cues; *Symphony* is never as explicit in its subject matter, at least at the level of sung or played musical sound, as Whitehouse.

A few more stops on our whistle-stop tour. British act Sutcliffe Jügend released *We Spit on Their Graves* in 1982 (Come Organisation). The album is based almost entirely around the victims of Peter Sutcliffe (the first thirteen tracks are named 'Ripper Victims I', 'Ripper Victims II', etc.), and as with Whitehouse feature piercing, sometimes chaotic distortion, and feedback, which is run through with wailing, screaming, and buried speech. In 1983, and again similarly, Italian artist Mauthausen Orchestra released an album entitled *Dedicated to J. Goebbels* (Produktion), where twisted, destroyed samples of speech are subsumed into crumbling, primitive synth loops, with interjections of unprocessed speech from Goebbels appearing at various points. Finally, in 1984, British musician Con-Dom released *Calling All Aryans* (Control Domination), on which warped samples of Nazi propaganda vie for attention with bleeping and pulsing noise. Later on, and in a similar vein, in 1997 Con-Dom released the pounding, pulverizing track 'Moor-Rapist', whose text is a sampled speech from a homicidal police officer in the British show *Cracker* (from *War against Society*, Praxis Dr. Bearmann). Con-Dom also subsequently released *Colour of a Man's Skin*, some of whose tracks have racial slurs in their titles (Tesco Organisation, 2001). (We'll return to Con-Dom in more depth later.)

These broad and varied examples get us into the general headspace of power electronics, where audio destruction and manner desecration, aggressive provocation and outright transgression, have been weapons in a kind of cultural war against conformity and polite common sense (and, for some, against reasonable, moral standards of behaviour). It's already clear that this power-electronics headspace can be a dark, potentially scary and even hateful place to be. Its artists focus on the most destructive and ugly sides of human nature, using titles, lyrics, and sound to evoke genocidal or murderous acts and individuals. We will explore the political/aesthetic intent and impact of these choices throughout this chapter. But it's important to acknowledge even at this point that, as per some of the quotes above, whilst the book treats power electronics as a serious attempt to grapple with very tough subject matter, this treatment is neither a moral imperative for others to treat the music in this way nor is it necessarily (yet) a judgement about its political and aesthetic efficacy.

As anyone familiar with murder-obsessed popular films, novels, and TV shows would attest, the subject matter of power electronics is hardly unique to it. And yet, whereas it's usually fairly easy for viewers to distance themselves from what they're watching – probably partly due to the visual and therefore perhaps less immersive nature of the medium but also due to the commercial nature of most TV and film production, which demands a kind of conventional gloss and detachment even in the context of gory subject matter – power electronics embodies the ugliness that such other art pushes away or objectifies. We can, ironically, look to a TV character for a summation of the approach: 'I become the thing we fear the most … I become the horror' (Frank Black, the near-psychic detective from the television show *Millennium*, describing his ability to get into the mind of serial killers).

Such an approach, where music steps into the perspective of a killer or abuser or similar, is not totally unknown even in mainstream music. But it's also not a tactic that's especially common; the lack of distance between subject and subject matter in power electronics can, after all, be deeply uncomfortable and even unseemly. Figures from both the left and right of the political spectrum have accordingly characterized power electronics as reactionary and even fascist; at best an immature and cheap attempt to shock and at worst a glorification of violence (a 2011 article in Indymedia sums up many of the familiar accusations against power electronics). And yet, as we saw especially in the Stevenson quote above, power electronics supporters and sympathizers prefer to emphasize its deliberate complexity and ambiguity. Indeed, in this spirit, one *might* argue that the extreme performances and topics of power electronics couldn't be intended as straightforward endorsement or tribute; that they contain some element of critique or satire; that the typical distance between personnel and persona is sublimated onto a deeper level for the sake of aesthetic intensity. For many this isn't good enough, of course.

The nature of power electronics' relationship to its subject matter, its seeming intent to challenge taboos and de-programme listeners, will clearly take a lot of parsing over the course of the chapter. As another way into this, the next section looks at various points of intersection and comparison between power electronics, industrial, and 'anti-music', styles whose cultural origin points, contexts, and approaches overlap. It starts with music before moving on to material, social, and cultural connections.

Music and cultural crossovers and contexts: Power electronics, industrial, and 'anti-music'

Industrial music, that provocative, transgressive blend of rock, electronic music, and performance art that emerged with artists like Cabaret Voltaire and Throbbing Gristle in the late 1970s, laid the groundwork for power electronics. It wouldn't be too much of a stretch to see power electronics as a slightly more extreme, deliberately rougher, and even more confrontational offshoot of industrial music. Accordingly, we can point to any number of parallel or preceding industrial artists as comparators for the power electronics scene. The audio collage work of Nurse with Wound and Cabaret Voltaire had clear parallels with an artist like MB, for example. Meanwhile, the clanging sounds, challenging themes, and political agitations of SPK, Einstürzende Neubauten, and Test Dept are close cousins of much of what we find in power electronics. But the most obvious musical precedent for artists like Whitehouse would probably be the foundational UK industrial act, Throbbing Gristle.

Throbbing Gristle's late 1970s music, as with Whitehouse just a few years later, focused on taboo subject matter and transgressive themes. It also similarly used abrasive electronic and/or amplified sounds and simple, often repetitive song structures as vehicles for and embodiments of that transgression. Richard Johnson underlines the connection between the bands in discussing Whitehouse's early releases: 'only by what some have seen as 'divide and rule' tactics coloured by austerity and industrial disputes on the largest national scale (Taylor 2016, Location 238). This filtered down to the music; whilst there's never a one-to-one relationship between art and its times, the connection in this case seems palpable. After all, the destruction and anger in each music, though often distinctively expressed, nevertheless resonated loudly and consistently with the unrest and anger in the society that surrounded it.

Whitehouse, *Total Sex* (1980) and *Great White Death* (1985)

As will probably be obvious by the amount of space given over to discussing the group already in this chapter, Whitehouse were the central driving force in power electronics. William Bennett, the group's founder and sole constant member – though others, such as Philip Best, were long-time contributors throughout the group's twenty-seven-year run from 1980 to 2007 – was likewise the scene's key figure and indeed gave it its name, as noted. This was true both in Britain and abroad, where, as we'll see especially in Chapter 3, artists as far afield as Finland, Australia, and the United States felt inspired enough by the group's work to start making music of their own. The incredible reach of even such an extreme, obscure act as Whitehouse underlines the global character of fringe networks by this late century period, where deep-rooted international cultural relationships and infrastructure could be seen to support both mainstream and fringe forms of artistic practice.

Where Whitehouse would go on to inspire various other artists to make music that echoed and altered their approach, they themselves had both taken inspiration from previous acts – primarily, the Sex Pistols and Throbbing Gristle – and similarly sought to push those sources into different areas. In their case, even farther and further; the story here is, in many ways, a familiar modernist tale of rejection of supposedly radical influences for not having pushed things far enough, for backing away from the precipice of the 'truly' radical or new. Parallels with earlier 'killing the parent' relationships, like that between Boulez and Schoenberg, are obvious. Bennett, in this spirit, adopted but adapted the force and shock of such earlier groups, creating an uncompromising electronic sound and aesthetic in which extreme shock and distress are the overriding characteristics.

This sonic and aesthetic template was in place from Whitehouse's debut album, *Birthdeath Experience* (1980), and, as we've seen at least in part with *Dedicated to Peter Kurten* above, remained in place right across their first nine albums (all released on Bennett's Come Organisation, 1980–5). And yet, even though the basic ingredients of churning synth waveforms, piercing high tones, and screamed vocals remained constant, it's also important to note the ways that their sound evolved in this classic period and beyond. Whitehouse's second album, *Total Sex* (Come Organisation, 1982), introduced a level of heavy reverb on the voice that would remain important on subsequent albums, for example, whilst their ninth album, *Great White Death* (Come Organisation, 1985), softened the group's previous sonic roughness somewhat and foregrounded slightly clearer vocals. I'll examine these two releases in more detail as a way of exploring both the group's ever-present power-electronics template and the shifts this underwent along the way, also calling forward to later releases beyond the general scope of this chapter at various points.

Total Sex repeated the extreme themes and imagery of *Birthdeath Experience*: its original cover featured an image of a victim of the Yorkshire Ripper, while the wholesale version that went to Rough Trade depicted a Guanajuato mummy from Mexico. The later CD reissue on Susan Lawly featured a passage from *120 Days of Sodom* on the cover (1994). *Total Sex* also maintained the tinny, abrasive synth sound from that earlier album but, as noted, changed the approach to Bennett's vocals, which were now heavily flanged and distorted and, for the most part, subsumed into the texture as one more element of noise. The sound across the album's six tracks – though one, 'Politics', is essentially a two-minute interlude featuring an initial blast of whirring noise and then tapping and silence – is indeed extremely rough-and-ready, with the vocals in particular feeling poorly recorded and mixed.

And yet, the lack of polish lends *Total Sex* a kind of murky, weird depth. 'Total Sex' and 'Phaseday', for example, feel so muffled and indistinct in both their impressionistic but emotive shouting about 'leather steel coitus' and 'domination' and their dark, reverb-heavy humming and clicking noise, that a kind of ambient sublime is achieved, the sound ricocheting around the room in mysterious, enigmatic anger. Even though the sustained bass tones of 'Total Sex' anchor things more securely than in the more fragmented razor glints of 'Phaseday', across both a kind of looseness and almost sound-art texture pervades, a proto-hauntological noise-crackle that is rich in suggestion. Indeed, there are moments in each of these tracks where one is reminded of the later stages of Alvin Lucier's *I Am Sitting in a Room*, discrete musical gestures subsumed into standing waves and acoustic-synthetic overtones, persona-becoming-aura. 'Dominate You' is more forthright and clearly defined in sound, a buzzing low drone offsetting a pitch-shifting, higher-toned dyad that whizzes up and down shrilly, before a middle-range Bennett enters to consume the centre of the track, barking like some cyborg lion. And yet again, here, Bennett and the rest of the track seems to be forever fading into pure digital code, abstraction haunting harshness throughout.

'Rollercoaster' and 'Ultrasadism' offer more of the same aggression tempered by rudimentary tools and/or wilful indistinction. 'Rollercoaster' contrasts whirring higher-range glissandi with a busy, glitchy low crackle and drone, whilst a high sine tone acts as organizing pedal point intermittently throughout. Bennett gives a particularly involving performance here, his resigned intensity playing well as contrast with the swarming crackle that enters and withdraws throughout. 'Ultrasadism', finally, continues the metallic harshness of other tracks, low bass tones, mid-range buzzing, and a trebly, silvery Bennett giving way at various points to more deliberately sequenced synth motifs or weird pattern-synchronicities of noise/static/groove. As with other tracks on *Total Sex*, the music very much plays in a strange space between harsh aggression and personal annihilation, chaos, and an intermittent, emergent sense of musical order and cohesion (again, we lean here to the music end of the noise/music dialectic or dyad).

As seen across these examples, within and across tracks the continuity of sound sources and textural types lends the album a cohesion that plays well against the murky depth of the actual sounds themselves. Particular moments are mysterious but, taken together, the whole makes sense; especially given the ever-present anchor of Bennett's rabid street-preacher, whose barks and screams step in and out of the fray throughout. It's in this latter aspect, indeed, where the 'Politics' interlude starts to make more sense as a structural device; the clear passages of silence between Bennett's interjections on tracks like 'Rollercoaster', like the clear space between different sonic elements in the title track, create an internal sense of definition and shape, just as the starker periods of silence on 'Politics' do for the album as a whole. This is not a work of simply ill-defined mulch and dirt: sound and silence, density and starkness, all interplay fluidly. The album's sense of cohesion, then, doesn't come through a particularly typical route, as with, say, a familiar melodic arc or conventional harmonic and rhythmic language. Instead, the continuity of sound sources, the overarching thematic focus, the repeated motifs within each track, and the regular formal structure of *noise – vocalnoise – noise – vocalnoise* infuse the music with a clear logical hierarchy of gestures and sounds. The disorder of sonic murk and shouted ferociousness plays off and with the order of form and familiarity.

For its part, *Great White Death* features a more developed, well-realised, and clearly defined sound than *Total Sex*. And yet, much of the same thematic concerns, sonic flavour, and musical ordering are present here, seven albums and five years later. Indeed, the very same themes of abuse, domination, and so on found on these early albums would persist in Whitehouse's later work; 1998's *Mummy and Daddy* (Susan Lawly), which focuses on domestic violence and child abuse (in a typically uncomfortable, confusing fashion), is a good illustration of the group's sustained thematic focus. Similarly, these same cutting, clanging, and piercing electronic sounds and loose-but-repeating forms – give or take the odd spoken word or ambient track, such as 'Baby' from 1995's *Quality Time* (Susan Lawly) – would likewise persist. This is even as Whitehouse adopted digital tools and recording techniques on albums like *Cruise* (Susan Lawly, 2001), which boosted the clarity and volume of their sound. And also even as tracks like 'Cut Hands Has the Solution' from 2003's *Bird Seed* (Bird Seed), and the group's last album, *Racket* (Susan Lawly, 2007), started to include the pared down, quasi-ritual drumming sound found in releases by Bennett's later project, Cut Hands.

Great White Death found the group working with an external producer for the first time (David Kenny). I've already noted that the sounds of the album suggest a new degree of clarity, but the songs also feature a greater degree of structural deliberation than on previous releases. And, though the harsh edges and pure intensity of earlier albums remain, the sound overall is now thicker, warmer, heavier. If anything, though, this depth and darkness means it is *more* menacing than the earlier rickety noise. 'Great White Death' itself offers a good illustration of this. A goblin voice, pitch-shifted down into the dungeon anchors but plays against slightly contrapuntal, stereo-separated scrabbling and busy high tones, and a glitching mid-range fuzz-drone that sits just to the right of the spectrum, holding the track in tension throughout. Each of these sounds feels balanced and clearly placed in the mix, register and tone-colour now being used carefully to create a sense of slowly creeping dread. 'Ass-Destroyer' (this and other titles below, extreme as they are, could be seen to be playing into the 'I become the horror' trope from earlier) is more chaotic, with reverb-heavy shouts and screams encased in watery, dripping loops of mid-range electronic sound and gesticulating high tones. But even here, the contrast is marked between the realization of these familiar Whitehouse tropes of watery noise, high tones, and hateful shouting here as compared to earlier albums like *Total Sex*, the one feeling darkly poised and the other like a vivid but chaotic nightmare. As with 'Rapemaster' and 'We've Got the Power', both the title track and 'Ass-Destroyer' benefit from the typically condensed forms favoured by Whitehouse, looping synth tones, sustained drones, and brief verses of spoken word, shouting or screaming all working together in tight formation before each track expires after 150–200 seconds.

The two longest tracks on the album – not including the pulverizing death-industrial drone and feedback of the thirteen-minute 'My Cock's on Fire', which was added to the album as a bonus track when it was reissued on CD by Susan Lawly – unsurprisingly contain both the most sonic variety and detail and the most exploratory forms, stretching out as they do to 8'28" ('You Don't Have to Say Please') and 7'28" ('I'm Comin' Up Your Ass'). 'You Don't Have to Say Please' offers a masterclass in careful tension-building and textural expansion amidst potentially hateful sentiment. The track opens with high whistling tones and Bennett grubbily growling that 'you don't have to say please, get down on your knees, suck my cock'. As he jumps an octave and several registers of calm, merging into the whistles as he repeats variations of the words, a dark electronic bass tone enters below him holding a subtonic tone, opening out the sonic space dramatically at about 0'25". That bass tone moves about within a narrow compass for about seventy-five seconds, as Bennett strangles and stretches the words – including other new lines, such as 'You don't have to beg me for it' – into submission, maniacally screaming or wheedling or growling (this contrast between speech, shouting, and screaming parallels a similar approach on the aforementioned 'Rapeday'). At 1'40", the bass tone moves onto a new pedal point one tone above the earlier one, suggesting a kind of tonic arrival, a note it holds until 3'09". Through this 'tonic' passage, whistling tones scratch about and Bennett moves between whispers, shouts, and lunatic screams, the sonics picking up some of the vocal utterances (as the whistles had earlier), amplifying or twisting them into new shapes; for instance, a stunning moment at 2'44" sees Bennett's high-pitch wails fade into a held, oscillating synth tone. We are far from chaotic noise here, the tonal contour and the timbral and textural detail feeling carefully, deliberately choreographed (or, at least, cohesive). After that held tone fades away, 'You Don't Have to Say Please' moves into a more fragmented texture, the scratchy, bird-like whistles and isolated bass from earlier now arcing around in a bare sonic space. Bennett enters with the original three lines of lyrics, building in intensity until a wild scream yields the return of the earlier 'tonic' bass tone, a busier texture, and more shouting at 4'02". The following four minutes serves as a kind of second verse, following that interlude of fragmented sound. Bennett again explores the repeated lyrics from earlier but from different angles, now shouting in echo, now breathing heavily between lines, now screaming in agitation or terror, whilst the scratching whistles and bass tone anchor the space around him. A feint beating enters at about 7'40", perhaps to signal a transition into the coda for the final 26 seconds, from 8'02", where the bass tone drops out and a reverb-heavy Bennett hushes towards the close.

'I'm Comin' Up Your Ass' is built from a similar contrast between largely sustained instrumental noise and sound, and a freewheeling Bennett playing constantly with vocal delivery and verbal shape. In this case, the latter is done through the (again, potentially disturbing) lines 'I'm Comin' Up Your Ass. I'm so bored of your cunt. You won't like it sugar. Take my cock you whore. It's what you deserve', which are treated less like a typical lyrical verse as they are elements to be extracted, manipulated, and merged into noise. The sonics in the first half of the track are narrower than those on 'You Don't Have to Say Please', consisting largely of microtonally dissonant held, high sine tones playing abrasively against Bennett's growls. As with that previous track, we now enter a brief, Bennett-less central segment of relative fragmentation, with a low bass drone entering at 3'04", and a mid-range fuzz at 3'24". Bennett then returns for the second half of the track, now in a lower register, angrily spitting out lines such as 'you cheap slut, you really are disgusting'. Here as elsewhere on the track, the delivery and the lines themselves are so lurid and over-the-top that they feel (or can feel) deliberately absurd or ridiculous (as in, ridiculed). At 4'22" Bennett drops out, and each sonic element ramps up in action for about thirty seconds, high tones ranging up and down and fuzz and drone cutting across each other aggressively. A passage from 5'01" is more concentrated on those high sine tones, with intermittent entries of the bass drone and other glitching noises. This starker sound palette serves as backdrop for a newly growling and disgusted Bennett at 6'01", who ranges wildly about during the next seventy seconds of the track, screaming in terrible abandon, before a final fifteen seconds of deliquescing noise draws things to a close.

As can be seen, both longer tracks are based on the same ingredients as earlier; notably, Bennett's characterful voice and hateful lyrics, and a concentrated range of sonic elements often splayed clearly across high, mid, and low registers. Their local forms are arrayed in tight sequences marked by vocal entries and exits. But the two tracks stretch the earlier, shorter ones out, in each case using an interlude spotlighting silence and/or fragmentation to create contrast before the bulk of the preceding 'verse' material returns for the second half. The relative sonic polish and dynamic use of registral contrasts and timbral detail help those tracks hold attention, too. Each one, for example, contrasts low depth with busier high sound. Again, a useful comparison can be drawn between the sonic vibrancy of *Great White Death* and the very different but parallel sonic vibrancy of *Total Sex*, where the sound was much more ramshackle but the character equally rich, and the force of expression as intense. These are all simple but effective strategies. These tracks' registral, formal deliberation demonstrates how easily the concentrated intensity of power electronics could lend itself to broader, more traditionally 'musical' exploration and language, the jagged, 'becoming' sound forming into and out of ordered, conventional shapes, these held in the kind of suspended dialectic discussed previously.

I've looked at these two Whitehouse albums very much from a musicological-analytical perspective, only alluding in passing to the nature of the words—and, by implication, the attitude and potential political intent and impact—of each track. Before moving to my next case study, I want to draw the discussion together by expanding the frame to consider how each element – the sound, the words, the attitude expressed in the words and delivery, and aspects such as imagery – might be seen to come together as an aesthetic, psychological, and political proposition.

As noted above, Bennett's performative aggression and his choice of upsetting imagery and what look to be deeply misogynistic or otherwise hateful lyrics quite predictably frustrated and angered some listeners. Bennett's goal seemed to be to shock and disturb, and the fact that the music, the titles, the cover imagery, and the performances (as with the infamous 1983 Whitehouse/Ramleh 'live aktion' at the Roebuck Pub where, following glasses being thrown amid violence in the crowd, the police raided the venue) did indeed shock or disturb is unsurprising. That, for the most part, Bennett wasn't prepared to explain or justify his choices seemed merely to aggravate this shock and disturbance. In response to later attempts to withdraw support for his work, Bennett *did* release a statement in 2013 in which he: explicitly distances himself from fascism and other ideologies, stating that 'I am not, never have been, nor ever will be, a nazi/fascist/racist'; points to irony and satire in his work; and defends his and others' approach as an 'artistic immersion in taboo areas of human expression' (2013). But this is an exception that proves the rule; Whitehouse usually deliberately avoided placing distance between themselves and the themes explored in their music.

I've considered, and will consider again in future chapters, the political implications of this sort of position; whether adopting the perspective of an abuser or misogynist and focusing on upsetting themes is an effective, responsible or morally justifiable strategy, or whether it just undermines the work. But a deep dive into the *sound* and experience of Whitehouse albums, such as we've just done, perhaps leads one to consider the political valence of the music from a different angle. Or at least, with a deeper perspective than the themes and lyrics sometimes allow. Heard as sound, these albums can easily come to represent a kind of sonic 'totalitarianism', in Paul Hegarty's words, where the combination of ugly themes, the overwhelming assault of Bennett's vocals, and the abrasion of the sound around those vocals put the listener into a state of abjection. Here is Hegarty on that very idea:

> Whitehouse raise the questions of misogyny and misanthropy perhaps more than anyone else, and are not particularly interested in justifying their purported outlook ... Is such as an aesthetic oppressive? Looking away from the content of Whitehouse tracks, and even the harsh electronic 'soundscapes', there is still another level where power operates, and it is certainly totalitarian, in that it seeks to be a total experience that inflicts itself. The purpose of the approach varies: on the one hand, the volume and difficult sounds try to convey the affect suggested in the vocals; while on the other, the text of a track is part of an overall bringing of the listener into a shared abjection ... The masochistic contract permits a temporary suspension of equality.
>
> (2007, 122)

This 'abject' position, where the listener becomes a kind of masochist submitting to the force of the sound and performance, is a useful lens to think about how the themes of domination and annihilation explored in Whitehouse's lyrics, titles, and imagery are borne into and out of the sound in a kind of process of aesthetic 'syncing'. Not that this implies a kind of 1:1 mirroring relationship between sound and theme. Instead, the one enhances the other, interactions of sound and shouted idea creating resonances of affect in which ideas or impressions from one area are transplanted into, and enhanced, in another; for example, the words being transformed by the sound and the sound anchored by the words.

All of this changes (or, again, can change) the political 'message' of the work, the sound and affect potentially mussing up any seemingly clear denotation in the lyrics or the attitude. For instance, that sound and affect can easily leave the listener themselves psychologically dissembled, temporarily neither subject nor object but instead, to use Hegarty's word, 'abject', caught midway between the hyper and depersonalization states discussed in the Introduction, arrested in a state of prone becoming without clear personal coordinates and agency. Tense, aggressive, febrile music like this, for all its formal order – or, at least, its powerful holding in tension of wild energy and loose sound on the one hand and underlying timbral, textural, formal order on the other – is always bursting at the boundaries of 'normal' reason and emotional regulation, the shouty vocals and ear-splitting sound creating a situation of high, often confused alert for listeners. You feel like you've been through something powerful when you turn off Whitehouse, almost as if you've returned from a difficult (or, depending on what you bring to it, hateful or undesirable) journey of some sort.

Finally, and separately from all this psychological and political interpretation, it's also worth pointing out that – considering the clear and distinct musical ordering, detail, and flavour we identified above – it's possible to bracket Whitehouse's sound from the pre-set themes of their words, images, and interviews. In that light, particularly from the perspective of decades' worth of similarly themed power electronics on the one hand, and harsher and perhaps sonically more all-consuming noise releases on the other, we can hear these albums simply as relatively moderate explorations of intense sounds, ideas, and moods. In this hearing, the albums wouldn't necessarily embody or endorse any of the hateful perspectives and ideas described in their lyrics or titles. Instead, these would be artistic scenarios that are fundamentally fictional in nature. With that lens, we might then as listeners be able to attune more closely to these albums' rich formal and timbral rhymes; their dramatic emotional outbursts; and their abrasive but appealing sounds, as aesthetic ends in themselves.

Ramleh, *31/5/1962–1982* (1982) and *The Hand of Glory* (1983)

As we've already heard a couple of times in this chapter, Gary Mundy's Ramleh and his associated label, Broken Flag, were another important presence in the power electronics scene of the early 1980s. Broken Flag, for its part, were responsible for (often infamous) releases from key artists on the scene, from Mauthausen Orchestra and MB to Consumer Electronics, Swastika Kommando, and Le Syndicat. The 1983 compilation, *Neuengamme*, was particularly important (and controversial), collecting and platforming as it did such artists as Sutcliffe Jügend, Whitehouse, Esplendor Geometrico, Consumer Electronics, and MB; Steve Underwood has even suggested that the album 'is considered by many to be the Power Electronics set by which all others should be judged' (2010, 84; this article offers a comprehensive overview and history of Broken Flag). Meanwhile, Ramleh shows and releases generated a lot of interest in this period and beyond; Rough Trade's well-publicized refusal to carry *Return to Slavery* (Broken Flag, 1983) due to the autopsy image on its cover is just one example of the group's notoriety (Underwood's piece discusses this incident).

Like many other artists I'll consider in this and subsequent chapters, Ramleh's beginnings can be traced directly to Whitehouse, whom Mundy went to see live after a friend of his had noticed an ad for one of their gigs in *Time Out*.

> I formed Ramleh after seeing Whitehouse. We didn't want to be Whitehouse 2, but we wanted that harsh electronic backdrop to add our own ideas to. I think Ramleh is almost a slightly psychedelic take on some of the Whitehouse sound. We also went for a more haunted and desperate sound. Whitehouse was more domineering, more of a macho approach. We were deliberately far more ambiguous.
>
> (Cited in Keenan 2009, 31)

As Mundy indicates here, he and collaborators in the group – Bob Strudwick and Philip Best (again) being amongst the most significant – took direct inspiration from the harshness of Whitehouse. Ramleh's use of a Wasp synth and an array of cheap effects pedals and microphones likewise aligned their sound with Whitehouse. But, as we'll see, Ramleh added a softer, (Mundy is right) more ambiguous sonic edge that marked their work out from some of their peers on the scene. Indeed, this marking out would go even farther, with Ramleh's later-period music moving more directly into Krautrock and psychedelic rock territories, albeit infused with noise textures and intensities; see *Circular Time* from 2015 (Crucial Blast).

And yet, despite this sonic and stylistic contrast, Ramleh directly mirrored Whitehouse in using morbid imagery, allusions to sexual violence, and Nazi references in their work. For example, their – and the label's, though it had to displace a couple of earlier cassettes for the honour – first release, *31/5/1962 – 1982* (discussed below, 1982), was named in honour of the twentieth anniversary of Adolf Eichmann's execution. Similarly, the group's name was taken from the town in which Eichmann was executed (Ramla in Israel, informally known as Ramleh). Mundy retrospectively frames these choices as an effort to match the intensity of the typical power electronics sound with a corresponding intensity of theme and image:

> We always dealt in complex and potentially controversial subject matter. The music was violent and depressing at times, and needed imagery that suited that. There was also a feeling of wanting to challenge the listener, not just for shock

value but to make people think and react. I think a feeling that runs through a lot of Ramleh and Broken Flag products is one of uneasiness. Some people have said to me that our music makes them feel uncomfortable, and I think to be able to get that sort of reaction is intriguing.

(Keenan 2009, 31)

Meanwhile, in the Underwood piece referenced above, Mundy emphasizes the importance of ambiguity in the group's use of Nazi imagery, and the role of offence in their work:

> I like the ambiguity, and I didn't want it to be obvious whether it was pro- or anti-Nazi, or whether it was ironic or not. I was certainly OK with the idea that it might cause offence at the time, although I think when you listen to a lot of the stuff it's fairly obvious that it's not pro-Nazi. It never really occurred to me that it would attract real neo-Nazis, and strangely, it didn't, which in hindsight is something of a relief. I think it was so extreme that it was assumed that it couldn't be for real.

(2010, 87)

Mundy's latter point here echoes my own suggestions both in more general terms in Section One and with reference to Whitehouse at the end of the previous section that, given the aesthetic extremity and chaos of much of this power electronics work, it would be difficult to see it as a straightforward endorsement of its chosen themes, to imagine actual fascists looking to the music for a confirmation or exploration of their views.

And yet, of course, whether intended and/or acknowledged or not, it's very easy to see how someone could take serious offence at these young artists' appropriation of Nazi (and, in other cases, misogynist) references. Looked at one way, Mundy's acceptance later in that interview that a lot of the choices he and others were making at that time could be explained by the natural arrogance of youth makes a lot of sense. The Monty Python phrase 'very naughty boys' sometimes comes to mind when considering power electronics artists' courting of shock. Indeed, Mundy describes getting to twenty-one and realizing that 'the people who were listening got what we were doing anyway and the ones we wanted to annoy weren't really paying attention' (2010, 87). It's also noticeable that the artists being considered in this chapter appear to be universally white and near universally male; without wishing to generalize, it's safe to say that these factors likewise probably influenced both their desire and their perceived capacity to speak out in this way. Finally, it should also be noted that these choices created a kind of 'scene' kudos (what Sarah Thornton would call 'subcultural capital'; 1996) for the artists, connecting them to peers and attracting such audiences as power electronics enjoyed in the period. On some level, the Nazi imagery can be seen as an attempt to create scene 'insiders' and 'outsiders', and to build an audience.

Though in one sense it gets harder every year to defend these artists' subject matter, as cultural attitudes to representation and to potential triggering content become stricter and stricter, it is *possible* to read their choices in a different way, as artistic decisions that aim towards powerful aesthetic effects. And as with Whitehouse, it's easier to do this, and to empathize with Mundy's point about ambiguity, when you tune into the sounds of Ramleh's music rather than just their titles and visual images. Ignoring the image of Eichmann on its cover, for example, it would be hard to hear *31/5/1962–1982* as an endorsement or depiction of anything beyond the consuming joy of immersing yourself in squelchy, hesitant, chaotic, dirty sound. Feeling almost totally lacking in structure – both in terms of larger song forms and more locally in terms of distinct phrases or metres – the album's six tracks move freely around a crumbling space of shipwreck-distortion, squalling feedback and fuzz, and gamma-ray effects, the sound in a constant state of emergence or becoming, form and shape never quite settling.

The sound of *31/5/1962–1982* is also never driving or overwhelming as it sometimes can be with other PE artists. 'Throatsuck', for example, blends space-echoed vocal shouts and sudden theremin-like divebombs with an almost tender sense of sonic interaction and flow, the sounds never quite getting in each other's way or pushing at the listener. 'Deathtoll' again tenderly offsets different elements, here a gently thudding gong and resonating feedback, all of it encased in the ever-present sonic gunk and crud that gives the album much of its character. 'May 31' is even more restrained, swirling held organ clusters rotting away in hiss and crunch as various phased shouts and sweeps struggle to the surface momentarily. The sound seems to get quieter as it goes on, the ramshackle mess only pulling the ear further and further in. As noted, the abiding affect here is a kind of crumbling enigma, the prone, tense, strident 'becoming' of Whitehouse turning to something warmer and fuzzier. We're therefore far from the throng and stomp of *Triumph of the Will* or even a Nazi-lampooning industrial group like Laibach on *31/5/1962–1982*. Instead, we're sucked into a dark swirl and haze of absorbing motion. The album certainly gels into moments of passing anger, but the atmosphere is murky and flecked not blood red. It is, accordingly, easy to lose oneself in the sound; less overwhelmed as more gently lured into mystery and flow.

Ramleh's *The Hand of Glory* EP (Broken Flag, 1983) is more sonically forthright and defined than *31/5/1962–1982* had been. But again, the approach here is more hallucinogenic than harrowing; loose, gently puzzling flows of sound and comparatively light hefts of gesture run across the four tracks. 'Squassation' starts with a high, isolated harmonic. An LFO'd low drone enters a fifth below and oscillates broadly towards the left of the picture, as higher synth sounds, very high feedback, and distant shouting thicken the texture. Those shouts, indistinct and echo-heavy but committed, gradually take over the focus of the track as high synth tones revolve around them. 'Prossneck' is built from similar elements, with drone on the right and distorted fuzz tone on the left, though its central speaking voice, again echoing, is clearer and calmer than the shouts on the previous track. A much more distorted second voice careens around that spoken word and eventually takes over, as synth tones modulate and sweep around the spectrum. Again, voice, contrast between low drone and high harmonic and feedback, and a crunchier mid-range define the sound. This is even as that definition tarries in haze. A subtle climax of thickness and intensity happens in both tracks, though that haze never quite lifts, amelodicism and aformalism winning out over anything more musically discrete. The two 'The Hand of Glory' tracks again build from similar elements, though across their ten minutes' various distinctive sonic features bubble out of the flow, from the oscillating laser-gun midway through the first track to the particular anguish conveyed by the distant, screaming voice throughout the second. That anguished voice, along with the particularly grating high tones and general frenzy of the texture at the track's climax, indeed ensures that Part 2 marks a particular intensification in what is otherwise a fairly continuous sonic and emotional journey across the EP. We swim in a gently immersive sea of sound, disturbing flotsam and jetsam washing up around us at various points, until we notice a dead body in those final few minutes.

And yet, even there, the gelatinous, spongy character of Ramleh's work (in this case, and in this period) seems to override any direct reference or reading one could draw from the sound. The music is a hazy puzzle, order and disorder in murky dialogue, and the listening experience hypnotizes us in its lure to gentle self-loss. Fascist politics seem far away, to this listener at least. So, whereas in Whitehouse the sound and the performances married up with the subject matter – even if, as we saw, the nature of the former could undermine the latter – in Ramleh, the relationship is more tangential. The aesthetic-political tenor of the work is even harder to pin down as a result. This doesn't mean the group's choice of subject matter was validated by their approach to sound but it does seem to change how we might react to and experience that subject matter. Ramleh's aesthetic proposition in these early years, then, was partially determined by the lyrical and thematic content but was ultimately defined by the particular emphasis on murky becoming and alluring haze I've been identifying in their sound.

Con-Dom, *All in Good Faith* (1988) and *The Eighth Pillar* (1991)

Con-Dom – short for Control-Domination – is the solo project of Mike Dando, based in The West Midlands region of England. Con-Dom started in 1983, inspired by industrial music and local power electronics acts such as Family Patrol Group. The first of Dando's 'live assaults', as he describes his live shows, took place in Wolverhampton in 1984. These 'assaults' were the focus of Dando's activity across the mid-1980s; a series of conceptually elaborate records came later, with *All in Good Faith* (Control Domination, 1989), *The Eighth Pillar* (Sounds for Consciousness Rape, 1991), *Colour of a Man's Skin* (Tesco Organisation, 2001), and *How Welcome Is Death to I Who Have Nothing More to Do but Die* (Tesco Organisation, 2016).

As might be guessed from the name, Con-Dom has a clear conceptual idea or 'credo' at its core: that modern society is based on various – sometimes subtle, sometimes explicit, always totalizing – forms of control and domination. Con-Dom's work aims to expose these patterns, often by exposing audiences to forms of control and domination as a way of potentially revealing their customary acceptance of, and entrapment within, these forms. As with other power electronics acts, Con-Dom is therefore motivated by a kind of didactic-pedagogic, 'cultural terrorist' (thinking of the Grey Wolves) political function. And whilst Dando's vision of societal 'control' and 'domination' is hardly original, the punishing, brutal nature of how the message is delivered perhaps is. Confrontation is the core method in that delivery, as expressed by Dando:

> Confrontation is the chosen method of education. Con-Dom generates brutality, pain, fear, hate (the instruments of control), so that the existence of the forces of control may be acutely felt, experienced and recognised. The aim is to provoke resentment / confusion / ambivalence, to upset and challenge conditioned expectation, to shatter preconceptions.
>
> (Dando in Taylor 1992)

Dando's 'live assaults' embody the method most directly. They have featured overwhelming, chaotic barrages of feedback and noise, aggressive shouting, disturbing rear-projected images of mutilation, disease, and destruction, and even outright physical violence and confrontation with audience members. Indeed, Dando very much sees Con-Dom as a kind of total sensory, multimedia experience; in the same interview just quoted, Dando suggested that 'Con-Dom is neither music nor art, film or theatre. It is all of these things. It is none of them' (Dando in Taylor 1992).

Episode 9 of *Art Demolition*, a Huang Mingchuan documentary about the 'Art Demolition' festival held in Taiwan in 1995 at which Dando appeared, vividly illustrates both the multimedia experience of Con-Dom's live assaults and Dando's conception of the confrontational approach taken within them. The documentary shows clips from Dando's set. We hear squalls of feedback, churning static, and indiscernible but very aggressive shouting. We see a shirtless and sweaty Dando moving about the darkened room – extreme, often morbid imagery projected behind him – actively pushing, pulling, prodding, and pawing at audience members. The mood is tense and chaotic and Dando's attitude hostile and challenging. (These are all typical ingredients at a Con-Dom live show. At Never Saw When, a festival celebrating thirty years of Broken Flag held in London in 2012, I witnessed first-hand the genuine hostility and raw anger that Dando – and even members of the audience – experiences during live shows, even after all these years and after all the inevitable familiarization of such approaches that's taken place.) The culmination of the show sees Dando trying to fondle a woman's breasts, which, as the video voiceover has it, sets off a chain of counterattacks. The documentary then cuts to Dando, who explains:

> I played for forty minutes last night, and for 99% of the time, I was physically abusing people, for want of a better word. Pushing them around, wrestling them to the ground, touching their private parts. Nobody did anything to stop me. It took to the 38th minute of the performance until somebody finally had the guts to stand up for themselves. And that's really what Con-Dom's all about, it's saying 99% of the population don't stand up for themselves, don't fulfil themselves properly, and 1% maybe do. And that girl is the 1% that we should all be aspiring to, not the 99% that were purely apathetic.
>
> (ArtDemolition n.d.)

Dando's work, as can been in this example, clearly echoes the aggressive sound and attitude of groups like Whitehouse. It's hard to justify his actions in the documentary: both passive shock or stupor and aggressive counterattacks seem like very reasonable, human reactions to an artist demanding that an audience member face up in that very moment, at his demand, to what he sees as the contradictions of human society. Who knows what has happened in that audience member's day, or indeed life, leading up to that point? And yet, there is at least a coherent aesthetic strategy and political view being explored through Con-Dom's performances, and one can see (and indeed I have seen) how Dando's shows could have revelatory consequences for audience members.

Dando's aesthetic emphasis on shock and upset as tools of potential political awakening was time-honoured by the 1980s. Locally speaking, Dando's use of shocking, usually racially inflected (or just racist) subject matter on his records echoes similar tactics in industrial and power electronics artists before him, if anything pushing them to even more of an extreme. Con-Dom's *Calling All Aryans* and *Even More Racial Hatred* (not on label) tapes from 1984 and 1986, respectively, illustrate this point, with the use of a swastika on the sleeves being somewhat genre-standard, but the tape and track titles, such as 'Kampf', 'Next Reich', and 'New Holocaust', pushing things into dangerous territory (I mentioned the racial slurs on 2001's *Colour of a Man's Skin* earlier). Even if we know there are good, thoughtful intentions behind such works, does that justify them? Are they worth the risk? Even more than with Whitehouse and Ramleh, it would be hard to disagree with someone who judges these works simply to be beyond the pale; hateful, racist material that is not worth the effort.

Later albums *All in Good Faith* (1988) and *The Eighth Pillar* (1991) took similar tacks to these earlier tapes and live assaults, infused as they are with extreme language, imagery, and sounds. But they also added more conceptual elaboration and new themes to the mix. I'll examine each one in detail to arrive at a fuller aesthetic analysis of Con-Dom's work.

Eighth Pillar was based on the life of T.E. Lawrence, the archaeologist and military commander who was one of the British/Allied leaders of the 1916–18 Arab Revolt against the Ottoman Empire during the First World War. The album took inspiration from Lawrence's 1926 book, *The Seven Pillars of Wisdom*, which is a poetic, fictionalized account of Lawrence's experiences during the war (2008). For Dando, Lawrence's masochistic, almost spiritual fascination with torture and control as paths to some form of sexual (or otherwise) enlightenment and transcendence, as well as Lawrence's experiences in the war and his interest in motorcycles (which would lead to his death in 1935, following an accident), provided rich thematic and sonic inspiration. Accordingly, across the album, chugging armoured vehicles and motorbikes; strange, distant choirs; buzzing, often insect-like drones; and Dando's wild-but-echoing growls and shouts evoke an intense, spiritual-infused, desert-esque struggle.

The album's centrepiece, the seventeen-minute 'Confession of Faith', provides a kind of suite-like sonic image of Lawrence's experiences. The first three minutes layer two twisting and unsynchronized distorted guitar figures that are seemingly modelled around the speech pattern of the Arabic speaker at the beginning of the track. These collectively sound like two free improv guitarists chattering away against each other in fizzy disharmony and disunity. Horses galloping and motorbikes and cars driving around a larger sonic space open the track out in the fourth and fifth minutes, the muffled sound of stentorian preaching from Dando or someone else giving way to a gradual thickening of loud and noisy fuzz and hum across the fifth to seventh minutes. This barrage then starts to give way, the noise now just a buzzing in the left speaker and a sustained mid-range oscillation across the picture. A (sampled?) scene of torture starts to play out, tinny whips and then responding whimpers cycling around in unforgiving repetition, whilst a now-clear-miked Dando screams out a litany, shouting in William-Bennett-esque (though having moved position from subject to object, or abject) terrible ecstasy that 'I crave the terror of the next strike ... I am completely broken'. The voice is more and more exhausted as it works through the pain, but feels mysteriously transfigured nonetheless, released by the abjecting, consuming pain. The staging of the track across these first nine minutes is expertly done, different passages of phonographic scene-setting slowly building towards the more direct, emotionally climactic terror just described.

At 9'00", 'Confession of Faith' shifts into the opening sounds from *Lawrence of Arabia*, Strauss-esque chromatic strings and orchestra arcing out a tense pattern as lightly thudding noise dirties things up on the left of the picture. This noisy texture exits at the end of the eleventh minute, the track taken over completely by the swooning, dark strings of the soundtrack. As this climaxes at 12'00" the sound of the whipping torture returns, now playing out against a yearning solo cello line surrounded by glistening, singing strings. If the earlier torture was the scene of a transfiguration, this one is the after-effect, the torture continuing but the soul singing in its release. Calling back to Whitehouse and Hegarty, we could say the track has moved from abjection to full self-loss in the contours of its torture. The *Arabia* soundtrack then fades away in the fourteenth minute as a thick layering of engine and static noise consumes the sound. This modulates into a slightly thinner, treblier noise wall as a double-tracked, muffled Dando speaks out dark reflections from within the noise. The final minute clears out the texture almost completely, a voice lamenting in the far distance and a minor-key synth line repeating and repeating mournfully. Again, staging and shape are key, each panel of sound slowly merging into the next one, the disparate whole coming together along an emotional arc of climaxing transfiguration, then decay, then rest.

As can be seen, then, 'Confession of Faith' arrays all sorts of idioms and reference points along its way. It creates a kind of loose-but-deliberate form, and a coherent-collage style, out of its disparate elements, moving in brutal flow from Arabic scene setting to noise, torture, and transfiguration, to allusive yearning, then back to torture and a kind of terrible final rest. Collage of this sort was common in classic power electronics, as it had been in earlier twentieth-century avant-garde practice, where layering and collision produce a kind of super-meaning through confrontation. This has more general echoes in power electronics' use of sampled news reports, historical events, and other 'found' materials. In the case of Con-Dom and *Eighth Pillar*, the different sound sources and reference points construct a loose musical psychobiography of Lawrence, the sonic narrative and the affective atmosphere of its central track evoking a kind of Lawrencian experience of submission and ultimate transcendence through pain. Dando's effort to transcend conformity and constraint through exposure to taboo-busting pain can be seen in this light as a kind of bastard offshoot of the kind of joyful, ecstatic self-loss discussed earlier in the book.

All in Good Faith (1988, though an expanded version incorporating material from *This Sickness Faith*, Control Domination, 1985, and *Have Faith*, Broken Flag, 1987, was released on CD in 1996 by Functional Organisation) mirrors the focus on faith and transcendence of *The Eighth Pillar*. This is seen most obviously here in the title and in the tape's housing in a refashioned *Songs of Praise* hymnbook. But the album adds racist themes and titles (most notably 'Sir N****r' – not censored on the release – and the opening track, 'Klan') to this focus on faith.

'Klan' opens with nineteen seconds of a woman singing 'God Bless America', before a distant droning spray of turbulence starts to move slowly left-to-right in the stereo picture, with an oscillating, rising-and-falling tone added to that drone on its left. These left-to-right and up-and-down sounds shape the rest of track, where the textures and sounds sometimes thicken into crumbling static or tapping and sometimes stay with the soft rising/falling tone and distant, moving drone. Dando shouts, subsumed in the texture, intermittently. 'Surrender 88' follows a similar path of sampled speech moving into thickening noise. The track opens with thirty seconds of sampled dialogue, a woman and a man talking about 'peace, love, a sense of progress and wellbeing … He's healed me of hatred and bitterness that I've carried for thirty-five years', before the following three minutes of dense, clipped cicada noise and shouts from Dando. 'Sir N****r', again similarly, opens with the sound of a group of people singing a cappella country blues about heaven's door, before cluster-bleeps phase and modulate busily for four minutes. A preacher enters for the last twenty seconds and portentously describes America's 'divine assignment'.

All in Good Faith continues in this vein, stacking up reflections on faith against enhancing or undermining noise and shouting. For example, the final song on the first half, 'Master Speaks', opens with a woman saying, 'I actually felt the presence of Jesus just put his arms around me, and I heard an audible voice telling me he loved me and always loved me', before giving way to a relentless ten minutes of distant ostinato-synth, swiping, wobbling noise gestures, and a semi-audible Dando grandly shouting about Jesus. The effect is destabilizing and thrilling, the track building across those ten minutes to a pitch of saturated noise and screaming voice, as if the nothing-God is finally speaking. The woman from the opening of the track finally returns to reflect on the emptiness she felt as a drug addict before Jesus came into her life.

The four tracks on side B broadly follow the same pattern just outlined. They open with vocal samples reflecting on religious faith and belief before various forms of chuntering, punishing noise and Dando's wild vocals take over. Each track indeed gradually thickens and spreads in different ways before climaxing in some form of consuming noise. 'Christian Voice' and 'Road to Total Freedom' are particularly remarkable mixes of each of these elements. The former's opening voices discuss fundamentalism and belief in the bible, and Whitehouse-esque sustained buzzing and high tones provide a tense backdrop. Different sampled speeches and preachers then describe 'coming out of the churches and changing America', 'child sacrifice', and the 'racial suicide' represented in the dwindling population of 'Western democracies', noise and hateful message intermingling ferociously. 'Road to Total Freedom' opens with a woman talking about being 'raped the first time when I was five, and the fifth time when I was sixteen'. The woman describes how her mother was in the room during one of the rapes, and how one of them was at the hands of 'a man of God'. The rest of the track marries reedy, juddering high tones to a repeated quasi-bassline groove below it, as a distorted, shouting voice martially tromps around the centre, a kind of dreadful looped crowd following most of his phrases.

What we as listeners should or can take from all this is somewhat unclear. It's tempting to hear the album as a condemnation of cheap faith, the supposedly naïve investments in down-home religious faith of the sampled speakers and singers undercut by what we might hear as the 'true' pain and horror of existence as evoked here in the unforgiving noise textures, in Dando's subsumption in and intensification of that noise, and in the brutal testimonies and hate speech especially on Side B. But this is probably too simple. Considering Dando's particular interest in a kind of annihilating, submitting, abject-ecstatic spirituality, we could after all *also* easily hear some of these tracks as expressing the humbling and consuming value of religious faith; the noise elements of these tracks, in this understanding, would perhaps be an attempt to embody and exalt the speakers' reflections on faith. These different interpretations are valid and indeed not necessarily mutually exclusive. Ultimately, though, in sifting through these interpretative options I would say that, for me, the titles, words, and sounds of each of these tracks add up to an ugly but compelling picture of the different kinds of extremes often evident around religious faith and religious communities. That is, the consuming self-loss, salvation, and group-security that faith and community represent on the one hand, but also the division and wild prejudice they can sow on the other. The overwhelming force of the thick, dense, brutal noise textures of each track would be heard here as amplifying both the self-loss of faith on the one hand and the hatred and/or squalid terror expressed by the speakers on the other.

As a final interpretative comment, I'd note the dual role of noise here as both intensifier of the album's verbal themes and an emotional engine in its own right. After all, the noise opens its own emotional spaces on the album, its charred, unpredictable grooves and repetitions, and its intricate, wild loops and layers, putting the listener into a state of nervous excitement as they try to catch the pattern or stay inside the feeling. So, even though 'Road to Total Freedom' ends with the unadorned statement, 'without the Lord there's no hope', the listener is as likely to find themselves replaying and restaging the buzzing noise ballet that danced out for much of that track as they are to contemplate the message of that line, which after all is striking but potentially semantically limited. The noise, by contrast, is endless in its unsettled becoming.

Conclusion

As we've seen, then, power electronics in the 1980s – primarily, so far, in Britain – took the focus on taboo themes and dirty electronic sound of industrial music and ramped it up to an almost absurd extreme (even as it remained more 'music' than noise). Angry white men screaming about sadomasochistic sex or race or religion, backed with hissing and buzzing Wasp synth sounds, is both the stereotype and, to some extent, the reality of the music in this period. We saw many examples early on that would broadly fit that description, whether we think of Sutcliffe Jügend or Whitehouse, or later, of some aspects of Con-Dom.

But there's much more to both that stereotype and power electronics music in general. For example, in MB we saw an artist broadly in the power electronics world whose music was much subtler than that blunt stereotype suggests. Likewise, the case studies of Whitehouse, Ramleh, and Con-Dom demonstrated a variety of approaches and sounds even as it's clear that their work aligned with the power-electronics template of provocative taboo and crud nonetheless. Con-Dom, for his part, used anger, confrontation, and controversial (often racial or just downright racist) themes as deliberate tools of provocation. But these sat alongside a capacious sonic spread, subtle use of form, and an arresting access to high-intensity and often notably submissive-orientated emotion. Meanwhile, Whitehouse developed their own array of sounds and formal shapes over and above their basic template, with Bennett, like Dando, managing to evoke a true abjection or personal annihilation in his vocal performances, albeit in his case often via an active, assaulting subject position. Finally, Ramleh's sound was more gelatinous, murky, swamp-at-night rich – but likewise as emotionally arresting and, on occasion, annihilating and 'abjecting' in its own way – as that of Whitehouse or Con-Dom. All these artists, then, created work of great thrust and force that, in its dirt and opacity, also emphasized both characteristic noise discursive 'becoming' and a kind of idiosyncratic psychological 'abjection' in which hyperpersonalization and/or strained self-loss was performed in the music and potentially felt by listeners; it's indeed easy to get lost in this stuff, caught up in panic or annihilated by the sound.

Considering the intensity of the subject matter and the approach of power electronics, in finishing it's worth thinking further about how these aesthetic and psychological points shape or overlap with the supposed politics of the work. I made the point earlier that we can hear the sound of this music at something of a remove from the words and images, as a variegated exploration of, for example, developing approaches to noise as musical resource, to extreme vocal performance, and to a mixed-media approach in which sound, performance, and visuals come together to articulate various 'credos'. I've also made the point that the sheer extremity of the sound and performances can be heard to push the themes and points-of-view into an uncertain state, the music being hard to parse as a straight-up endorsement of the views. These interpretations argue for nuance and ambiguity as key qualities of power electronics music, despite the bluntness of its style. But I've likewise tried to acknowledge the many people who choose to reject power electronics outright as a music whose subject matter and attitudes are beyond the pale of what is acceptable. And it's not unreasonable to suggest that the topics and performance styles commonly found in power electronics should not be given airtime and tolerated. This is even if I personally tend to hear power electronics as an attempt to explore and perhaps expunge dark emotions and topics – as an opportunity for emotional release around subjects like male violence. This may come, for example, via identifying with, or feeling catharsis through, the intense abjection of the performers and the sound. For myself and many others the value of retaining a fringe, isolated, extra-mainstream and extra-academic stream of avant-garde expression that makes a space for such intense, shocking experiences and extreme themes, cannot be underestimated. Power electronics, in this interpretation, brings ugly subjects, events, and emotions to the surface. It is a kind of noise-musical reckoning with the Jungian shadow that, in the end, serves to release the dark energies that are otherwise compacted up within that shadow.

2

Anti-music?

'Anti-music' doesn't describe a scene, a movement, a genre or even a subgenre or substyle of noise or any other form. As much as it's possible to point to previous usage, it is one of a set of terms put forward by artists such as The New Blockaders to describe aspects of their work. And yet, expanded out onto a broader canvass, it is a useful category that allows us to draw together some important strands of pre or proto-noise music from the 1980s and early 1990s, serving as an important building block in our emerging story of noise. For the purposes of this book, then, I'm treating 'anti-music' as a proto-noise/noise style of Dada-influenced practice in which traditional conceptions of music in general and, more specifically, of musical form, technique and tools, are somewhat – 'somewhat' because I continue to find elements of musical form and style here as elsewhere – abandoned. Instead, anti-music expounds a philosophy rooted in nonconvention, destruction and negation and a noisy approach to sound making based chiefly on the amplification of non-traditional sound sources such as saws, power tools, chairs and modified vinyl. This sound making often takes the form of the destruction or manipulation of such 'concrete' sound sources.

A wide variety of practices might fit under this broad definition. As such, I'll spend a little bit of time in the chapter looking at aspects of anti-music in a broad array of noise and non-noise music. But the focus is very much on what I see as the core of what I'm calling the anti-musical style: The New Blockaders and The Haters. The first section expands on the social and cultural background of anti-music. The second examines the general tenets of anti-music in the context of various examples, notably The New Blockaders and The Haters. Sections 'The New Blockaders – *Changez Les Blockeurs* (1982) and *History of Nothing* (2001)' and 'The Haters – Performances (1979-present) and *In The Shade of Fire* (1986), with *Ordinarily Nowhere* (1995) and *Death-Defying Sickness* (2002)' dive deep on these two artists' work. The extended (relative to other chapters) Conclusion, finally, argues that the conceptual and sonic destruction inherent in anti-music can be placed into a rich tradition of psychoanalytic and mystical nihilisms stretching back through Lacan and Bataille to Meister Eckhart, Krishnamurti and others. There, ideas of nothingness, the void and divine darkness all similarly (and, seemingly, contradictorily) anchored productive, creative, transpersonal visions of the universe. The musical detail and specificity of various examples of anti-music offer support to this line of argument. But they are also examined, separately, as aesthetic ends in themselves.

Social and cultural background

In the previous chapter I described anti-music as sharing cultural roots, social contexts, and, to some extent, musical aesthetics with power electronics (and, in turn, industrial music). It's therefore useful to remind ourselves briefly of the social conditions and material infrastructure around these musics. As with groups like Whitehouse, the anti-music featured in this chapter emerged out of (or alongside) conditions of austerity, neo-Conservatism and free market economics in the UK and the United States (and, to some extent, Europe). Many saw these systems and ideologies as leading to forms of cultural decay and social taboo, especially in the Anglosphere, from rising unemployment and the decline of social-democratic safety nets to the emergence of a kind of culture-war puritanism and social conservatism. As far as we can draw direct lines between these broader social effects and specific forms of cultural production taking place within them it's fair to say that both power electronics and anti-music can justifiably be seen to be acting in response to their social context.

Anti-music likewise existed within the same ecosystem of post-punk, cassette and fanzine culture that so directly supported the heavily localized and marginal practices of power electronics and industrial music. Mail art, gigs in disused or derelict venues or small art galleries, and an international fringe network of magazines, zines, college radio, independent labels and so on all supported these musics. This ecosystem also existed within the same broader cultural dynamics explored in the previous chapter, where the centre of gravity of exploratory, perhaps even 'avant-garde' music making was gradually spreading outwards to the fringes, away from traditional bastions of high-art culture such as concert halls and major art galleries. This global fringe network wasn't an entirely new phenomenon; even Dada itself started somewhat on the margins, whilst as Bernard Gendron (and others) has noted, cultures as separate in time and place as cabaret in *Fin de siècle* Paris and Downtown Music in 1960s and 1970s New York had already fomented much cross-cultural, non-traditional experimentation (2002). But the emerging fringe musical network or ecosystem of the 1970s and 1980s in which the values and networks so important to anti-music were developed nevertheless represented something new.

Anti-musical destruction

> We are The New Blockaders. Blockade is resistance. It is our duty to blockade and to induce others to blockade … It is time for change – make way for The New Blockaders: The Discipline of Absolute Freedom! Abolish Everything! … Anti-books, anti-newspapers, anti-films, anti-art, anti-magazines, anti-poetry, anti-music.… We will make anti-statements about anything and everything, we will make a point of being pointless. … We must destroy in order to go forward! We are the creators who destroy.
>
> (Extracts from the *T.I.C. Manifesto*, included on the sleeve of The New Blockaders' *Changez Les Blockeurs*, self-released, 1982)

The New Blockaders (TNB) were a group from Newcastle in the North of England. Their core members were brothers Philip and Richard Rupenus, and they began releasing music in the early 1980s. TNB's work is often described as anti-music; not least because, as can be seen in the extract from the *T.I.C. Manifesto* above, they used this term themselves. The 'anti-musical' aspects of their work arise in its apparent (and actual) resistance towards conventional musical sound, to what we saw Hainge call 'musicality' (i.e. tonal, formal hierarchies) in the Introduction, and in the group's resistance towards conventional visual codes of performance. These resistances manifest, amongst other things, in their lack of typically deployed 'musical' instruments and in their insistence on wearing leather gimp masks on stage (though one could easily argue that the latter actually honours theatrical performance tropes as much as it might destroy them), both of which can be seen in Figure 2.1. The group's general emphasis on resistance and an 'anti' worldview, which can also be seen in the extract above, was in fact taken to such an extreme that they were known to resist not only art but also even anti-art. They wanted to resist absolutely everything; except for resistance, perhaps.

As will be obvious to anyone with even a passing familiarity with twentieth-century art, TNB's manifesto echoes earlier manifestos and movements. It takes clear inspiration, for example, from the Futurists' 'Art of Noise', from Dadaism, and from Gustav Metzger's auto-destructive art in its emphasis on provocation, novelty, absurdity and destruction. There are also obvious parallels with 'cultural terrorist' thinking in power electronics. But the group's – and anti-music in general's – most obvious forebear is probably the Dada-inspired, 1960s Fluxus anti-art position most

Figure 2.1 The New Blockaders live in Kortrijk, Belgium, 2017.

readily associated with Henry Flynt (via Metzger), where the avant-garde Dadaist challenging of institutional art from earlier in the century was turned inward on avant-garde art itself. Flynt's concept of 'cognitive nihilism', where dialectical reason is founded on a self-referencing contradiction that ultimately destroys itself, is also relevant here.

Alongside TNB, the LA-based, GX Jupitter-Larsen-led The Haters are the most obvious standard bearers of anti-musical destruction, conceptualism and performance art. As with TNB, The Haters wear masks in performance, subscribe to a philosophy of destruction and agitation, and use unconventional sound sources – in The Haters' case, drills, staple-guns, sandpaper, calculators and more – to make sound and/or noise. The two main case studies in the chapter are therefore dedicated to these two groups, as mentioned above. But other examples will give a broader sense of the threads of 'anti-music' that run through twentieth-century avant-garde culture.

I mentioned Fluxus in the context of Flynt above. The broader school of Fluxus composition is an obvious and important touchstone here. This is whether we think of La Monte Young's concept-music cycle *Compositions 1960*, with their various absurd, mostly text-based stage directions, including prompts to 'draw a straight line and follow it', or to push a piano through a wall (more on this in the TNB section below, but see Potter 2000 for context on these pieces). Or of Dick Higgins' *Danger Music* series, text scores that instruct performers to do everything from 'spontaneously catch hold of a hoist and be raised up at least three stories' (*Danger Music Number One*) to 'volunteer to have their spine removed' (*Danger Music Number Nine*). This Fluxus-originating strain of conceptually driven, non-traditionally musical performance practice carries through to the present day, with artists such as Mattin and Brandon LaBelle using verbal instruction and, above all, the social relations embedded in performance space as their artistic material. We'll consider Mattin again in Chapter 9 but it's worth explaining what I mean by 'the social relations embedded in performance space'; this would be where performers like Mattin and LaBelle set up scenarios where the social rules/norms/etiquette governing crowd behaviour in concert settings explicitly become part of the material of the performance, as for example in the Mattin performance where, à la one of the Young pieces, he sat silent in front of a crowd awaiting their reaction, recorded that sound and then played it back to them, again sitting silently.

Another important – this time parallel – anti-musical example comes in the destructive performances of early Japanese noise rock (or proto-harsh-noise) groups like Hijokaidan and Hanatarash in the late 1970s and 1980s, where venues were trashed, performers urinated and vomited on stage and musical instruments were destroyed. These performances echoed The Haters in their efforts to cause havoc and mess through carnivalesque destruction, chaotic sound and violent performance situations. In the case of the Japanese acts, somewhat more traditional musical tools and aesthetics were also deployed, however, with both groups named above, for example, using guitar and drums to produce noisy, extreme, but more somewhat more straightforwardly 'musical' sounds.

Perhaps the most important point of comparison here is the practice of making 'anti-records' that various US-based artists, from Boyd Rice to The Haters'

Jupitter-Larsen to Ron Lessard of RRRecords, explored in the late 1970s and 1980s. These 'anti-records' represent an important rejection and reuse of traditional musical materials. As with other forms of anti-music, the result conceptually subverts traditional modes of musicality and yet also generates and plays in and with traditional musical forms, patterns and sounds. For example, Jupitter-Larsen released records played by the listener scratching them (*The Haters 7*", Jupitter-Larsen, 1983) and records pressed with random, overlapping grooves that would sound different on each turntable (*A Basic Introduction to the 'T.N.U.'*, Alamut Records, 1990). The Haters' *Wind Licked Dirt* from 1988 (RRRecords) remains perhaps the most famous noise example of an anti-record. The album was released as a blank 12" with no grooves, with the packaging including both dirt and the instruction that 'This record is played by rubbing dirt on it' (C.D. and cassette versions were later released; Jupitter-Larsen, 1993, Hanson Records, 2008).

Lessard has had a sustained focus on the anti-record, with various RRR releases subject to treatments such as painting, melting or drilling. As his alter-ego Emil Beaulieau, Lessard used these 'anti-records' in live shows, in combination with his four-armed 'Minutoli' turntable, producing thick, gurgling, but often funky noise as a result (the funk coming in large part from locked grooves scratched into the vinyl). The 1991 tape, *Anti-Performance* (RRRecords), features a series of performances of anti-records from artists such as AMK, Kapotte Muziek, Billboard Combat and The Haters; in the latter's case the 'anti' action was doubled, since the album used was *Wind Licked Dirt*. *Anti-Performance* can be seen, in many senses, as an apogee of the conceptual and sonic potential inherent in the 'anti-record' idea.

As with TNB, these anti-record, Fluxus and post-Fluxus and noise examples attempted to resist or destroy key ingredients of conventional music making and social relating, whether in terms of tools, sound or performance tropes. As we'll see below, none managed to oppose or destroy music or social norms completely – musical protocols and hierarchies, aesthetic judgement and social rules have a way of returning even when they are repressed – but they provide important examples of alternative, noise-anchored approaches to music and social life nonetheless. Principles and parallels established and general cases discussed, the next case study dives directly into the sound world of TNB as a key example of anti-musical approaches to idea and sound.

The New Blockaders – *Changez Les Blockeurs* (1982) and *History of Nothing* (2001)

Changez Les Blockeurs opens with what sounds like a heavy, metal object being dragged slowly and haltingly across a cement floor. This sound revolves and repeats, gaining musical profile as distinct phrases and even aspects of phrasing and pulsing emerge, punching in and out almost as a digital sample would. As the sound gathers its forces, I myself lean in further and further, attention held. This dragging metal sound acts like a kind of cantus firmus throughout the album, a central sonic point of reference around which everything else is defined. Back to the early seconds of the album.

In the distance, more to the right of the stereo picture – though this isn't true stereo separation, since the effect is achieved by putting microphones at different distances from the sound source – metal is scraped in small melodic gestures. This sounds like a bowed cymbal but in reality is much more likely to be a saw scraping off metal. These scrapes or bows feel tense and grating in their thin sonic tactility; I can almost feel my skin crawl. But they also carry an emotional charge, embodying a kind of sonic argument where each gesture feels like an insistent and searching answer to some unheard question, an impression of sonic becoming that infuses the album's forty-five minutes of sound. The scraping-bowing sound disappears about three minutes in, with a more insistent, continuous, high-pitch squeaking joining the centre of the picture. This sound carries even more nervous tension than the scraping, its busy, filigree, chipmunk notes feeling like ants running over the skin. It's not a nice image but the sound does create a strong sense of forward momentum and energy.

These three sounds – dragging heavy metal, scraping-bowing and squeaking – dominate the whole album. As I said, the dragging sound is a kind of central cantus firmus but the other two motifs are important throughout. Back to the music. The scraping-bowing returns a minute later. Throughout this passage a distant sound of rain on a tin roof comes through as a background texture. At 5'42" things start to get chopped and screwed; the central dragging motif percussively beats and chops and a new version of the high-pitch squeaking comes back as grating, nails-on-chalkboard sounds. Things return, about a minute later, to the central motif mixed with distant bowing-scraping and rain. Over the next few minutes each of these elements, textures and techniques repeats, develops, evolves. For example, a gentle, thwacking or tapping, hammering pattern takes on various playful shapes during the ninth and tenth minutes. Following this, the central motif withdraws somewhat from 9'20", with the high-pitch squeaking taking centre stage for forty seconds or so before the central motif returns but in chopped sound blocks, almost like a solo being followed by a stop-chorus in jazz.

At 11'00" the central motif returns with more force, the album moving comfortably back in to its familiar, by now comforting territory. This carries on for two minutes, until at 13'04" the texture clears again somewhat, the distant bowing giving way to the squeaking and the rain briefly returning, as the central motif again withdraws slightly. A minute later the bowing returns and we're back into thicker textures, with aspects of thwacking and scrimmaging popping up here and there in the fifteenth and sixteenth minutes, the music busy with assaulting event. The remaining six or so minutes on the first side and track continue in much the same manner, adding small details and contrasts – the rain becomes heavier in the twenty-first minute, for example, while some clip-clopping shoe sounds briefly enter towards the end of that minute and the following one – but essentially moving around the same musical environment as the previous sixteen. All 22'33" are based on a shared set of musical materials, arrayed in slowly developing shapes and hitting various peaks and troughs of energy.

I've offered a lot of descriptive detail so far, and we'll have a little more on the second side before we get to more extended interpretation. This is deliberate: music like this is often dismissed or idealized in different ways, perhaps as party trick, or pure concept, or non-musical chaos. Getting inside its sounds in such detail is one way to dispel this.

The second side of the album is drawn largely in the same shapes and colours as the first. We start by flowing naturally on from the ending of Side One, though the central, metal-dragging sound enters especially aggressively at the start of the track, and indeed takes on a particular weight and force in the first few minutes, once again calling me to attention. The squeaking, too, feels more forceful and tetchier to me in these early minutes. The scraping-bowing sound returns towards the end of the second minute, joining the other two, but it now sounds with more reverb; wetter and more distant. A particularly exciting and energizing episode in the fourth and fifth minutes sees the scraping-bowing cut through sharply in a series of exclamatory gestures.

A long passage of relative quiet then runs from the sixth to the fourteenth minutes, where the central motif, now more percussive in attack, largely dominates. Even though some distant speaking and barking, with clip-clopping and passing cars, can be heard in the thirteenth and fourteenth minutes, a great deal of space surrounds that central motif in terms of both the silence between gestures and its isolation in the sonic environment. This passage contrasts sharply with the much busier textures and gestural language of the preceding five minutes, just as it does with the remaining seven to eight minutes of the track. The scraping-bowing and the squeaking both return for those seven to eight minutes, tag-teaming in and out, finding new sounds and gestures along the way – there is a particularly interesting and engaging marriage of high-pitched scraping, dog yelping and door shutting in the sixteenth minute – as the different motifs continue to dialogue and develop. The final minute or so of the track gradually leaves the harsher scraping and squeaking behind, turning inward into thudding and creaking, the listener pulling back from the sound, before a somewhat abrupt ending.

Putting all this detail together, we can see the second side of the album as a kind of ternary (i.e. A/B/A) form with a short coda. To wit, the busy first five minutes lead into a broadly solo passage of relative stillness and quiet, before the more frenzied, recapitulatory but still playfully developmental final section and the brief coda. And, stepping back and looking across the whole album, we can see a consistent set of motifs and gestures running across both sides, which vary as the musicians play with the sound and capability of their sources but remain relatively stable as reference points within the sound. The traditional terms I've just used – ternary form, coda, motif, variation – are perhaps somewhat alien concepts to place on to this brutally rudimentary 'anti-music', which on one level it would be reasonable to hear as relatively spontaneous, sonically unpolished noise. And yet, these two reactions don't seem mutually exclusive to me: a piece of music can be sonically unpolished and feel relatively spontaneous whilst also gelling together – or, again echoing Hainge, 'encoding' – into something that can be read as or feel like traditional musical language and form. This is something we'll see again and again with later forms of noise music. These traditional terms, then, clue us into some of the ways that noise can work *qua* music, as emerging form and structure; the 'becoming style' layer of the book's overarching interpretative argument. After all, on both sides of the album these various motivic mutations and mirrors create a sense of structural coherence in their evocation of distinct patterns of space and syntax. In addition to structural coherence and spatial definition, musicality *also* comes through in the character of the other two main motifs, the scraping-bowing and the squeaking. As I've said, these motifs carry energy and excitement both in their sonic profiles and in their constant interplay, the one entering as the other retreats or each drawing out different aspects of the other as they overlap. And finally, though it might seem a very basic element of the sound, the periodic presence of distant rainy pattering likewise calls to mind a sense of musical texture and colour. This is all even as the brute roughness and remaining unpredictability of the sound ensure things are never fully settled or hierarchized. So, whilst the sense of structure and space evoked across the album – space between and across musical or sonic 'phrases', or literal space between the sounds – is perhaps one of its chief musical attributes, we never lose the sense of noise tension that is so important to the sound; noise and music are held in a suspended dialectic throughout.

TNB therefore create musical noise filled with definition, rise-and-fall and recurring detail. These details come together to create a sense of linguistic play and puzzle, the distinct motifs speaking to and answering each other and the jumble of dirty, abrasive sound never quite settling into clear meaning but always heading in that direction. For the attentive listener – stepping into the psychological dimension for a moment – though the sound, for this listener at least, never quite overwhelms to the point of intense depersonalization, the sonic puzzle, volume and aggression are such that the listening experience could easily lead to lighter, more passing forms of self-loss of the kind described in the Introduction to the book. *Changez* distracts and disturbs enough to draw one out of oneself.

These same impressions of structural becoming run through TNB's later music, where, again, a rudimentary approach to sound making nevertheless leads to a whole variety of sonic results. The 2001 compilation album, *History of Nothing* (released on Japanese label Siren, and then again in curtailed form on Hanson Records in 2010), illustrates this point well. *History of Nothing* gathered tracks from various 7" and other releases from across the 1980s and 1990s. Though the range of its music is broadly in keeping with the rough-hewn sounds and largely everyday sound sources heard earlier on *Changez*, the assorted tracks nevertheless point to different kinds of textures, sounds and energies as had been present on that earlier album. For instance, the busy scrapes and slow-winding feedback of 'First Offensive' contrast sharply with the title track, 'History of Nothing', which is ASMR-like in its gentle, friction-driven phonography. 'Epater Les Bourgeois' is different still, its unrelenting chewed-up electronic sound surrounded by clattering, collapsing piles of pots and pans in a frenzy of propulsive noise. 'X-Nihilist Assault' matches the intensity of 'Epater' but adds a greater sense of individual gesture and figure to the tumult. Other tracks add yet more different layers of sound sources, sound qualities and densities of musical texture and detail. 'Viva Negativa!', for example, is particularly interesting, with its foregrounded streams of quiet feedback and distortion, its mid-level click-clacking and chuting and its deep background, periodic swelling of voices and hum. 'Blockade is Resistance' is built from the same kinds of metal dragging sounds heard on *Changez* but adds thick, unrelenting layers of clatter, feedback and static, the track approaching the density and abrasion of harsh noise. 'Hidden Agenda' is made from two, slightly misaligned in both time and stereo space clumps of churning static. These clumps shift in texture and density, moving into contrasting pulsing noise and static periodically and gradually incorporating ricocheting woodpecker hammer blows that add gestural speed and tension to the sound. As with 'Blockade', the harshness here, though a little warmer and wetter than on the previous track, is unrelenting, feeling at times like it broaches harsh noise wall territory.

The sound on all these tracks, then, is once again built out of distinctly 'musical' layers, gestures and interactions, even as the sonic character of each layer and the unpredictable, dialectical play of the whole never quite settles into order or resolution. And yet, if TNB's manifesto and billing are to be believed, the sounds on both *History of Nothing* and *Changez* that I've described in distinctly musical terms are nothing of the sort. Instead, they are 'pure sonic nihilism', to echo one of TNB's slogans; a kind of anti-music meant to destroy music. To destruct musical identity into nothingness. As a rhetorical idea, such nothingness is a neat and seductive one. The notion that TNB's sounds are so extreme and beyond the pale that they transcend music and art, attaining a kind of nth degree of nihilistic power, feels therefore both appealingly dangerous and convincingly clean, simple and right. The problem, or rather the fact, is that humans can and will find order – form, art, music – in anything. This is writ large across this book, where one of the two main strands sees me identifying moments or passages where noise music coheres into a kind of language or musical code. My close listening of *Changez* above can be seen as an embodiment of this process of noise-becoming-music, of noise and music fusing in held dialectical tension.

TNB themselves know that a true anti-music can't exist, that a 'Gesamtnichtswerk' (to take the name of a 2002 compilation of their music), or a 'total nothing work', is impossible. Everyone knows it: I'm not saying anything surprising in pointing this out. But this 'reality check' doesn't make TNB's manifesto any less powerful, nor does it detract from the force of their approach. Even if TNB's work submits easily to cognitive ordering and manipulation, and even if *Changez* has various direct conceptual and sonic forebears – I've already mentioned the artistic lineage it exists in, but on both conceptual and sonic levels a piece like La Monte Young's 1960 *Poem for Chairs, Tables, Benches, Etc. (Or Other Sound Sources)*, where the titular objects are dragged across the ground to create a cacophony of noise, is a direct ancestor – the group can still be recognized as important pioneers of proto-noise music in which ideas of sonic convention and social tradition are turned on their head. This is therefore (proto-)noise that's sold as musical and social destruction but that in the end is more like distortion and creation ('we are the creators who destroy', to quote TNB). We'll come back to this idea in the next section, and then again in more depth in the Conclusion.

The Haters – Performances (1979-present) and *In The Shade of Fire* (1986), with *Ordinarily Nowhere* (1995) and *Death-Defying Sickness* (2002)

The Haters is the name GX Jupitter-Larsen has used since 1979 for his various activities and collaborations as performance artist and musician; for many of its performances the group has included local musicians and 'agitators' as collaborative members. As we started to see above, The Haters' work is anchored as much in performance, performance art and conceptual art as it is live or pre-recorded sound.

The article that Jupitter-Larsen wrote for *As Loud As Possible* in 2010 contains a useful précis of the philosophical impetus behind the project, as well as summarizing many of Jupitter-Larsen's key performance pieces and techniques. In terms of that 'philosophical impetus', Jupitter-Larsen suggests that,

> Free thought fused with non-confrontational violence became the untitled ideology of The Haters. For a mess to be a truly BIG mess, you have to destroy only discarded rubbish and let the mess mean something clutter has never meant before ... Socially, what could be noisier than plain confusion? ... The purest form of social noise is doubt.
>
> (2010, 28)

As can be seen, Jupitter-Larsen here emphasizes freedom of thought, non-confrontational violence, mess and rubbish and confusion and doubt. As is typical for Jupitter-Larsen, the quote also features a poetic description of how, somehow, destroying something that is *already* rubbish infuses that rubbish with a new kind of meaning; makes clutter transcend into value, aesthetics cathecting an object such that it shifts from being present-at-hand to ready-at-hand. Above all, Jupitter-Larsen emphasizes a kind of social noise that, we could surmise, might lead people into a different sense of themselves and the society around them. This, of course, echoes the power electronics' (and, as we saw, Viennese Actionist) emphasis on provocation and challenge. It seems that all these artists felt that something valuable arises from such challenge and provocation, perhaps a kind of frisson or reprogramming that pushes people beyond habitual associations into a new relation to the world.

In the case of the early period of the Haters in the late 1970s and early 1980s, these ideas were first applied in performances in which sound was either absent or a secondary concern. This was such that pre-recordings of 'fuzzy, lo-fi soundtracks' would simply be started and stopped as audio bookends to the visual, physical performance of the group (2010, 29). Sound – at least sound beyond the sound arising naturally from the actions on stage – was something to be used merely to signify the beginning and end of performances. Jupitter-Larsen indeed suggests that,

> In 1979, confusion for me meant the kind of noise I was looking for wouldn't be the audible kind. What I was looking for was a sociological transmission. A social distortion instead of sonic feedback would be my personal post-punk mandate.
>
> (2010, 28)

Such 'social distortion' was explored through performances in which piles of garbage were destroyed in exponential order, from paper tearing to wood breaking to glass smashing and metal wrecking, with pre-ordained 'agitators' in the audience being cued at various points to encourage communal destruction. Such performances were not intended to threaten people's personal space and safety as much as they were to channel collective energy through non-confrontational violence. And, in so doing, to produce a kind of catharsis or 'reprogramming' that might prove both healing and transformative.

The Haters' approach shifted its emphasis (if not its objective) over the course of the late 1980s and 1990s. In this period, different forms of live sound became pivotal to the group's performances, in many cases acting as an audible representation of a narrative or concept being explored in the piece. Indeed, by 1995 the group had stopped using pre-recorded sound in live performance altogether. The Haters' work also moved from an emphasis on *destruction* to one of *erosion* around this time. To wit, from the late 1980s on live sound in the form of the destruction of various objects became more and more important. From 1992, erosion came to the fore. The first example of the latter can be seen in a Paris performance in which a live microphone was slowly pushed into a power grinder. The piece 'Mind The Gap', from a few years later, used an amplified staple-gun to shatter a stack of LPs (with two versions of this captured on *Mind The Gap*, Vinyl Communications, 1996, alongside another track). The 'Drunk on Decay' performance series suspended an amplified funnel on heavier and heavier objects and allowed it to 'drag and erode on a spinning sandpaper turntable' (this was captured on the 1997 album of the same name on Release Entertainment). 'Building Empty Holes' used 'amplified electric drills to turn large wooden objects into sawdust'; *Building Empty Holes* was released in 2011 (Skeleton Dust Recordings) as an audio device with tape player, mini amplifier and a six-minute looped cassette packaged inside a handmade wooden box (2010, 29–30 for details on all these performances and others. See Jupiter-Larsen's 'performance journal', *Digging through Time*, 2020, for a fuller account). Finally, in a glorious *coup de theatre* that brought together the various threads from the previous twenty years of violence and destruction, everyday objects and noise, from 1999 on Jupiter-Larsen began to use as his main sound source what he called an 'Untitled Title Belt'. As can be seen in Figure 2.2, this is a literal belt worn around the waist designed in the style of a championship wrestling belt but with built-in distortion pedal, microphone and noise generator.

The 'Untitled Title Belt' has been far from the only sound source in this later period though. 'Loud Luggage', for example, placed radio transistors inside briefcases, using microphones on the surface of the briefcases to draw out potent wails of feedback and noise. As Arvo Zylo has said, 'I have seen incredible sounds come out of the simple rubbing or pounding of these briefcases, not to mention when someone takes an angle grinder to them.' A separate stream of live radio performance should also be acknowledged as an important dimension of the group's work throughout their existence (Zylo 2019).

In parallel to the 'anti-musical' – though even here, as wood gets drilled into sawdust or objects are ground down, conventional musical protocols of spectacle, performer, and form are clearly present – performance work I've just been surveying,

Figure 2.2 The Haters, 'Untitled Title Belt'.

The Haters released a series of records throughout the 1980s, 1990s and into the twenty-first century. I've already mentioned some examples of Haters anti-records above, notably *Wind Licked Dirt*. In the rest of this section, I'll look at one of the group's most important 'conventional' albums, *In The Shade of Fire* (Silent, 1986), as well as selected later works. This is done to convey a sense of what their music – or, in Jupitter-Larsen's term, 'entropic noise collages' (2010, 29) – sounds like, and to explore how it does or does not relate to the destructive philosophy mentioned above.

In the sleeve notes to *In The Shade of Fire*, Jupitter-Larsen describes the album – and the group's work as a whole – as a form of 'destroyed music': 'My destroyed music is the sounds of anything getting literally or conceptually smashed, crashed, demolished, vandalized, slashed, ravaged with fire, or cut up, bombed, uprooted, or undone'. (This description has obvious parallels with the views on the destruction of rubbish outlined above.) But 'destroyed music' is not conceived negatively. Instead, Jupitter-Larsen sees positive transformation in the act of destruction.

> To destroy is the transformation of an entity from one state to another. This transformation can be done in a positive manner. The act of 'positive destruction' is the deliberate and active breaking up of entities into more dynamic pieces to be collaged together into new forms. It could also be said that 'positive destruction' can also be the making of something more efficient by shattering away any and all nonessentials. My 'destroyed music' acts as a kind of audio account or authentic evidence of the said transformation that takes place during the act of 'positive destruction'.
>
> (1986)

Destruction transforms and creates, according to Jupitter-Larsen.

When an artist is as eloquent as Jupitter-Larsen in describing the conceptual and aesthetic programme they see as defining their work, the analyst or critic is easily seduced. It's very tempting in cases like this either to take the artist's hand and be led blindly into their house, using your analysis simply to pause and marvel at what you are being shown. Or, on the other hand, to see the power of it and go in the other direction, trying to poke holes or offer alternative readings perhaps merely for their own sake. As a way of attempting to find the best route through this impasse, I do both, hearing the album in the terms set out by Jupitter-Larsen but also thinking about others.

In the first respect, it's easy to hear different forms and processes of destruction in the album; to honour, in a way, Jupitter-Larsen's aesthetic vision. I'll run through key tracks to establish this point. The opening track, 'Glsam', consists of five minutes of shattering glass locked into a repeated groove, with hints of a crumbling chromatic synth gesture underneath. The next track, 'Explosions 3', is even more suggestive of destruction, its five minutes of sound working through an extended series of crashing bombs in the left channel and perhaps a volcano exploding in the right. The track has a strong sonic presence, the sound whooshing and banging all within a pall of overbearing heaviness. 'Iny 1', next, is a minute or so of paper being cut up with scissors; 'Iny 2', jumping ahead to the end of the album, is similar though slightly weightier in sound. 'Bebas', following 'Iny 1', is more in line with the smashing loops of 'Glsam', though the sound is pitched lower, draggier, and has more thwack. It is less like glass smashing than, in the right channel, a car slowly going through a grinder and, in the left, things repeatedly crashing to the ground in a large warehouse. The loops here are simple and brief but the slight misalignment of the two channels and the internal sonic detail of each loop are such that the track remains compulsive throughout. 'Diti', later on, again suggests 'Glsam', but the sound is a little more varied and less straightforward than earlier.

As these descriptions indicate, the album is based very much in simple, concrete (or 'concrète') materials that often suggest destruction. Repeating, iterative processes, natural or otherwise, feature throughout. Many of the tracks are also built on interesting musical contrasts between their left and right channels, both in terms of sound and in terms of alignment and misalignment of loops. Two final examples add more flesh to these points. The eight-minute 'Thuch' is built on precisely this kind of light variation between left and right channels. Both channels feature ASMR-like clanking gravel slides, like pebbles dashing down a stone hill, with the right pitched slightly higher and ahead and the left slightly lower and almost in close answering canon with the right. Another eight-minute track, 'Fire 5', is similarly pictorial and similarly dyadic, though here there is more of a contrast between the two channels. On the left, we hear a 1.5-second loop of a rising/falling drum stutter over a bed of embers. On the right, a more sustained sound of fire burning that yet contains a hint of rising/falling buried deep in flames. Each side, in this way, resembles but expands on the other.

Across both tracks, in any case, as on the rest of the album, we hear simple but seductively 'designed' material built on puzzle and unresolved flow, sounds rich in character and interaction locked in perpetual flow. With their quite literal pictorialism and their concentrated, minimalist character, many of these tracks feel like phonographic etudes, meditative studies both of the sound quality of various events or phenomena – from fire burning to paper tearing, explosions to pebble dashing – and also of the temporal, processual flow of these phenomena. It's easy to make a connection to Pierre Henry and Pierre Schaeffer's early musique concrète' cataloguing of sounds in studies like Schaeffer's *Etude aux chemins de fer* (1948) or in pieces like the duo's *Symphonie pour un homme seul* (1949–50). It is also easy, in the case of The Haters, to get lost in these tracks, lightly trancing and self-losing in tandem with their cyclic, looping repetition and their inviting, detailed, but simple lattice-sounds. It's true that some tracks are coarser than this description suggests: the almost DJ-like cuts and scratches in the banging, clattering sounds of 'Cassas' are hard to relax around, even if they are based in the same complementary but contrasting two channel, looping repetition as the other tracks. And it's important to acknowledge the sheer noisiness of tracks like 'Explosions 3'. These are not necessarily easy listens for non-noise fans. Nevertheless, much of the sound here flows comparatively gently, sketching small sonic images filled with simple but enigmatic musicality and detail and shimmering in slight blur. The longest track on the album, the 11'37" 'Taisic', is an excellent illustration of this summary point. Built on a bed of quiet, centred static and hiss, which cuts in and out unpredictably but gently, the foreground of the track consists of a simple swiping or tearing sound. This sound starts out towards the right of the stereo picture before moving to the hard left at 2'50" and then back again at around five minutes (it goes left again at 7'24" and becomes slightly more regular and lower pitched before returning for good to the right at 9'24"). This sound is more gestural and defined than the central static, but is still essentially tender in profile, returning every few seconds for a swipe or two or three, in almost-but-never-quite-predictable patterns. As with other tracks, the effect is hypnotic, musical in spirit even as the sound is anything but traditional in nature.

Where does this leave either GX's 'destroyed music' philosophy, or any other interpretation we might offer in response to the album? As I've said, many of these tracks are indeed based on (actual or evoked) sounds of destruction, either literal (glass smashing, paper tearing, fire burning) or more metaphorical (the erosion and deposition of pebbles, the impression of exploding). These are, often, acts of 'undoing' that yet become a kind of positive *doing* in their being documented, constructed or perceived. These tracks present pictures of things – pieces of music – being *made* even amidst the unmaking that is inherent in their destructive imagery and processes. Moreover, and in the same vein, these tracks are, to use one of Jupitter-Larsen's favourite terms, *entropic* in their somewhat unadorned presentation of random processes of decay. But entropy, in our order-making minds, invariably expresses new possibilities, suggests change, transformation and, above all, opportunity for novel creation. We find it hard to look at a campfire burning away and not on some level think of the new day coming tomorrow. We find it hard to think of the world falling apart and not think of our part in putting it back together. In being frozen as recordings these tracks play into that cognitive preference for order and for creation over disorder and destruction. They give us opportunities to make of them and of ourselves anew each time, each listening a chance to find meaning and to find a small part of ourselves once again through different processes of destruction and death. It's the classic hero story of walking through the fire and then returning home again. These tracks are destructive only in the sense that destruction, as Jupitter-Larsen himself seems to suggest, is always also a form of creation.

Setting aside – or perhaps just adding to – these Jupitter-Larsen-set interpretative coordinates, we can note once again what I would describe as the *musical* design of the album and recognize this as an aesthetic end in itself. As I've pointed out, on this note, though the materials and musical processes here are quite simple – most of the tracks being made from a simple, or simple-sounding, source split into two closely related and largely repeated stereo-separate loops – the musical results contain enough sonic detail in terms of colour and gesture, as well as in terms of counterpoint and rhythmic interrelation between and within the loops, to offer new things to the listener with each new hearing. Those listeners are likely to be sometimes hypnotized in trance, sometimes left confused and sometimes tickled by a left-brain desire to decode and solve the puzzle of the musical design. Likewise, the album's offsetting of its sonic harshness either with quiet mixes and emphasis on the one hand, or with softer and more gentle sounds on the other, also adds to the rich character of this (noise-)musical design. We can attend to this character without considering any broader semiotics of destruction.

Though the study-like concentration of *In the Shade of Fire* has its own particular character, its approach to material, musical design, process and form nevertheless has parallels across The Haters' recorded output. *Death-Defying Sickness* (Banned Production, 2002), for example, is much more sonically aggressive than *Fire*, feeling more like harsh wall noise than anything else. *Sickness* consists of two long tracks (18'29" and 26'59" respectively) filled completely with a relentless buzz saw drone, which is surrounded by tearing, scratchy and abrasive feedback and static glinting around and above it. The mulch of this sound is immersive for listeners, who can easily disappear in the restlessness and complexity of the noise marginalia or get pulled into local micro-patterns and dialectics. Either way, *Death-Defying Sickness* ultimately sounds like someone has stuck contact mics onto a large, buzzing angle grinder cutting slowly through metal. And yet, in its working through of a steady process, and its concentration of material and detail, the album echoes the trancing pull of *In The Shade of Fire*.

Ordinarily Nowhere (Pure, 1995) sits somewhere in between these two albums. For starters, it is more resolutely noisy and harsh than *Fire*. 'Smack', for example, adapts the smashing glass of 'Glsan' but adds churning static and a drawn-out length, at 12'23". 'Fireback' is fifteen minutes of burning fire with insistent but distant crackle and feedback above it. 'Make a Fire and Be Happy', meanwhile, contains a surreal, computerized verbal tribute to a 'magnificently beautiful' fire destroying an 'edifice' only 'to be created into a thing even more beautiful', as noisy churn is phased and delayed across eighteen inventive minutes. 'Mangle Whack' is almost like conventional harsh noise, various crunchy dive bombs, explosions and static dancing around each other wildly for ten minutes. *Ordinarily Nowhere* is therefore dominated by harsh, difficult sounds. And yet, as well as evoking the concentration of *Fire*, these tracks never quite settle into the broader brutality of *Sickness*. 'Fireback', in particular, feels of a gentler persuasion, whilst the cyborg hook of 'Make a Fire and Be Happy' keeps reasserting a strange kind of joy and wonder that likewise suggests a more obviously welcoming impression than is created on *Sickness*.

We can draw some broader interpretative points from these three albums. First, that The Haters' recorded work is dominated by drawn-out, process-focused sound that is often simple in source but full in subtle or not so subtle detail. Second, as with TNB, these sounds are both usually noisy in character, sometimes harshly so, but ultimately musical in orientation. Third, that destruction and entropy are clear thematic touchstones, both in terms of explicit conceptual framing and in terms of sound and deteriorating sonic processes. Destruction and entropy are indeed potent creative drivers in The Haters' work, serving as energizing stage directions for a play about the creative or transformative power of alternative modes of thinking and artmaking. In a sense, then, what happens in The Haters' recorded (and, indeed, non-recorded) work is that existential concepts of destruction and decay are turned first into aesthetic principles and then turned back again into enriched existential statements where destruction and decay become alternative frames in which to think existence.

Conclusion: Destruction, distortion and creation

Whether we describe their work as 'anti-music' or not, it's therefore clear that for both TNB and The Haters (as well as, perhaps, for the other composers and artists mentioned above), ideas of 'destruction', as well as, in the 'anti' of TNB and the 'distortion' and 'confusion' of The Haters, resistance, represent the highest of creative (and perhaps existential) ideals. Put simply, their work destroys in order to create.

It's not hard to see connections between this artistic emphasis on destruction and resistance and extra-musical, even transpersonal – to use an important term from the Introduction – and nihilistic ideas of negation, nothingness and the void. Nihilism and nothingness are indeed both explicit touchstones for TNB: see for example the aforementioned *History of Nothing*, or their 2015 album on Klanggalerie, *Nonchalant Acts of Artistic Nihilism* (not to mention the 'pure sonic nihilism' referenced above). As was the case in our discussion of destruction, it's easy to see the 'nothingness' of nihilism in purely negative terms. But as many have argued, nihilism has more often been seen as an opportunity to transcend traditional cultural attitudes, social norms and etiquette in a search for deeper meaning (see Brassier 2007). Nihilism, like anti-music, perhaps negates in order to create. Moreover, such nihilism embodies a position in which annihilation – of self, of physical and/or musical materials, of social or aesthetic norms – provides productive, transpersonal transformation and perhaps even release. Underlying this position, it's fair to say, is an account of the universe as orientated round a lack or a void rather than as something as unsustainable as humanistic life. There is much more to say about this; given the importance of destruction, nothingness and nihilism across anti-music as a whole, in closing I'll briefly explore these broader dimensions of anti-musical nihilistic and destructive creativity.

In addition to the super-egoic, transpersonal aspects of annihilating destruction, the further psychoanalytic dimensions of anti-music's turning towards destruction, resistance and, perhaps, the void are hard to miss. For instance, it can be connected to the universal 'nothing' or 'lack' that, for Lacan, sits at the very core of our psyches generating desire and energy for wholeness but in a manner that occludes the lack itself (1977). Lacking psyches (aka psyches) can never be made whole, will always search for the missing piece of their happiness until they recognize that there will always be a missing piece, a void, at the core of life. Anti-music, perhaps, recognizes and tries to realize that fact.

Another, complementary, way to think about anti-music's destruction or negation is offered by the widespread and deep-rooted, proto-nihilist spiritual-literary mystical tradition that we can trace back through thinkers as varied in time and geography as Georges Bataille, Jiddu Krishnamurti, Meister Eckhart, Dionysius, Angela of Foligno, Nagarjuna and beyond. For all of these thinkers and mystics, ideas of the divine, or simply of being, are synonymous with darkness, the void, emptiness, nothingness. Or, 'no-thingness', as Krishnamurti often emphasized (this emphasis recurs throughout his recorded talks, but his 1975 dialogues with physicist, David Bohm, are a particularly useful source in this respect; 2016). For example, Nagarjuna focused his cosmology on the 'way of emptiness' – 'sunyata' – where no entity or thing underlies worldly appearances (see Westerhof 2018). Similarly – and as we'll see more of in Chapter 8, where the liberating, abject 'nothingness' of masochistic submission is explored in the context of musicians such as Atrax Morgue – Georges Bataille's preoccupation with sex and death, and the supposed ecstasy of death-in-sex, was underpinned by ideas of a God of negation and nothingness, and of an unknowing and impersonal poiesis. Eugene Thacker quotes Bataille on this point in *Starry Speculative Corpse* (2015), a book that indeed stands as a useful précis of some of these spiritual-mystical threads of nothingness and divine darkness: 'I hold the apprehension of God … to be an obstacle in the movement which carries us to the more obscure apprehension of unknowing: of a presence which is no longer in any way distinct from an absence.' Thacker expands on this:

> This darkness-mysticism has to be placed in the context of Bataille's own version of political economy, a non-human, 'general economy' based on excess and expenditure. In the same way that divine darkness is in excess of the individuated human being, so is there a divine darkness that is in excess of the world – at least the world that we as human beings construct for ourselves and fashion in our image. Divine darkness is precisely this negative movement that cuts across self and world, the human and the non-human – not by virtue of a bountiful, vitalistic life-force, but by way of an emptying and a darkening.
>
> (2015, 35–6)

Divine darkness, for Bataille and others, therefore constitutes a kind of ultimate level of reality, underlying or supervening both human and non-human objects alike. Darkness and unknowing, void and aporia, as truth.

What has all this divine darkness and nothingness/no-thingness to do with The Haters, TNB and anti-music more generally? I've already drawn parallels between these groups' focus on destruction and negation on the one hand and broader transpersonal and nihilistic ideas of transformation through negation on the other. The point in mentioning Thacker, Bataille, Krishnamurti and the broader spiritual-literary tradition we might see them as belonging to is to establish the deep, wide roots of such thinking in cultural history. The rhetorical emphasis on destruction and negation in anti-music plugs into this deeper history, articulating its practice as yet another iteration of void-love, of finding something in nothing. But it's not just that: I haven't emphasized the point as yet, but it's important also to acknowledge the somewhat 'impersonal' nature of anti-music's creative process, something that likewise plugs it into that tradition of the 'no-thing' (including no self) just mentioned. For instance, though we could easily see Jupitter-Larsen as a kind of 'strong author', given his cult status within the noise scene (as we could TNB's Rupenus brothers), it's also the case that he and others like him have deliberately avoided any sense of traditional mastery and virtuosity in their practice. The use of anonymizing leather masks in performance undergirds this. In neither do we find a particular cultivation of virtuosity or notable markers of a traditional 'compositional' voice. Instead, objects are destroyed, power tools amplified and processes left to run. And yet, as with similar contradictions in figures like John Cage, both anti-musical groups are anchored in clear and strongly voiced manifestos and opinion. And, as I said, both Jupitter-Larsen and the Rupenus brothers have attained cult, even guru-like status on the scene; like John Cage in his milieu. The artistic self is therefore both present and absent across anti-music, asserted strongly in interviews, promotional materials and performances but deliberately effaced or destroyed in aesthetic process along with musical and physical material, perhaps in an attempt to court the power of the void that Bataille, Nagarjuna and the others have written about. Destruction of various kinds (metal on metal; saw on piano; sticks burning; authorial control) here therefore perhaps serves above all to open a portal into creativity and creation, the one leading naturally to the other.

For listeners, too, the sense of absented self and the courting of the void that is inherent in both anti-music's sound and in the ideas circulating around that sound presents opportunities for self-transcendence and loss. For example, trancing concentration on the loops or the unfolding sonic processes of this music can lead to a slippage into unconscious reverie and imagination, or into an engaged leaning-in where self is strengthened. In a different sense, the everyday sounds and happenings of the music – the pattering rain or the metal sawing of TNB, the fire burning and explosions of The Haters – can create for listeners a kind of everyday sublime in which the aesthetic frames that are put around sounds that you might encounter in your environment or through media can lead the listener into reverie or light depersonalization. There are many paths to ego dissolution; this music can guide audiences down some of them. The ideas of anti-music therefore cue the listener into a nihilistic negation and no-thingness just as the sounds themselves offer moments of self-release and even transformation.

Of course, as I've been saying all along, even if these lenses of destruction and negation are both strongly pushed on the work by the artists themselves and indeed make a great deal of sense as interpretative lenses, we can (also) easily hear this work at a remove from ideas of destruction or negation, whether these are put in psychoanalytical, spiritual or literal frames. *In The Shade of Fire*, as with some of the other Haters' music mentioned above, contains all sorts of musical devices – loops, canons, stereo-separation, cycles – that can be heard and interpreted in purely (and conventionally encoded) musical terms. The motivic array and formal patterns of *Chungez* can likewise be read in purely musical terms, as plays of structure, shape and space. These two critical approaches, the one interpretative and the other formalist, are not, needless to say, in conflict. Instead, they help us think about the many valences of anti-music (as with other forms of proto-noise and noise); as noise-musical form and dialectic, as avant-garde artistic performance art, as political statement and as spiritual exercise.

3

Global harsh power

This chapter moves our story forward in time and outward in geography and style. So, we go forward to the mid-to-late 1980s and early 1990s and outward to Europe, the United States and Australia. Finally, we stay with power electronics whilst *also* starting to blend in tropes from what would come to be called harsh noise (hence 'harsh power'). Our first section explores the transcultural dynamics of noise and, relatedly, the style blend of harsh power. Subsequent sections use geographical frames to organize a series of case studies of key artists working in this area; we start with the United States, move to Australia, before finishing in Europe.

Transcultural noise

I described noise as 'transcultural' in the Introduction. This description echoes Deena Weinstein's observation about heavy metal, that it is a fundamentally 'transcultural' music in how it generates 'varieties and hybrids while maintaining a continuity of code and a self-conscious tradition that remains determinative wherever it travels' (2011, 56). The same has been true of noise. It has moved around the world, inflecting and being inflected by local trends and tastes but maintaining a degree of stylistic continuity all the same. As we saw, this transcultural character has depended on the late twentieth- and early twenty-first-century global infrastructure of international mass media and mass music markets. Though this global infrastructure is sizable and sturdy enough to support a wide variety of culture it's also true that the anglicized titles and band names pervasive in both Weinstein's metal and in noise have allowed these musics to circulate relatively freely across national and/or cultural boundaries. Moreover, in noise's case, the general lack of vocals (or, at least, the invariable lack of clear lyrical content) increases its ability to circulate widely in this way. Noise's mutually reinforcing intercultural presence across both Japan and the United States in the 1990s is an excellent illustration of noise's more general transcultural character. This Japanese-American intercultural noise network was, typically, made possible both by broader channels of economic interdependence and cultural exchange – from tourism to mass-market film and TV – that already existed between the two countries, and by local nodes of connection such as college radio, underground zines and micro-tours.

The case of power electronics is salutary in terms of transcultural variety and continuity. As power electronics spread across the world in the 1980s – often via the kind of 'fringe benefit' reliance from afar on global mass-media and mass-market channels of exchange and infrastructure that we see in many fringe musics – it took root in the United States, Europe, Australia and, to some extent, Japan. As it did so, many of its original characteristics evolved in ways both subtle and not so subtle, even as an underlying thematic and stylistic core united these different international offshoots. An illustration of this comes in the fact that many artists took direct inspiration from the topics and techniques of acts like Whitehouse but shifted these into new subject areas and more varied musical approaches. The chapter is organized geographically to bring out these transcultural dynamics and the musical stories running through them.

The chapter's most notable musical story is the way in which power electronics develops into a kind of hybrid harsh noise/power electronics style in this period; the 'harsh power' discussed above. As we'll see, many of the artists examined here blend what would later be recognized as harsh noise textures and sounds into the power electronics template of extreme sexual subject matter and performance. A related phenomenon is the blending of power electronics themes into death-industrial sound that can be heard in acts such as Anenzephalia. In both cases, we hear power electronics evolving into new contexts and styles across this late 1980s and early 1990s period. In the broader, first case, we even trace the emergence of harsh noise as a discrete genre, the global chains of power electronics influencing and taking influence from the often co-located and co-extensive global chains of underground noise just then coming into focus.

The artists examined in this chapter, from Blackhouse and Intrinsic Action in the first section, to Grunt, Streicher and Genocide Organ in the following ones, therefore helped to effect a transition from various early or 'proto' noise forms and micro-scenes – industrial, anti-music, power electronics, early Japanese noise – to a more clearly defined and cohesive international harsh noise scene. The chapter tells this story, exploring how power electronics and other styles slowly and fragmentarily spread across the world and, in so doing, blurred into newly formed musics, primarily harsh noise. Chapters 4 and 5 build on this story in looking at harsh noise directly, first in the context of Japan and then the United States and Europe.

The United States: Blackhouse and Intrinsic Action, with Master/Slave Relationship and Anenzephalia

Power electronics' impact in the United States was built on the networks of mail art, cassette and fanzine culture and micro-independent labels described in Chapter 1; in particular, on the mail networks in which industrial and/or proto-noise artists such as Throbbing Gristle, Boyd Rice and Monte Cazzaza were embedded. Magazines such as Vale's Re/Search and, a little later, Peter Sotos' *Pure* were likewise pivotal in building or focalizing US interest in industrial, early power electronics and related topics such as serial killers and sadomasochism. Meanwhile, broad-based experimental and/or industrial labels such as Cause and Effect, Banned Productions, and AWB Recording

Label all sprung up in the mid-to-late 1980s and served to channel and encourage interest in the nascent power electronics scene. Though Ron Lessard of RRRecords wasn't a fan of power electronics, that label likewise played a role in the scene in its support of industrial/PE artists like Blackhouse and Master/Slave Relationship.

Power electronics had been around a few years by the time its influence started to be felt directly in the United States. With a number of key power electronics releases in circulation by the mid-1980s, an image of the movement as being fixated on shock and upsetting subject matter related to murder, sadism and so on had begun to emerge. This image proved inspiring to a range of US artists in both positive and negative ways. The rest of this section moves through examples that demonstrate the range of this inspiration. It starts with two briefer examples, Master/Slave Relationship and Anenzephalia, where the influence was positive. It then moves to two extended case studies – of Blackhouse and Intrinsic Action – where the influence was more complicated.

One can draw clear thematic and, to some degree, musical parallels between the typical power electronics' approach and an American industrial act like Debbie Jaffe's Master/Slave Relationship. This is such that Master/Slave albums like *Soundtrack to Black Leather Bondage* (Cause and Effect, 1987) and *Being Led Around by the Tongue* (MSR, 1990) married uncomfortable or extreme S&M imagery and louche or aggressive (spoken, whispered or shouted) vocals with a pounding and/or gleaming synthetic industrial sheen. The latter was often made from battering drums and a simple, repeated distorted synth motif that climbs one or two notes away and/or back to a home tone, though some tracks veer away from such common tropes into harsher, looser noise territory; 'The Pain of the Chains of Love', from *Soundtrack*, is a good illustration of this.

Various tracks on *Being Led Around* demonstrate Jaffe's hybrid style well. 'The Desire to Castrate Father' marries swirling, Kosmiche-style synth-organ motifs with a darkly confessional spoken word whose delivery, as is typical for Jaffe, portends threat and lust all at the same time: 'I no longer wish to castrate him, I just want to know what he felt; why did he have to suffer in this relationship? I reject his last wishes.' The crisp but jagged industrial/no wave thumping of 'Hexus Sexus' again circles around the expression of extreme, 'ugly', but thoughtful feelings: 'If I can repulse you today, I know I've done my job well.' The discussion of sadism and master-slave sexual dynamics in 'My Pleasure Should' is more sonically aggressive, hovering as it does on a serrated, distorted motif that moves, drone-like, from a tone to a tone a minor second below, and back, and filled as it is with thick, sometimes glitching processed speech and feedback. Meanwhile, 'Force' mixes chopped and clipped but pummelling drum-machine hits with another jagged, distorted synth line circling around a repeated home tone, as an animated Jaffe aggressively but seductively instructs someone to 'come here, lie down, play with yourself'. 'Wet' again mixes choppy drum machine sounds with slightly unwieldy distorted synth and processed vocals (Jaffe's characteristic whispers and squeals alongside pitch-shifted growls), as the speaker enters an erotic state: 'You know I wanna be fucked … make me feel like a fucking slut … you make me feel like a man … you make me feel like a little girl.'

The sexualized aesthetics (and aestheticized sexuality) of these tracks provide a clear illustration of the power-electronics-infused industrial style of Jaffe's work. As she herself puts it in the aforementioned 'Hexus Sexus': 'I want so bad to piss in your fucking mouth … that's what I call art.' The emphasis on sadomasochistic themes (from her artist name down), and on a snarling, often aggressive vocal persona that tends to assume the 'Dom' position in the sexual fantasies staged in many of the tracks, creates clear parallels between Jaffe's work and artists such as Whitehouse and Con-Dom. And yet, at the same time, the comparative lack of politically upsetting content (this arising not least through the inverted gender dynamics in play here), and the aforementioned industrial sheen – the music's basic tunefulness and wholeness, notwithstanding the pervasiveness of distortion and other noisy elements – sets Jaffe's work apart from these forebears all the same.

Anenzephalia, a project primarily of Brigant Moloch (also a sometime member of Genocide Organ), operated in a similar hybrid space to Jaffe. As noted above, Moloch was positively inspired by various aspects of power electronics and industrial music, something that comes through most obviously in Anenzephalia's dense, complex and sometimes even contradictory approach to social-political issues. This approach was expressed in their mix of, on the one hand, controversial sampled speeches and titles – such as 'Transcendental Suffering', 'Meat Grinder' and 'Successive Torture' from their 1993 debut, *Fragments of Demise* (RRRecords), or 'Planet of Slaves' from 1998's *New World Disorder* (Tesco Organisation) – and the more atmospheric, cavernous, slow and low sounds characteristic of death industrial music on the other. The latter sounds rendered the speechifying and explicit content of the music even more ambiguous than it might already have been. To wit, the murky, smoky, amelodic and aperiodic atmospheres of *Fragments*, where German, likely Nazi speeches are buried in a haze of low, distant drones and jagged, oscillating mid and high tones (see, for example, 'Megalomaniac 2'), represent a kind of nightmare re-hearing of power electronics where intention and impact are even harder to parse than they were there. Similarly, the LFO-driven, phased and reverb-heavy bass tones and distant, muffled vocals of 1995's *Ephemeral Dawn* (Tesco Organisation), as on tracks such as 'Regime' and the sepulchral 'Thaum', represent a distinctive melding of power electronics themes and sounds with death-industrial, almost dark-ambient inflections – inflections we'll return to in Chapter 7 – of space and texture.

As can be seen, Master/Slave Relationship and Anenzephalia are two acts who had a constructive, positive relationship with power electronics. Other US artists had a more openly conflicted relationship to that same source even as they took direct inspiration from its style and sound.

Blackhouse

Blackhouse's Brian Ladd is an excellent example in this respect. As an avid listener to experimental music in the early-to-mid 1980s, Ladd was inspired by Whitehouse's extreme sound and their attitude of audience confrontation. And yet, Ladd rejected Whitehouse's thematic emphases and subject matter, replacing these with more outwardly Christian themes (like many later industrial acts). Indeed, Ladd saw Whitehouse's approach as negative, hate-filled and even formulaic. Ladd's choice of 'Blackhouse' as his artist name sums up well this dual relationship to Whitehouse and other power electronics and industrial acts, the sound and intensity welcomed on the one hand but the transgressive shock rejected on the other.

> Whitehouse inspired me to create power electronics as … Blackhouse. This was 1984. I wanted to create a band like Whitehouse, but without all the negative stereotypical hate Whitehouse was projecting. The industrial 'philosophy' was about shock. Unpleasant stuff. Murder, ultra-sadism, rape … Toss in some grainy photos of cadavers or Auschwitz or sex. It was a formula. That stuff became the norm. I'm not interested in the norm. Blackhouse was not just an industrial noise band. I declared it to be a Christian band, as well, with positive messages about Christ and Pro-Life and Be Good and all that. Of course, that upset a lot of people. That inspired me even more!
>
> (Cited in Candey 2016, Location 792–8)

Blackhouse's 1984 debut album, *Pro-Life* (Ladd-Frith), honours this intent. That is, at least at the level of its culture-war-baiting title (the Pro-Life movement being well established by the early 1980s in the United States) and its cover, which depicts a transparent crucifix with a glowing light coming from its centre. The track titles, too, deliberately invoke Christianity; 'Born Again' and 'Jesus Loves You' are the two most obvious examples. But the music tells another story. Though self-described as a Christian Industrial act, which might suggest a more commercial sound than someone like Whitehouse, if anything much of *Pro-Life* is murkier, more abstracted and more abrasive in sound than the music Whitehouse was releasing at this time. Though the shorter tracks typical in power electronics are again present – eight out of eleven tracks here hover between two and four minutes (the others are 5'29", 7'16" and 7'52", with the two longer tracks actually each coming in two parts) – other elements are turned to something of an extreme. For instance, the pounding rhythms and insistent narration or shouting of British power electronics are largely absent, replaced by sheets of proto-harsh-noise static, gurgling drones and piercing high feedback.

Elements of such sounds are present throughout the album but the division of its two sides into 'No Rhythm' (the first six tracks) and 'Pro-Rhythm' (the second five) indicates clearly where the concentration of less rhythmic, more abstract, noisier sound lies. Indeed, Side A tracks like 'Love' and 'Long Live Life/The One Truth' are particularly notable examples of such noise-heavy looseness, filled as they are with unpredictably phrased and organized minimalist ballets of static and feedback. Meanwhile, where vocals are present, as on tracks such as 'Born Again', 'Jesus Loves You' and 'Apparition/Abolition of Strife' (the last of these is from Side B), they are basically unintelligible, processed into crumbly distortion and fuzz; essentially one more element of sonic gristle and atmosphere. Even on the first couple of minutes of 'Apparition …', where megaphone-like shouting feels crisper and less abstracted than elsewhere, the words are impossible to make out.

Despite the 'No Rhythm' heading, Side A actually does feature elements of rhythmic drive, though where this is present it is usually caked in noise and based in some off-beat repeated sonic feature rather than any pre-set drum loop. A thrusting pulse emerges from 'Pro-Life', for example, but it's the result of a glitchy filtering of a static noise wall. Such off-beat beats, as it were, are present on Side B, too. For example, the last six minutes or so of Side B's 'Apparition/Abolition of Strife' are based entirely on the steady repetition of a heavily distorted two-note synth-bass gesture and a tapping, quasi-hi-hat keeping pace through each iteration, as shards of tearing hiss and static fly around. Though based in sustained repetition and a clear pulse, the sound quality of both the anchoring gestures and the intervening noise means the track is already in abrasive territory even before the stuttering delays and increasing fuzz of the last minute or two.

'Power of the Lion' and 'Be Good', both from Side B, act as the exception that proves the overarching abstract-and-harsh-noise rule on the album. 'Power' is based on a steady, 4/4 loop of slightly stereo-phased high synth melody and thudding drum, whilst the remarkable 'Be Good' is almost industrial-techno heavy in the driving sparseness of its bass-note-to-fried-treble-tone ostinato. But even on these two tracks, fuzzy noise and chaos intervene to twist things into harsher territory; sprays of static and absurdist megaphone-shouting bring flavour to 'Power', whilst the steady drive of 'Be Good' is constantly undermined by overloaded shouting that is interjected between and over iterations of the beat.

As can be seen, *Pro-Life* is filled with proto-harsh-noise gestures and sounds, even as clearly 'musical' design is present likewise. The Christian message of the track titles and album cover are completely absent from the sound, which veers from strangely parsed dances of static, feedback and shouting, to aspects of wall and harsh noise, to, in the two Side B tracks just discussed, studies in quasi-techno-noise loops and patterns. Through all these elements, the sound never quite settles into anything like a clear, transparent statement of intent and style; this is music mired in murk, enigma and mystery. So, whilst the brevity of the music, the outright political messaging in the titles, and the intensification of the industrial template of abstracted electronic sound align the album with power electronics, for whatever reason – personal preference, point in time, geographical distance from centres of production – this album is very much its own unique stylistic proposition. In this, it can be seen to pivot around a typical sense of noise stylistic becoming; this is, unusually, both in terms of the expected suspended dialectic of order and disorder that's present here in the unresolved tussle and dance of the music's beats and static *and* in terms of its being caught between different substyle poles.

Key aspects of *Pro-Life* carried through into Blackhouse's later work, where aggressive vocals, harsh, staticky sound and Christian themes are dominant. But much of that later work tended to emphasize the rhythmically straightforward sounds of *Pro-Life* more than it did its charmingly strange, even restless noise walls. Indeed, in adding a dose of sonic polish and gleam, clearer vocals and more balanced forms to those driving drum loops, Blackhouse's sound aligned with somewhat more commercial forms of industrial music as these were evolving across the late 1980s. 1987's *Holy War* (RRRecords) provides a good illustration of all this, with its fuzzy but chiming synth loops, repeated hooks, crisp vocals and clear-cut dynamic profiles. Even with typically characterful sonic intensity and vocal themes running through the album – the breathy, sin-laced 'Whispers of Love' is a good example of this, even as its death-industrial ambience contrasts well with the more thrusting beats and shouting of tracks like 'Repent' and 'Make A Choice' – *Holy War* presents a more commercial, more conventionally musical proposition than the ramshackle, abrasive *Pro-Life*. As noted, the latter stands somewhat alone in Blackhouse's output as a power electronics/harsh noise hybrid emanating far from what had been or would be the centres of these genres in the UK and Japan, combining their aesthetics in an unusually dirty, restless, searching way.

Intrinsic Action

As compared to Ladd's Blackhouse, Mark Solotroff's Intrinsic Action (a largely solo act, though John Balistreri, who later became serial-killer-focused power electronics act Slogun, occasionally participated) was a little more directly aligned with power electronics as it was being practised in the UK in the early 1980s. This can be seen both in the harsh electronic pulsing and bleeping of Solotroff's music and in occasional song or album titles based around sadomasochistic themes, for example 'Rope Trick' (from *Five*, AWB Recordings, 1988), or the collection *Sado-Electronics* (Tesco Organisation, 1992). Meanwhile, the raw, shoutier tracks on albums such as *Five* have been seen as 'foundation stones of American power electronics' (Candey 2016, Location 828).

And yet, much of Intrinsic Action's earlier work eschewed clear (or any) vocals or speech, whilst tracks were often in high single, and sometimes double, figures in length. 1987's *II* (self-released) is an interesting illustration of Solotroff's indebtedness to the particular sonic extremity of power electronics, whilst also – to some extent like Ladd before him – betraying as much of an allegiance to what would become harsh noise. The most obvious example of this latter point comes with the opening track, 'II'. Both the track's unusual length – forty-six minutes – and its varied sound palette mark it out. The first eighteen minutes or so are taken up with a slow, death-industrial build of low, modulating and sweeping tones and slowly thickening atmospheric effects. These drones and tones gradually thicken in intensity and texture, with the odd moment of withdrawal and quiet increasing intensity amidst the build. In the nineteenth minute, a louder – though still instrumental, aperiodic, abstract – passage of distorted clattering and fuzz brings out a more violent, disjunctive effect for four-and-a-half minutes or so, sound panning left to right and left again. The next eleven minutes, from 23' to 34', mooch about the same death-industrial space from the earlier build, with the passage from 23' to 28' feeling particularly withdrawn and fragmented. Though the sound palette is continuous throughout these eleven minutes the language is gestural and event-filled, with brief dynamic swells, or contrasts in gestural density, adding restless, almost dialectical flavour and variety. Four or so minutes of relative silence and restraint follow, bringing us to the thirty-eighth minute. Finally, the last eight minutes of the track return to the louder mood of 18'–23', though the loudness and relative violence are more fragmented and varied, less sustained, than earlier.

As can be seen, the track therefore contrasts long passages of death-industrial build and mood with briefer moments of climax and overwhelm, expressing a somewhat straightforward A-B-A^1-B^1 form that is yet belied by the murky warp and weft of the sound. Figure 3.1 below illustrates some of these points. It shows the sustained profile of the sound, with gaps only really appearing in that gulf between minutes 23 and 28. Meanwhile, the spikes in energy at minutes 18–23 and 37–45 are visible clearly in the appearance of two bands of frequencies around 188–215Hz and 470–520Hz, indicated here with the two downward arrows.

The remaining four songs on *II* are much shorter than that opening track, even though the two nine-minute tracks likewise stretch out the typical power electronics template. The first of those nine-minute tracks, 'Monitor', consists of a barrage of churning low synth tones, hiss, high bleeping and consuming static. Processed vocals are buried deep in the mix, abstracted as another element of the noise. As with 'II', the density of event here is high: the churning swell, inconstant and eventful, anchors proceedings, but some passing feedback tone or sweeping synth note is always on hand to liven up the surface of that swell, setting listeners back in their attempt to still and order the sound. Both the abiding noise-swell and the combination of that swell with the passing events that intervene on it are indeed in a state of unrealized becoming, so many sonic details rushing by that the whole never settles or resolves. Similar could be said of the other nine-minute track, 'Denial', where the underlying anchor is much buzzier static and bass than on the other track, but the overriding atmosphere (and, effectively, style) is similarly harsh and unsettled. The two shorter tracks, 'Universal Time' (5'04") and 'Libidinal Ramblings' (4'36"), are also harsh and unstable in effect. 'Universal Time' features somewhat distinct sampled vocals, though these verge into abstract noise soon after each appearance. Its anchor of a repeated, pounding bass-synth gesture gives the overwhelming noise-swells around it a driving, pulsing profile, even as those swells consume any emerging order the pounding bass gestures towards.

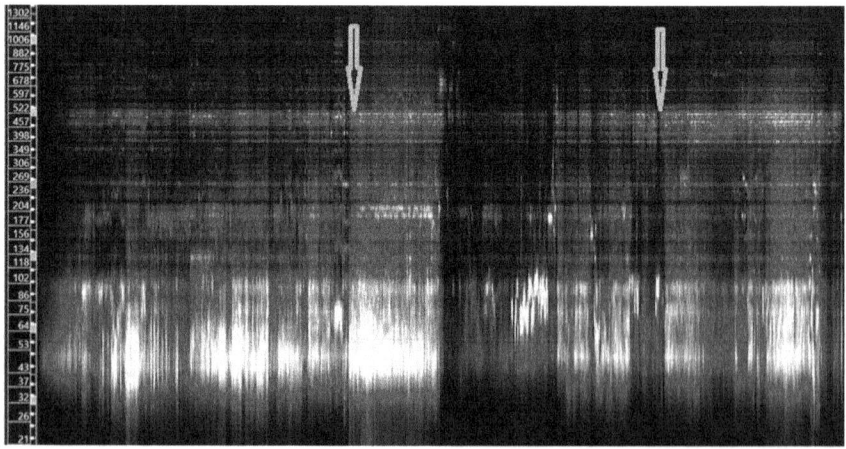

Figure 3.1 Melodic range spectrogram of 'II' from Intrinsic Action's *II* (1987).

'Libidinal Ramblings' focuses on the contrast between relative silence and a squealing, bleeping noise wall, stark, searching interplay between the two shaping the first forty-five seconds and reappearing throughout as a key motif, now marking out a noise-then-silent-then-noise flow, now overlaid as a kind of noise/quasi-silent array.

Solotroff's music as Intrinsic Action therefore honours but also expands on the power electronics template; relative distance in time and space may lie behind this stylistic expansion though it's hard to say for sure. Solotroff's later work under aliases such as BLOODYMINDED moved away even farther from power electronics, in any case, dropping the sonic overload and occasionally overt politics or sadomasochism of Intrinsic Action in favour of a more minimalist, concentrated (though no less violent or raw) electronic sound. And yet, Solotroff's importance to the development of power electronics in the United States can't be overestimated: apart from his own music, from the harsh-noise-anticipating *II* to later albums like *Five* and *Bad Jack* (both Arbeit Group in 1988), Solotroff's aforementioned label, AWB Recording Label, played a pivotal role in boosting the presence of power electronics in the United States, for example by releasing work from artists such as The Grey Wolves and Slave State. Solotroff therefore expanded power electronics in both noise-musical style and space, ultimately strengthening the power electronics tradition even as his work eventually moved farther away from its roots.

Australia: Streicher

The same central point could be applied to Ülex Xane, aka Streicher, who in many ways pioneered power electronics in Australia – often in potentially troubling ways, as we'll see. As with Ladd and Solotroff, the touch paper for Xane was very much Whitehouse, one of whose LPs Xane picked up in a local record shop in Melbourne on a whim in 1982. (The very presence of this UK LP in that shop on the other side of the world, incidentally, demonstrates how even a micro-genre such as power electronics benefitted in the aforementioned 'fringe benefit' way from the global networks and channels of cultural exchange discussed earlier; the obvious cultural links between Australia and the UK are just one of the factors that allowed such an encounter to take place.) Xane subsequently got involved in a lengthy mail correspondence with William Bennett. Whitehouse, Come Org, Philip Best's Iphar label and Mundy's Broken Flag were indeed to prove hugely influential on Xane's development as an artist. For example, in addition to making music in the same spirit as those artists and labels, in 1984 Streicher started a similarly small label of his own, Extreme, which was focused on a comparable range of transgressive music. (Xane, it should be said, didn't start releasing work as Streicher until the late 1980s; the official Streicher releases on Xane's successor label to Extreme, Zero Cabal, which were re-workings of the mid-to-late 1980s Streicher recordings, didn't start coming out until 1992.)

Xane's music, which in this period was single-mindedly focused on the crunching and thumping sounds of the Korg MS-20 analogue synthesizer alongside aggressively shouted vocals, has been labelled 'Oi! Noise'. From his own perspective it was indeed was very much based on a desire to bring 'an Oi/skinhead attack to power electronics for the first time' (2014), with the act's original name, Streicher 84, being inspired by the Oi! bands Combat 84 and Condemned 84 (more on Oi! in a moment). For Xane, the power electronics aesthetic 'seemed to emanate a seething violence, couched in an inscrutable web of illicit imagery' (Xane 2016, Location 645). But like Blackhouse and Intrinsic Action before him, Xane wanted to expand on his power electronics sources.

> Whilst I was interested in and admired the kind of subjects that the Come Org artists were dealing with, I didn't want to copy that, and it needed to be based more on personal experience. I mean, the serial killer thing was cool, but how does that relate to your own life? At the time, in the early 1980s, the whole skinhead phenomenon was a source of fear and loathing to the mainstream public. Even when I was growing up in the mid-seventies, the skins and sharpies of Melbourne were perceived as a genuine threat to law and order by the authorities, and there was a lot of violence.
>
> (Xane 2016, Location 688)

So, in order to replicate what he saw as the 'danger' of power electronics, Xane combined it with aesthetics derived from Oi!, a skinhead movement that grew out of punk in the late 1970s and was, by the early-to-mid 1980s, a threatening subset of Australian (and British) culture. Oi!, in Timothy Brown's words, provided 'an artistic forum for [the politicised wing of the] skinheads to express their own ideas'. Oi! thus 'became a mirror of the left-right divide within the skinhead scene', out of which polarization 'the genre of "Nazi rock" developed' (2004, 158). The 'Nazi rock' reference here is important. Xane's work, like artists associated with Broken Flag, Come Org and indeed Industrial Records deliberately drew on Nazi references and imagery. The most obvious of these comes in the name itself, 'Streicher'. Xane took this name from Julius Streicher, who was a member of the Reichstag and the editor of *Der Stürmer*, which was a weekly Nazi propaganda paper published from 1923 to 1945 (and also the name of Xane's first Zero Cabal release, in 1992). These reference points in fact permeated the work, with Streicher's image and other Nazi-associated symbols and imagery being used on covers, and military sounds and language appearing across many different tracks.

Such blatant use of Nazi material gave Xane's work an extremist, racist and reactionary reputation; for instance, the online marketplace, *Discogs*, has blocked a number of Streicher releases for sale, including *Der Stürmer* and the 2003 compilation, *War without End* (Cold Spring; this is discussed below). Xane himself defends the use of such material:

> what people fail to understand is that my interest derives largely from the perspective of transgression and the abhorrence of any current societal consensus, in moral as well as political terms. As Throbbing Gristle demonstrated, there are many and diverse weapons and tactics that can be used against the establishment and this vacuous corrupt world.
>
> (Xane 2016, Location 694)

So, much like Throbbing Gristle, Whitehouse, Con-Dom, TNB and The Haters (and others not examined in detail here, from The Grey Wolves to SPK), Xane's basic position was one of opposition to what he saw as a 'corrupt' and 'abhorrent' social consensus. His method of expressing this opposition was to choose subjects seen, in turn, as abhorrent by that society. A corrupt society, for Xane and others, should have its corruption turned back on itself.

The political effectiveness or validity of this kind of approach is of course not at all clear cut; for many people, subjects as ugly as Streicher's should essentially be verboten for musicians, where the seeming distance and objectivity open to, for example, filmmakers who want to make art about Nazism, is perhaps not present. For most people, engaging with this material via the immersive, often first-person-defined medium of music is dangerous, and should at the very least be subject to intense critical scrutiny, if not outright banned. After all, using divisive, destructive, racist imagery in music (or any form) to oppose corruption can easily add to and intensify such divisions, merely piling corruption on top of corruption. Moreover, any supposed critical intent behind the work can easily get lost in the face of listener confusion or hostility. And, of course, such work could and indeed has been taken as purely hateful examples of shock for shock's sake. On the other hand, one could argue that the adaptation of troubling – even Nazi-associated – imagery or reference points doesn't necessarily equate to uncritical endorsement or simple shock tactic. Or that artists like Streicher (and Whitehouse) may intend, or have, a critical – satirical, parodic, subversive – impact. We've rehearsed some of these points already as regards Whitehouse. They are even more pressing in the case of Streicher, where the Nazi allusions and material are more dominant.

Moving to the music more directly, it's clear that, despite the bluntness and brutishness of the work, both the sound and the textual elements of Streicher's music are filled with levels of detail, power, tension and richness that could – *could* – be seen to belie the reactionary label sometimes given to it. 'Nihilist Assfucks Manifesto', the opening track from 1995's *Annihilism* (which had been recorded between 1989 and 1991 originally and then reworked; Zero Cabal), is a good illustration of Streicher's dual quality of complexity mixed with blunt directness. The track is composed of a woman reading out the titular 'manifesto' for three and a half minutes; a notable increase, from 0'54" on, in the intensity of tape hiss below her is the only clear 'musical' event in the track outside the vocals. And yet, even though the sonic elements here are somewhat limited they are key to its impact: the relative restraint of the tape-hiss backing serves to create a clear but quietly bristling, tense space for the delivery of the words. Meanwhile, the blank-and-yet-saturnine affect of the speaker's inflection underlines the nihilist brutality of the message:

> Reap the winds of terror. Sow the seeds of hate. Life is useless; death just so. Noise gives birth. Noise kills. Infernal, eternal noise. All else is marking time. To work, marry, have family, be entertained. The final score is zero. You and your world are ultimately nil. To fuck, kill, die. There is solace in the energy of destruction. Force is pure. The evil is a construction of frightened minds. Existence is merciless. The importance

ascribed to anything is futile, pathetic fiction. All ends in nothing. The zone of the nil is the only constant. Annihilation the only certainty. You cling to the vanity of glory, success, status. It is all for nothing. The noise continues. A psychosis to saturation. And you go on with your empty routine, a walking corpse. Daily you shrink from the ravages of decay. Postponing the inevitable. The warfare all around, and in your mind, cannot be overcome. Death wins, always. The apocalypse has no beginning, no end. Nothing at the start, nothing at the finish. Pray to the void, your destiny. Futile prayer, vain hopes, pitiful fears. Nothing is the not-positive. Nothing is the not-negative. You are doomed, regardless. Happy the man free of hope. Desire satisfied in a moment, and the emptiness closes in again. Humanity has no common will. Conflict is intrinsic. Pain the deformed twin of pleasure. Extermination awaits your feeble breath. Suffer the angst of existence. To cease is your reward. Take your consoling pleasures where you find them. Kill everything and everyone repeatedly, over and over and over again. Piss, shit, and assfuck your way to oblivion.

This text, as can be seen, is graphic, unrelenting and extreme. But it's also packed with rich ideas, many of which connect the track both to other noise music and to important strains of thought reaching back centuries. For instance, the emphasis on, and even the existential elevation of, annihilation, the void, oblivion and what is poetically called 'the zone of nil' chimes with similar nihilist messages in The New Blockaders and The Haters. As we saw, the transcending, transpersonal void is a source of ethical and aesthetic vitality for these artists, who see it as some kind of cosmic truth principle.

Meanwhile, though not explicitly courting oblivion in quite the same way, the buzzing crunch, wild distortion and shouted, growling gesticulations of fellow *Annihilism* tracks like 'Destroy You Motherfuckers' and 'Nothing Has Any Meaning' convey a related message of complex, blunt force sonic trauma that belies any simple affect or intent that their brutal surface might suggest. Streicher's void is anything but empty; instead, it is a place of great, restless energy and force, sound clasping and cleaving in apparent freedom and chaos. The music, in these ways, suggests an unceasing becoming even, or especially, in the face of total existential oblivion. Pray to the void, your destiny.

Streicher's *War Without End* compilation, which was released in 2003 but consisted of tracks recorded in the late 1980s and early 1990s, offers a range of examples of that core dualist quality of brutal bluntness and restless complexity. 'Let Slip the Dogs of War' is a 14'30" sonic battlefield, the track being a kind of phonographic exploration of the sounds of war. It gradually layers up distant artillery, aircraft and bomb sounds into a sonic collage that ingeniously blurs these concrete sound sources into and out of musical gestures and effects, from sustained synth tones and sine waves to chugging percussion and the dark, cavernous synth pads that lurk deep in the atmospheric background. The track is brutally aggressive at times. For example, its dark-ambient textures fade into the background across the eighth and ninth minutes as machine guns rat-a-tat loudly in the foreground; this rat-a-tatting modulates lower from the eleventh minute on as an array of artillery, explosions and divebombing aircraft thicken the wild sonic field. At other times it is delicate and subtle, as for example in the hushed detail of those sustained synth tones. The track is therefore an excellent mission statement both for Streicher's blunt/complex duality and for his typical thematic focus on war and battle. Its concept, the musicality of war, is old and simple, but its execution is both subtle and brutal.

Tracks like 'Voltage Liquidation' and 'EOD Ordnance Detector' are more consistently harsh and raw in sound. The former starts with a guttural, groaning shout, as a swarm of cicada-static oscillates in the centre of the picture. This sound builds over the next three minutes, with glitchy distortion and thickening static adding a sense of frenetic, wild sonic activity, before the texture winds back down to the cicada-static for the last thirty to forty seconds. Even given this clear arch form, however, the overall impression here is one of intense action and movement, the staticky, inharmonic centre of the track never settling into a stable, periodic sound. 'EOD', for its part, contrasts a tone of wailing feedback with more restrained, low crumble and, in its middle passage, distant sounds of cooking and eating. This is, again, a kind of collaged and phonographic-esque harsh noise mired in cruddy movement and becoming. Meanwhile, another *War* track, 'Martyrdom's Call', places what sounds like a keening-but-melodic shawm over sustained churn. The title and sonic references of this track, along with the Morse-code-bleeps of 'World Trade Centre', can be heard as direct allusions to real-world, US-Arab conflicts. 'Coded Channels' is a kind of interrupted noise-wall, a humming drone cutting through spitting static; again, sonic inharmonicity and aperiodicity suggest relentless irregularity and disorder, just as the anchoring drone and musicalized distribution of the static pull things to order. 'Terrorist Reality (S.N.A. #1 Live)' is twenty minutes of disjointed clatters, pitch-shifted and heavily distorted screams and shouts and crashes and explosions cut-up and chopped to the point of near chaos. Disorder and order once again vie for supremacy throughout, never resolving one way or the other. The track feels a little like a peek into an aggressive Dada noise carnival.

As can be seen, Streicher mixes a variety of approaches across *War without End*, from carefully controlled near-ambient sound to ramshackle noise collage to thick and churning power noise. As with Blackhouse and Intrinsic Action above, the style both on this album and on other Streicher work is therefore hybrid, clearly indebted to some of the reference points, sounds and political bluntness and brutality of power electronics but both turning these to what can easily be seen as an even uglier, hateful and potentially racist extreme, and mixing them with emerging harsh noise, death ambient and industrial tropes of abrasive, aporetic and/or atmospheric sound.

Power electronics, then, as it spread in space and evolved through time, clearly proved itself to be a viable template and inspiration for a whole host of noise tributaries. Some of these took inspiration from its abrasive approach to sound and some of which aped and even intensified its taboo-baiting, often nihilist or transgressive political gestures. These tributaries continued to flow through the 1990s and beyond, as we'll see both in the next section and in subsequent chapters.

Europe: Genocide Organ, *Leichenlinie* (1989); Grunt, *The New Form of the Organic Machine* (1995)

We've looked at the spread and evolution of power electronics across the United States and Australia in the mid-to-late 1980s. What was happening in Europe around this time? Different forms of noise, harsh noise and noise-adjacent music had taken root in Europe by the early 1990s. We've already discussed the importance of England to industrial and power electronics, and we'll encounter many English or British noise acts from the 1990s and beyond in the rest of the book. We'll also encounter French, Italian and Scandinavian artists, labels and scenes. Noise was thriving across Europe at this time, as we can see in looking at everything from Atrax Morgue and their Italian Slaughter Productions label to Roger Karmanik's hugely influential Swedish dark-ambient/death-industrial label Cold Meat Industry, home to Scandinavian acts such as Mortiis, Megaptera, Arcana and Karmanik's own Lille Roger and Brighter Death Now.

The spread and development of noise in Europe at this time was made possible by the global economic and material infrastructure described at the start of the chapter, which was of course as deeply embedded in European societies as it was anywhere else. Harking back to the 'fringe benefit' point from earlier, where there is already relative economic stability and a well-established infrastructure of musical venues, scenes and traditions, it after all only makes sense that smaller forms would find cracks and corners to exist within. Our two examples in this section, Germany and Finland, prove the point. Their respective cultural depth and variety – which covers everything from mainstream to more experimental musics; electronic artists such as Pan Sonic in Finland and German movements like Krautrock are good examples here – and their concomitant economic and cultural embedding in European and global channels of exchange meant that conditions were ripe in each country for the emergence of more marginal, but still globally connected, forms of music.

Genocide Organ

This idea of marginal but globally connected music perfectly describes a group like Genocide Organ. Based in Mannheim, Germany and originating in the mid-1980s, Genocide Organ's work was based from the start in a typically aggressive, post-Whitehouse power electronics mould. An almost minimalist concentration of materials runs through their music; distorted, shouting vocals (usually by frontman Willhelm Herich), churning static and piercing feedback and thumping drum-machine loops all encase controversial themes and subject matter. In this case, that subject matter tends to orientate around topics such as imperialism, racism and the Ku Klux Klan and war. That so much of Genocide Organ's approach and subject matter overlap directly with acts from other parts of the world, notably the Australian Streicher and the British Con-Dom, supports the transcultural point made earlier.

As with other power electronic artists, Genocide Organ's intense sounds and ambiguous treatment of upsetting themes – the group very rarely explain, interpret or defend their work – have generated a great deal of controversy. Like Streicher above, for example, *Discogs* have blocked the sale of their 1997 live album, *Remember* (Tesco Organisation). And, as with the other contentious acts we've been looking at over these first three chapters, it's easy to sympathize with this kind of reaction. 1991's *Save Our Slaves* (Tesco Organisation), for example, deals with topics such as the Klan, slavery and the far-right-wing John Birch Society in potentially confusing, non-condemnatory ways. Alongside the album's harsh, often grimy and pulverizing sounds, the packaging of the album plays its role in this, with its brutal cover image of a corpse burning on a pyre with a gaggle of nonplussed white people looking on, and its stickers reading 'Save Our Christian America!' and/or 'Let the Legend Live in the Grand Ole South!'. This is difficult stuff to defend.

Genocide Organ's debut album, *Lechenlinie* (Tesco Organisation), sets out their polemical stall very clearly. The title, translating to 'line of corpses', is matched by the cover's black-and-white image of corpses (seemingly, the corpses of soldiers) lying strewn across a field. The opening track, 'Ave Satani', matches and qualifies the cover and title, offering an oscillating, synth-laden rendition of the 'hail Satan' music from *The Omen*. This opening melds into the droning, staticky, shouty mulch of 'Mind Control'. Tracks like 'Stalins Orgeln' (Stalin's organs) and 'Negros in Sky-Wars' move in similarly dirty, rough sonic territory. Thudding, echoing thumps anchor the former in a relentless, shadowy march, as metallic feedback cuts in more and more aggressively and regularly as the track moves on. The latter offers a lo-fi, broken, weird-noise-facsimile of what sounds like both the droning engine and the cutting blades of a helicopter. Here as elsewhere the group do much with sonically little, the loose-limbed phasing and chopping of the two basic sonic elements always leaving the listener askew, unsure, whilst the distorted, noise-rich sounds themselves never settle or stabilize. The stuttering, jabbering staticky noise loop in 'Klaus Barbie' offers similar variety, its percussive charge always holding tension and suggesting irresolution through unpredictable patterning and the gradual addition of new sonic colours, such as the changing filters in the latter half of the track. Noise never sleeps, as shown in the constant, unpredictable movement in these tracks, where musical shapes and language constantly form only to be unsettled or complexified. A final couple of examples from the album. The minimal thuds, abstract, distant German speechifying and whirring synths of album closer 'Keiner Kommt Zurück' (Nobody Comes Back; at almost seven minutes, the longest track on the original 1989 release) presents another key aspect of Genocide Organ's style; concentrated and grimy, again, but quieter, turned inward, more menacing in its dark, threatening sounds and its distant, terrible theatre. 'Face of Horror', earlier in the album, offers another example of this quieter but still restless and *moving* noise music.

So, we are not in pleasant territory here, either in terms of sound, image or word; the potentially dog-whistle titles, disturbing images and the group's avoidance of any supporting context or interpretation leave many listeners in a difficult position. However, again as with other power electronics artists, it is perhaps understandable that fans would defend the music as a deliberately intense, ambiguous meditation on or engagement with dark, often taboo themes and material. In this spirit, Richard

Stevenson argues that we should see Genocide Organ's overwhelming aesthetics and political material, alongside their refusal of explanation, as part of a broader programme of 'total sensory overload':

> Genocide Organ are clearly striving for higher aims beyond mere 'music' and 'lyrics', and their approach could be considered their Gesamtkunstwerk: to synthesise musical, visual, and thematic materials into a comprehensive and all-embracing aesthetic art form. With their particularly weighty approach, which includes the convergence of visceral elements (visuals, titles, text, and dialogue samples set to extreme electronic sound and overlaid with shouted or distorted vocal delivery), Genocide Organ evoke a form of sensory overload that ensures that ambivalence towards their releases is almost impossible. When the extreme sound and visual art of Genocide Organ acts as the point of stimuli, does a negative emotional reaction negate the validity of the art form itself? Yet for those listeners intelligent enough, and uninterested in forming simplistic, polarising views of the group, the fascination lies in this extremity of approach, provoking myriad intellectual questions.
>
> (2016, Location 3469–80)

Here, we're back in familiar territory to where we were in discussing the political (and aesthetic) validity or valence of Con-Dom, Whitehouse and other power-electronics artists in Chapter 1, and Streicher above. As in those cases, what Genocide Organ actually intend for their work, or what they might personally stand for, is not necessarily irrelevant but is perhaps less important than what is put into the work itself.

In terms of the latter, to be crude about things, on one side we could (legitimately) condemn it as empty taboo-baiting shock. Or as fascistic propaganda; and this reading has a different gravity to it given the group's nationality, notwithstanding the transcultural points made earlier. On the other, we could instead accept Genocide Organ's right as artists to engage with the material they choose to engage with, without explanation. And, in the same vein, we could likewise recognize their deliberately confusing, overwhelming presentation; particularly in terms of the music's coarse, unpredictable rhythmic patterns and tone colours. The sound is often aggressive and dirty but it is also just as often quiet and dark, the detail so intricate in its looping subtlety that the music perhaps transcends its specific verbal content in evoking an unresolved state of feeling that is charged up with political and stylistic gambits. Structure and meaning here can derive as much, or more, from the steady varying repetition of drum or static loops, or the building intensity of interjecting shouts, as much as they do an album cover or track title (even if these more immediate elements sometimes stop the discussion before it can get going). This is all such that the work's aesthetic effect can become more unsettling than anything else. Finally, to echo the point about the shadow with which we closed Chapter 2 and to extend the point about the complexity of the music's ultimate political meaning or function, since we know that death, mass murder, slavery, racism and so on are not necessarily topics that have been properly reckoned with and faced up to by western societies, we could suggest that using ambiguous, complex art in some way to process our relationship to these histories and experiences is an effective strategy: a shedding of light into very shadowy spaces. Approaching these topics only at a safe, pre-packaged distance means we might not see as fully into the darkness as we can with groups like Genocide Organ, who, for better or worse, guide our attention fully and directly into it.

Grunt

Our second example in this section, Finland's Grunt, presents a related, but also contrasting, relationship to the power electronics source, one that we'll see is once again fundamentally transcultural in nature. Grunt (aka Mikko Aspa) played a key role in the burgeoning 1990s Finnish noise scene, alongside U.N.D. (Unseen Noise Death) and Bizarre Uproar (see Aspa's own history of Finnish noise in 2016). Grunt's music draws on the tough, clanging percussive sounds and the sado-masochistic imagery and intensity of power electronics. Its live presentation likewise draws on familiar power electronics visuals, with leather and other elements being prominent. But it often abstracts these elements into somewhat purer forms of harsh noise. As Aspa himself has said, 'there was never [an] intention to focus [on] any particular side, à la "harsh noise" or "power electronics" scenes, but to remain somewhere between, where all the noisy sounds melt together into [a] bizarre mix' (Aspa 2020).

Grunt's later work is dominated by heavily delayed, shouted vocals overlaid on churning distortion and clanging sheet metal. That style is germinating but not yet fully formed on *The New Form of the Organic Machine* (Freak Animal Records). This is a two-hour double album of 'harsh audio art' (as described by the tape's J-card) in which what we might call 'Japanese' overloaded harshness and cheaper and looser 'American' sound sources (more on this opposition over the next two chapters) come together in a vivid way. The album's twenty-three tracks run across a variety of moods and colours. Much of the effects are achieved by looping a four-track into and out of a stereo system, creating droning internal feedback which is then processed through effects pedals. (This kind of internal feedback system can be heard across a whole variety of harsh noise from this period, usually in the kind of 'mixer feedback' heard throughout MSBR's 1992 album, *Ultimate Ambience*, MSBR Records.) This feedback is then combined with radio sounds, heavily processed vocal interjections and assorted metal junk sounds to produce a wide palette of harsh sounds and textures. (Some tracks, such as the wild 'Discharge Frustration', eschew this set-up and are instead dominated by screeds of loud, detuned-guitar feedback.) The moods and colours of *Organic Machine* vary widely, despite this relative consistency of sound sources. They go from the exciting, pulverizing, Merzbow-like beating static and feedback of tracks like 'From Development to Obliteration', 'Ulkoisen hyvaksynnan hylkaaminen' and 'Gorelegion', to the rollicking cymbals of 'Destructive Species'; the overwhelming static and distorted vocal churn of 'Mental Health'; the subtle thunder and e-bow ballet of 'Audio Funeral'; the backwards-processing of sheet metal in 'Overdose of Knowledge'; and the more sustained, though still mutating, liquid droning wall noise of closer, 'New Generation – Degeneration'.

'Plastic Revolution', the first track on Side D, is worth looking at in more detail. As can be seen in Figure 3.2 below, much of the energy of the six-minute track is concentrated in two areas. Firstly and most consistently in a low-range static drone that sits across the 60–200Hz region (with emphasis on 135Hz), foaming and churning throughout. Secondly, the high-pitched feedback tone at around 360Hz, with the odd related glint right up at 1080Hz, which enters, cuts out and re-enters unpredictably, almost like damaged Morse Code. These sounds contain enough linear and, in the case of the drone, vertical variety to invite attention and perhaps even immersion; though this music is not as overwhelming and therefore immersive in volume, density or pace as some examples of harsh noise we'll see in the next chapter, its intensity is such that it's easy to slip into trancing, puzzling reverie while listening.

What the spectrogram doesn't really show, however, are some of the distinctive gestures and detail in and around those two key elements of the drone and high tone. Most obvious of these is the two-note, low-register pattern that suddenly emerges from the fuzz at 0'43". This pattern burbles away for about a minute, hovering back and forth on a seesaw fifth like a battalion of fugitive double basses. As with the percussive beating referenced above, this two-note pattern pulls us into a separate idiomatic space, the discourse of noise obscurity blurring into a kind of compositional, even orchestral sound that leaves the listener pulled between different gestural and textural languages. Even though much of the rest of the track sits in more familiar harsh noise territory of unpredictably mutating static and feedback, with interjected screams intensifying things here and there, echoes of that bass pattern never leave the picture. For example, the second half of the fourth minute come very close to sounding it in its original form. Meanwhile, the lower tone of the motif anchors the music throughout.

'Plastic Revolution' therefore double layers discursive or stylistic becoming. Such becoming can be heard here both in the inharmonic, aperiodic, unpredictable shapes and sounds of the central noise material itself and in the way that material is offset by, and offsets, the mysterious bass pattern throughout, both elements creating the kind of suspended noise-music tension we've already heard across a number of other examples. On another note, as noted, this track, as with the rest of the album, never quite achieves

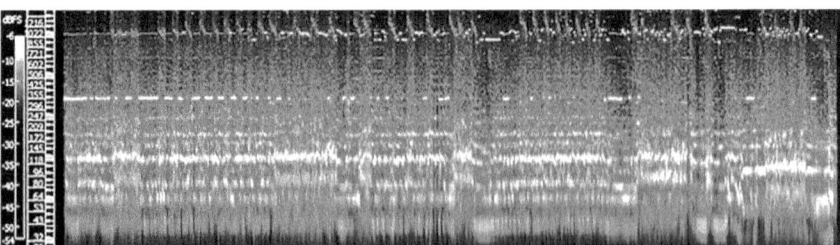

Figure 3.2 Melodic range spectrogram of 'Plastic Revolution' from Grunt's *New Form of the Organic Machine* (1995).

the kind of overwhelming depersonalization potentially activated by harsher, more frantic noise music. But its idiomatic push and pull nevertheless lures listeners into cognitive games, unsettling ego sanctity in its challenge to musical identity but in the end probably elevating ego through its relative consistency of style and reference. This is the sort of 'light', puzzling personalization discussed at various points already.

It should also be noted, though it will be obvious, that neither this track nor the broader album it comes from ever engages overtly in the kind of taboo extra-musical themes and disturbing material as some of the other artists examined in this chapter. So, even though Aspa himself is no stranger to controversy on those kinds of grounds – Aspa has indeed been accused of having ties to National Socialism, though largely in the context of his black metal work as Clandestine Blaze – and even though Aspa's live presentation, his favouring of power electronics artists on his Freak Animal label, and his own explicit framing of his work connects him to the earlier power-electronics source, *The New Form of the Organic Machine* is nevertheless perhaps the most sustained illustration of the dominant musical 'story' mentioned at the beginning of the chapter: the blending of power electronics and emerging harsh noise in 'harsh power' I've been discussing throughout. In the case of Grunt, we indeed see a power-electronics-indebted artist moving more exclusively into the kind of 'purer', less taboo and vocal-laden, forms of harsh noise making that would come to dominant noise in the 1990s.

Conclusion

Through each of the case studies in this chapter we have seen the various ways that international artists existing within a globalized context of freely circulating fringe culture and music both mirrored and moved beyond their British power-electronics forebears. As with those earlier power-electronics influences, the politics in these international examples are often disturbing. But they are likewise often rendered in such a way as to leave open the possibility of engaging with the work not as mean-spirited hatred but instead as an attempt to reveal something new both in listeners themselves and in subjects whose sharp edges tend to get bevelled away in other artistic representations. As attempts, perhaps, to construct truly challenging, tough and twisted exercises in compassion and empathy. That so much of the noise we've considered here has pivoted around restless, searching, unpredictable musical language and sound, suggesting unresolved becoming as it did so, only strengthens these latter impressions, even if other, less accommodating interpretations are both available and justifiable.

Perhaps most interestingly, at least in terms of tracking the musical history and story of noise, these various case studies have shown us a range of international artists drawing out earlier artists' formal interest in intense, involuted sound and generalizing it, in their 'harsh power' music, into an inchoate but distinct generative aesthetic principle. This aesthetic principle, this emerging interest in noise for noise's sake, embodies very well what would become a broader scene focus over the next couple of decades on generally more abstract 'harsh noise'. The next two chapters start to track that story more directly. Mirroring the relationship between Chapter 1 and the current chapter, they look in the first instance at the emergence and establishment of their chosen genre in a key location – harsh noise, and Japan in the 1980s and 1990s – before expanding outwards to look at the spread of harsh noise across the globe in the 1990s.

4

Harsh noise in Japan

Harsh noise is the most important and largest subgenre or substyle of noise music. Subgenre or substyle is probably not broad enough, in fact, given that for many people 'harsh' noise and noise music in general are interchangeable concepts – harshness, indeed, is found across all forms of noise (even if it's in harsh noise that the quality of harshness is most pronounced). I retain the distinction, however, to allow 'noise music' to encompass forms such as death industrial, power electronics, noise rock and so on. Emerging slowly and fragmentarily across Japan, the United States and Europe in the 1980s and then exploding in the 1990s, harsh noise draws on the sounds and aesthetics of earlier avant-garde, popular, industrial and power electronics artists – as we saw in the last chapter with 'harsh power' – in building a music of extremes in which severe static and distortion, unpredictable forms and intense sounds and images are a central focus.

This chapter and the following two look at harsh noise head on. Subsequent chapters then consider offshoots and hybrid forms. The book dedicates this much space to harsh noise because of its importance in the broader history of noise music. Collectively, this suite of 'harsh' chapters analyse harsh noise's permanent, suspended, unresolved dialectics of order and disorder, the ways in which the music's often-overwhelming linguistic uncertainty and sheer volume and mess allow it to lock into the dual processes of becoming style and becoming self(less) I identify as core qualities of noise music. On this last count, as we'll see, harshness (of both sound and style) is often a source of great power in noise, immersing listeners in the consuming spectacle and allowing them to experience intensity and even catharsis as a result. The current chapter focuses on Japanese proto/early noise in the 1980s and, particularly, what we'll see is perhaps the harsh noise high watermark of the 1990s. This approach allows me to track back and spend some time on the origin points of noise whilst nevertheless keeping focus on examples of 'classic' Japanese harsh noise. Chapter 5 moves on to look at American and European noise in that same classic period. Chapter 6, following a brief Interlude that moves our noise 'story' on into the twenty-first century of Part Two, looks widely across the international harsh noise scene of the 2000s, 2010s and early 2020s. The first section below offers a brief history of the Japanese scene, before delving into its cultural and social background and context. The subsequent three sections are dedicated to case studies of specific artists; Hijokaidan, Merzbow and Masonna (we revisit Merzbow in Chapter 6, whilst other Japanese noise artists will be considered at various points in Part Two).

Japanese noise history and transnational culture

The Japanese noise (or 'noizu') scene – which would come to be described colloquially, at least by some western audiences and critics, as 'Japanoise', though this is not a term I'll be using here – developed throughout the late 1970s and 1980s. It became established and defined as such, both locally and internationally, by the late 1980s and 1990s.

The Japanese scene was based initially around Osaka records shops and labels such as Alchemy Records, whose impressive catalogue of noise and, latterly, psychedelic and other musics, started to build from 1984 on. The scene also featured artists like Hanatarash, Solmania and Hijokaidan; Hijokaidan were active from 1979 and all three were releasing tapes by the mid-1980s. All of them also made music and staged performances full of chaotic, relatively freeform noise, even as they also all had either obvious or underground connections to rock, though 'rock' is a bit of a misnomer here since rock elements such as guitar and drums were turned to new, wild, often performance-art indebted ends. The scene quickly expanded outwards across the 1980s, to cities like Tokyo and to more psychedelic or electronic artists such as Nord, Fushitsusha and Merzbow. Later still, in the early-to-mid 1990s, Tokyo artists such as Government Alpha and MSBR (and Merzbow) focused on a 'pedal noise' approach in which guitar pedals, synths, tone generators and internal system feedback – where, as mentioned in the previous chapter, mixing boards would be used without input but with gain turned up in order to generate feedback that could be filtered and processed – were used to create an often intricate, always overwhelming and sonically rich noise aesthetic.

As described by Kato David Hopkins in his peerless 2020 history of Japanese noise, *Rumors of Noizu*, the noise (Hopkins prefers the aforementioned 'noizu') scene grew organically out of 'a variety of backgrounds in Japan's postwar culture, both mainstream and underground', all of which provided the 'seedbed' for noise (2020, Introduction, unpaginated). Hopkins discusses the gradual loosening of state control of the arts that took place in the post-war period in Japan, where things like the Armed Forces Network – linked to American military bases but popular among a significant cross-section of Japanese society – exposed Japanese audiences to western (popular and art) music and culture on an unprecedented scale. In further describing that seedbed, Hopkins identifies key figures and movements working within more avant-garde or experimental traditions in Japan at this time, from the Jikken Kobo group led by poet Takiguchi Shuzo to composers such as Toru Takemitsu and Yuasa Joji, both of whom were heavily influenced by the post-war generation of European avant-garde composers. The 1955 foundation of an Electronic Music Studio by the state broadcaster, NHK, was to prove especially important in fomenting cultural expansion, with a weekly programme of contemporary music ('Gendai no Ongaku', 'Music of Today') being broadcast from 1956 on (2020, 6–10). Meanwhile, artists such as experimentalists Group Ongaku and jazz musician Sadao Watanabe built on these beginnings in securing further national and international attention for western-influenced Japanese music throughout the 1960s and beyond.

These artists, as with later noise and non-noise musicians in Japan, relied on the strong cultural kinship that developed between Japan and western countries such as the UK and United States in that post-war period (and before). Channels of cultural exchange via tourism, globalized mass media, specific phenomena such as the Armed Forces Network, and so on were crucial here. Takemitsu, Group Ongaku and Watanabe are exemplary of that kinship since each extended an essentially western – or at least, transcultural – tradition. This intercultural dynamic continued into subsequent generations. For example, mainstream Japanese musicians in the 1970s and 1980s all relied to one extent or another on the Japanese-western kinship just described, whether we think of western-moulded rock and electronic acts such as Happy End and Yellow Magic Orchestra, J-Pop scenes such as Shibuya-kei or more experimental rock or free music artists such as Taj Mahal Travellers.

The same intercultural and, ultimately, transcultural point likewise held true for proto-noise/noise artists in this 1970s/1980s period. For example, David Novak quotes from Mikawa Toshiji, founder of Incapacitants and member of Hijokaidan, who by his own account was directly inspired by western 'free improvisation, punk rock, and German "Krautrock" records' in starting to practice what we now call noise and in forming groups like Hijokaidan (2013, 2). But the transnational, transcultural nature of harsh noise didn't just manifest in its western idols. Style and mode of presentation in live shows and on records; use of instruments like guitar, bass, drums, effects pedals and so on; reliance on media forms such as vinyl, tape and print; and a related reliance on the fringe cultural circuitry of zines and specialist magazines, mail order correspondence, college or independent radio and small venues: all these paralleled other music scenes across the world. By this late century period, after all, transnational exchange and connection was more the norm than the exception. This was such that cultural products from film to TV, art to music, could all circulate relatively freely through economically prosperous territories like Japan and the United States. That's not to say that such circulation was unmarked, as if these cultural artefacts could travel unmolested from place to place like so many bits of Esperanto. The uneasy, colonially inflected promotion of western composers such as Bach in countries like Korea and Japan in the late nineteenth and twentieth centuries is just one example out of many of the antagonism that has often arisen in the wake of globalizing culture (Lee 2013). Transnationalism has supported global systems of cultural and economic homogenization at least as much as it might have contributed to diversity.

And yet, the twentieth-century development of global culture has ultimately proved a boon to fringe cultural practitioners, as discussed previously. A 'global periphery' has in this way developed on the fringes, underground, relying on the media and material infrastructures of transnational capitalism for dissemination but sending weird, obscure material through those channels. This global periphery has seen connections forming amongst internationally located but small groups of hobbyists and specialists and ultimately building into nascent fringe nodes and networks. This is precisely how Japanese noise developed, in tandem with related scenes in Europe and the United States. Artists and fans traded tapes and zines by mail, musicians visited other territories, performing and often collaborating with local musicians and far-flung labels released music by foreign artists. Novak expands on this point, describing the mutually beneficial relationship between the Japanese and American noise scenes in the 1990s – something that was expressed in various examples of collaboration and crossover, but whose most obvious exemplar was probably *The Japanese/American Noise Treaty*, an album collecting leading American and Japanese noise artists that was released on Relapse in 1995 – and also enumerating some of the ways in which tours and publicity in America impacted Japanese noise artists:

> Japanoise surfaced in North America from within a larger framework of reception that included not just Noise but 'noisy' Japanese music. A host of recordings by strange Japanese groups had begun to filter into independent distribution: Boredoms, Haino Keiji, Melt Banana, Omoide Hatoba, Ruins, Ghost … By the early 1990s, recordings by Hijokaidan, Incapacitants, C.C.C.C., Solmania, Masonna, Monde Bruits, Astro, Aube, Government Alpha, Pain Jerk, K.K. Null, k2, msbr, Geriogerigegege, Violent Onsen Geisha, and Merzbow had swept into North American reception. College radio stations and independent record stores circulated releases from Osaka's Alchemy, Public Bath [Hopkin's label], Japan Overseas, and New York's Shimmy Disc and Tzadik labels. Underground fanzines like San Francisco–based Mason Jones's Ongaku Otaku informed fans of the archetypal examples of Noise and helped them assemble a rudimentary map of its generic boundaries in Japan. North American tours, especially by Merzbow and Masonna in the mid-1990s, allowed select fans to experience Japanese Noise live and relate legendary stories for those who missed the chance. It was increasingly possible to talk about a 'Japanese Noise scene,' and maybe even see some of its representatives in live performance. By the time I really began to tune into what was going on, the layers of feedback from North American reception had already shifted the ground for Japanese musicians.
>
> (2013, 11)

As we can see, the US-Japan noise networks represented here in zines, labels, musicians, shops and radio stations were vital in boosting the success of each scene. Such networks were not, of course, confined to the United States and Japan; as we've already seen, power electronics and other proto or early noise musics circulated widely across cultural channels shared by Australia, Europe, the United States and so on. Given all this, Novak indeed argues that 'any story of Noise must account for the transnational circuitry of its subjects … It was exchanged as an object of transnational musical circulation that touched down in particular places and eventually came to be imagined as a global music scene' (2013, 15 and 5).

Transnational contexts and transcultural dynamics clearly played key roles in the development of noise in Japan, then. But it's also important to acknowledge that specifically local cultural factors came into play too. C.C.C.C. and Astro's Hiroshi Hasegawa, for example, paints a dim picture of noise's local place in Japanese culture.

> I know many foreign people regard Japan is as [sic] the center of unique noise music culture. But in fact, in Japan, it's very rare that noise is recognized as a culture, a music genre or a study subject. It's just regarded as bad taste music for maniac people.
>
> (Zimmerman 2017)

Others have focused on the broader social dynamics around noise in Japan. Japanese post-industrial musician Masahiko Okubo, whose work as Linekraft I examine in Chapter 10, has described the relative popularity of noise in Japan, particularly the country's typically harsh and relatively wild forms of live and recorded noise, as a reaction to the supposed rigidity of Japanese social etiquette and behavioural norms. Okubo accordingly describes the 'suppressive mindset' of Japanese society and the way in which noise music acts as a corrective and release for musicians and audiences:

> Japanese society is a form of 'mutual surveillance society' and people think like *Fuwaraidou* (meaning: to behave like a flock of sheep). Everyone observes each other and watches for rule breakers: Do people think the same way? Do they have the same belief? Are they different? Are they a 'guilty man' as a consequence? That suppressed mindset gets completely eradicated through explosive noise, and this is surely one side of Japanese noise music. So, a music style which delivers explosive hysterical high-volume noise functions as a form of therapy and is quite popular in the noise scene.
>
> (In Stevenson 2021, 5)

Whether this is true or not is open for debate. An artist as famous as Masami Akita (the main, latterly sole member of Merzbow) comes at this from a different angle, suggesting that it is precisely the clatter, tumult and *noise* of consumer-culture Japan that noise is trying to cancel or correct: 'Sometimes I would like to kill the much too noisy Japanese by my own noise. The effects of Japanese culture are too much noise everywhere. I want to make silence by my noise' (cited in Cox & Warner 2008, 61; see also Wilson 2015). Either way, though, even this latter point is a transcultural one, given that the cultural noise being responded to is global, circulatory in nature. Whatever explanation we offer for the founding, spread and (apparent, given Hasegawa's point) relative popularity of noise and harsh noise in Japan, it's clear that the music both started and spread as an intrinsically transnational, transcultural form.

Moving back to musical aesthetics before we get into case studies, it's clear that all the artists described above, whether from Tokyo, Osaka or otherwise, are united by an emphasis on musical and affective (as opposed to thematic) intensity, excess and harshness. Adam Potts indeed describes Japanese noise in terms of a 'a sonic excess that overflows the form and contours of music ordinarily understood'. 'Japanoise', Potts goes on, 'aestheticises excess in such a way that the possibility of it being a type of music is wagered ... Japanoise wills a world of formlessness and pure chaos, away from the material world of bodies, meaning and formation' (2015, 379–80). As we've already seen at length, my overarching interpretative argument about noise *music* moves us away from such ideas of 'formlessness' and 'pure chaos' towards an idea of unresolved, suspended dialectical processes of becoming in which formlessness and chaos are suggested but always held in tension by countervailing musical form and order. Nevertheless, Potts' emphasis on excess captures one of the essential points about harsh noise style.

This quality of excess indeed manifests across all examples of harsh noise (and even noise in general), whether from Japan or not. And, of course, we have already identified a certain intensity in artists like Whitehouse, The Haters and Genocide Organ. But it's also true that Japanese artists like Merzbow and Masonna have pushed the sonic intensity of noise to something of an unprecedented extreme, and as such can be seen as pioneers of affective and aesthetic extremes in noise music. We'll explore this point across the three case studies to come, starting with key Osaka act Hijokaidan.

Hijokaidan: *King of Noise* (1985) and *Noise from Trading Cards* (1997)

Hijokaidan have been one of the leading lights of underground/fringe music since the 1980s, both inside and outside Japan. As noted, they share a member (Toshiji Mikawa) with the similarly influential group Incapacitants; their leader, Jojo Hiroshige, spearheads the scene-leading, Osaka-based Alchemy Records and Alchemy Music Store (the latter of which was managed by Maso Yamazaki, aka Masonna, whose music is discussed below); and they pioneered a kind of freewheeling, extreme, performance art-inspired noise aesthetic that's proven both enduring and inspiring.

King of Noise (Alchemy Records) caught Hijokaidan at something of a transition point, moving towards the freewheeling harshness of later records. As such, it is an interesting album to discuss within an overview of the development of harsh noise. The style here is hybrid in its combination of influences. On the one hand, there is the skronk and honk of earlier free music artists such as Borbetomagus and Peter Brötzmann; indeed, I alluded to Hijokaidan's 2007 brain-frying free noise collaboration with the former, *Both Noises End Burning* (Les Disques Victo), in the Introduction. This 'skronk and honk' is evident most obviously in the wild guitar playing of Hiroshige, the gloriously unhinged screaming of Junko (the third key member of Hijokaidan), and the clattering drums from Mikawa. On the other hand, the album displays a burgeoning, unwieldy noise ethos in which remnants of free jazz licks and more traditional musical organization are pulverized, torqued by howling walls of theremin, amplifier and synth noise. This sort of hybrid approach was characteristic of this moment in Japanese noise music; the wild outpourings of Hanatarash, a hugely important group consisting of future members of Boredoms and Zeni Geva, are a useful mid-1980s comparison point for the Hijokaidan of *King of Noise*.

The style map below illustrates how we might see this mix playing out across the five tracks on the album. Unfastened noise rock merges into ambient harsh sounds,

Table 4.1 Style map of Hijokaidan's King of Noise

'The Wreck of a Once Promising Youth'	'Tod Dem Marximus'	'Konzentrationslager'	'Self-Mutilation'	'In Touch of Abe Kaii (Part 1)'
Free/noise/rock	Ambient harsh noise	Free/harsh noise	Ambient harsh noise	Noise/punk

which flow into freer and harsher noise and back again, before a punkier, 23-second conclusion.

What's notable here, in addition to the mix of styles from track to track, is the variety and detail of the musical material *within* each track. The deliberately rough and ramshackle feel of the playing is both at the heart of generating this variety and, sometimes, responsible for its loss.

Opening track, 'The Wreck of a Once Promising Youth', leans hard on unmetered, undeveloped drum explosions and mostly 1-string, heavily distorted guitar clanging. It starts out with potent energy and gestural unpredictability but gradually loses ensemble force over its seven or so minutes. Similarly, the excitable whelps of 'Konzentrationslager' add flavour and contrast but eventually decay into repetition. On the other hand, the elegantly spaced, constantly searching guitar and electronics harsh shimmer of 'Tod Dem Marximus', like the more restrained but densely packed feedback ballet of 'Self-Mutilation', demonstrate both the group's inveterate interest in harsh sounds and their subtle coordination of those sounds. I include these evaluative judgements not for their own sake but more to reflect the point that this album is an example of noise in transition and formation, the music a little uncertain and stuck as harsh noise style struggles to the surface gradually. Simply put, this is exploratory music not yet settled into stylistic shape, although the 'meta-stylistic' dimension of noise, its unresolving, suspended dialectical feel, is already present. But by the time we get to albums such as *Romance* (Alchemy Records, 1990), Hijokaidan's harsh noise assault has become more uniform, more sustained, playing out over sixty or seventy minutes of quasi-noise-wall. Hegarty describes *Romance*, indeed, as 'a constantly changing mess of howling feedback, residue overpowering the possibility of a musical centre to fix upon … permanent suspense replaces the ebb and flow of noise and not-noise or different types of noise' (2012, 20). I've already connected this 'permanent suspense' to my notion of 'becoming', but the point is worth underlining: albums like *Romance* are firmly rooted in a stable harsh noise style (or meta-style), which is founded in uncertainty and irresolution, on a productive mix of 'noisy' and 'musical' elements and tendencies.

Noise from Trading Cards (Alchemy Records, 1997) continues in the same vein. Blistering, festering walls of electronic static, guitar feedback and submerged drum clatters play out across three tracks and fifty-one minutes. The sonic harshness and relentless movement are overwhelming. And yet that's not the whole story. What is important here – beyond the shredding intensity of the total sound explosion –

are more subtle, fine-grained musical details, such as the stark contrasts of texture and weight found across the three tracks. This contrast is shown well in Figure 4.1 (whose arrows demarcate track divisions). As can be seen, the first track, 'What a Nuisance!', concentrates its 27-plus minutes of noise in mid and high range, retaining a remarkably consistent texture throughout. The second, 'Knocking on Hell's Doors', is more fragmented in flow, using held feedback tones and distortion to slowly unspool fourteen minutes of more delicate – though still very loud and harsh – noise interplay. The third, 'April 8 1996 San Francisco', is built on lower-range sonic tunnelling, with shards of high-pitched feedback and noise glinting throughout (the latter are more evident in Figure 4.2, which we'll get to in a moment).

What also holds attention on the album are the momentary features of order, form and shape that bubble up here and there amidst the chaos, from mysterious standing waves to curious distorted sound cells and gestures to unexpected moments of synchronicity. For example, at 6'07" in opener 'What a Nuisance!' a lower guitar tone aligns with a thwacked, slack snare drum, briefly grounding the trebly, tundra-like atmosphere in shared gestural and sonic weight and momentum. In addition, from 12'01" a series of events spool out that feel dramatic and climactic, from the appearance of discrete feedback motifs to a repeated lower guitar gesture to a powerful increase in percussive intensity. Again, these are elements that easily, effortlessly (thinking yet again of Hainge) encode into conventional musical gesture, signifying intent, contrast and structure as they do. Meanwhile, the whole of second track 'Knocking on Hell's Doors' feels like an unpredictable but constantly revolving cycle of noisy but distinctly *musical* tension and release (and back again to tension). Finally, the emotive shouting and screaming of Jojo and Junko, from minute two or so of closer 'April 8 1996 San Francisco', act as intermittent node of audience identification, grounding the wailing noise explosions with a sense of scarred, vulnerable human drama. In the same vein, there is also a compelling consistency to the total sound picture of *Noise from Trading Cards*. As well as sound sources remaining broadly the same throughout the album, there are notable continuities of pitch amidst apparent sonic chaos. Perhaps most interesting of these is the sustained high tone audibly concentrated at around 1850Hz, something that can be heard throughout the first and third tracks. This can be seen in Figure 4.2, which displays

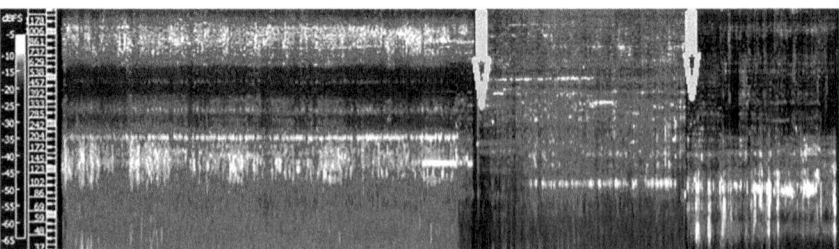

Figure 4.1 Melodic range spectrogram of Hijokaidan's *Noise from Trading Cards* (1997).

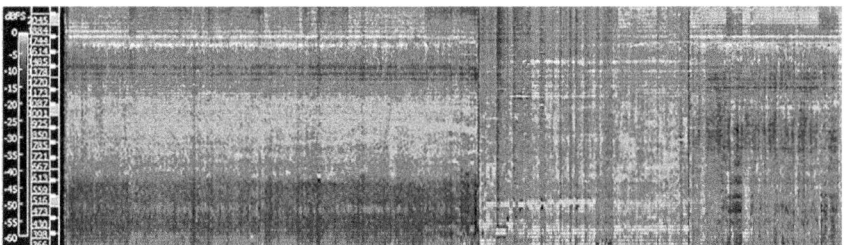

Figure 4.2 Peak frequency spectrogram of Hijokaidan's *Noise from Trading Cards* (1997).

a higher frequency range to Figure 4.1 and highlights peak frequencies rather than more traditionally isolatable 'musical' events.

Noise from Trading Cards, then, presents an unwieldy, wild sonic proposition with few clear idiomatic touchstones. And yet, as I've shown, the album features (or, at least, affords to listeners) discursive variety, drama and even some notable aspects of musical continuity and structure across its thick fifty-one minutes of noise. The elements of continuity and variety I've identified across the album increase the richness of its sound and pull audiences into its play of action and drama; most listeners tend to need something to hold on to, and consistencies of sound and texture, momentary suggestions of order and repetition and energetic, emotive screaming and playing all serve that function. I'd also note, finally, that the peculiar peaks and unrelenting assault of Hijokaidan across these albums, especially by the time we get to *Trading Cards*, create a particularly fertile affective, narrative space for listeners. Those listeners can jump back and forth between moments of order and identification into a more cognitively overloaded, hyper-processing state in which normal flows of information and secure, egoic feelings of self are hijacked by the churning, agitating flow of the music. This toggling of ego and id – or, to use my earlier terms, hyper and depersonalization – creates moments of rich tension for listeners trying to find ways through the sound.

Merzbow: *Noisembryo* (1994)

Masami Akita (founding and, latterly, sole member of Merzbow) has been perhaps the leading noise music artist over the past few decades. Akita has produced literally hundreds of albums, often in collaboration with musicians from within and far beyond noise, been reviewed many times in mainstream publications, and appeared at all sorts of popular venues and festivals. It's a kind of (relative) crossover 'success' that hasn't cost admiration and respect within the noise scene; indeed, the *Noisextra* podcast frequently referenced in this book started life as 'Merzcast', until a run-in with Akita over the hosts' comments about the BDSM content and focus of his earlier work encouraged them to change direction. In recognition of Akita's prominence, we both spend a lot of time on his 1990s music now and then return to his music at length in Chapter 6, where we'll focus on his twenty-first-century releases.

The 1990s represent the peak of Merzbow's so-called 'analogue' period. Where the 1980s Merzbow of Akita and Kiyoshi Mizutani had often used guitar and drums, in addition to metal plates, contact mics and other found or constructed junk and industrial objects, the 1990s was a decade in which Merzbow produced a whole slew of albums primarily using EMS and Moog analogue synths and a variety of effects pedals and units (though some of the contact mic'd junk from earlier often made appearances too). These albums – coruscatingly harsh, rhythmically pulverising and overwhelmingly intense pretty much to a release – made a huge splash inside and even outside the world of noise, driving the 'crossover' success just alluded to. This was partly because of Merzbow's five-album 1990s run with Relapse Records, an American label that otherwise specialized in extreme but comparatively popular heavy metal acts such as Obituary and Pig Destroyer. This run did much to get Akita's work into record shops and music magazines. But the 'splash' these albums made was also because of the undeniable power and force of the music, which brought the harshness of earlier acts into concentrated, compelling focus across hours and endless hours of spuming walls and electric spasms of noise.

Of those 1990s analogue releases, it is probably *Venereology* and *Noisembryo* (Release and The Releasing Eskimo, both 1994) that get the most attention, though albums like *Pulse Demon* (Release, 1996) and *Hybrid Noisebloom* (Vinyl Communications, 1997) are also important examples from the period. David Keenan described *Noisembryo* as the 'quintessential Merzbow release' (2000, 33), whilst Hospital Productions, the label responsible for its lavish 2018 reissue, called it 'the holy grail, not only of Merzbow's obsessive discography, but of the entire 90's noise movement' (2018).

My choice to focus on *Noisembryo* here is largely in response to this reputation, which is well-deserved and reflects the importance of this release in establishing Merzbow's analogue style. But I could have analysed any one of those 1990s albums and ended up with a representative picture. This is not to say that these albums are seamless parts of a greater whole – distinct sounds, from the vocals on *Noisembryo* to the emphasis on, you guessed it, pulse in *Pulse Demon*, mark each album out from its companions. But it *is* to suggest that a consistent style or meta-style runs through them. Paul Hegarty, analysing 'Ananga-Range' from *Venereology*, described this in terms of 'microphases of sound', which 'acquire consistency only to be caught within as the layered whole moves on, closing over whatever looked to emerge'. This 'patterning and seaming of layers' is seen by Hegarty as a characteristic feature of Merzbow's music in this mid-1990s period (2007, 159). This is well said. Across Merzbow's work from this time the listener is regularly confronted with a kind of chaotic 'order' or musicality flickering into and out of existence as, say, a steady pulse pattern emerges, or an oscillating bass drone throbs into existence, or a panrhythm of clashing noise layers suddenly locks into polyrhythmic place. In such moments, aperiodicism, ameldocism, aformalism and inharmonicity crystallize into perceptible rhythms, or shapes, or sonorities. And yet almost always this emerging order or 'crystal', as Hegarty puts it, 'is no sooner established that it unforms' (2007). The steady pulse, or sustained bass drone, or textural hierarchy, or polyrhythmic groove disappear almost as they appear. The prevailing effect of this is of a constant tussle between order and disorder, between compositional logic and entropic discomposition, where hints of distinct musical references and compositional alignment briefly come to the surface and recede amidst waves and waves of consuming noise. The dialectic never synthesizes. This is related to the similar phasing in and out of order in Hijokaidan, even as Merzbow's music feels sonically very different; harder, more propulsive, more directed.

Merzbow's 1990s music plays in these ways as a theatre of action in which both musical language and the listening self are in a constant state of becoming or tension. In this sense, the 1990s albums are prime examples of my overarching interpretation of how noise music can be understood to work. To explore these points in more detail, I use a two-pronged analytical approach with *Noisembryo*. First, I take a broadly descriptive, technical look at Part 1, which was chosen for this purpose both because of its relatively compact nine-minute duration (the 2'54" of Part 4 would have been too short, whilst the remaining two tracks are over twenty minutes each) and its representative density of music detail and event. Then, I immerse myself more impressionistically and selectively in Parts 2 and 3, using the deep listening, auto-ethnographic approach discussed in the Introduction to tease out events and potential plays of self and self-loss in response. First, the descriptive analysis of Part 1.

Merzbow's propulsive, jerking muse is obvious from the get-go in this track; the openings of all four parts of the album indeed throw us headfirst into a staticky dancefloor. Multiple irregular beat patterns thump out over each other, drilling, vibrating and shaking as they go. This is Skrillex twenty years too early and gone very awry. At about 0'44", a more isolated, driven, singular clump of static consumes the audio field, lavaically popping and roiling against an arrested lower pulsing. We are now in a more uniform noise world. That lower pulsing, suddenly more regular in pulse and profile (with a fast 3-3-3-3-2-2 pattern emerging), takes over at 1'38", gradually being consumed over the next minute or so by a lacerating piece of distortion, then the clump of static from earlier, then a huge rubbery coil of sound. Static and scrawl come to the fore again at 2'35". Even in these first few minutes all the elements are in place: multi-layered noise, intermittent clear pulsing and distinct gestures and supervening sheets of noise.

The next minute of the track absolutely bristles with noise, four or five or six separate loops and layers of static (including a particularly busy and condensed tattoo of noise far in the right channel) drawing attention this way and that. At 3'36" a more sustained low blast runs for twenty seconds, busier crackle above playing against it excitingly, before all of it starts to glitch and tremor at 3'56". The low blast and higher, spattery static cut in and out unpredictably over the next few minutes (with a particular moment of contrast at 5'02", where the sound completely cuts momentarily). This middle passage, then, is characterised by high energy and dense textures but also by clear contrasts, with, for example, the entry of the low blast marking out a moment of distinct textural change. Once again, the sound holds chaos and order in tension.

At 6'17", following about ten seconds of a juddering oscillation in the low blast, gestures spread out, different filters and rates of delays and, strangely, breathy sounds vying for attention amidst a brief but general cooling of temperatures. A sheet of coruscating noise cuts in at 6'31", driving the track to its close after this brief respite, momentum never letting up for the next 100 seconds or thereabouts. In this intense climactic passage, the sound is concentrated in the mid and higher registers. Volume and frequency are high and texture dense, as noise and quick stabs and scratches come in from all quarters, completely overloading the sonic space. We now arrive at the final movement, as it were, of the track. A brief call back to the low blast at 8'10", after a few seconds of a slightly cleaner texture, prepares the ground for the final fifty seconds. These, typically, see a gradual reduction down in event and density on the way to a more concentrated final fifteen seconds, where a single oscillating piece of distortion whirrs and judders in a slightly modulating looped delay (with subtle hints of bass below), before a final, unexpected higher tone and random bit of static close us out.

As can be seen, Part One of *Noisembryo* is packed with sonic and musical event. Sheets of noise, storms of clashing textures and rhythms and, periodically, distinct sounds, patterns and call backs come together to produce a broiling mix of order and disorder. Moments of clear compositional transition and cohesion – the repeated low blast, the higher static, the itinerant pulsing – anchor the track in a fairly uniform set of materials even as this anchor is constantly yanked away. We never quite settle. Harsh noise here therefore relies for its effect both on the shock of exorbitant detail and disorder and on subtle but strong threads of continuity and change. All this creates a rich interplay of logic and fall, of musicality and noise, throughout.

Parts 2 and 3 – the first 25'07" and the second 20'59" in length – work on much the same basis, though the scale is grander and the drama more drawn out than it was in Part 1. Unalloyed and densely drawn noise and static get wrestled into pulsing, throbbing life, before arrest and explosion of that life destabilizes emerging form and logic. This creates a compelling and often overwhelmingly exciting sense of chaotic forward momentum. Sounds always feel both on the verge of coming apart and together: these two tracks exist on a line of oscillating torque and tension, the wiggling vitality of the universe manifest as sound. I highlight one notable passage from each track – 10'59" to 14'25" in Part 2 and 5'40" – 10'41" in Part 3 – where this wiggling vitality is most wiggly and most vital. I am doing this both to get into more detail and to chart what this oscillation of order and disorder does to the listening mind and body; to my listening mind and body.

Part 2: 10'59" to 14'25"

I'm lost in the noise early in the track, static coming at me from all sides. At three minutes in a flanging, wild, guitar-finger-tapping-like scrabble resolves the tumult momentarily. At 8'19" what sounds like a quick, repeated dialling up and down of a volume swell pedal creates a propulsive one-TWO, one-TWO beat (a version of which had been heard, in part, at the opening of the track), which has that characteristic Merzbow impact of making harsh noise feel like the most danceable, pulsing music in the world. Moments like these, with noise and periodic beat dissolving into and out of each other in frenzied dialectic, bring me into my body and out of my mind [if these two can be talked of in this way], phasing me into the present with the music as I attune to its heteromorphic energy. I flow into the beating world, staying there as the music keeps changing and pulsing; it's possible to transcend – trance – in this way with more conventional music, but the low rate of repetition and high rate of density and strangeness in noise means that such trancing can have a particularly rich tensile quality when it's achieved. As the noise continually melts into vicious, lacerating beats, I have become, for a moment, an 'egoless centre through whom the principle of emptiness is made manifest' (Campbell 2008, 141). I lose myself. There are many other ways to describe this kind of experience – as with Guesde and Nadrigny in The Most Beautiful Ugly Sound in the World, we could for example choose a complementary focus on the role of the body in experiencing noise: 'awareness of the body's role in listening is particularly remarkable in the case of noise – unlike a formal listening that appeals more to the intellect. The noise listener is an embodied listener, whose body intervenes not only as a way to access sound, but also as a way to appreciate music' (2018, 71) – but this one feels right to me: this music takes me out of (my) self and makes me cosmic.

The most extraordinary example of such cosmic feeling arrives at 10'59", when the music gets taken over by a series of remarkable grooves (anticipated only seconds before by some itinerant beating at 10'49"). First, what initially sounds like a snare drum roll but materializes more clearly as drum machine blasts arrests my body with martial direction. Next, at 11'13", 27 seconds of another march-like, one-TWO throb, with a low bass tone on the one and an opened, wah-wah spray of static on the two, gurgles out of the melee. This bristling march causes involuntary movement, the unexpected force of the beat ricocheting against my nerves and sending me out to my edges. The throb is varied after a few cycles with a high pass filter throwing light onto higher scratching overtones and feedback, frissons now all over my skin. At 11'53" we vibrate deeper into the noise with a further development of the one-TWO throb, the '1' now divided into three smaller beats and the high, trebly '2' into a 2 and 1 pattern. After thirty seconds that sliced and diced throb starts to become submerged, ducking underneath squalls of feedback, before an explosion of crumbling at 12'44" tunnels us into oblivion for a few seconds. The beat keeps coming to the surface but intervening wah-wah noise and static push it away again and again. By 13'39" we've lost the throb completely in a wall of high-pitched noise and static. A new, lower-range presence emerges at 13'54" that partially ushers us back to the beat but that beat now feels farther and farther away, just about tethering us even as the noise increases in intensity and density. By 14'25" I'm surrounded by noise and far from the beat, Akita's heavily distorted vocals just one more element in an overwhelming, disorientating mix that has me pitching and rolling between poles of depersonalized trance and anxious, neurotic, hyperpersonalisation.

These whole tumultuous three or four minutes have seen me lose, find, and lose myself all over again, ego and self dissolving into a larger, cosmic context just as the tussles between beat, noise, and overwhelming volume kept pulling me into and out of that dissolved state.

Part 3 5'36" – 10'41"

The early-going here is looser, more chaotic than Part 2, but the emergence of what sounds almost like a steady, sequenced synth beat at 0'24", followed by unloosed vocalisations soon after, alert the listener to the fact that this track will be operating across the borderline of focused musical intensity and noise chaos.

The tension of order and disorder reaches a peak at 5'36", where a dancing, bobbing low-register beat pulls us into flow as tones glint and tear around it. At 6'00" the texture cleans out completely and a chugging, four-square rhythm thrums out for thirty seconds as stereo-active modulating noise tones scan back and forth. Over the next few minutes different versions of these two beats, the first echoing the one-TWO throb from Part 2 and the second in more regular 4-time, are chopped up and screwed about. At 7'11', for instance, a sliver of the low-register beat is cut-up amidst fragmented, spare textures. About a minute later, the oscillating throb of that same one-TWO beat returns, now submerged and overwritten. At 8'41" a kind of hybrid of the two beats throws us into one of the most exhilarating passages of the whole album, where chugging static and throbbing one-TWO combine to form a fearsome wall of hitting, pulsing, vibrating noise. A pummeling beat then enters at 9'40". It is consumed in static and feedback, even as its compulsive force persists over the next minute. It pulls us along with irresistible momentum even as every other sound cuts against or into our dancing bodies, my dancing body, which is lost to the sound, present with and immersed in the music, beyond time.

Both the music and the listening self feel here as if they are 'dissolving into undifferentiated energy'; shooting stars and meteors of sound mass into a consuming celestial fire, rational thought running faster and faster to keep up before it outruns itself and the body grooves ludicrously: 'thought goes. The mind rests in its pure state' (Campbell 2008, 149 and 140). This affords me the feeling of the kind of 'freedom from the known' discussed by Krishnamurthi, where we attain a state 'that cannot be disturbed by circumstances, by thought or by human corruption' (2010, Chapter 1). Big words but these are big feelings.

Noisembryo, as can be seen in these two passages as well as in the broader technical description above, makes its bones out of typical noise strategies of cut-up, modulated, oscillated sound – which is often inharmonic, aperiodic and aformal in nature but equally is often periodic and hierarchical – as well as frenetic edits and action, and overwhelming volumes and colour. But the intensity of its micro-structures, its microcosms of shifting and interpenetrating order and disorder, leaves the music in an especially fertile place, repeatedly resolving into language and back out to chaos as it goes. And it likewise, perhaps, allows the listener to explore a fertile communion between sense and sensation, acuity and awareness, where thwacking, staticky beats pulse them into the present moment and in so doing momentarily take them out of our their anxious, split, neurotic selves.

Masonna: *Spectrum Ripper* (1997)

At thirty-one minutes, twenty-five tracks and a million screams, shards of feedback, and bulldozing clumps of static, *Spectrum Ripper* (Cold Spring) is an absurdist masterpiece of cognitive overload and hyper-arousal. This is typical for Masonna, who alongside Merzbow, Keiji Haino, Hijokaidan and others has been a key figure in

Japanese for decades now, and who invariably makes dense, fast-paced, compulsive sound. Masonna's music frantically pushes onwards like a madman running through a fireworks festival, seemingly largely impervious to rational order and logical form. This is part of its power: it lands on the listener as a mess of squealing, scratchy, hysterical emotion. This is harsh noise as terrible sonic joy ride, driving us into and out of order and controlled self as it sparks wildly along the highway. But as we'll see, there can also be a kind of sense and order present amidst the madness.

Spectrum Ripper is built on two central motifs or gestures. First, out-of-body, distorted, high-pitched screams and guttural shouts, which usually last for about three or four seconds each. Second, fuller spectrum, though still light on low end, static explosions of roughly five to ten seconds. Both elements are achieved via amps turned up high and a typical array of analogue synth, filterbank and distortion, delay, wah and fuzz effects pedals (including the Boss PS-2 pitch-shifter/delay pedal so often found on noise releases from this period). Sometimes the two motifs are twisted together, toyed with, even developed in tandem. But mostly they play out as brief, separate microphases of either distorted scream or static. The music is in this sense astonishingly simple in its narrow range of material; either scream, or static, or scream-and-static.

And yet this narrow range generates great emotional impact. This is both through the bulldozing affective intensity of the central motifs and through the level of subtlety in how they are drawn out. Listen closely, slowly, and you hear fine-drawn contrasts of material, moments of dramatic shape and contour that are vital for the album to sustain listeners' interest. For example, after four tracks of high and mid-range, exciting but seemingly disordered distorted screaming and static, at the beginning of Part V we get five seconds (five 1-second iterations) of a distinct pulse marked by contrast between high- and low-end sound (see Table 4.2). The sound here is still dominated by static and distortion. And yet clear pulse and registral contrast mean that this brief passage works as dramatic punctuation in the flow of unrestrained sound. Even at only five seconds, with the rest of the track composed of the usual gesticulatory screams and fuzzed-out static, this gesture creates a sense of narrative definition; since this is especially compacted, concise music, five seconds can after all have more impact than it might in more drawn-out, spacious contexts.

Similarly, a 21-second passage from 0'05" to 0'26" of 'Part VI' focuses around a single, relatively undistorted mid-range tone in such a way as to create narrative shape. Within those twenty-one seconds this tone is gradually filtered and modulated. A low

Table 4.2 Motif from 'Part V' of *Spectrum Ripper* (1997)

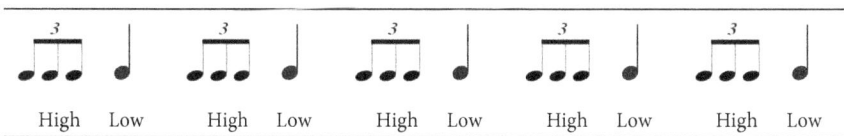

pass filter creates a beating pattern and then a pitch shift down an octave and back up (and down and up) again creates further beating and movement. The tone then slides up by the interval of about a major second for a few seconds, this serving as a kind of cadential transition back into more disordered distortion. And again similarly, 'Part VII' is even more varied in material and in its use of space and texture; its first nineteen seconds consist of a delicate interplay of stereo-separated high tones coming into and out of close alignment with each other, rising by step a couple of times to ratchet up tension once again as we transition back into distortion.

Spectrum Ripper features such subtleties of detail and pacing throughout, amidst its more general litany of screams and static. The first twenty seconds of 'Part X' use steady delay reflections of a held texture, and then slowing, lowering distortion of that pattern, to set up contrast with the ensuing noise (the delay pattern returns at a different pitch at 0'59", too). 'Part XV' cleans out the texture for fifteen seconds or so of a watery beat. 'Part XVIII' features seven seconds of a held tone in the right channel, with a simultaneous oscillation an octave below between dominant and tonic in the left channel (though terms like dominant and tonic aren't quite right here, given that these tones shift, crackle and slide about in a pitch space that is far removed from equal temperament). 'Part XXI' starts out with six seconds of exposed high tones, arcing out a weird remnant of a flattened sixth to fifth cadential climax.

'Part XXIV', at 4'04" the longest track by far, is astonishing in this regard of creating contrast with, and drama within, the rest of the album. It's worth delving into in some detail to round out my *Spectrum Ripper* discussion. The track's first sixty-six seconds consist of the usual splatter and verve, though the first five seconds have aspects of the registral contrast and beating delay patterns from earlier. But 1'06"–3'00" are given over completely, and abruptly, to 109 iterations of a repeated, siren-like tone chorused across a couple of octaves and, within each iteration of approximately a second, a sliding down of about a minor third. This is a remarkable passage in which radical change and hyper-momentum suddenly give way to iteration and stasis in a totally unexpected way. These iterations then just as abruptly give way at 3'00" to a gently ricocheting, repeated dyad spread an octave apart, where the lower note feels like percussive patter and the higher one like a thin synth tone. The fundamental note of this dyad is roughly a major third below the lowest tone of the siren iterations. This once again suggests a kind of cadential function or resolution, in this case the siren sounding out scale degrees $\hat{5}$ and $\hat{3}$, and the ricochet sounding $\hat{1}$. Deliberately or not, harsh noise here uses basic templates of western music to suggest (at least to some listeners) narrative closure and definition. The dyad continues for the rest of the track, gently modulating in spectrum and decreasing in volume from 3'33" on, like a ball dropped into an empty barn left to bounce out its remaining energy. Figure 4.3 conveys both the clear three-part structure of 'Part XXIV' and the stark contrasts of material across those three parts. As can be seen, the dense spectra of the first section contrast with the robotic siren glissandos of the second and the slightly fuller, drawn-out ricochets of the third.

All this drawing out and relative stasis leaves the listener prone for the last track, which is, in stark contrast, composed of nine seconds of utterly berserk scream-distortion. The dramatic shift between the stasis of Part XXIV and the blasted explosion of Part XXV is illustrated clearly when looking at the latter's spectrogram in Figure 4.4 (this time a peak frequency spectrogram, so that distinct frequencies and events can be more easily perceived in the noise chaos), which shows the brief track's wide frequency spread and textural density.

'Part XXIV' works beautifully in this way to create contrast with everything that had come before it, its relentless repetition and reduction of material feeling chasm-like after the hyper-glossolalia of much of the first twenty-three tracks. It hypnotizes the listener into a state of stillness and calm, ego repose and repletion, that is brutally wrenched apart by the brief cognitive overload of the final track. This is the album's key dramatic strategy in macro-microcosm, sprays of seemingly improvised, spontaneous noise given unexpected form and relief by contrasting passages of ordered pattern and space.

Spectrum Ripper, like Masonna's work as a whole – this approach being generally consistent across his discography with some notable exceptions; the almost-minimalist repetition and patterning of Side B of 1995's *Filled with Unquestionable Feelings* (Coquette) is a good example – is harsh noise taken to an absurd extreme of information-density and seeming disorder. Sounds are harsh in their volume, chaos and screeching distortion. Forms and gestures are, on the surface, spontaneous and loose. Flow is, again on the surface, secondary to spectacle. Such an impression is enhanced in the context of Masonna's live shows, where two- or three- or four-minute

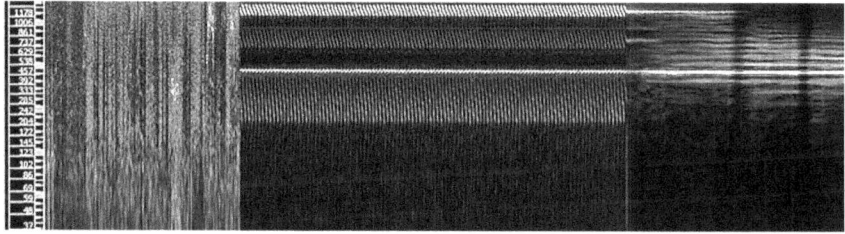

Figure 4.3 Melodic range spectrogram of 'Part XXIV' from Masonna's *Spectrum Ripper* (1997).

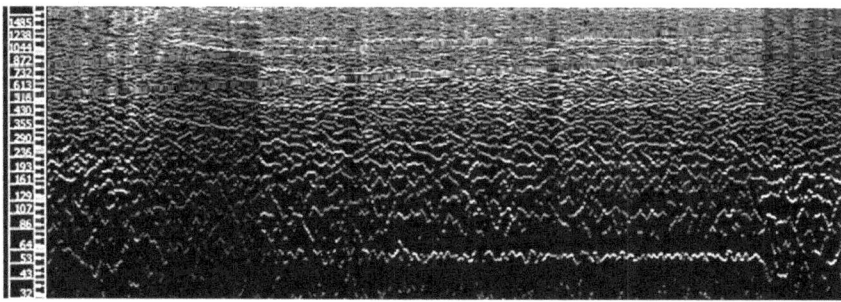

Figure 4.4 Peak frequency spectrogram of 'Part XXV' from Masonna's *Spectrum Ripper* (1997).

blasts of distorted noise and screaming are delivered with all the pomp of 1970s stadium music; black clothes, long hair and rock god poses all playing with and against the cut-up, tearing intensity of the sound to create irresistible spectacle. And yet as well as all this, as we've seen, Masonna's harsh noise pivots around subtle directions and details, where moments of sudden contrast, or rest, or repetition, arrest the otherwise unceasing onward flow. Whether these moments arise out of careful planning or the kinds of controlled accidents the best improvisers rely on is immaterial: they are there, and they play a vital role in creating an unresolved dialectic of disorder and order that, to me, evokes a kind of endless becoming to listeners. This all amounts to dramatic discourse, a cohesively incoherent narrative of flow, change and climax.

Conclusion

As is demonstrated in my close reading of *Spectrum Ripper* and in my discussions of Hijokaidan and Merzbow, it's clear that classic Japanese harsh noise pivots around a beautiful tension between cognitive overload and restorative order, noise-musical chaos and cohesion. In this aporetic tension, harsh noise likely plays a dual function for listeners. On the one hand, we listen to artists like Masonna to be taken out of ourselves, transported into a realm of febrile, hyperpersonalized activation, the sheer density of the music forcing us first to race to try and catch up with its puzzle and then out of rational processing mode and into a space of feeling and instinctive pleasure or pain. This space of feeling can even slide into a depersonalized zone in which activation blurs into ego transcendence, the self snapping for just a moment as it loses rational mooring. But, to make something of a new point for this chapter, we also listen to pick up on the patterns and the flow of the sound and to be confirmed in our egos, parsing the chaos into something that at least feels like it can be processed and perceived as something other than what it first appears. As with the similarly intense and dense music of Japanese artists such as Monde Bruits or Pain Jerk or C.C.C.C, it's clear that this music is both ego-shattering pyrotechnic and ego-flattering puzzle. We don't always lose ourselves in listening to classic Japanese harsh noise; we can just as easily find a stronger, more secure self, buoyed up by its pleasurable tussle with overwhelming sound. It's important to hold on to this in our talk of hyper or depersonalization; sometimes, noise just helps with our personalization.

The next chapter picks these aesthetic and psychological thoughts up with reference to American and European harsh noise primarily from the 'classic' 1990s period examined here.

5

Harsh noise in the United States and Europe

We're now in the middle section of our 'book within a book' triptych of harsh noise chapters. (Chapter 6 updates the story in looking at the international harsh noise scene of the 2000s, 2010s and early 2020s.) Whilst I once again divide the chapter into geographically determined parts – the first on America, the second Europe – it's nevertheless recognized, thinking about the transcultural idea discussed in the previous chapter, that all the examples are part of similar music-historical lineages and likewise share music-stylistic DNA. Our two American and three European examples indeed embody the transcultural mix of global continuity and local variety that characterized harsh noise throughout the 1990s.

American junk

Macronympha: *Pittsburgh/Pennsylvania* **(1995)**

Harsh noise thrived in America in the 1990s, hot on the heels of the 'harsh power' artists discussed in Chapter 4. A range of gonzo approaches and artists sprung up, partly in the mould of earlier experimentalist outsiders like Harry Partch, partly picking up directly from harsh power artists like Intrinsic Action and partly emerging *sui generis* out of a cocktail of Japanese influence, new technological resources and cultural opportunity.

Consisting primarily of Joseph Roemer and Rodger Stella and coming out of Pittsburgh in the early 1990s, Macronympha are a great example of this burgeoning US-harsh-noise tradition. Their focus on rudimentary sound sources is characteristic of a lot of US artists in this period, for example. Similarly, their typical eccentricity and extremity of persona and image; as well as lurid, taboo-baiting and often offensive titles, the group became well-known within the scene for ill-advised interview pronouncements – most notable of these being an infamously juvenile interview focused around body parts and sex in *Bananafish* #10 (Glass 1995). Finally, their wide exposure and collaborative energy on the US and international noise scene are characteristic, with many artists and labels driven by such fertile cross-pollination and relationship-building. After all, without having to worry about barriers like money, rights, intellectual property, scaled-up distribution and so on, and with relatively cheap materials, easily exploited channels such as mail order, and a lot of energy from producers and audience members, fecund, dense scenes like the international harsh noise scene of the 1990s can easily develop.

Though I've just described Macronympha's 'eccentricity and extremity' as typical for US harsh noise artists in the 1990s, it's worth acknowledging that there are often political dimensions to their work that were not necessarily typical, harking back as these did to the taboo-busting and hatefulness of power electronics. On *Pittsburgh/Pennsylvania* (Praxis Dr. Bearmann, 1995), the political dimensions emerge in two primary ways. Firstly, the album explicitly engages themes of Rust Belt deindustrialization and 'urban decay', to steal a title from another Macronympha cassette. It does this through its title, which plays on Guy Mitchell's homonymous 1952 hit about pawnshops and millionaires in pointing to a key Rust Belt location (and the band's hometown). And it does it through its music, which consists of amplified scrap metal sounds processed through effects pedals and recorded to Tascam four-track, these scrap metal clangs and shudders seeming to evoke industrial soundscapes. Secondly, and this is where we broach taboo and offense, the titles of the album's three Side A tracks tread into apparently white supremacist ground, being grouped under the heading 'Critical Determination of Genetic Malfunction in Three Racial Groups' and called, in turn, 'Negro', 'Hispanic' and 'Semite (Arab and Jew)'.

Echoing political discussions in earlier chapters, an obvious and not unreasonable political reading of these track titles, and of the album as a whole, would condemn Macronympha for their, at best, retrogressive and ill-conceived use of tried and tested noise and industrial shock tactics, and at worst for their drastic reduction of complex economic and cultural dynamics into a white supremacist politics of racialized resentment. The only existing sustained scholarly analysis of *Pittsburgh* indeed adopts this sort of condemnatory position. In that analysis, William Hutson acknowledges the album's 'multi-layered' complexity but suggests nevertheless that it can ultimately be heard as 'expressing a deeply confused and reactionary perspective on white supremacy within performative codes of white trash masculinity' (2015, 93). It does this by taking what Hutson describes as a 'nostalgic', 'melancholic' attitude to Pittsburgh's steel industry past, an attitude that Hutson argues acts as 'an elegy for a sound no longer heard in [the group's] depressed and desolate, impoverished neighborhoods, a remembrance for the phantom booming of now-silent factories' (114). This 'backward-looking' attitude means that 'the record performs a frustrated, impotent, re-sounding' (115). Addressing the titles mentioned above, Hutson comes to the crux of his argument:

> For Macronympha … the frustration of poverty becomes conflated with racial hatred. In this ideological move, minority groups take the place of neoliberalism as the perpetrators of whatever social and economic problems Macronympha experience. They see themselves as oppressed and, in turn, out of misdirected fear and anger, blame superficial markers of racial and cultural difference and ignore a situation of shared material conditions.
>
> (2015, 118)

Given the evidence Hutson cites – not the music itself, which he only briefly describes and indeed summarizes as 'simple' and 'rudimentary' (93) – from interviews with the band to track and album titles and the broader cultural context these point to, this political reading makes sense. And yet to my mind, whilst I recognize its validity, it is a little too unidirectional, too deterministic. All music is inescapably multi-layered and even ambiguous, difficult to pin concrete political readings on. This is particularly the case with noise such as *Pittsburgh, Pennsylvania*, with its dense textures, confusing sonic details and unpredictable organization. We've already identified such ambiguity even in extreme, seemingly hateful music from the likes of Whitehouse. And it's possible to hear *Pittsburgh, Pennsylvania* both through this lens of ambiguity and in terms of industrial and PE-derived tactics of risk and overidentification, where repressed social tensions are exposed via risky embodiments of unpalatable perspectives (*becoming* the horror). This is not to discount Hutson's condemnation but merely to expand on it.

So, when we hear the album's track titles alongside both the broader transgressive tradition in noise and also the dense, bulldozing and profoundly complex sounds of each track, singular political interpretation becomes tricky. Yes, we can read the album and its broader semiotic context as a statement on or of racialized political economy. But we can also, for example, hear it as an attempt to expose the narrow-mindedness of white supremacist attitudes. Or as a cocktail of different cultural flashpoints put together without any clear intention uniting them. Or, in primarily aesthetic terms, as a typically problematic noise release filled with fascinating atmospheres and ideas. On this latter point, after all, even though Macronympha's decision to amplify scrap metal sounds has obvious cultural resonances with their Rust Belt setting it is also completely in keeping with 1990s American noise tropes, where cheap, junk aesthetics were common. We can see this in everything from artists like Werewolf Jerusalem and Bacillus using rudimentary radio or tape and speaker setups to Chop Shop using salvaged materials and speakers to Emil Beaulieau making noise out of destroyed or deformed records. The Rita's Sam McKinlay has indeed commented in this regard that 'American harsh noise back in the 1990s was noticeably dirtier, concentrating on the crunch and rumble a lot more than the squeal and jolts of some Japanese artists, with their cleaner feel' (2010, 14). Scrap metal may be culturally significant but it might also simply be heard as a genre trope. And the actual *sound* (as opposed to sound sources) of *Pittsburgh/Pennsylvania* is also in keeping with other noise releases from the period. Hutson indeed acknowledges this point, comparing the album's 'forty minutes of constant, screaming feedback and chunky, crumbling distortion' to artists like Merzbow. And it's an excellent example of the genre: tough, immersive and unpredictable throughout, psychedelic in its intensity and in its flickering between overwhelming disorder and emergent order and contrast. As we'll see in more detail in a moment, the music doesn't provide much support to Hutson's political reading, even if the track titles and interview pronouncements are hard to mitigate.

The concentration and continuity of the music on *Pittsburgh/Pennsylvania* can be seen clearly in Figure 5.1. As the image shows, apart from a sharp edit for the last two minutes of the first track (where the sound spreads in range suddenly; this is denoted with the first arrow from left to right), the four tracks (separated by the second, third and fourth arrows from left to right) hover around the frequency range of 75–220Hz, and at broadly the same volume and dynamic intensity.

And yet within this broad continuity lies a world of micro-events and internal struggle and tussle, which bely Hutson's claim that 'timbre remains as the album's sole musical gesture' (109). The first couple of minutes of the album alone demonstrate its density and variety. Figure 5.2, which is a peak frequency spectrogram of these 118 seconds, shows a whole host of sounds (right up to 1300Hz or so) jumping out briefly to lure us in, and a whole series of textural breaks and contrasts likewise.

In fact, the experience of listening to both these opening couple of minutes and to the rest of the album is one of utter musical contrast and variety. This can be shown with a deep dive into the nine-minute track one, along the lines of my present-tense, impressionistic descriptions of *Noisembryo*.

I start to listen as a child cries not far from me. I'm already on edge, present and not. The bustling sounds of the first thirty seconds or so are a comfort, like being in a crowded cafe or thoroughfare with reality turned up. But at 0'35" this introduction gives way to shredding volume and noise (this break in texture can be seen clearly about a third of the way through Figure 5.2). Suddenly I'm tunnelling into stereo confusion, picking out patterns, feeling out terrible struggles, making sense here and there of wild beat patterns, hovering feedback, wonky sci-fi. Nothing feels steady; I don't feel steady. I feel the thrill and the fear of both depersonalization, of becoming the kind of 'egoless centre' mentioned previously, and hyperpersonalization, fight/flight kicking in. This is even as, around it all, rational habit energy and aesthetic feel kick against that defensive instinct, grabbing on to recurring touches like a stray high pitch that starts to be heard about sixty seconds in. I start to adjust, to attune to the information. My ego gains ground. Somewhere in the third

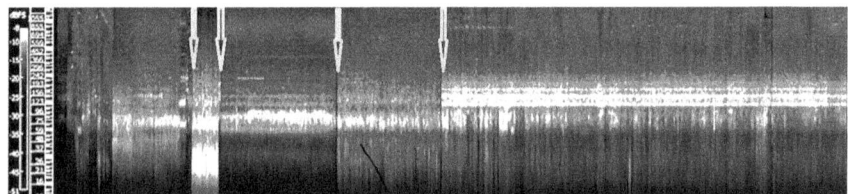

Figure 5.1 Melodic range spectrogram of Macronympha's *Pittsburgh/Pennsylvania* (1995).

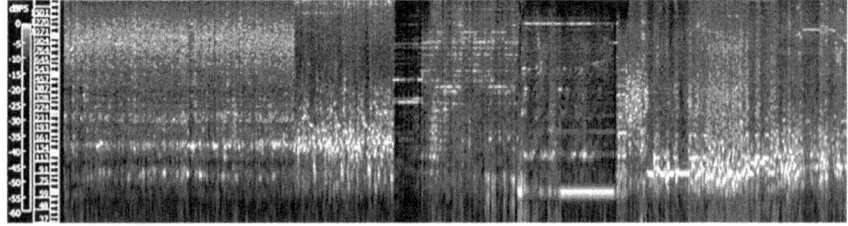

Figure 5.2 Peak frequency spectrogram of the first 118 seconds of Macronympha's *Pittsburgh/Pennsylvania* (1995).

minute I hear a version of that high-pitched sound, followed by a rush of wind, a one-two pairing that feels somehow familiar. By the fourth minute small emblems of recognition build as I get used to the sonic palette and energy swirl, even as the rate of change stays relentless, the random jerking and whooshing feeling like gravity, my body flexing and responding where it needs to. Then, musically, things start to draw out. For example, the steady, stereo-busy layering of scratchy, inconstant mid-range distortion and choked screams over intermittent looped, fuzzy low drones in the fifth, sixth, and seventh minutes provides a powerful but subtly realized contrast with the relentless bustle of earlier. It draws me into a sustained musical intensity. This represents a steadiness of idea as well as creating a steadiness of identification, the erotic fear from earlier now graduated in my mind and body into a lower-level affect of attunement and pleasurable poise. By 6'31", higher frequency screams or feedback start to interject, unsettling me in my poise but equally both calling back to the earlier high pitches and preparing me for change and new information. This is compositional, I realise, detail and affect working in tandem to create narrative and flow.

At 6'53" to 6'55" the texture suddenly cleans out [the brief passage just before the first arrow from left to right in Figure 5.1]. Rudimentary, trebly whizz-bang sounds à la early Musique Concrète or 1960s science lab sound effects usher in a mysterious rising bass figure (at the blue arrow). This figure arcs out a simple, short-short-long, $\hat{1}$-$\hat{5}$-$\hat{6}$ motif, semi-submerged behind and within spread-wide static and noise that's now quieter, less invasive than the overwhelming harshness from before (the splash of white at this point in Figure 5.1 is misleading; here's one of those moments where the imperfection of spectrograms must be acknowledged). This bass figure lasts for about twenty-five seconds, before a version of the fuzzed out, tunnelling effect from earlier returns, low in the left channel and an octave above in the right. Seven seconds later, blocky gestures in right and then left channels push the track into a smothered static-crackle sound that is placed right in the centre of the stereo picture. Again, compositional contrast and detail create musical drama and flow. This smother-pedal lasts for most of the last eighty seconds or so of the track, playing as a coda that maintains notes of tension and fever from earlier, but turned quieter now, resolved in some way. Or, heard in hindsight, perhaps just a final effort to keep away the storm, which explodes in the wild feedback and static of the final six or seven seconds.

As can be seen, as the rate of change in the track became more manageable, more articulate in musical terms, and overarching connections and shape started to emerge from what felt like sonic chaos in the first couple of minutes, my own presence in the analysis withdrew. From a place of feeling marked by elements of de- or hyperpersonalization I moved into a more secure, rational, distanced analytical position. The burden of interpretation shifted in this way from my own experience to the musical frame of the track. As analytical detail thickened in this way I gained distance between myself and the track, my affect accordingly gearing down from a consuming erotic to one shaped by pleasurable, rational consumption; that safe state of personalization discussed at the end of the last chapter.

The harsh intensity and compositional variety adduced here in the first track continue through the rest of the album. For instance, the long final track skulks much more consistently than the opener in that tunnel-esque, staticky place I described above, with a sustained blast of distorted fuzz and busy bustle above and below the tunnel for much of the track (as can be seen in broad strokes from Figure 5.1). But even there, micro-events within that sustained sound hold interest from second to second, new gestures emerging for seconds at a time, drawing attention from the centre of the image to smaller characters around it before the music drifts or jumps back again. And larger change happens here and there too; at 15'12" or so into the track a distinct rising bass synth gesture throbs out below the texture for a few seconds. About fifty-five seconds later, a held bass tone roughly in the same register sounds for about six seconds. Just over a minute after that, a distinct contrast between more exposed higher-range static and then lower tones, and then back again, prepares the ear for a more final reversion into lower-range, anchored tunnelling sound, eighteen minutes into the track. This is all typical for *Pittsburgh, Pennsylvania*, an intense and wild album that is yet full of musical event, cohesion and contrast. Whether by high-level design or not, there is a kind of musical intelligence at play here.

As I chase these sonic phantoms on the final track, finding order amidst seeming disorder (or, at least, an unresolved trucking between order and disorder), the sheer intensity and relentlessness of the sound keep pushing me out of myself, the harshness feeling like a question I need to answer, if I can just regain my composure for a moment. Even here, with rational analytical brain fully engaged, both the level of confusing detail in the sound and the violence of the volume and timbres mean that the mastering analytical self ends up blurring into something less defined. Paying close attention to the music of *Pittsburgh, Pennsylvania* therefore gives the lie to Hutson's claims about its music – this album is full of moments of musical contrast, continuity and cohesion, even as its sonics overwhelm and potentially throw listeners throughout. And, whilst none of this disproves Hutson's political condemnation, it does complicate or add to it.

Black Leather Jesus: *A.N.T.I.* (1993) and *Torture Machinist* (1995)

Black Leather Jesus [BLJ] are a harsh noise collective centred around Richard Ramirez; Ramirez also operates under his own name and a variety of aliases, such as Werewolf Jerusalem and Crash At Every Speed. BLJ have been active since 1989 and have included a variety of figures from inside and outside the (largely Houston, Texas) noise scene as members. These range from friends of Ramirez such as Randi Shrum-Houston and Scott Houston in the early 1990s, to Sawgasm's David Gilden in the early to mid-1990s, Fetus Furs' Kevin Ogg in the mid-1990s and Kevin Novak (aka T.E.F.) in the late 1990s. Ramirez' husband, Sean E. Matzus, has been a key member of the group in the post-1990s era.

In keeping with trends identified above in relation to the 1990s American scene, Ramirez often works with cheap, found sound sources. Ramirez describes the specific approach he takes in Werewolf Jerusalem, expanding from there to discuss his general approach to noisemaking:

> It had to do with a handheld radio I have, and still have. I was using it specifically for Werewolf Jerusalem. And it just gave this really nasty, crunchy static sound.

And the first time I toured doing that project, I took that radio on tour. And I was just using that radio with one distortion pedal – and that was it … There's people that love their gear. It's never been my thing. I've always liked to use found objects to create something, and just maybe run it through distortion. I can use a floor fan, and I have. A leaf blower. Things that I find. I've had a microphone near an air conditioner and just recorded the sounds from that. It's just various things I can find to get sounds out of. A lot of times I just use sheet metal and feedback.

(Leyva 2019)

BLJ share this philosophy, albeit spread across different contributors and tools, from contact mics to guitars. Ramirez describes the approach he has taken with the group, echoing the emphasis on found and basic sound sources from above:

The first recordings, I used television sets. I'd have them on the static channel. Radios, have that on a static channel. Just dead air. And I would just have 'em playing at the same time in a room. And I had an old 70s turntable/tape player that I used to record. Because the turntable, when you put it on the setting of a turntable and you messed with it, it would give a weird metal sound. And you would twist and it would give a creaking sound. So I utilised that a lot in my early recordings. Another early recording that I did, I turned on the television set and I had two radios on, and I just let it record, so it was all just static noise. But the BLJ stuff, it was mainly that turntable and television set and radio, and I just blasted it really loud and recorded it.

(Leyva 2019)

Noise outdoes punk's so-called 'DIY' ethos by some margin here! This basic set-up of old radios, turntables and televisions, scrap metal and other found sources on the one hand, and minimal processing tools on the other, is emblematic of the 1990s American harsh noise scene, as we've already seen with *Pittsburgh/Pennsylvania*. It contrasts with the contemporary use of synths, guitars and other more traditional instruments by harsh noise musicians in Japan, Europe and elsewhere. And it led to very different sound worlds as a result; if not in terms of qualities like density – Ramirez albums such as 1997's *Memorial* (Praxis Dr. Bearmann) are exemplary in their simple means but complex sounds – then certainly in terms of timbre and line. It also, obviously, contrasts with the emphasis on digital, laptop-based sound that would become significant across the noise world in the 2000s, as we'll see in the next chapter.

I examine two BLJ releases here so that I can demonstrate something of the variety of their style. In the latter respect, these two albums present contrasting propositions. *A.N.T.I.* ('Anything Not of Traditional Interest'; Deadline Recordings, 1993), on the one hand, is an important early example of what would come to be called harsh noise wall, a genre that will be examined in more depth in Chapter 7. *Torture Machinist* (Chaotic Noise Productions, 1995), though retaining some droning, wall-like qualities, is more striated and varied in texture.

A.N.T.I. is a warm, dare I say it even comforting album (Tara and Mike Connelly compare it to ASMR in the Fatal Impact episode of *Noisextra*; 2020a). Its music is anchored in a brown noise-like sustained bass drone, with a steady fuzzy nimbus of crackle and crumble adding tension, colour and texture above and around that brown noise. The prevailing continuity of *A.N.T.I.* is clearly visible in Figure 5.3. This shows, on the one hand, the sustained, low-register saturation of the frequency spectrum below about 100Hz, which runs almost throughout the whole fifty-seven minutes of the album, and, on the other, the more dappled, tense, dynamic crackle above it.

And yet, *A.N.T.I.* contains sonic variety as well as continuity. In the first instance, the dappled crackle that overlays the brown noise adds a consistent impression of movement and tension, a sense that even if we're in a comparatively warm zone of harshness we can never fully slip into trancing, self-losing meditation or repose. The sheer variety of that crackle, which meets the ear like contact mic'd popping candy and leaves one always just a little on edge, always caught in the process of decoding and decontaminating, is better shown in the peak frequency spectrogram of Figure 5.4, which covers a wider frequency range as well as highlighting sound events in a different way. Moreover, the album contains peaks and troughs that create a sense of texture and movement throughout. For example, midway through the thirty-third minute the central fuzz drone loses some of its abrasive quality, shifting for just under nine minutes into a narrower and more pockmarked frequency range

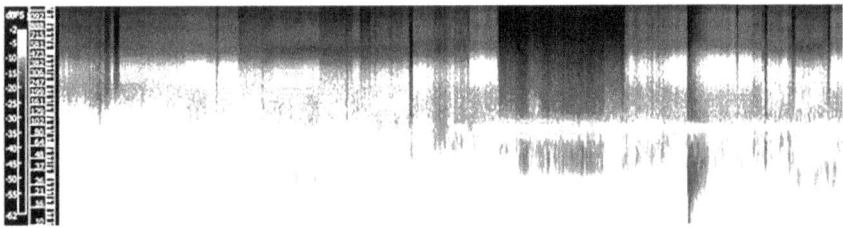

Figure 5.3 Melodic range spectrogram of BLJ's *A.N.T.I.* (1993).

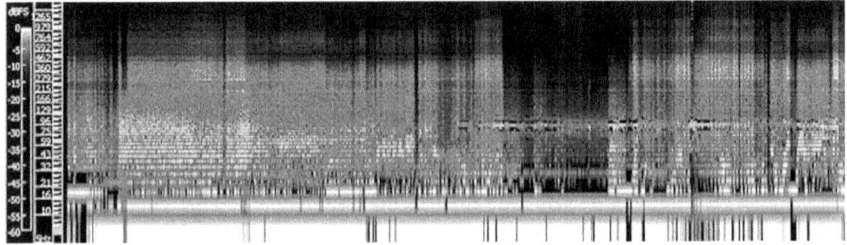

Figure 5.4 Peak frequency spectrogram of BLJ's *A.N.T.I.* (1993).

dominated by pure, low-range sine tones and warm crackle. This passage reframes the tension between the low tones and interfering static and crackle, giving weight to the former, easing tension as a result. A passage that starts towards the beginning of the forty-seventh minute likewise plays with this contrast further, its first thirty seconds concentrating low tones in the left channel, and the next thirty seconds seeing the gradual and steady emergence of overwhelming static in the middle of the stereo picture. This static revolves in density and tapers in volume throughout the rest of the album. So, even though *A.N.T.I.* can be characterized in broad terms as fuzzy, warm and continuous, listening a little more closely reveals a whole range of subtle details, structures and microevents.

Listeners' responses to these musical details will of course themselves create further peaks and troughs throughout. I find the album both comforting and unsettling. I hear the sustained low tones as a kind of warm hug, even as the febrile staticky sounds above them make me feel like I'm wearing a hairshirt while getting that hug. Meanwhile, the drawn-out, droning nature of the sonic information on the album draws me into a dynamic of light trancing, slipping into the rivets and cracks of the noise wall, gently puzzling and bristling depending on the moment. But I never quite flow away through those cracks as they are too quick to shift and bristle; I slip for moments but mostly retain my border. *A.N.T.I.* in these senses feels like well-ordered, delicately drawn, immersive sonic havoc.

Torture Machinist was released in 1995 and was split into just two tracks: 'Mechanical Rape (Fuck with Metallic Fists)' – S&M themes are often important to the band's work, and as a survivor of rape himself Ramirez has defended his use of that term in track titles and group names (Leyva 2019) – and 'Man and Machine (Engines of Destruction)'. Both tracks run for just over half an hour in length. This album shares some sonic DNA with the concentrated droning of *A.N.T.I.* whilst also including much more textural and dynamic variety. The overriding impression with *Torturing Machinist* is of a constantly moving electrical storm: jerking feedback and piercing high tones; brief but pummeling low beat patterns; juddering and shuddering distortion and fuzz; churning static – elements such as these revolve frantically for much of the 63-minute running time. It's hard to get a handle on the flow at times. The music plays like a wild, often joyous and hilarious outpouring of pent-up noise energy. The listening experience, as a result, is one in which cognitive overload undermines one's sense of rational self, the joyous dialectic of dis- and re-assembling of self mirroring the patterns of disorder and order that tumble over each other as you struggle to make sense of the music. And yet some clear moments of contrast and change create stark dramatic contours in the flow of noise; the musicality identified above in relation to *A.N.T.I.* is in clear evidence here. For example, twelve minutes into the first track the texture clears out, and high pitched feedback and pummeled beats interplay. A quick glissando downwards at 12'13" leads us right into an echoey scrapyard or mechanic's shop, isolated banging, sawing, cutting and sparking glinting out amidst cavernous silence for about forty seconds. We're then thrown back into sustained static and noise, but we don't get there without warning;

in the last few seconds of the clearer texture hints of a harsher lower tone leap out to prepare the ear.

This contrast between sustained static and drones and sparer, more fragmented textures continues throughout the album. For example, a passage from about 21'40" into the first track plays pummelling low static off against yawning chasms topped by isolated shards of feedback. A heavily processed voice enters about ninety seconds later, interjecting words or phrases to intensify the sprawling action. A string of words at about 26'20" lead into the final passage of the track, where phrases such as 'cut up his throat' can be heard amidst increased sonic tension and violence, a repeated lower tone offsetting scrawled higher register looping gestures. A more concentrated, condensed couple of minutes of drawn-out static transitions us into a climactic final explosion of scratching and pummelling. As can be seen, contrasts – whether simultaneous or successive – between sustained sound and more fragmented gestures characterize these final eight to nine minutes of the track, creating *musical* textures and flow amidst overbearing noise unpredictability.

The second track occupies a similar sound world and plots out similar arcs and movements, with feedback, static, bass-like drones and busier high frequency scratching and wheedling all playing off each other to create constant motion and action. Both tracks therefore share an emphasis on dynamic linear change and vertical density. The last six minutes of the second track offer a remarkable illustration of how BLJ build such dynamic musical drama out of raw, thrashing noise sounds. A sudden edit at 25'15" into that track – prepared a moment before by the texture reducing to the pummelling low drone from the first track, offset by brief glitchy silence – throws us into an unexpectedly 'musical' passage. A summary of the main sonic events in these six minutes can be seen in the table below, around which I offer present-tense description of my experience of that same passage.

Initially, loud, crumbling static and shards of fuzz underly a repeated, short-short-long synth gesture that spins out a hypnotic Db-D-Eb motif. My attention is rapt. After 100 seconds of this, an array of material plays out 24 seconds of sonic fireworks. This array includes: slowed down organ arcing out a slow motion Eb-Gb-Bb motif (which had been heard in different forms in the fourteenth and fifteenth minutes); snatched but

Table 5.1 Description of 25'15" – 31'05" of 'Man and Machine (Engines of Destruction)', from Torture Machinist (1995)

25'15"	26'55"	27'30"	28'05"	28'35"	28'55"	29'05"	30'35" to end
Crumbling static with Db-D-Eb motif	Sonic 'fireworks' passage, with Eb-Gb-Bb motif	Static and high feedback tones	Industrial beating	Eb-Gb-Bb motif returns, with elements of 'fireworks'	Decrescendo	Sparer textures, portentous thwacks	Pummeling garbage chute noise

steady drum patterns; buried vocals; fizzy noise; and skronking sax. All this piles onto and around the Db motif, which has continued into this passage though it is now harder to hear. The whole makes for an intriguing mess, dissonant polyrhythms pulling the ear and body this way and that, though it should also be noted everything pivots around Eb as a kind of displaced, fragile tonal centre; that Eb acts as a kind of centre-of-gravity amidst the fireworks. At about 27'30", the music shifts back into more familiar territory of crumbling static and isolated high feedback tones; strangely, even though the sound is restless, I find myself resting into the relative calm. This lasts for thirty-five seconds before that crumbling static congeals into a steady beating pattern akin to industrial thumping, into which I lean instinctively, entraining and dropping further into the sound. After fifteen seconds of that and then another, more familiar fifteen seconds of fuzz and fizz, the Eb-Gb-Bb organ gesture from earlier returns, with drums and other elements from the 'fireworks' passage bubbling up to increase textural density. Sounds, noise, and beats tumble over each other in glorious misalignment for twenty seconds, hard to hang onto but joyous to misalign with nonetheless.

A softening, slowing descrescendo built around downward pitch shifts bring us into a much sparer cavern, where a quiet turntable crackles over portentous industrial thwacks on echoey metal. This runs from 29'05" for about ninety-two seconds, with snatches of voices from a radio station and more disordered noise gestures thickening texture here and there. The last 50 seconds of the track throw us back into harsher territory, pummelling low drones playing against garbage chute chaos, the listening body pummelled and exhausted in turn.

These six minutes or so of 'Man and Machine (Engine of Destruction)' are highly exciting. They feel compositional, almost, musically detailed and dramatic in how they lay out and connect different kinds of sounds, moods and textures, creating momentum and drama amidst bristling, often overwhelming and destabilizing noise as a result. As with all the other harsh noise we've looked at, 'noise' and 'music' here are not antinomies but overlapping partners in constant dialogue. And whilst these six illustrative minutes serve as a particularly concentrated example of BLJ's taste for musical drama it's nevertheless true that the whole album is organized around similar principles. Various sonic continuities and consistencies support this reading, from the pervasive importance of the low, rumbling static sound to the broadly sustained emphasis on change and momentum to the recurrence of the Eb organ motif in the second track. Aspects of gestural, thematic, motivic and even post-tonal integrity therefore bind *Torture Machinist* together.

As with other music discussed in this chapter and others, my argument is not that these elements of compositional nuance on *Torture Machinist* are necessarily the result of any higher-level executive design. Instead, this nuance, this toggling between different textures and sounds and between order and disorder, emerges simply from the musicality of the group, who pull back, transition, intensify and so on as any musical group would, and from the innate narrativization of listeners, who constantly parse, puzzle and dream with the music. Harsh noise here leans into harshness and commotion, then, but inflects that commotion with enough torque for it to feel discursively driven, held-in-tension and permanently becoming.

European dirt, polish and gunk

Italy – Murder Corporation: *Victims* (1993), *Disturbance* (1995) and *New Crimes* (1996)

The Italian tradition/s of harsh, electronic noise and post-industrial music is a proud one. I mentioned MB and Mauthausen Orchestra in Chapter 1, and we'll look in detail at Marco Corbelli in Chapter 8. Corbelli's label, Slaughter Productions, was both crucial in supporting the Italian scene in the 1990s – as well as Corbelli's own work, it released music from key Italian noise artists Murder Corporation (aka Moreno Daldosso) and Dead Body Love (aka Gabriele Giuliani) – and hosted a number of prominent international figures, such as Taint, Subklinik and Richard Ramirez.

Italian noise, like the American examples considered above, has often been cruddy, crusty, dirty and dark, in terms of both sound and imagery or theme. For example, as we saw in Chapter 1 MB's music is dark and dank in sound, though it's also built around aspects of sonic sophistication and layering. And as we'll see, Murder Corporation's sound is often brutally basic and dirty. Dead Body Love's noise is slightly more polished, though it still revels in filth and crud. Similarly, a taste for extreme imagery and subject matter runs through Italian noise, this often being based around sex and/or murder and death. We'll explore this in much more detail with reference to Atrax Morgue, but a thematic focus on serial killing, (mass) murder and mutilation is found in both Murder Corporation and Dead Body Love. This fixation on extreme subject matter serves as a through line back to the Italian industrial, power-electronics roots of the scene in MB and Mauthasen Orchestra. It also resonates with the powerful strain of sex and death that runs through Italian culture more generally; Giallo and 'zombi' films, and filmmakers such as Tinto Brass and Pier Paolo Pasolini, provide some obvious points of comparison here.

Murder Corporation's thematic focus on serial killing, (mass) murder and mutilation, as I just put it, is obvious from the name of the project down. Dead, mutilated bodies on album sleeves (see 1993's *Butcher Meat* or 1997's *Insane Pleasures*, both on Murder Release); gruesome track or album titles (*The Final Solution* from 1993, self-released, or 'Mutilated Corpse', 'Flesheater', 'Strangulated' and 'Bleeding Face', all from the eight-tape 1995 version of *The New Crimes*, Murder Release); and references to serial killers and violence (e.g. Gerald Eugene Stano, an American who was convicted of murdering twenty-two women, on 'Stano's Method', from *Insane Pleasures*, or the home invasion and rape depicted in 2015's 'Torture Chamber', from *Nekro*, menstrualrecordings): all these lend the project a particularly scuzzy demeanour. Though, of course, it's also important to note that the grimy, non-salacious presentation of the images and the somewhat ambiguous nature of the references perhaps move the work into more of an aesthetic than a political or documentary framework. Murder Corporation's sound plays its role in this ambiguity too. The unrelenting, almost wall-like blasts of static and distortion on the one hand, and the murky, menacing, enigmatic lo-fi passages of oddly rhythmic or hooky, quiet hiss or fuzz or feedback on the other, reinforce the intensity and ugliness of the subject matter. But they can also evoke a nebulous affective atmosphere, re-signifying the messages of the titles and images as so much charcterful noise. I'll focus now on the sound world of a few key Murder Corporation albums/tracks to draw out further the aesthetic texture of the work.

Victims (self-released, 1993), *Disturbance* (Slaughter Productions, 1995) and *New Crimes* (recorded in 1994 and extracted in 1996 from the eight-tape version, for RRR's Pure series) are dominated by short wave static, tape hiss, distorted voices and other cheaply produced noises. Daldosso would incorporate an Akai sampler and a tone generator into later work – as heard in the washed-out Whitehouse samples on *Insane Pleasures*, for example – but his sonic palette remains dirty and cruddy even on those later releases. All three of these albums, in any case, can be heard as forerunners of harsh noise wall in the sheer sustained intensity of many of their tracks. But as with many other examples considered in this book, when one leans into the sound one hears worlds of what can be described as musical detail, order and form. *Victims*, for example, seems from a distance to be comprised of harsh low-range rumble and hiss with the occasional higher tone of sustained feedback or distortion periodically cycling out to alter the texture and intensity of the music. But go closer to the sound and you start to hear patterns and correspondences; all sorts of small local cycles of tension-and-release; and sudden moments of textural contrast and repeated 'anchor' sounds. *Disturbance* is the same: the track 'Exophagy', for example, is anchored to different versions of crumbling, mid-range staticky waves and low-range wind-blown distortion for the whole of its twenty-six minutes. But whilst these elements act as sonic touchpoints throughout, the track also moves through a whole range of thicker and busier, or louder and more insistent, passages, using several unexpected breaks in flow and sound to get there. The thickening textures in the second minute, giving way in the third to a hooky melodic feedback pattern (itself glitchy and unpredictable in shape and interrupted in flow), and in turn giving way in the fourth minute to a more saturated return of the opening crumble before a shift into landslide static and churn in the fifth and sixth, provide a nice microcosm of the kind of fast rates of change and rhythmic and textural variety that are found across the album. Similarly, the vocal sample and relative calm of the ninth minute, moving in the tenth to a more restrained, concentrated version of the opening low rumble before a noise wall of searing highs and thick lows crashes in late in the eleventh, illustrate well the breadth and variety of Murder Corporation's sound palette. The nine untitled tracks of *New Crimes* work through a similar set of endlessly inventing, expanding variations on some basic sounds and sound sources, from sustained blasts of loud static to short-lived noise melodies and motifs and passages of relative quiet: these all flow seamlessly through the album's near-seventy minutes. But one is always aware of a kind of internal logic or order – or at least, a held-in-tension, unresolved dialectic of disorder and order – to the sound.

This is, therefore, musically rich, cohesive but variegated, work. Its sheer intensity and harsh sonics place it squarely into the international harsh noise genre, even as its unrelenting concentration and periodic but sustained blasts of static also call forward to the harsh noise walls of Part Two. In these global connections the music once again reinforces our transcultural point about the broad continuities of noise music, even as its dirty, cruddy tone and its bloody focus also chime with other examples of specifically Italian culture. This harsh noise is locally inflected but, fundamentally, internationally configured. Finally, like other examples of harsh noise we've looked at here, its tallying with different layers of order and disorder, its negotiation and play between syntactical musical language and more freely articulated moments of sound, present a characteristic discursive play, with which listeners themselves can play, reflect and identify as they see fit.

France – Zone Nord: *Marche Noir/Denrées Diverses* (1993)

Where the other artists examined in this chapter have a degree of prominence inside and outside the noise world, Zone Nord is a somewhat more obscure proposition. A short-lived project of French musician Jean-Luc Angles, Zone Nord's small discography has long been a source of fascination for noise audiences (Chris Sienko's overview of Zone Nord's work in *As Loud As Possible* reflects this; 2010, 18–20). Coming up just short of the all-out sonic assault of contemporary Japanese releases but also pushing the synth-based loops and rhythms of industrial and power electronics music into a crunchy extreme, Zone Nord's music provides a nice contrast with the sound palette and extreme emotional tenor of the Japanese and American releases examined elsewhere in this chapter and the previous one. As such, although this case study is more compacted than others it is included to demonstrate other possible approaches within the broader harsh noise family.

Sienko's article captures a key quality of Zone Nord's music; its enigmatic, emergent feel. Sounds and pattern never quite settle here even though aspects of continuity and repetition can be found in all of Zone Nord's work. Instead, the music feels rather like it's somehow searching, even fumbling, for stable ground that it never quite finds. Each track serves in this way as an emotional-technical study in which the tensile strength of different synth sounds and flanging noise textures are pushed and prodded at from different sides. Tracks rarely end in answers though; we leave feeling like we travelled but didn't quite arrive.

Marche Noir/Denrées Diverses (self-released) plays out like this. The album is composed primarily of bubbling, fizzing synth drones or loops infused with or surrounded by textural crunch and crackle. Figure 5.5 conveys the relative continuity of the synth bed running through each of the five tracks; Side A, 'Marche Noir', consists

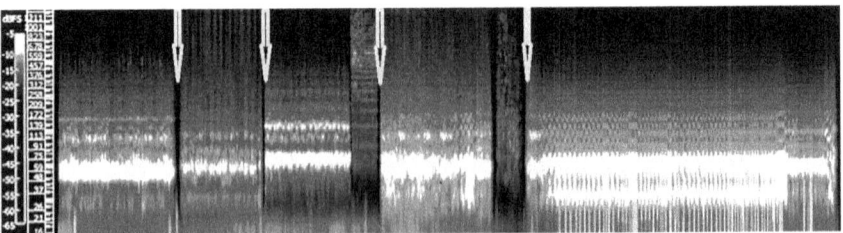

Figure 5.5 Melodic range spectrogram of Zone Nord's *Marche Noir/Denrées Diverses* (1993).

of three shorter tracks, and Side B, 'Denrées Diverses', two longer ones (all tracks are untitled; they are separated below with arrows).

But the spectrogram gives little sense of how both these steadier patterns and the overall sonic picture are deformed by destabilizing noise and fray. Whether it's the glitchy cracks and edits throughout the opener; the overloaded but underconfident, even halting static and chatter of the second track; the more assaultive, continuous bass rumble and skittering daubs and smears of the third; the harsher, skating higher tones and wails firing off lower crackle in track four; or the slow, decaying static effect on the comparatively sustained oscillating drone in the long final track – all of these elements work to create a sense of digging around in some blasted, black-and-white landscape. Harshness and unresolve pervade.

The searching quality of this release, where drones and patterns shimmer or crumble into noise and texture and skulk back out again or fade out before they can do so, presents a different discursive proposition to other harsh noise music. Instead of overwhelming disorder smelting into recognizable form and language, the proposition here is reversed; familiar language and order reveal their flimsiness either through overlay or extension. These tracks therefore don't form into anything legible but ultimately put their seeming legibility into question. The music does not bury order in chaos but rather sees chaos as propping up and ultimately, perhaps, consuming order.

UK – Evil Moisture: *Gak* (1997)

Though Japan and the United States boasted probably the most concentrated harsh noise activity in the 1990s, as we've seen in the examples of Italy and France above, a variety of European scenes and musicians had come through by this time. Many of these built on earlier developments in places like the UK, as covered in Chapter 3. On the back of some of those developments, the British noise scene was thriving by the time we get to the 1990s. Artists as varied as Mlehst, Smell and Quim, Facialmess, Prick Decay and many more built in different ways on the rich British heritage of industrial and power electronics on the one hand, and idiosyncratic sensibilities of lurid whimsy, junk and freakery on the other, to produce a whole host of fascinating music and art.

Evil Moisture (British artist Andy Bolus) has been a leading light of the international harsh noise scene since his first tape releases in the early 1990s. Across different kinds of media, from homemade delay pedals, filters (or 'filthers'), oscillators, circuits and heterodyne mics, to drawings, paintings, cartoons, films and, of course, noise music, Bolus' style is one of gore, spazz and trash, an avant-garde B-movie in sound, electronics and image. Like some of the other examples considered here and elsewhere, then, Evil Moisture's music presents a kind of puzzle and dialectic to listeners. However, the pacing and affect here are exaggerated to a point of absurdity, the musical character and listening self both pushed into a kind of hyper-position of total movement. The music uses reel-to-reel loops, homemade pedals and other sources to produce audio collages of cartoon intensity. Tom Smith's 'genre is obsolete' description of noise is never more appropriate than with reference to Bolus' busy, frenetic work (see Brassier 2007).

Gak (Howard 1, 1997) is Bolus at his most humorously bizarre and whizzy. From the opening thirty-second zip through snatched acoustic guitar strum, careening high feedback tone, static, backwards tape, more static and found noise, 1980s hard rock sample, and then that same sample drastically pitch-shifted down and out, we're thrown into a runaway train of audio collage that never lets up for the next forty-seven minutes and thirty-three tracks. Sound events steal by like meteors, often staying in sight for no more than about six or seven seconds. Many micro-snatches of noise and distortion indeed last only a second or two. This is truly sound 'chopped, mangled and re-re-mangled', as the sleeve has it. The album is not without clear sonic markers, however, despite this density. The sustained rate of change just described is one example. Similarly, the album features a steady stream of detours into faithfully reproduced pop or rock samples; in addition to the hard rock from the opener, the fifty seconds of overloaded 1990s lounge trip-hop in 'Gak 5' (at 21'20" into the album), the brief move of a radio dial from disco to house in 'MetaGak' (at 31'35") and the '70s theme tune in 'Super Hyper Mega Gak' (33'33"), stand out. Finally, the album is based on a small set of recurring sounds and effects. These range from everyday household sounds, to churning static and distortion, high feedback tones, tape whirr and weal, high-speed fuzz and bustling noise collage. These recurring features add texture to Bolus' zippy musique concrète, balancing out its wild surface filigree with an off-kilter sense of continuity and consistency.

Indeed, the density of presentation on *Gak* itself eventually levels out, for this listener at least. This happens both because of the album's sonic continuities and because of the consistency of its rate of change. These aspects, in the end, convert what initially feels like cognitive overload into something more like alert and amused attention, our brains and bodies rewiring to the manic style and energy of the music. We ourselves become cartoon as a result, a haze of colours, movements and energy. Noise's facility for taking apart ego through either de- or hyperpersonalization can be seen in a different light here, speed of sample melding with sharpness of sound to push us into an instinctual, fight or flight quality of consciousness that feels unsettling but not quite as all-consuming as the same instinct felt in response to something like Masonna. Personalization, but sped-up.

Gak's mix of unusual, often harsh sources and sounds with rudimentary processing techniques and a junk surrealist aesthetic leaves the album feeling like a fruity cocktail, somewhere between the more abstract electronic music of someone like Luc Ferrari and the rickety, collaged 'mock' and roll of Los Angeles Free Music Society acts such as Le Forte Four and Smegma. Connections can also be made to the avant-garde collage weirdness of The Residents and Nurse With Wound, and even the music hall absurdity of psychedelic jokesters such as The Bonzo Dog Doo-Dah Band (who themselves of course connect to the rich English seam of nonsense that goes back through Lear, Carroll and others). This is not even to mention noise acts such as Prick Decay and Smell and Quim; a very British taste for brutal, lurid imagery and humour can be seen to run through all these acts. Meanwhile, parallels with the postmodern pastiche compositions and miniature collages of John Zorn, in particular his thrash metal/soundtrack/whatever band Naked City, are loud and clear, even if Zorn's music tends to be more obviously referential than Bolus' more deliberately distanced noise. *Gak*'s genre-obsolete idiomatic mix, then, is rich and broad. Evil Moisture's emphasis on humour, constant sonic change and collage aesthetics, as well as the idiomatic mix just described, contrasts sharply with other noise acts examined in this chapter. His music likewise displays a somewhat unusual emphasis on a kind of schizophrenic consciousness that contrasts sharply with the pulverizing depersonalization one can experience with acts like Black Leather Jesus and Merzbow. Evil Moisture tickles where these acts pierce the skin. This is even as Evil Moisture's taste for extremities of perception and intensity of harsh sound aligns him with those artists all the same.

As can be seen both in this final example and more generally across the chapter, then, harsh noise in the 1990s was much more of a broad musical church than some might think. *Gak* and Evil Moisture shows just how broad the idiomatic mix of harsh noise could get in individual examples. But equally notable is the musical variety and intricacy on display across the work of all these artists, where detonating and often delirious excitement rubs shoulders with delicate or chaotic, dialectical design in many unexpected and subtle ways.

Conclusion

Trying to capture the overwhelming variety and wealth of harsh noise across this classic period of the 1990s is incredibly difficult to do in the space of only two chapters. But the selection of artists covered here and in the previous chapter has given a sense of that variety and wealth, conveying something both of the transcultural and the aesthetic dimensions of the music in this period. This was a scene that rapidly expanded across the globe in the 1990s. It exploited the kind of fringe cultural network of mainstream social infrastructure and webs of aesthetic and artistic affinities formed across that infrastructure that I've described. In doing so, it drew on local cultural traditions and proclivities but fundamentally expressed a global continuity of style and aesthetic orientation. That style, as we've seen, was based in all cases on a taste for intense, extreme sound and, in many cases, constructed unresolved dialectical webs of order and disorder, stability and chaos, noise and music, which I've read in both formal musical and symbolic terms. We'll pick this story up in the twenty-first century in Chapter 6. An Interlude follows that wraps up the progress we've made in Part One of the book and prepares the ground for Part Two.

Interlude: The story so far and to come

So Far

In Part One, we saw noise grow and expand from late-1970s and 1980s pre- and proto-noise musics such as industrial and avant-garde free music, into proto- and early noise with the likes of Whitehouse and Hijokaidan. It spread across Japan, Europe and the United States as it did so, mutating into different forms and gathering weight and depth as it went. By the late 1980s and the 1990s, a substantial, global fringe ecosystem of noise artists, labels, venues and zines had developed. In terms of musical style, power electronics and a kind of free noise rock dominated the early goings of noise in the 1980s. As the decade went on, 'harsh power' mixes of power electronics and emerging harsh noise tropes started to appear, even as earlier forms of free noise and power electronics persisted alongside them. By the 1990s, harsh noise had come to the fore as a creative focus for the broader noise scene. Through all these styles and stages of development we've seen broad continuity of tone and some continuity of theme; intense sounds have been a hallmark of all the artists we've considered, whilst extreme, often upsetting and offensive subject matter characterized much of their work too. This is even as anti-music fixated on nihilism and destruction without broaching taboo, and even as many harsh noise artists dropped extreme subjects in favour of a focus on what we might call 'noise-for-noise's-sake'.

To come

As we move into the twenty-first century of Part Two we'll see both continuity and change with respect to the story of Part One. Extreme subject matter continues to recede whilst remaining important. In some cases, artists have continued to work in the tried-and-tested death-and-sex realm of power electronics. In others, artists have shifted their political lens into more obviously progressive (though still often grimily or ambiguously expressed) points of view, from the sex-work focus of Himukalt to the liberatory, often anti-capitalist politics of Mattin. Extreme and intense sounds have remained the *raison d'etre* of noise. However, picking up on the change side of things, the sonic flavour of those sounds has expanded in several directions. The emergence of distinct new subgenres or substyles such as the harsh noise wall genre originally developed by The Rita in the late 1990s, off the back of the pile-driving harsh sounds in acts like Murder Corporation and Black Leather Jesus, is a notable example of this expansion. Another notable example of the expansion of noise sound comes in the widespread adoption of digital tools and sounds that has taken place in twenty-first-century noise. The presence of laptops and associated software in noise music from the late 1990s on is obvious; Merzbow beginning to focus on laptops in 1999 is merely a well-known tip of the noise iceberg. Building on earlier tape and computer work in granular synthesis, digital signal processing indeed opened new worlds of granular sound. It suddenly became possible, for example, for non-specialists to make unpredictable, dense, algorithmically derived patterns of microsound where everything from envelope to waveform, spatial position to spectra, could be stretched, morphed or disintegrated at digital speed. Pita and other Mego-affiliated artists produced noise-infused digital music that leant into digital software's capacity to shudder and splinter time and tone in this way. Pita's 1999 album, *Get Out* (Mego), is a particularly good example of this, as can be heard on the feedback-rich, stuttering and jittery glitch micro-noise of tracks 1 and 6.

New digital tools and infrastructures also affected the consumption of noise in this period. Noise in the 2020s is indeed unthinkable without web databases, blogs, forums, social media, streaming platforms and so on. Because whilst physical zines, record shops and music venues have survived, these now occupy a relatively marginal space on the scene, dwarfed by the ease of accessibility and breadth of function of the web. That's true even within such a supposedly DIY, self-reliant, obscurantist and sometimes technophobic scene as noise.

A final example of the sonic expansion of noise in the twenty-first century comes in its growing hybridization, which we can hear in the widespread blending that has taken place between noise and styles like rock, experimental and dance music. Indeed, alongside the persistence and deepening of transcultural trends, perhaps the most important area of continuity and change in the story of noise music in this period is its further, now-near-universal hybridization. We'll begin to see the extent of this hybridisation in Chapter 6, where we track the evolution of harsh noise and see how its native hybridity has become even more intense. Across Chapters 7 and 8, hybridity is a kind of satellite frame as we look at some of the divergent streams coming out of harsh noise, power electronics and so on, first with harsh noise wall, death industrial and dark ambient in Chapter 7, and then a range of power electronics, harsh and other noise styles under the banner of 'noise erotics' in Chapter 8. Chapters 9 and 10 bring the story of noise hybridity up to date. First, we look at how noise has blended into related styles such as experimental music and rock. Second, we consider the more straightforward 'noise' hybridity that, I argue, characterizes the scene in the 2020s.

Part Two therefore tracks and teases apart various high-level narrative shifts in noise's sonic and stylistic, thematic and political, orientations. As before, it uses the interpretative concept of 'becoming' as an organizing lens for the music it examines, whilst also constructing a music-historical narrative around that lens. Unlike Part One, Part Two does not chronologically 'feather' its chapters; instead of the basically forward-moving chronology of Part One's five chapters, the five chapters of Part Two each range across the 2000s, 2010s and 2020s, using thematic frames – harsh noise, harsh noise offshoots, noise erotics, genre/style hybridity – to focus activity as they do.

Part Two

Noise music now

6

Harsh noise in the twenty-first century

This chapter updates the story of harsh noise from Chapters 4 and 5, looking at a range of continuing and new artists. As noted, the geographical divisions used in previous chapters are dropped here and across Part Two in general. This is in recognition of the increasing importance of the 'transcultural', globalist frames previously discussed, as the internet and other contemporary phenomena continued to flatten noise and other forms. As Government Alpha's Yatusoshi Yoshida remarked in 2012: 'nowadays, noise music seems rather borderless for each culture. There are some US noise bands showing style elements usually regarded as typically Japanese, on the other hand, some Japanese noise bands have been influenced by European and American styles such as gothic, dark ambient or power electronics' (cited in 'Like Hunting in the Wild' 2012). Noise music has always been transcultural and hybrid but in the twenty-first century has become ever more so.

The current chapter explores all this more directly as it moves the book definitively into the twenty-first century. It is divided into two main sections. The first section covers artists originally active in the classic 1990s period but who continued to make interesting work into this century. Its focus is Masami Akita/Merzbow though it also looks at Government Alpha. The subsequent one moves on to look at newer and/or younger harsh noise artists Torturing Nurse, Rusalka and Body Carve. Other harsh noise, or harsh-noise-adjacent, artists will be examined at various points across the subsequent three chapters.

Continuing classics

Merzbow

Masami Akita's approach to noise making has gone through a few changes in the twenty-first century. As noted previously, Akita's 1980s and 1990s work was focused in various evolving ways around analogue, acoustic and junk sound sources, all of which were used to produce pulverizing, often driving noise. Akita incorporated the laptop as a primary instrument from 1999, a choice that persisted into the early years of the new century. Akita then reintroduced rougher analogue and junk/industrial sound sources into his live shows and recordings towards the end of the 2000s. His work since, as we'll see, has ranged widely across these various sound sources. Akita's political and personal perspective likewise shifted in this period; Akita developed a strong interest in animal rights and in leading a 'cruelty free life', as his 2005 book has it, after he started keeping Bantam chickens in 2002. Akita's interest in animal rights has remained consistent; many of his albums are accordingly animal or nature themed, again as we'll see.

In checking in again with the twenty-first-century Merzbow we are faced with an utterly bewildering array of music. Already busy in the 1980s, Akita released a barrage of noise around the 1990s; notably including the infamous fifty-CD *Merzbox* (Extreme, 2000), which consists of thirty discs of repackaged material and twenty discs of previously unreleased music. In the decades since Merzbow has released literally hundreds more records. To wit, as of June 2022, *Discogs* has a total of 556 items attached to Merzbow, the majority having been released since 2000. Some of these are old recordings that have been reissued or released for the first time. Many are new. Some are studio based and some live. And many are collaborative. Given this depth and range, this brief case study can't offer a comprehensive updating of the story of Merzbow. Nevertheless, given how interesting the various hybrid threads Akita has followed have been, I try to capture as much as I can. Accordingly, I use four primary lenses to get at key aspects of Akita's diverse, hybrid work so far this century: 'laptop' music; transitional music featuring drums and other 'analogue' sources; collaborations; and then, finally and briefly, a more recent album, *Aodron* (Automation Records, 2017), which features a mixed range of sources and sounds.

In terms of laptop-focused digital noise, Merzbow presents an interesting case, since his work had always been quasi-digitally dense, dizzying, driving, even as its unrelenting, almost granular sense of change and self-disintegration (Hegarty's 'total suspense') were always leavened by a sense of rhythmic character and a cohesiveness of approach. Those qualities persist into his digital era but, in line with the changed capacity of digital processing, are sometimes handled differently and placed into new contexts. The 22-minute long 'A Ptarmigan', from 2003's *Animal Magnetism* (Alien8 Recordings), is a good illustration of the continuities and contrasts that run across the 'analogue' and 'digital' periods of Merzbow's work. Undoubtedly brutal in focus and tone, the track nevertheless moves through a variety of sound colours, moods and intensities, many of which feel new to the digital period. The dark-ambient opening, for example, is very carefully wrought in terms of weight and sonic atmosphere. Sub-bass and glitchy micro edits create a sense of architectural poise and control that has echoes of other digital-era tracks, as for example 'Inside Looking Out' Parts One and Two on 2002's *Merzzow* (Opposite Records; another potential comparator, 2010's *Merzbient* on Soleilmoon, is a repackage of analogue-era recordings). Nuance in sound design continues even after the expected explosion in wild, filter-sweeping distortion and crackle, which happens here in the fourth minute; for example, stereo separation of fuzz and trebly feedback, and careful scaffolding of registral details, anchor the flow throughout. The central section of the track reconciles the two earlier sets of materials. Serrated and cutting sound is framed with dark, weighty low tones and a sense of space extending around the clustering noise. Elements such as a repeated, wave like sweep in the eleventh and twelfth minutes; steady, insistent beating underlying a held mid-range tone soon after; and cutting, thickening static throughout much of the rest of the track add further to its sense of construction and intent.

The 2005 album, *Bariken* (Blossoming Noise), doesn't feature quite as much digital intricacy as 'A Ptarmigan'. But its relative control in terms of sonic layers, semi-regular periodization of sounds and careful textural build and flow nevertheless mark it out from the looser, at times more chaotic sounds of analogue releases like *Venereology*. The title track, 'Bariken', for example, is built on a bedrock of clomping, stomping fuzz, steady in beat and pattern, with four regular beats being followed by four wah-wah-infused beats, the twist in sound creating a kind of closed/open motif across the ('closed') four-beat to ('open') four-beat phrase. Layers of crumble and distortion are added in slowly over the second to fourth minutes as the beat drives on, before the texture is stripped back in the fifth and sixth minutes. Another heavy climax builds from the seventh minute, with familiar Merzbowian squalls of feedback and grinding distortion gradually consuming the texture in the tenth and eleventh minutes. The clomping beat is sometimes obscured but always returns to the fray. The relentless digital grind continues until the end, however, with both this clomping ostinato and the careful insertion and interaction of layers creating a different feel and atmosphere to the looser, more chaotic *Noisembryo* tracks discussed in Chapter 4. Finally, the thirty-minute closing track, 'Bariken (Reprise): Mother of Mirrors', which returns to the same grinding beat of 'Bariken' but varies its profile, colour and setting to a much higher degree than in the earlier track. The second half of the track sits on top of a 3-3-2 bass pattern that squarely anchors squalling walls, the whole being sometimes arhythmic and sometimes polyrhythmic as the noise jams against or interlocks into that pattern. Again, there is an element of sonic chaos or becoming here but fundamentally this music is controlled and driven by beat, pattern and texture.

Despite some of the periodizing I did above, Merzbow's music can't really be neatly divided into different eras. For one thing, re-releases or archive releases are peppered throughout his career, mussing up any teleological stylistic evolution. At the same time and as we'll see, collaborations introduce a whole other layer of changing style into his work. Nevertheless, as noted, it's largely true to say that the late 1990s and 2000s period of laptop-focused work began to give way across the 2000s to a more hybrid style of working where digital tools would be combined with analogue and/or electric instruments, or where the latter would simply replace the former. The monumental, thirteen-disc, *13 Japanese Birds* (Important) set was released across 2009 and 2010, with a 1000-run edition of each album – all of them named for an individual bird that was depicted on their cover – coming out every month.

The set features a caterwauling array of sound, though across its thirteen discs Akita's drums – if not quite ever present, then certainly a dominant feature – serve to contain and channel the noise. Akita is a wild, free-indebted player but also leans towards a traditional approach to drums as sound source. To wit, rather than deconstructing the drum kit à la Chris Corsano or using extended techniques à la Eddie Prevost (and many others) Akita essentially fills up time, trance-like, playing rolling snare and tom fills and whacking and whacking his cymbals. His style would fit right into the freak-out portion of a psych rock live show. Akita's approach to his drumkit means that we hear discrete, gestural sounds across the set. These sounds are clearly defined in attack and quasi-periodic in pattern; whilst we rarely fall into routine, steady pulsing it is nevertheless easy to pick out hypermetrical two- or four- or five- or seven-count patterns in amidst the noise. The drums therefore add definition, shape and gesture to the sometimes-undomesticated noise of *13 Japanese Birds*.

This interplay of wild, but defined, drum sounds with more familiarly Merzbowian electronic and electric, dialectical noise both frames the whole set and is heard in different formations across each album. To take some examples from across the thirteen discs: the thwacking drum kit and sine-wave motif of the set's opening track, 'Red Bird of Summer Part 1' (from *Suzume*), which, somewhat typically, moves through wild, then more restrained and then climactic sections, offers an exciting tension and interplay between different levels of sonic play. The continuous drum rolls and hits and swelling noise of 'Once the Human Meat Is Do' (from *Shirasagi*, Part 11) are cut from the same cloth. Other tracks work with that same psychedelic, free, noise-and-drum harsh cloth but cut it differently. 'Tori Uta', again from *Suzume*, pushes things into a brutally harsh zone, with criss-crossing lightning strikes of fuzz-drums and trebly, bird-like noise. The quieter, death-industrial thumping of 'Wind of Pain' (from *Kujakubato*, Part 7) is one of a few tracks that shift emphasis and offer contrast with the more common high-volume assault. Other tracks move us into a more psychedelic, sci-fi space, as with the spacier, wonkier electronic sounds and ever-rolling drums of 'Black Headed Gull' (from *Yurikamome*, Part 3). Meanwhile, other tracks still are more trad in harsh noise outlook and tone, as for example in the variegated but intense and ever-becoming noise burbles and static of the 51-minute, album-length 'Resurrection' (from *Chabo*, Part 13). This last track is the set closer, which is perhaps strange given its atypical album-length nature and its relative lack of foregrounded drums; as on the previous album, *Tsubame*, the drums here are submerged underneath the noise in a way they aren't on other albums. And yet, its wide dynamic arcs, its distinct moods and, above all, its characteristic dialectical restlessness, feel of a piece with the harsh but musically rich worlds created across the thirteen discs. This disc, as with the set as a whole, catches Akita in something of a moment of reconciliation. Different approaches to noise from throughout his career come together with his native intensity, rhythmic drive, formal detail and searching quality in a kind of summation and affirmation. Resolution on top of persisting local irresolution.

Collaboration has always been important to Akita, but became especially so in the twenty-first century, as his reputation and reach continued to grow. Of many interesting collaborations in this period, Merzbow's ongoing work with Japanese noise rock group Boris, as heard on albums such as *Megatone* (Inoxia, 2002), *Rock Dream* (Daymare, 2007) and *Gensho* (Relapse, 2016) is probably the most well-known. Merzbow's approach to collaborations can feel blunt but it does vary somewhat according to the style and type of artist he is collaborating with. For example, with the grindcore metal group, Full of Hell, Merzbow sticks with, but sometimes finds it hard to insert, his trademark churn-funk and blasting static. It's not until the last two tracks of their 2014 collaborative album, *Full of Hell & Merzbow* (Profound Lore), that distinctive noisy elements come through to shape the mood and surface of the sound: until then, Full of Hell's scything beats, shreds, growls and screams dominate. On the other hand, with Throbbing Gristle's Genesis P-Orridge on *A Perfect Pain*, first released in 1999 and reissued more widely in 2018 (Cold Spring), the sound feels much more productively mixed, with drum and synth loops, serrated, bristling static and skulking, menacing spoken word gelling together to evoke an updated, noisier Throbbing Gristle or a magic-spell Merzbow. A similar sympathy and mutual re-identification take place to greater or lesser degrees with artists with whom Akita has long-running collaborations, as for example Mats Gustafson. The 2020 noise improvisation with Gustafson and Balázs Pándi, *Cuts Open* (RareNoise Records), is a good illustration of the perhaps unexpected musical sensitivity of Merzbow's approach, where, as on the 23-minute first track 'I Went Down to Brother', for example, Akita's glitchy livewire feedback and system noise is pushed out and pulled back just enough that the clanging percussion and sly winds of the other two musicians are able to come into the light when they need to. In such examples, the alinguistic, aformal semblance conjured through noise, where language (and style) itself seems to be in constant formation or becoming, suffuses the sound and approach of the other musicians. On *Cuts Open*, for instance, the dialectical searching native to improv is infused with the sonic bristle and propositional uncertainty of noise. Such is the promise and, sometimes, the gift, of noise collaboration.

Since *13 Japanese Birds*, the emphasis on both collaboration and the rapprochement of earlier noise approaches that we've already seen continued apace. Post-laptop albums have been many. *Aodron* is a good place to finish, given its characteristic, somehow-still-full-of-energy-and-chaos blend of synths, noisy metallic clanging and filter-heavy squalls of feedback. These sounds hark back to albums like *Pulse Demon* (Release Entertainment, 1996), as on the churning beats and static of 'Tetsu TO', and career highlights like *Venereology* (Release Entertainment), as on the pulverizing though rhythmic and pattern-heavy synths and feedback of 'Ao Part 2' and on the wild formal breaks and fissures of the silence-riven 'Ao Part 3'. And yet, the album also sounds somehow sonically polished, even controlled, at points; see for example the subtle, and then lavish, presence of synth strings on 'Melo'. This polish and control is such that *Aodron* aligns to some degree with the variegated DAW-focused approaches to noise making that have become common, Akita making use of the precision and extended capacity of digital software but also, in *Aodron*'s dirty wildness, retaining an interest in analogue and/or electric and acoustic sound sources.

Given all this, it's tempting to see works like *Aodron* as a smooth dialogue or reconciliation between analogue and digital methods and sounds. But this is too neat a story, even as it makes some sense. *Aodron* feels like it draws on lessons learned throughout Akita's extensive career but it might also be accused of re-treading earlier work, digital influences failing to challenge or transform its core focus on broiling, uncertain surfaces and bubbling depths. Akita's post-laptop music therefore puts reconciliation and a kind of late-style serenity on the table in how it draws together tools from across the decades. This is even as the sounds themselves demand a more interesting critical response that would be able to attend both to this possibility and to other, messier readings.

Government Alpha

Government Alpha, aka Yasutoshi Yoshida, is a new figure for us (excepting the quote above). However, Yoshida has been making rip-roaring harsh noise since his debut release, *Doze*, came out on his own Xerxes label in 1994. Before getting to Yoshida's twenty-first-century work I'll spend a little time on his 1990s music by way of background.

Notable Government Alpha albums such as *Erratic* (Xerxes, 1996), *The Garden of Eternity* (Less Than Zero, 1997) and *Sporadic Spectra* (Ground Fault, 1999) resemble the kind of intense, loud, brutal, but somehow musically controlled and/or dialectically poised fuzz, noise and static found in concurrent Japanese noise from the likes of Merzbow and Monde Bruits. Drawing on a typical 'pedal noise' set-up organized around Boss Fuzz and DOD Buzz Box and Death Metal effects pedals, the music on these albums is both incredibly detailed and subtle on the one hand and free and looser in flow on the other, incorporating unexpected and even psychedelic elements as it goes. In terms of that subtle detail, Yoshida's taste for relatively compressed and internally referential forms creates a sense of cohesion within and across tracks on these albums. This can be heard in, for example, the shared frequency range and sense of density and texture on *Erratic* tracks like 'Philosophically' and 'Persecution Mania'. In terms of that freer, looser, even restless flow, loud volumes and a creeping sense of abandon and unconscious play permeate even short, relatively sonically and gesturally circumscribed tracks like 'Comatose Lily' (from *The Garden of Eternity*). Meanwhile odd, unexpected sounds such as quasi-ray guns and lasers in tracks like 'Perceptual Juncture' (from *Sporadic Spectra*) often crop up to colour the otherwise pervasive buzzsaw, staticky harsh flow. The sense of play represented in such moments has always been in strong evidence in Yoshida's live shows, too, where he adds screamed and sung vocals to the array of mangled distortion and fuzz. Not for nothing does Yoshida point to what he sees as a 'spiritual state of selflessness', a feeling of being 'connected to an inner space of the unconscious' while he makes music and performs (cited in 'Like Hunting in the Wild' 2012). Meanwhile, split releases and/or collaborations with acts like Macronympha (*Obliteration*, Xerxes and Mother Savage, 1996), Skin Crime (*Unnatural Disasters*, Xerxes, 1998) and Bastard Noise (e.g. *The Relic*, Xerxes, 1999) likewise yielded pulverizing results, which in these cases drew out and intensified the core emphasis on harshness across American and Japanese noise in the 1990s. As can be seen, then, with releases on leading labels such as Ground Fault (*Sporadic Spectra* coming out as part of the Ground Fault Series III sequence) and relationships with key acts from the American scene, not to mention the appeal of Yoshida's Gilliam/Rauschenberg-like visual collages, Government Alpha's work in the 1990s was an important part of the harsh noise scene.

Whilst Yoshida has never attained the degree of impact and cut through of acts like Merzbow or, to a slightly lesser extent, Masonna or Torturing Nurse (more on the latter below), his importance and his noise vitality have persisted into the twenty-first century. Yoshida's music in the 2010–20s presents an interesting picture of the way in which characteristic 1990s Japanese harsh noise both retained key elements of its style and, as could be expected of this none-more-shocking style, also moved into new collaborative areas and new sounds. Government Alpha albums such as 2017's *Inevitable Phenomenon* (Xerxes) indeed felt old and new at the same time, continuing the former emphasis on pedal-mediated overwhelm and restless sonic mangle of earlier releases but adding new elements all the same, for example tools such as a Kaoss Pad and an iPad. Meanwhile, collaborations such as the 2013 split with Halanihil, *Inhuman Culture of Psychoacoustics* (L.White Records), likewise split the difference between continuity and change. In that case, Yoshida's typical blitzkrieg onslaughts were slammed up against, and twisted into new shapes by, Halanihil's power electronics screams and digital loops and edits. 2020's *Affective Imagery* (Abhorrent Creation Tapes) is an excellent illustration of the persisting intensity and challenge of harsh noise in the twenty-first century. I'll spend time going deep on this album to illustrate this point in more detail, using passages of auto-ethnographic impressionism to get at both what's happening in the music and some of the psychological affordances of the album.

We begin with 'Stridor'. This track starts out with a heavily filtered sample of what sounds like metal going through a blender, the sound loud but glitchy and low-bit digital in detail and flow. Unexpectedly, at around 0'21" that sound is brought lower in the mix as a sustained, distant organ or string pad fades up. The blend of choppy, abrasive sample and continuous, warm pad is pleasing, the one softening or hardening the other. These two layers move in and out of the foreground, with a held tone a major second below the original organ drone adding a sense of shape and tension as we go on. I feel myself moving with the relatively clear patterns of the music. The last forty seconds – apart from a brilliantly placed glitch and stretch in the final couple of seconds that transition us into the buzzsaw noise of second track, 'Invisible Area' – see a resolution of these sounds, as a low, repeated fuzzy drum strike gradually comes to the fore, this gesture repeatedly sounding out the same pedal note of the organ pad but now an octave below. As a listener I process the material in these rational, organizing ways even as I get pulled into a less rational, more personal response that is affective and experiential in nature. The mix of sounds and textures in 'Stridor', always anchored in noise-detail but with some musical sense of flow and logic all the same, pulls me in and out of myself, mind solving but slipping all the while.

It's easy to get lost in the overwhelming barrage of continuous sonic evolution in this sound; later tracks are again packed with unexpected detail and textural and formal subtleties. I sometimes find myself losing conscious intentionality and flowing along with the music; approaching depersonalization. But it's just as easy to get pulled into analysis, into the pleasurable, puzzling noticing of detail and structure; re-personalizing. The longest track, the 9'28" 'Pale Idolum', finds me toggling between these two states each time I listen. The track is filled with loud, consuming sound whilst also boasting a high degree of designed variety and scope. Its first two minutes or so of blistering, screaming high frequencies and feedback contrast with a choppier passage of noise and silence early in the third minute. A climactic passage of overweening, busy, mid-range churning follows, with fuzz and saw sounds crashing and skating into and over each other across the fourth, fifth, and six minutes. I dive into these sounds with glee, never quite sure where I stand or when I'll emerge, even as I'm pulled into feeling out the sharp contrasts and shapes of the sound. A lower-range, more saturated noise drone pulls things to a head in the seventh and eighth minutes, temperature raised as we (seem to) race to a close. But the final ninety seconds or so are then filled with quieter, albeit still pockmarked and hysterical, digital bleeps and modulation. I fade out of the tumult here and align with the formal elegance of the whole, appreciating the cooling effect of the quieter volume even as I still bristle and flicker with the sonic detail of the coda.

I continue to toggle for the rest of the album. For example, the serrated mid-range and bulldozing lows of wall-like closer 'Transience' and the stereo-separated delayed-drums and sustained, oscillating synth pad of 'Sacred Tree' are both unrelentingly harsh and overwhelming but also contain a variety of textures, sounds, and shapes that allow me to moor myself. We therefore get the kind of loudness and brutal earthquakes of static and distortion of classic harsh noise across Affective Imagery. But we also get moments of silence, of glitch, and of unexpected colour and easily encoded musicality. Moreover, form both flows freely and feels controlled, each track containing peaks and valleys of carefully layered intensity and density. There is also, finally, enough sonic continuity across the album, notwithstanding the unexpected bursts of colour or music or silence, that it feels cohesive, the sounds coming from the same palette even as the painter throws in unexpected combinations and inflections as we go. All this leaves me in a pleasurable place, puzzling at the sound, rational brain engaged but also slipping into something less observant as we go. As the musical form flows but fixes I mimic or move away from the sound's logic, forming into focus but drawing away, feeling a degree of release and contentment when I recover myself at the end, now changed, lighter somehow.

As we'll see in the younger artists examined below, this kind of approach to harsh noise, where brutal static and overwhelming noise suggest relentless movement but can also just as easily blend into silence or glitch, or organ and even melody, or some other unexpected element, is characteristic of a scene as free with its creative expression as it's ever been. We'll also see – as already illustrated in the examples of Akita and Yoshida – that twenty-first-century harsh noise artists have often enthusiastically engaged with new, digital tools and with web-enabled scene infrastructure. These new contexts have added even more hybrid flavour and colour to the scene even as these artists' work has retained a characteristically harsh and unrelenting approach to sound.

New classics

Torturing Nurse

Torturing Nurse are a Shanghai-based harsh noise act led by balaclava-clad Cao Junjun, aka Junky. They have moved through various line-ups since their founding in 2004, out of the ashes of cult no wave group Junkyard. Their music, in Junky's words, is 'analogue harsh noise/pure noise' and 'extreme harsh nihilistic noise!' (these descriptions are taken from the group's Facebook page; Junky n.d.). This is well said: Torturing Nurse use effects pedals, junk metal and other familiar noise methods to produce rackets of static and clatter in the vein of a whole variety of earlier harsh and other noise acts from across Europe, the United States and Japan. But Torturing Nurse have managed to cut through the fragile international networks of noise and experimental music to become what journalist Josh Feola has called 'a household name in harsh noise circles around the world' (2019). Torturing Nurse are an exciting and powerful act, which at least partially explains this cut through. But they're also a good story. I'll get to why in a moment.

Torturing Nurse are inspired by and imitative of both the kind of aggressive, lurid, sadomasochistic performance-art shenanigans explored by Japanese groups Incapacitants and Hijokaidan in the 1980s, and the audience-baiting and even confronting tactics of power electronics artists like Con-Dom. A favourite *YouTube* clip features Junky haranguing somewhat nonplussed (and amused – it is a funny, not especially threatening spectacle) onlookers in Lu Xun Park in Shanghai in 2012 (JunkyChaos). His face is covered, his Ecoute La Merde leather jacket is on, and he wields a small battery amp, mic and sheet metal, the latter of which he strikes with a hammer to produce a clattering static. More conventional settings usually see Cao and colleagues in similarly playful but confrontational mood; notable performances have incorporated everything from bondage to raw pork.

Torturing Nurse's uniting of S&M and/or violent stage performance on the one hand, and rudimentary effects-pedals-and-junk-metal noisemaking on the other, very obviously honours noise music tradition. Moreover, Torturing Nurse's bewildering array of solo, split and collaborative releases likewise slots neatly into noise tradition. Junky maintains live Google Docs on the group's *Facebook* page which list all their gigs and releases; as of June 2022, the latter runs to 464 releases. This outpaces even Akita. So, Torturing Nurse might be seen as chips off the old noise music block.

And yet, the group also represent something new. And here's where they offer such a particularly good story, over and above the innate fun and excitement of their approach. Because, although looking at Torturing Nurse through a distant, exoticizing lens would place the group into a wider, shared East-Asian noise-cultural ecosystem with some of the Japanese artists we've examined, their Chinese origins and identity mean that many audience members will naturally and rightly place them into a different ethno-cultural frame and context. Putting on risqué, grotesque or extreme live noise shows featuring nudity and fowl was after all a very different proposition in 1980s Tokyo or Kyoto compared to how it was even in 2000s or 2010s Shanghai. Indeed, although China's cultural and economic opening up to the world since the 1980s and 1990s has been profound and dramatic, it's nevertheless the case that Chinese culture remains both internally focused and conservative. This is certainly the case when we compare China to neighbouring countries such as Japan and Korea. Those countries' long history of modernization (and, arguably, westernization) stretches right back to the nineteenth century. In the case of Japan, this includes everything from the Meiji Restoration of 1868, with its slogan 'Japanese spirit, Western technology'; to the 1872 incorporation of western classical music into the new national education system; to the post-war boom of western pop and rock. In the case of Korea, the signing of the Kanghwa treaty with Japan in 1876 provided a signal moment, opening the country up to western culture and education as it did (see Lee 2013 for a wider discussion of the reception and presence of various western composers in Korea between 1900 and 1945). China, by contrast, endured long periods of twentieth-century isolationism; Wham!'s April 1985 concerts in Beijing and the southern city of Guangzhou were notable for the international attention and shock they generated. As late as 2002, as a BBC article put it, a Chinese show by Kenny G 'was considered big news'. Even internationally famous western acts such as the Rolling Stones have been subject to censorship when they performed in China, as for example with their 2006 concert in Shanghai, when they were forced to cut five songs from their set (Savage 2016).

Torturing Nurse therefore present a fascinating example for noise audiences West and East: both familiar in sound and approach but also new in context. And whilst not entirely singular in this Chinese regard – the improv, experimental pop and noise scene around Yan Jun in Beijing, for example, features a host of interesting musicians and events – Torturing Nurse's role in and representation of the Shanghai scene, where for example Junky helps organize 'noise/free/avant series gigs NOIShangha' and 'harsh noise/HNW/power electronics/grind noise series gigs EarAgainstTheAmp' (Junky n.d.), is both important and notable. It is notable both for its accomplishments in promoting and spreading noise culture in China and for how it presents a new noise story to audiences outside (and perhaps inside) China. In this latter sense, Torturing Nurse's harsh noise offers an image (whether real or imagined) of tantalizing tension between still censorious Chinese society and supposedly free-loving and boundary-baiting noise performance. It's an intriguing mix.

Given the 464 releases mentioned above, sifting out significant examples to examine is difficult. Though it's hard to assess this point objectively, the 2005 and 2007 albums, *NanaNanaNanaNanaNanaNana* (Obscurica) and *Eeerie* (Indie-ziert), are probably the group's most significant releases. In both thinking about my sense of which of their albums have had longevity on the scene and then in looking at the amount of reviews their discography has generated on *Rate Your Music* (n.d.) – a useful yardstick for measuring audience impact, in noise as in other forms – this is indeed confirmed, with the former album, for example, having 180 ratings as at June 2022, and the latter 117, both far more than their other releases. I'll therefore discuss these two, alongside 2015's *All Bastards+* (which, incidentally, had 18 ratings, a relatively healthy number; Cruel Nature), to give a flavour of their style over time.

Like a lot of Torturing Nurse's work, *NanaNanaNanaNanaNanaNana* is built on sonic spasms, cuts and churn. The track names (see Table 6.1) and lengths on the album demonstrate this well, with their deliberately pointillist, additive style on the one hand and condensed lengths on the other.

The playful interconnections of the titles here – na, becoming nna, becoming Ann, becoming Nann and later, Ann (twice!) and Anna (and annA) – are reflected in the sound. For example, the 'daaaaa' screamed intro of 'na' jumps nicely into the stereo-roving, jerking drone and Yol-style throat gurglings of 'nna', whilst the bare high screams with low, filtered bass drone of 'Nann' are qualified by a reappearance of that filtered drone at the start of the busier, eight-bit flanging drones and textures of

Table 6.1 Track titles and lengths of Torturing Nurse's *NanaNanaNanaNanaNanaNana* (2005)

1	Na	0:04
2	Nna	0:46
3	Ann	0:56
4	Nann	1:44
5	N.A.	0:48
6	Nsae	1:23
7	Anna	0:46
8	AnrA	0:02
9	nAcra	0:10
10	Ncsda	1:06
11	dfAn	1:05
12	Lan	0:44
13	Qan	0:51
14	WnA	0:50
15	a.n.	0:50
16	Cdna	0:59
17	Noka	1:16
18	Noknda	0:28
19	NeAcc	0:21
20	eaCn	0:53
21	WaPn	0:41
22	maNq	0:49
23	Anna	1:03
24	NanaNanaNanaAnanAnanAnan	2:05
25	annA	1:03
26	qNam	0:49
27	nPaW	0:41
28	nCae	0:53
29	ccAcN	0:21
30	Adnkon	0:28
31	Akon	1:16
32	Andc	0:59
33	.n.a	0:50
34	AnW	0:50
35	naQ	0:51

Table 6.1 (Continued)

36	naL	0:44
37	nAfd	1:05
38	Adscn	1:06
39	arcAn	0:10
40	ArNA	0:02
41	ArNA	0:46
42	annA	1:23
43	easN	0:48
44	.A.N	1:44
45	nnA	0:56
46	Ann	0:46
47	An	0:04

'Ann' a few minutes later. The music here is frenetic and cut-up but it is also consistent and cohesive.

Correspondences such as those just listed can be heard across the album. Most abiding throughout is a sense of continuity amidst (and of) change, the frantic, interrupted, glitchy flow of high feedback, scratchy video game sounds and, above all, distorted screaming creating a consistent sonic palette even as those sonics rarely settle into anything like a repeated pattern, sustained tone or steady texture. Instead, the impression is often of striated lines or cuts collaged together to create a pointillist whole.

And yet, the album is not without moments of collision and connection. The music seems indeed to work around complementary notions of cut or splice, where frantic and often fleeting sounds are either cut apart or spliced together. So, the more discrete, striated gestural units just mentioned are isolated from each other with silence or a track break, working like sonic analogues for the spasmodic, herky-jerky motions that Junky seems possessed by in concert (a December 2020 concert at yuyintang illustrates this well; TorturingNurse 2020). At other times, these units are spliced together, combined into consuming earthquakes of sound. This can be heard, for example, on tracks like the bulldozing, threshing 'a.n'. The sound is always glitchy and frenetic but it can be more-or-less separated and striated on the one hand, or stacked together on the other, depending on the moment.

Given this cut-or-splice approach and given the striated or stacked phrases it is based on, we can ultimately say that the album amounts to something like Masonna's wild lightning strikes of tearing static, feedback and screams as further condensed into dense, trebly gestural units of sound that are cut apart or spliced together. And even though the generally cut-up nature of the sound means we don't quite get the same impression of burbling sonic lava in Torturing Nurse as we sometimes do in artists like

Merzbow, Torturing Nurse's sound contains such force and restless forward-momentum that, in the end, it feels in constant motion, its stylistic integrity always in question, its basic orientation one of becoming. The listening experience here is correspondingly wild and frenetic, as it likewise often is in Masonna. *NanaNanaNanaNanaNanaNana*'s splenetic sound and performances can create an intense sense of anxiety and perhaps even hyper-personalization, as listeners struggle to get a foothold in the fast-forward, high-wire sound. This can of course shade into the kind of pleasurable, puzzle-centred experience I've described as personalization, depending on your mileage, but ultimately it would probably be hard to settle in and truly lose oneself in the sound as might be possible in other, perhaps less frenetic and jittery forms of noise.

Eerie lives in a broadly similar sonic space to the earlier album; for example, the principle of 'cut and splice' mentioned earlier is evident across it. In that respect, *Eerie* is full of the kinds of striated, cut-up sharp yowls and feedback interjections heard earlier. But here the emphasis if anything shifts to the splicing, combinatorial aspect mentioned above, to such a degree that the sound often moves away from the glitch of the earlier album and approaches the lava of other harsh noise. The latter can be heard in particularly potent form on the near-27-minute 'None of'. About twelve minutes through the track, after all, we move into an absolute cavalcade of churning metallic sound, like a JCB being put through a giant metal crusher. This whisking tumult and onslaught last for three to four sustained minutes of intensity and obliteration, before just a little more space and silence are let into the clattering fray. In passages like this, the noise becomes so total and all-consuming that it is very easy as a listener to get lost, connect and even depersonalize, as the noise fries any sense of personalized, rational remove on the one hand or panicky anxiety on the other. The music demands total surrender.

Eerie, more generally, is an interesting proposition when set against *NanaNanaNanaNanaNanaNana*. On the one hand, the two albums are strongly connected. As just noted, both feature moments of high intensity and sonic near chaos. The sound palette of both is broadly similar too; though we don't get any video-game-like sonics on *Eeerie*, and though there is a heavier low-end presence on the album as compared to the earlier one, both are relentlessly assaultive and wild in tone. They are, in this respect, filled with feedback, divebombing globs of distortion from Kaoss Pad, and frenetic gesticulation and screaming. On the other hand, however, the albums have a clear difference in texture and atmosphere, as indicated by my point above about the 'splicing' emphasis on *Eerie*. The sonic textures on *Eerie* are simply more drawn-out and sustained than the earlier album. The fact that *Eerie* consists of three longer tracks as opposed to the 47 bitty, shorter tracks of *NanaNanaNanaNanaNanaNana* obviously contributes to this impression. But it is more than that; the sound here is often undergirded with a churning mid-range noise wall or drone, which both anchors and pummels everything into blistering, caustic static and crumble. It's true that 'Jubilation', the middle track, is bittier, more scream-laden than the relentless churn of opener 'Ys', but even there the sharded high feedback, scratches and screams tend not to come up for much air. Meanwhile, the aforementioned 'None Of' is brutal throughout, over and above its central climax; again, some sense of flowing, arcing gesture is introduced through Kaoss Pad swoops, but the track is dominated by tearing, trebly distortion and never-stopping clatters and industrial blending. The sound across all three tracks on *Eerie* indeed contains such a density of event that we approach a kind of noise wall here, though it's a very different wall to those of Vomir or (as we'll see) the Rita; almost micro-polyphonically structured rather than monolithically walled.

Later Torturing Nurse music continues in much the same vein of cutting, trebly sound that can veer into lavaic, dialectical density. This is even if albums such as the 2007 collaboration with Zbigniew Karkowski and Dickson Dee, *Penetration* (PACrec), inevitably work in different sonic territories and contexts, in that case blending noise frenzy with more deliberate compositional control and detail. The aforementioned 2015 album, *All Bastards+* (Cruel Nature), is a good illustration of how Torturing Nurse – like harsh noise artists more generally – pursued a twenty-first-century approach that we could characterize as 'continuity with variation'. In terms of such variation, *All Bastards+*'s sound palette is more concentrated than that of the earlier albums examined above, with a focus on distortion, fuzz and feedback as core sonic ingredients maintained pretty much throughout. And yet, in terms of continuity, the kind of striated or stacked intensity and blast found on the earlier albums is once again front and centre here. The title track, for instance, contrasts blasting low distorted churns with isolated high feedback tones, the one answering the other in relatively bare, intense discussion. 'Sunday 22.22' is a little busier and thicker, but even there the sound is concentrated around tensile static fuzz drone, which is pulled and whooshed both subtly and grandly. To wit, inner details shift and bristle as we go along, whilst large redirections of sonic flow and focus happen from time to time too, as for example with the shift into rubbery, scratchy distortion and feedback across the second minute, or the more spaced-out passages of feedback and fuzz in the eighth. Meanwhile, 'For ZK' brings in (what sounds like) a heavily distorted and processed sample of screaming, which it pairs with and meshes into glints of feedback across the stereo spectrum as a lower drone gurgles underneath, the whole once again creating a characteristic sense of strained, sometimes wild movement.

The long closer, 'Relentless Joy', is initially less assaultive than the other tracks, building up slightly quieter drones in the left and centre with similarly thickening metallic feedback on the right. By the time we get to the fourth and especially fifth and six minutes we find ourselves in a harsh wall, layers of buzzing distortion enveloping a screaming Junky, as various feedback pedal points ring out, resolve or wink out barely heard higher or lower tones. As we move deeper into the track, the gestural language becomes busier and the texture less monolithic. This is such that we can hear different sonic events much more clearly. Intensity is, however, maintained; the shifting of musical detail from wall to avalanche in this kind of way creates a sense of shape and flow even as it ensures that our attention and, perhaps, our anxious or immersive consumption in the sound are maintained. This lasts right up to the close at 17'10" – the fact that the track fades out in its final seconds rather than just ending playfully suggests that the track's picture of a becoming noise cosmos is still somehow becoming – even as the final few minutes somehow ramp things up even further. In those final minutes, distressed screaming, metallic clanking and the thick buzzing wall from earlier combine to create an impression of heavy event, static wall and frenzied activity somehow held in dialectical tension even as we as listeners perhaps (pleasurably) struggle to stay with the detail and the flow. As with the broader arc of Torturing Nurse's work just identified, this long closing track expressed both change and continuity. After all, it features a kind of monolithic fixedness built around, and with, variety and activity.

As we saw with Merzbow and Government Alpha earlier, this sense of continuous but evolving intensity, harshness and sonic brutality runs across the twenty-first-century harsh noise scene. Our next example, Body Carve, evinces this continuity and evolution, both retaining (the ever-evolving, unstill) harshness and intensity from earlier harsh noise artists, and expanding that harsh palette in different ways, for example twisting harsh noise gruesomeness into a thematic focus on body horror and disease. Our final example, Rusalka, again retains harshness and intensity but adds new flavour, in this case compositional control and polish akin to sound artists and composers like Bernard Parmegiani or Karkowski. Both artists provide an illustration of the continuing power of traditional harsh noise in the twenty-first century whilst also showing how the music continued to evolve and grow in that period.

Body Carve

The artist behind Body Carve, N. Desuah, has been releasing music under the Body Carve alias since 2016; they also operate as Ligature Impression and under their own name. As Body Carve, Desuah produces harsh noise that is very much in the American tradition of Richard Ramirez, Macronympha and others, where junk metal and other cheap sound sources are used to produce rough, abrasive sounds that yet combine to produce subtle textures and unusual, restless forms. But Body Carve's work is also organized around a sustained thematic fixation on body horror and abjection (though the negative slant these terms suggest might be an external projection). This is common on the noise scene; we've already seen various gruesome topics and treatments across the first half of the book, and we'll look at body-focused thematic obsessiveness aligned closely to Body Carve across Chapter 8. Indeed, in many ways the current case study should be read as presaging and preparing the ground for that eighth chapter; it is being included here due both to Body Carve's harsh style and for how it opens our harsh frame in preparation for further, hybrid-orientated opening in the next and subsequent chapters.

Body Carve's thematic fixation is obvious from the artist name down. Albums include *Scrap Gash* (White Centipede Noise, 2017), *Autoamputation* (New Forces, 2019) and a split EP with Slit Throats, *Penetrating Neck Traumas* (Phage Tapes, 2017). Track titles include 'Frantic Cavity Hollowing' and 'Bore to Bone' (from *Scrap Gash*), and 'Aerating a Bloated Body' (from 2020's *Macro Induced Orgasm* on Cadre). Album art usually depicts bodily innards or other abject, grimy images. The album I'll examine in more detail, *Guts in Red Plastic* (Gutter Bloat, 2018), is an almost comically on-the-nose condensation of these themes. Consisting of two 21-minute tracks of crunchy, crumbling static and shards of piercing feedback, the album's sounds are derived from a 'necropsy' performed by the artist themselves (on what looks from the album art like an animal corpse purchased or obtained legally). In their own words,

> For over 20 minutes, I mangled and mutilated the organs while listening to the amplified, wet mush of the bloody innards and the crackle of the plastic as the sounds recorded to tape. These recordings were created by amplifying and overdriving the respective source recordings and supplementing with raw and distorted junk metal sounds as they played.
>
> (2018)

A special edition of the album was released in a VHS box with colour collage and insert depicting the original 'procedure', with 'tape guts' in a hazardous bag packaged along with the recording adding to the effect.

The music itself doesn't entirely betray its wet source, perhaps until some notable squelching at the end. Instead, each track offers dense, dynamic slabs of crunchy noise. As with Macronympha, the surface can be dense but the innards (excuse the pun) are full of give. Straight from the off on 'Necropsy (Entry/Excision)', brutal scrapes and then tunnelling distortion open a dynamic push and pull between high glint and punishing static low. These two poles define the sound in broad terms but every second is filled with dialectical movement and colour. This is both because of the dirty, murky spectra of the sounds themselves and because of the way they are processed and manipulated. For example, thicker, lower, loud rumble dominates the third and fourth minutes, before a relative pulling back into sharded, crunchy higher tones and feedback in the fifth and sixth. Later, in the tenth and eleventh minutes, a sparer rumble evolves into coruscating high tones and static. Throughout, the sound crackles and burns, never stopping, never refining.

The second track, 'Mangled (Guts in Red Plastic)' continues in much the same vein, though the sound is often noticeably more fragmented, more gestural here. The first few minutes, for example, contain much more empty space and suggestions of discrete actions than the first track. Later, the track becomes busier, crunch and bustle largely overwhelming the earlier fragmentation. Things climax in the last few minutes with a trebly cacophony of scratches and scrapes, almost like forks in an industrial garbage chute. However, we are never quite in overwhelming wall or Government Alpha territory here; for all its molten, searching burble, the sound always feels somehow smaller, more contained, more human scale than what we find in artists like Yoshida. Indeed, underlining this point, the last minute or two of the track sees a gradual thinning out, with things getting quieter and more focused around individual waves of crumble and high glint before the aforementioned coda of squelchy, crackly organ mangling.

This, then, is very much trad harsh noise, mic-on-metal overload and distortion. Its effect is defined by a restless sense of becoming – musical 'peaks' offset by noise troughs – and a consuming sound in which it's easy to get lost. This is even if, thinking of the dual points of both continuity and change mentioned earlier, Body Carve's thematic focus aligns Desuah with a broad array of noise artists from beyond the core harsh lineage.

Rusalka

Rusalka is Canadian – Vancouver, to be specific, like other noise artists The Rita, Flat Grey and Broken Sleep – musician Kate Rissiek, who has been releasing music under the Rusalka name since 2008. Working primarily with theremin and other electronics, Rissiek's music offers an interesting contrast with the artists considered above and with the harsh noise wall of the next chapter. This is because its harshness and its sonic resources are both more modulated and more dynamic than those other artists. With Rusalka, we hear an artist clearly invested in, but not constrained or imprisoned by, the affective and sonic traditions of harsh noise. For whatever reason – whether age, location, personal preferences or whatever – Rissiek's work strikes out for new sonic territories. In this respect of musical hybridity and innovation beyond harsh noise's innate hybridity and innovation, Rusalka provides a harbinger of some of the artists we examine in Chapters 9 and 10; what comes next for a scene to some extent still defined by seminal artists from previous generations.

The Way of All Flesh, released on Skinwalker in 2010, embodies this dual looking back and forwards across its two long tracks (which are 14'03" and 15'13" in length respectively). The first one, 'Flesh', layers familiar noise tropes – low, buzzing drone, which here plays out unadorned for about two minutes, priming us for something more, before it starts to get modulated and manipulated across the third minute and, from there, expands outwards; staticky, wall-like textures; piercing electronic tones that arrest attention and cut into the sound; and wordless, heavily processed, textural vocals – and builds these up gradually into a thick, immersive climax. But the piece is both more polished than much of the music discussed above and also more carefully choreographed, the sounds themselves detailed in tonality and arranged more with deliberation than abandon. The poised way in which the track's sonic envelope gradually opens out from that bare drone to a more modulated sound, and then into more overwhelming noise, is a good illustration of the point. The compositional control of the material here, which carefully evolves and unspools along the arc of the track, therefore doesn't so much suggest a becoming of grammar as it does a grammar of becoming (to call back to a phrase from my Introduction). This is still noise, given the abrasion, inharmonicity and aperiodicism of much of the sound, but the music shifts emphasis from a becoming that can't resolve into a kind of becoming of resolution. The listening experience, as a result, is exciting but more distanced and personalized than it is with other harsh noise.

The second track, 'Dots', works in much the same way, tipping the scales slightly to the order side of the order/disorder dialectic. Fairly blunt crackle and static occupies the centre of the field for much of the track, following the echoey, sampled vocal introduction. But delicate gestures and details can be heard at both low and high ends throughout; the centred static, for instance, is built on a play between busy higher crackle and a lower oscillating tone. Meanwhile, dynamic movement throughout creates a sense of flow and story. To wit, the crackle and low tone shift and spark throughout the first few minutes, whilst a largescale swell about halfway in creates a sustained peak for a track already filled with motion. This peak is hard won: following a rise in volume and presence for the low tone across the seventh minute and an encroaching staticky field in the eight, the ninth and tenth minutes are consumed with a swarm of buzz and fuzz, the anchoring low tone lost now as the sound hovers like a digital bee colony. Harsher tones cut in here and there as that swarm roves up and down, back and forth, across the eleventh to fourteenth minutes.

As with 'Flesh', the sense of sonic polish and control of flow on 'Dots' is impressive. For instance, although the music is both thick and noisy, and evokes spontaneity and restlessness in how it evolves and moves, its thickness isn't the thickness of a scrambled Torturing Nurse or even an ear-splitting Government Alpha, and its restlessness always leans towards some grander rest. On the first count, the sound always feels quantized, controlled and clipped, as if (and perhaps actually) digitally choreographed. On the second, the fact that 'Dots' resolves in the final five seconds of fifteen minutes of building noise from a higher-end buzzing into a much lower, repeated bass tone, makes complete sense and reaffirms Rusalka's gift for compositional shape and story. That gesture could feel random in other artists' hands but here, because of the way the swarm had gradually become concentrated around one note and because of the trust we've developed in the music's sense of internal form and outer purpose, feels hard-earned and logical. It lands like a twist that is both surprising and, once it's realized, obvious.

Base Waters, released on Absurd Exposition in 2019 and again consisting of two long tracks (this time 18'06" and 17'43", respectively), exhibits similar controlled intensity to *The Way of All Flesh* but moves along a tenser line, busier with event and less predictable in its arcs. The second track, 'Reflection underneath Waves', is focused and thick in its early stages, and fragmented and volatile in its latter. It is built initially on a huge central sound, crunchy but also steady and warm, which slowly evolves over the first half of the track into the sparer, higher shrill sound of the middle section. We are then given unpredictable passage through lapping water and arcing, modulating high tones, before, finally, isolated, filtered versions of those high sounds are set against low, depth-charge interjections across the final minute or two. The whole thing ends with a return to those lapping splashes. Form, as noted, winds more here than it does on *Flesh*. Nevertheless, a clear overall arc and shape, from focus to fragment with various detours, presentiments and reprises along the way, comes through. The first track, 'Sinking Blood Deep', is just as varied in flow, shape and sound as 'Reflection' whilst also nevertheless displaying clear control and choreography in its sounds and structure. I'll describe its minute-to-minute flow before stepping back to sum up my analysis.

'Sinking Blood Deep' *is anchored around a central low, staticky drone. But the oscillations of that drone are jerkier and the static more windblown, more chaotic, than, for example, the drones of 'Dots'. It makes for a quietly tumultuous opening, clicking our attention into gear without intruding on our security. Wave-like intrusions of higher-range distortion arrest flow as we move through the first few minutes, pushing us into a more uncertain state. All the while the anchoring drone gradually rises in volume, tone, and thickness. The sound becomes choppier in the sixth minute, gaps in the drone and various invading gestures unsettling and creating further tension, the tumult of the opening never quite resting or resolving.*

We move into a new section at the top of the eighth minute. The drone is now gone, a busy held high tone creating a force against which various sonics crash and break. This tone moves up and down over the course of the next few minutes, holding but rocking the listener. The texture gradually evolves in the eleventh and twelfth minutes as an oscillating mid-range drone comes to the foreground and largely takes over from the high tone. The track wobbles and falters as the sound struggles to get a footing, restlessness and disordered tension creeping in. This wobbling and faltering is then consumed by the return of the high tone from earlier, the sound moving into a more fragmented, glitchy piercing texture in the fifteenth and sixteenth minutes. It's hard to get a bearing through all this uncertainty and change even as it's fairly easy to hear continuity and control in the repetition of material and the steady rises-and-falls in tension.

The final few minutes offer a little breathing space in their spare exploration of that higher tone, now filtered and glitchy, now thick and surrounded with crumble. Harsher sounds interject here and there but the feeling is largely one of a fire starting to burn away. That is before another surprise ending, the quiet noise of lapping water now suddenly meeting our ears almost as answer and question all at the same time; this is where we've been heading all along, it seems to say, though it's hard to work out exactly why.

As is obvious from my description, 'Sinking Blood Deep' revels in the detail of noise. Its fairly internally consistent set of gestures are turned over, placed in new contexts and brought back, all with a keen ear for resonance within and across different sections. Once again, Rissiek's sounds are harsh in themselves and in terms of their fealty to the tropes of the tradition but also grasp towards something new, a personal voice in which compositional control, sonic character and noise freedom come together. Where becoming and become, tension *and* resolution, are perhaps equal facets or features of the sound. Even if personal, though, this approach to harsh noise, where digital and compositional control rub against rough and intense sounds, is not uncommon in the twenty-first-century scene – we've already seen elements of this digital control in Merzbow's work, but artists like Blind Date similarly blend traditional harsh noise tropes, such as the use of junk metal and cheap effects pedals, with more contemporary approaches to editing and production (see, for example, 2020's *Judy Garland Pavilion, Monorail Trespassing*). Such work clearly benefits from digital resources and thinking whilst nevertheless drawing directly on wilder, more restless aesthetic frames as it does so. Although Blind Date doesn't quite approach the same balance of order and disorder we could hear in Rissiek's work, it's clear that both nevertheless in their own way tip the scales a little differently to previous artists.

Conclusion

As we've seen across our five main examples, harsh noise continued to thrive in the twenty-first century. It expanded into newer territories, China most obviously, whilst making use of new digital tools and infrastructure. Its core stylistic template and touchstones stayed familiar though, with many continuing and newer artists displaying an abiding interest in sonic harshness, intensity and unresolved tension.

That template's potential for mystery, for immersion, for play, and for pleasure seemed (and seem) not even close to being exhausted.

And yet, the scene had to change to survive. This change can be seen both in terms of its embrace of new digital technologies and ever-expanding transcultural channels of exchange, and in terms of the many personal stylistic advances on the core harsh-noise stylistic template. For whilst, as just noted, that template continued to provide powerful inspiration for musicians in this period, many artists explored new ways of realizing noisy harshness, intensity and tension, whether it was the digital technologies of Pita and Akita, the compositional nuance of Rusalka and Blind Date or the body horror of Body Carve. The next few chapters explore other new ways that artists have realised and expanded on earlier templates.

7

Noise walls and atmospheric chambers

This chapter picks up the story of twenty-first-century noise begun in Chapter 6. It gathers different offshoots or related subgenres or substyles of harsh noise – harsh noise wall (HNW) and death industrial/dark ambient – to expand the stylistic frame of our twenty-first-century story, which is hybrid and mongrel from here on out (not that it hasn't been so far: noise was hybrid from its origins).

The chapter uses the metaphors of wall and atmosphere to frame the music under discussion and highlight connections between them. The first section explores these metaphors as a way of establishing the history and main aesthetic features of HNW and dark ambient/death industrial. The following three sections provide case studies of key artists whose work embodies different aspects of the HNW aesthetic; Vomir, Macronympha side project OVNM, and The Rita. I use spectrograms and description to get at what is happening in the sound and in my response to it without going all the way to the kind of auto-ethnography we've seen so far (since this approach could get lost in the impressionistic walls and chambers of this music). The final section looks at the death industrial/dark ambient music mentioned most directly in Chapter 3. It focuses on Subklinik and Gnawed as notable examples.

Walls and atmospheres

Harsh noise wall is a subgenre or substyle of harsh noise that developed in the late 1990s as an intensification and even logical endpoint of the extreme sonic (and affective) tendencies of noise music. HNW is a logical endpoint in other ways too. For example, of the move from more song-like, traditional 'musical' features in 1980s power electronics and industrial music into harsher, more abstracted sonics in late 1980s harsh power and 1990s harsh noise; and of the growing separation of harsh sounds from harsh themes that took place across 1990s noise. HNW mostly evacuates such traditional features and themes from noise, focusing instead on a profound slowing of musical rates of change and a transformation of relationships of form and time. (As we'll see, elements of traditional 'musicality' persist nonetheless.)

The metaphor of the 'wall' is both perfectly appropriate *and* inappropriate to the music. On the one hand, noise walls sonically embody many qualities of walls; their loud, densely packed, blockily textured sounds are brick-like in their unrelenting, monolithic, hard to penetrate surfaces and edifices. As many have pointed out, there is something of the monumentality of minimalist artists like Richard Serra in HNW. Noise walls are even, as Sara Ahmed suggests of walls more generally, personally confronting and uncomfortable to some listeners.

> A wall is a technique: a way of stopping something from happening or stopping someone from progressing without appearing to stop this or stop them, even by appearing to start something or even by appearing to allow them to progress. But you arrive, and it becomes uncomfortable. It is so uncomfortable, that you are not willing to stay. The discomfort can be tangible to you, like a thing, a wall, which you know is right there because you have just knocked into it. When you leave you do so willingly; it appears that you have left in accordance with your own will.
>
> (2014)

In this sense, all harsh noise could be described as wall-like; indeed, the metaphor and sonic image of the wall haunts pre-HNW noise, appearing again and again in a range of disparate noise examples. We have seen this throughout the book every time I used terms like 'wall-like' to describe a particularly dense passage of harsh noise. It is almost as if the wall is a kind of 'limit-case' of the sonic intensity and density of earlier examples of noise.

The Rita's Sam McKinlay, who we'll get to below, indeed traces the lineage of HNW through earlier noise artists. McKinlay starts with the 'cascading walls of noise' of 1980s and 1990s Japanese artists such as Hijokaidan and Monde Bruits. He then moves on to 1990s 'Americanoise' artists such as Macronympha/OVMN, Skin Crime and Richard Ramirez/Black Leather Jesus. McKinlay argues that the dense 'crunch and rumble' of these artists – as opposed to the 'squeals and jolts' of some Japanese musicians – expresses an ideal of 'grit' and 'darkness' that we can also trace in HNW (2010, 14). McKinlay's capsule pre-history is useful in highlighting important precedents for HNW. There are other precedents we could name, of course. Andrew Chalk's Ferial Confine is an obvious one, as is clear on releases like 1985's *The Full Use of Nothing* (self-released on tape and issued on vinyl in 1999 by Fusetron). Meanwhile, aforementioned artists such as The New Blockaders and Intrinsic Action often feature passing moments or impressions of walls.

Noise 'walls' therefore reach an apex with HNW but appear as a sonic resource and tendency throughout noise music history. And yet, looked at another way – staying with the wall metaphor as a way of understanding the wall music for a moment – neither the sonic walls of HNW nor the forerunning walls of harsh noise, anti-music, harsh power and other noise subgenres or substyles are actually walls at all. They are, instead (or also), immersive, porous, mobile and moving; the sonic architecture of these noise walls contains great, evolving variety and detail. As we saw in our brief discussion of Vomir in the Introduction, even in examples where the sound doesn't seem internally to change much or at all, the sound-as-phenomenon is always shifting, our psychoacoustic experience conditioned by and conditioning the sound in terms of affect, form and pattern, change. Indeed, in his questions to noise wall artists in the article referenced above, McKinlay focuses on the contrast between a static 'wall' and the dynamic spaces and relationships that emerge in, or in reaction to, the sound. In these respects, Pat Yankee of Paranoid Time suggests that 'spaces and dynamics lurking about the crunch pile take care of themselves'. Eric Stonefelt of Hum of the Druid similarly argues that 'effective crunch and cracking is suggestive of some sort of organic movement or acoustic presence' (2010, 16–17). Sound, or noise, never sleeps.

Calling once again on Ahmed, a fantastic theorist of material and spatial affect, noise walls can be said therefore to function more like *atmospheres*.

> Maybe an atmosphere is most striking as a zone of transition ... We might describe an atmosphere as a feeling of what is around, and which might be all the more affective in its murkiness or fuzziness: a surrounding influence that does not quite generate its own form.
>
> (2014)

In this sense, the evocative, resonant, kinetic qualities of noise walls infuse those walls with the feel of atmospheric movement. This atmospheric movement aligns HNW with the other styles being examined here, the more clearly 'atmospheric' death industrial and dark ambient. The immersive, resonant, echoey sub-bass, drones and careful sonic layering of these musics indeed typically create the feeling of being inside a kind of atmospheric chamber, evoking quasi-spatial or zonal territories filled with murk and chill as they do. The 'dungeons' of the black-metal-infused dark ambient sister style, 'dungeon synth', are often an apropos metaphor here as they are there.

Though HNW perhaps puts more emphasis on static walls than it does explicit atmospheric movement, and though dark ambient and death industrial may by contrast focus more on atmosphere, these musics therefore share common ground. Sonic walls move and have atmosphere; chambers have walls as well as atmospheres. Both HNW and dark ambient/death industrial are, in this sense, centred around a duality of wall and atmosphere. This duality charges each with dialectical force, the seemingly static volume and density of HNW always prone to spark off into countervailing movement and change, for example, and the haunted zonal chambers and dungeons of dark ambient and death industrial music always threatening to congeal into death and stillness. Given all this, we can see HNW, dark ambient and death industrial as interesting parallel and/or derivative streams of harsh noise, likewise built on dialectical tension and conflict but this conflict twisted in unique ways here. Considered collectively, they help paint a picture of the continuing story of noise's expansion and hybridization across the twenty-first century.

Vomir

We discussed an example from Vomir (aka French musician Romain Perrot) in the Introduction. I described Vomir's music as being based largely on unchanging walls of static; as he himself describes it, 'no ideas, no changes, no development, no entertainment, and no remorse' (2017). Vomir's approach in this respect is brutally simple and indeed easily realized. This has led to Perrot producing a huge quantity of work; as of June 2022, his catalogue runs to 395 solo and split releases (Discogs n.d. [c]).

Vomir's albums and live shows are filled up with seemingly static slabs of harsh sound. These slabs, or walls, *seem* to be absent of much in the way of traditional features of musical form, change or contour. Figure 7.1, which depicts the sixty-four minutes of the first disc of the six-disc 2007 release, *Claustration* (which, appropriately, means 'confinement'; At War with False Noise), illustrates this perfectly. As can be seen, except for a striking tapering at about 57'58" (indicated with the arrow), where some of the higher partials fall away and the weight of the sound thins out, the piece is dominated by a loud, crackly, but sustained blast of low-to-mid range white noise.

The effect of those 57'58" is striking, the dense sounds perhaps suggesting some kind of droning sonic monolith, and finally the tapering rocks crumbling off its huge edifice. But, given what I said in the Introduction about the sonic and psychological variety buried in Vomir's work – and given my overriding argument about what I see as the dialectical tension and restlessness of noise music, its overriding evocation of a permanent becoming of style and language where 'noise' and 'music' interpenetrate – it will be unsurprising that I hear atmospheric change, form and contour in this piece. For starters, as can be seen from the striation of even this high-level, zoomed-out spectrogram, the sound is not actually unchanging or unified; all sorts of phased events can be seen within its droning surface. This is obviously true of the seismic final tapering already discussed, which hits *hard* if you listen patiently and align with the long-held patterns leading up to it. But it's also true in those first fifty-eight minutes, where, once you tune in, align with the music, and accordingly rescale your expectations of information density and rate of change, the sound absolutely shimmers with internal phase-patterns, beating and rises-and-falls.

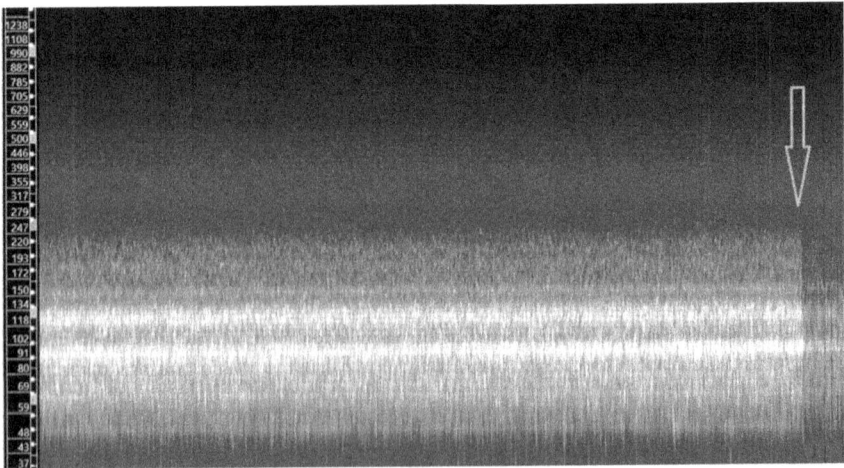

Figure 7.1 Melodic range spectrogram of disc one of Vomir's *Claustration* (2007).

I've moved from (at least more) objective sonic description here to my own psychological, psychoacoustic experience of the sound. I can't provide much external evidence for this experience. Some phasing and regular patterning can be seen in the spectrogram and easily heard in the piece but mostly what I'm talking about are more subtle 'internal' patterns that emerge only in listening. For instance – and here I'm citing examples from only one listening experience; psychoacoustic interpretation is not entirely unique but is hard to reproduce – the subharmonic beating I hear clearly across the sixth minute, or the stereo movement in the tenth, or the busy micro-polyphony in the twenty-second. Immersion into *Claustration* produces a raft of these experiences, the blunt and dense sound moving as you move with it, its arrested musical language engaged in a tussle of order and disorder in every pore of its frequency-saturated skin. I'd wager that for any listener willing to give themselves over to the sound, to immerse into another affective, informational reality, similar impressions of noise-music – and perhaps even psychological – becoming will come through. Certainly, the varied and evolving reactions of audiences at Vomir live shows, where people can usually be seen moving through their own narrative experiences of the work, support this point. This is what art does: sets its own sense of scale of action. Art and aesthetics are fields of true relativity. HNW is particularly potent in this regard, its toggling of information-density and sparsity allowing listeners to decompress, immerse and depersonalize in a range of different ways.

OVMN

OVMN, or 'Optimum Volume, Maximum Distortion', is the side project of Joe Roemer from Macronympha (with Macro's Rodger Stella joining him for some releases, particularly early on). The group released its first album in 1996 (self-titled, on Mother Savage Noise Productions), went on hiatus in 1998 for about twelve years, before returning with *II* in 2010 (Mother Savage Noise Productions). They have released a stream of albums of either new, reissued or rescued material since then.

Like Macronympha, OVMN's sound is cruddy, bristly and rough. Unlike Macro, though, the emphasis here is very much on unrelenting, often lower register, walls of noisy static. For some, including Sam McKinlay, this emphasis means that OVMN can be heard as the harshest of harsh noise, the music pushed to a static and intimidating extreme: 'OVMN is a virtual avalanche of harsh noise that is purposely the harshest possible, culminating in massive walls of sound' (2010, 14). And yet, compared to Vomir, the sound and form here are downright polylithic. Earlier OVMN tracks, such as 'Cocaine Erection' (on Roemer's own 1995 *Americanoise* comp; Mother Savage Noise Productions), feel less like HNW and more like particularly brutal and abrasive harsh noise, with their spaced out, evolving soundscapes. The same is true of important early albums like *Throbbing Pulse* (SE Productions, 1996), whose textures are wall-like but intensely crumbly and destructive/destroyed. The churning, pile-driving static found across *III* (Mother Savage Noise Productions, 2010, but recorded by Roemer and Stella in 1995) is another good example of this. The fifth (untitled) track from 2010's *Version* (which contained alternate versions of OVMN's first, unreleased 1995 tape; Mother Savage Noise Productions) provides a particularly eventful example, with its piercing, wilding feedback and its jousting crackle and noise. Later, post-hiatus OVMN music can sometimes be denser and more totalizing than the earlier examples just cited. But essentially it picks up from the dynamic, evolving, harsh crumble and rumble of that earlier period. To wit, the walls in this music are internally frenzied and eventful, sounds crumbling or moving as we go; doubling or halving in density; and even changing entirely within tracks.

2018's *Womblicker* (Bizarre Audio Arts) provides a sustained illustration of that later work. Consisting of two long tracks, 'Duration of Suppression' (28'06") and 'The Scent of Sex' (25'32"), the album is a blistering, postulating listen, with overwhelming noise walls holding the listener in place even as the sound changes or revolves along the way. 'The Scent of Sex' features a mid-to-low range distorted rumble in the centre of the track, which gradually, almost imperceptibly evolves in scope and colour throughout, around which hairshirt crackle and static disturb the ear frantically. The track provides a pulverizing listen, hypnotic in its concentration and intensity but absolutely packed with event; as unpredictable but strangely comforting as the sound of a gale of wind slamming against a microphone.

'Duration of Suppression' pivots on a similar, held tension between droning stasis and crackly event, though here a clearer emphasis is placed on the latter, high rates of change characterizing much of the track. For instance, the first few minutes alone feature several notable, explicit and unmistakable moments of formal transition. At 0'44", the somewhat arid, quiet, higher-range static of the opening suddenly explodes with the insertion of a loud, cracking static drone on the right of the stereo picture. The static grows to become a field. A wheedling high feedback tone cuts in and out from 1'26", and a loud fuzz tone enters in the centre at 1'39". At 2'35", following hints in the previous few seconds of a change in material and focus, the whole track seems to get confused with a panoramic churning drone, which combines and qualifies all the discrete elements heard so far into one mecha-monster.

Figure 7.2, which is a melodic range spectrogram of the track's first four minutes, conveys these global changes very clearly. The dominance of the barely visible white in the opening forty-three seconds gives way suddenly to sharp white gestures and spikes with the entry of the staticky drone (see the first arrow from left to right). The spikes at 1'39" and 2'35" mentioned above are also clearly indicated in the spectrogram via the increase in density and sharpness of white in the image at those points (see the second and third arrows). These are clear musical delineations of form and shape.

The approach heard across these opening minutes, where distinct sounds are layered up within the texture or across time and eventually brought together or qualified in a new sound and/or climactic passage, is therefore deeply musical in nature. This approach to form and texture continues for the rest of the track. Loud, howling, droning tunnels of noise are parlayed and then overlay each other as atmosphere. The build and then unleashing at 6'30", just like the careful, more concentrated exploration of lower range, slightly more spaced drones and static in the twelfth and thirteenth minutes – which leads gradually into an extended, overwhelmingly frenzied and intense central

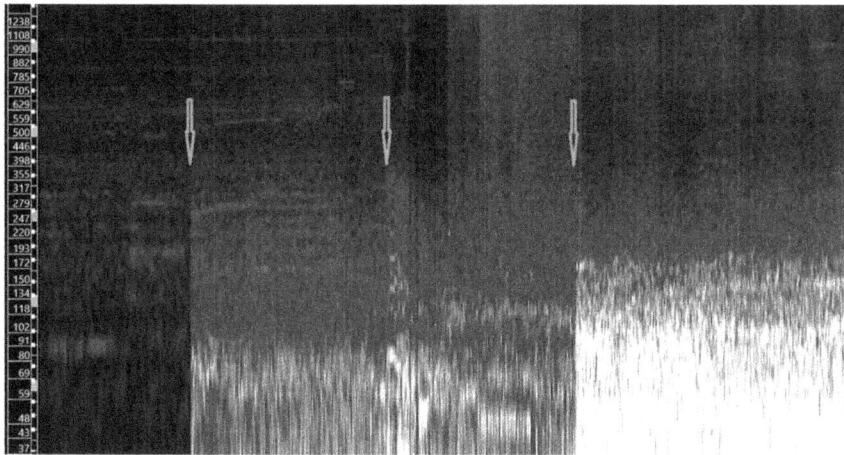

Figure 7.2 Melodic range spectrogram of the first four minutes of 'Duration of Suppression' from OVMN's *Womblicker* (2018).

climax from the fourteenth to twenty-first minutes – are excellent illustrations of this. The rest of the track arcs out a similar flow, from burbling concentration to volcano and back again (and again). The two states overlap to the point that discerning one from the other only becomes possible by zooming out and skipping across minutes of the track at a time. This is liquid, atmospheric wall building, as imperceptible in its movements as a fire spreading slowly through a massive forest but as inescapably active and dynamic as that fire would be. That the track *does* move, does create affect-rich atmospheres rather than just confront and bully with a somehow static, dense wall of noise, opens out huge possibilities for listeners, who will likely find themselves immersed and even productively lost in the overwhelming tension and puzzle of the sound. As with Vomir, this is wall noise filled with movement, atmosphere and held-in-tension order and disorder, the fissures and flow in the form creating pushes-and-pulls of stability and movement to which it's easy to attune and entrain.

The Rita

This gets us close to what Sam McKinlay described in his *As Loud As Possible* article as the 'sensation of being almost hypnotized by the vicious wall of distortion'. McKinlay indeed went on to suggest that,

> the sense of being overwhelmed by harsh noise was one of the original goals of some of the 1980s and 1990s artists: create such a high-volume wall of white noise and sound that the listener (and in most cases the artist as well) goes from cognitive interest to just staring blankly into space, physically overwhelmed.
> (McKinlay 2010, 16)

I've been pointing to this quality throughout the book. It is one that other noise artists or writers have identified using different language; Pat Yankee compares the sensation McKinlay characterized in terms of overwhelming blank staring to 'zoning out in kid-world' (cited in McKinlay 2010, 16). And we heard about the related trancing of Dave Philips and others in the Introduction.

But whilst this quality of depersonalized blankness is something I've pointed to throughout, and is certainly an ever-present quality of harsh noise, it's also true that the particular density and intensity of HNW mean that it is especially well-placed to hypnotize listeners in this kind of way, making them abject, pushing them beyond consciousness into a kind of unconscious connection (or dissociation) or self-loss.

McKinlay's own work as the Rita is a good note to finish HNW on in terms of this kind of hypnotizing, overwhelming noise wall affect. Active since the late 1990s, as of June 2022 McKinlay has been involved with 195 releases. These have included splits with a range of important acts, from Torturing Nurse to Rusalka, Vomir, and Richard Ramirez (as both Werewolf Jerusalem and Black Leather Jesus), as well as his own well-regarded albums, EPs and singles. McKinlay is clearly a key figure on the wall and harsh noise scene. Not only one of its original artists, he also gave HNW its name. As Tommy Carlsson describes in the liner notes to the Rita's eight-tape 2009 release, *The Nylons of Laura Antonelli* (Utmarken) – an album that, typically for McKinlay, pays homage to a recurring obsession, in this case genre film actresses and European exploitation films from directors like Jesus Franco and Andrea Bianchi; we'll see other obsessions below – his influence has been profound:

> If the 'wall of sound' approach by Phil Spector was a reference in name only, it does give a couple of helpful pointers as to what The Rita has accomplished in defining a new sub-aesthetic for the harsh noise world … The compelling impact of The Rita has been very much evident, seeing as there are legions of followers that have since adopted some of Sam's terms, like 'harsh noise purity' and 'militant walls', to such an extent that there is now a uniform group of noisicians clinging to a wall noise ethos.
>
> (2009)

Even though the relentlessness of McKinlay's noise walls sometimes gives way to quieter, almost pointillist static and glitch in works like Ballet Feet Positions (Old Europa Café, 2014), from his earliest releases McKinlay has been interested in pushing harshness to new levels. In what Carlsson describes as 'heavy static sheets of fuzzed out, dark and distorted workouts completely stripped of any sudden shifts and dynamic spasticity' (2009). McKinlay's work, like other HNW, pushes tendencies within harsh noise to a limit. And yet, at the same time, McKinlay's work clearly builds on both the sonic and thematic obsessions of earlier noise artists and subgenres or substyles. For example, on this point of continuity, those heavy sheets of static sound quite a bit like passages of noise attack in Macronympha, Black Leather Jesus, Skin Crime, The Haters and many other earlier artists. Similarly, the thread of fetish and sleaze that runs through power electronics and harsh noise continues through The Rita. The covers, track titles, sleeve imagery and other paraphernalia of albums like *Swingers Get Killed* (1998, Solipsism), *Possessed Nun Sleaze* (1998, Labyrinth), *Flapper Influence From French Prostitutes* (2005, Monorail Trespassing) and the above-mentioned *Nylons* are all testament to that.

The Rita's 2006 album, *Thousands of Dead Gods* (PACrec, Troniks), is one of McKinlay's best-known releases. It provides an excellent illustration of both the continuities and contrasts in HNW as compared to earlier harsh noise. *Thousands of Dead Gods* is based on recordings of shark cage dives. (Sharks are another of McKinlay's lifelong obsessions.) It combines audio from video recordings of cage dives that McKinlay made on a trip to the Isla Guadalupe with sound from vintage late 1960s and early 1970s shark cage footage. McKinlay processes these sources using 'analogue distortion and custom fuzz effects' (Anomaly Index 2020). The result, as we'll see in more detail below, amounts to fifty-nine minutes of overwhelming, confrontational, blunt crunch and jabber. The album is without much in the way of let up or space, or discernible concrete points of reference such as aquatic or cage sounds, the latter of which seem essentially processed out of existence. There is little to grab on to, at least in conventional terms. *Thousands of Dead Gods*, in these senses, sounds like much of McKinlay's other work.

And yet, it's also true that the story of its composition, its name, and its cover image of a carcass of a great white shark being looked at by a group of people all programme a particular sensibility. McKinlay himself makes the argument that the sound sources and thematic framing underlying his work are crucial to its aesthetic effect: 'No matter how deconstructed the original sound is … I believe firmly in the fact that the subtle nuances of the various sounds directly affect the final work' (Anomaly Index 2020). In this sense, according to McKinlay, the programmes assigned to different The Rita albums are important as scene-setting, providing keys to their atmosphere and tone. This is notable, given the supposedly none-more-abstract aesthetic of other HNW. However, I don't see formalism or pictorialism in music as mutually exclusive. Where we end up on the line between hearing the music formally and hearing it as a picture depends on a variety of factors, most notably how the sound and the themes are anchored to each other. Wall noise signifies, it doesn't just churn, but that signification can take many routes; musical, emotional, narrative and so on.

If we zoom out and think about the album's fifty-nine minutes as a whole, setting aside the extra-musical programme, the sound appears as a monumental, monolithic block of thick, fuzzy static, without much apparent internal change and variety. Listened to this way it could appear somewhat monotonous. And yet its volume – like all of McKinlay's releases, it is mixed very high – and its surface abrasion mean it is anything but monotonous or boring. Figure 7.3, which spans across the whole album, visualizes this monolithic, perhaps monotonous quality in the blob of white running throughout. But, even at this zoomed-out distance, the spectrogram also starts to make clear some of the particular, differential qualities of the album; the wide frequency spread as compared to other noise walls examined in this chapter, for example, or the unpredictable, stochastic sense of change and crackle encased *within* the (roughly) 0–50Hz and 200–1200Hz ranges of the wall, outside the uniform blob.

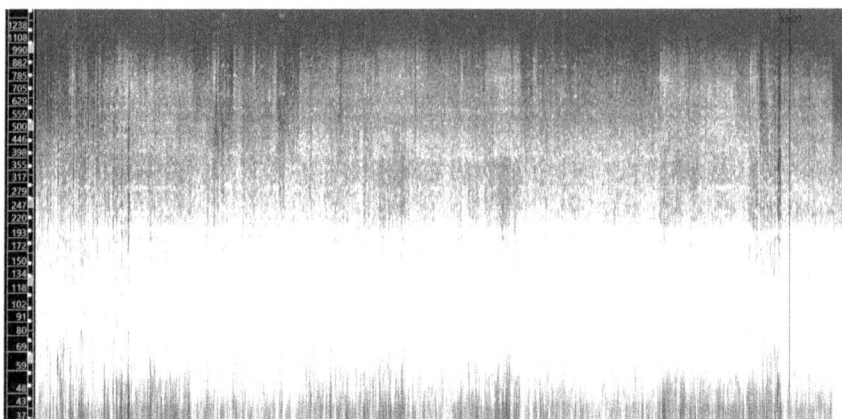

Figure 7.3 Melodic range spectrogram of The Rita's *Thousands of Dead Gods* (2006).

Zooming in to the sound a bit more, we pick up even more on the stochastic sense of change just mentioned. *Contra* the perhaps monolithic feel of the sound at a distance, the rockfalls and rubble slides of these non-blob regions feel relentless and overwhelming when listened to up close. Attuning accordingly, we pick up restless detail and micro-tensions between stasis and movement, surface bubble and fizz and ever-present shifts in the density, weight and colour of the sound. All this opens out a vivid sense of questioning change and tension. To put more flesh on the sonic bones of this point, Figure 7.4 picks out a representative one-minute passage, from 23'40" to 24'40". In that passage, the bubble and fizz is evident in the cracked, rent, broken (or, cracking, rending, breaking) drone hovering around 70–150Hz throughout the excerpt. On the other hand, an example of the album's many (relatively) clear shifts in density and colour appears at 23'56"(as indicated by the arrow), where the previous ten seconds' spatters of distorted crunch in the 150–250Hz range suddenly thin out, leaving a kind of striated pedal point at about 193Hz, all of it gradually, slowly thickening again towards the end of the excerpted minute.

Shifts like this last one are *audible* once you're paying attention. The shift I've chosen to focus on here sounds like a somewhat internalized but nevertheless dynamic textural shift that pulls the ear in to a sense of pulling out and then pushing back in, the latter coming through in a kind of serrated trebly sound that appears at about 24'01" (the striated pedal point mentioned above). *Thousands* is full of such small changes in texture and amplitude; this is especially the case in the (roughly) 220–500Hz range of Figure 7.4, where the envelope of the distorted sounds gives chaotic way to vapour and silence. Many of these changes track with the more general Figure 7.3, moments of fissure in the image matching a sudden thinning or opening in the sound. But others don't: throughout the album, the listener will find themselves hearing all sorts of patterns and shapes that can't be captured by a frequency and amplitude map. For instance, the lower ranges of the churning static drone often, for me, throw up a kind

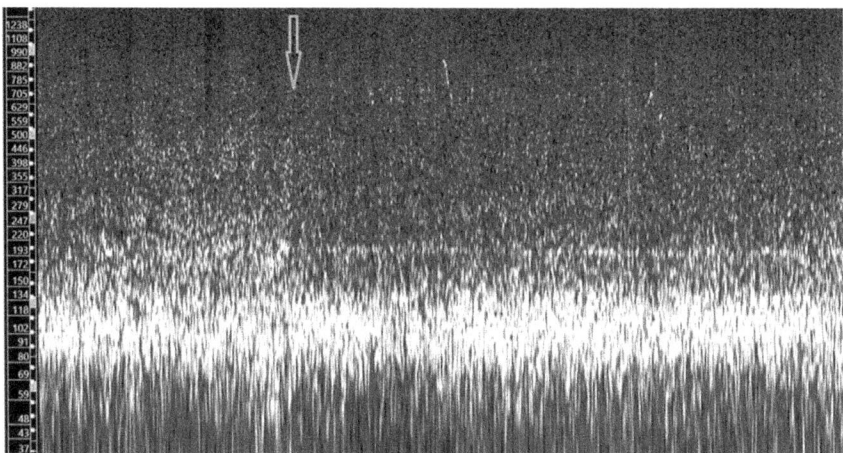

Figure 7.4 Melodic range spectrogram of 23'40" to 24'40" of The Rita's *Thousands of Dead Gods* (2006).

of beating pattern somewhere between an industrial, techno bassline and a drum loop. Meanwhile, the higher-range sounds set up a kind of polyrhythm against that lower drone that feels skittery, almost bouncy. *Thousands* is full of event in this kind of way, musical and psychoacoustic micro-details and tensions suggesting dynamism even as the sound's general surface and contour can appear wall-like and inert from a distance.

All this creates a clear sense of movement throughout the album. But this movement never resolves into a stable pattern, or periodic rhythm, or tonal goal; it is always a motion-to-nowhere, the order it grasps at always suggested or becoming, but forever in abeyance. This is McKinlay's work, and even HNW and harsh noise in general, in microcosm. Thick with detail but also forbiddingly blunt depending on how closely, and how, you listen, the music moves back and forth between monolithic wall heft and, as detail shimmers and shimmies, more mobile, flickering atmosphere we can't help but encode to 'music'. This toggling between wall and atmosphere can be found across all our noise wall examples, though probably more so in OVMN and The Rita than Vomir. Just as it can, too, in many dark ambient and death industrial artists likewise. The next section, accordingly, steps aside from HNW to update the story of death industrial and dark ambient that we heard a little about in looking at earlier artists such as Anenzephalia and Blackhouse in Chapter 3.

Subklinik, Gnawed and dark ambient/death industrial music

Dark ambient and death industrial are two closely related post-industrial musics that were first developed in the 1980s. It is important to consider them in some depth here both because of their aesthetic sympathy with HNW in particular, and also because they represent notable satellite or substyles within noise more generally, significant inflections of the core noise musical spirit and approach and close brethren on the broader fringe scene: the amount of times I've used the latter two terms as adjectives throughout the book is testament to that.

Both dark ambient and death industrial emphasize droning, echoing, spaced-out and dark atmospheric sound. Dark ambient leans more to the atmospheric, ambient end of things than the often percussive, growled music of death industrial; the one is ambient in orientation whilst the other retains many of the markers familiar to us from our discussion of power electronics and industrial music. However, as per the 'atmospheric chambers' of the title, both are based fundamentally on droning, often resonating dissonance and a kind of architectural approach to sound and texture.

There is a lot more to these musics than I have space to go into here. Excluded but vital parts of the story, for example, are labels like Cold Meat Industry, whose head, Roger Karmanik, gave dark ambient its name and, as Brighter Death Now, many of its most interesting albums; earlier composers and artists such as Nocturnal Emissions, Jeff Greinke and Lustmord; and a host of particularly important and/or genre-spanning albums. Of the latter, it's worth citing the seminal 1994 Slaughter Productions compilation *Death Odors*, which is a key reference point for death industrial music of the early-to-mid 1990s (and indeed includes many artists first associated with Cold Meat Industry), as well as Yen Pox's similarly important *Blood Magic* (Malignant Records, 1995). In examining two important albums and artists, nevertheless – the first, the death-industrial-leaning artist Subklinik, closer to the period captured on *Odors*, and the second, dark-ambient-infused death-industrial artist Gnawed, more recent – we'll at least get a sense of the aesthetics of these musics and, through this, a broader sense of noise style more generally.

Subklinik

As a profile written by Per Najbjerg Odderskov has it, Chad Davis' work as Subklinik

> began in early 1995 after suffering a devastating amount of tragedy within his personal life within the span of just a few short months. The isolation of loss had begun to permeate the sounds inside the mind and the exposure to negativity reached an all-time high. Subklinik was born on the basis of therapy – the mutating of thought to sound as a means of understanding the mental changes and challenges within the mind.
>
> (2017)

As stated here, the early impetus for the Subklinik project arose out of personal loss and pain. Though this personal dimension has shifted through time, Subklinik's music has retained a consistent focus on death and suffering. This is reflected in track and album titles (death, decomposition, death and cremation all appear multiple times), sleeve imagery (skulls are a common touchstone) and, above all, the dark sounds and style of his work.

Cremator (Slaughter Productions, 2000), Davis' third full-length release, provides an important early example of his approach. That approach was unrelentingly bleak in terms of theme and sound. It drew together a classically death-industrial set of ideas and images in the track titles (which include 'Decaying Innards', 'Deathchamber' and 'Feasting on Souls', the latter also being the title of Davis' second album) and skeletal sleeve art (a 2020 cassette reissue on Deathbed Productions even included a small vial of ash), with a similarly well-trodden set of death-industrial analogue synthesizer sounds drawn from the Roland Juno-106. The latter sounds include slow, skulking low bass tones, whirring higher tones and insistent (though usually muffled) rhythmic patterns, all of it spaced out carefully in time and acoustic space. A clear melody, or beat, or sense of forward motion is almost always absent from Subklinik's work at this time, replaced instead by a penumbra of atmosphere and intensity to which the ear naturally but perhaps sightly fearfully inclines.

The first track on *Cremator*, the 6'50" 'Dementia', keys us into this aesthetic directly. 'Dementia' starts out with a bare, fast-beating synth dyad, like tapping on wood sped up to 1000BPM, which fades in slowly over the first forty seconds or so. Small glitches in the sound over the next thirty seconds prepare the ear for further build and change, which comes with the addition of low, resonant drum thwacks from 1'11" on. These two sounds get subtly but gradually louder, as an intimidating but indistinct dark atmospheric sound (probably a very low-register synth pad) consumes the centre-right of the picture across the third, fourth and fifth minutes. An apostrophizing upward dial of the original dyadic sound gets more active from about 4'56" on, the track reaching something of a (shadowy, murky) climax for about forty-five seconds, before the final seventy seconds of this 6'50" track gradually taper into an echoing abyss. 'Dementia' provides a salutary lesson in constructing a dungeon-like sonic atmosphere – the build of dyad and drum is based on a clear sense of space between the sounds, just as the synth pad evokes a surrounding, atmospheric hum and clank – that yet has movement and flow to it.

Later tracks stick within this moonlit world of low drones and spacey textures. 'Mortuor lesson', for example, provides a hypnotic listen in this vein. A slowly insistent, low-bass-tone gesture (composed of two soft strikes and two beats rest) repeats almost throughout the near-ten-minute track. Various low pads – first, humming and sub-bass-like towards the left of the picture, and later, slightly more gesturally distinct and mid-range; though the precise nature of the sound is hard to pinpoint until we get to a quietly whirring pattern from the fourth minute on – circle around that gesture. That whirring pattern revolves and evolves gently from the fourth to the ninth minutes, occasionally expanding out to an almost *fp* dynamic, but mostly advancing and receding softly like waves on some dead moonlight shore. This central passage of the track creates a cavernous feel out of very minimal elements: low repeated bass tones (always with two beats on and two beats off – the evocative space and silence of the track in microcosm), background humming and soft ramblings through crepuscular surface event. The final ninety or so seconds, following a minor climax with a kind of 'landing' gesture at 8'18", gradually ebb into shadow. Other tracks work in similar ways. 'Cremator' offsets invasive sub-bass and low-register presence with intermittent clicks and jangles. Similarly, in closer 'Decaying Innards' we hear an almost on-the-nose quiet spook and spackle in the humming sub-bass and growingly pronounced surface whirr and modulations of the first six minutes of the track's 10'58", which ends with almost four minutes of silence before a 60–70 seconds coda of distant, thudding bass drum sounds. Once again, atmospheric, ever-moving and creeping opacity is evoked here through a clever use of low-register sound, acoustic and production space and contrasts between drawn-out tones and busier, briefer gestures.

In all these tracks, Davis exploits two key qualities in creating high-calibre death-industrial sound: space/time and relative quiet or silence. On the first count, the nature and number of the elements used to build each track are critical. Large, long, dark, resonant drones and similar gestures create a sense of shadowy slowed-time and extended space in themselves. Piling up too many of these, or adding too many other elements, would detract from that sense of slow extension and muddy up the sonic colour and scope. And so, Davis restricts each track to only a handful of such elements, in this way creating a sense of evolving, architectural composition, as the listeners move about an acoustic environment of shadows and whispers. Relatedly, and on the second count, Davis uses quiet and silence to refocus how we hear the work. Listeners' attention is attuned and retuned through the music's almost total insistence on quiet, hushed gestures (volume and inflection in sympathy with the dark tones and sounds favoured on the album). Here, what might float by as nothing in other, more eventful or louder music – a whirring crackle or a quiet oscillating tone evolving into something more rhythmic and distinct before receding back again – assumes centre stage, our attention pulled into the flow of micro-event and murky sonic shadow, mini-dialectics of becoming playing out on the music's surface and its depths likewise. As I said earlier in this chapter, this is one of art's great powers: it can reorder our sense of the world's scale, of time's contour, such that our being contracts and adapts along with the sounds of the music. That is one of the key contributions of both death industrial/dark ambient and harsh noise wall: a sense that normal 'musical' rates of change are norms not laws, suggestions rather than obligations. The code of music can contract and expand.

Gnawed

Grant Richardson takes a similar approach to space and scale in his work as Gnawed, a death industrial/power electronics project that began in 2009. I described Gnawed as 'dark-ambient infused' earlier, and indeed sepulchral, drawn-out atmospheric sound tends to dominate Gnawed's approach. On that note, although an earlier album such as *Terminal Epoch* (Phage Tapes, 2012) foregrounds power-electronics vocals and aggressive, churning feedback (and these elements are often likewise to the fore in Gnawed live shows), even there the template of darkly coloured loops and drones from later albums, such as *Pestilence Beholden* (Malignant Records, 2016), was already largely in place.

2020's *Subterranean Rites* (Cloister Recordings) very much works within that death industrial but dark-ambient-infused atmospheric space. Quite literally so, since, as

Noise Walls and Atmospheric Chambers 163

outlined on the sleeve, the album is based on sounds and voices 'recorded in various sewers, concrete vaults, and tunnels systems' between 2017 and 2019. These sounds were subject to the usual manipulations via effects rack and synths. Richard Stevenson of *Noise Receptor* sums up the album's aesthetic, highlighting the atmospheric evocations of sustained drones, thudding beats and distorted vocals:

> With [the] chosen methods and locations of recording, a real sense of forbidding atmosphere has been generated and has been completely infused within the recorded sonics … Ultimately it is a case where thick and grimly echoed catacombic atmospheres abound, as other sustained synths drones, muted sub-orchestral tones, and weighty thudding 'beats' provide structure. The vocals, when sporadically used, are duly smeared with distortion and rendered mostly as an additional sonic element. The further addition of controlled raw scrap metal sounds gives significant sonic detailing and provides the material in a dank and decaying 'real-world' aesthetic (as opposed to the 'cleanliness' of computer program creations).
>
> (2020b)

Spread across six tracks ranging in length from 6'53" to 9'14" and uniformly slow and stretched in profile and black in colour, *Subterranean Rites* does often evoke the 'catacombic' atmosphere mentioned by Stevenson. Literally and metaphorically, this is dungeon-crawl music filled with menacing, terrible sonic phantoms and monsters.

Subterranean Rites skulks around slowly but with portent, then, using a contrast between roomy, echoing low and long sounds and busier passing sounds to suggest action and tension. To wit, harshly distorted vocals and thickening, often higher-end-inflected textures and gestures on tracks such as 'Vivisepultre (In Rubble and Spoil)' and 'By Ropes Abseil' add a more forthright, goblin-Whitehouse vibe to the resonant thuds, low drones and watery tinkling that serve as background resonating chamber throughout much of the album. This sort of contrast between slowly unspooling low-end ground and busier, higher-range figures agitating on the surface creates productive tension on every track, the black stillness of the sound constantly being pushed into a kind of hysteria, the inner subject of the music forcing confrontation with whatever power is holding it in place. Other subtle musical details across different tracks add to that unspooling tension and sense of quiet, portentous becoming. For example, the shifting plateaus of the drone on 'Subfuerat', where the main tone slides down a major third and back up again (microtonal shades are sometimes brought out in the phasing of the swoop), in a seemingly irregular pattern, offer a subtly shifting anchor point around which the rest of the swirling, chiming track floats. In the same vein, the slow expansion from one to three hits of the grounding percussive loop of 'Subterranean Rites', as the rest of the texture thickens with leviathan growls and loose lunges of abstracted distortion, lends the track a kind of massive and ancient shipwreck energy. Finally, the unadorned, straightforwardly rainy, drippy sounds that backdrop 'Through Sunken Stone' contrast with the more obviously synthetic pads and drones that take up much of the centre of this comparatively stripped-back, even ambient track. The album has a kind of musical formula, then, such that long and low sounds create atmospheres whose depths are set in relief through various surface sounds. But the album is refined and subtle in how it realizes that formula.

Subterranean Rites, in sum, emphasizes dark, resonant, often thudding or watery sounds. It uses drones and other drawn-out sounds to build a sense of space. The slow, sustained profile and the low-end colour of these sounds create a kind of time-bending breadth and enlarging weight in which the listener can disappear. The barrier between listener and listening thus blurs here as it does in the best ambient music. Meanwhile, busier, more gesturally distinct surface crackle and noise are added to these droning sounds to create tension and movement within the music's huge, shadowy, atmospheric chambers. Gnawed's aesthetic, as sketched briefly here, is little different from previous dark-ambient or death-industrial artists in these respects. Even though, like Gnawed with his power-electronics growl and noisy churn, death-ambient artists such as Lustmord and Brighter Death Now have their own sonic touchstones and idiosyncrasies, the overall approach and effect of their music is strikingly similar. The sound changes but the song remains the same. And yet, the sounds and sonic spaces of dark ambient and death industrial are so rich, so mysterious, so full of dark journeys and movement, that the shared aesthetic yields much variety, irresolution and change.

Conclusion

Considering dark ambient and death industrial alongside HNW has proved instructive. All of these musics reframe listeners' sense of scale and space/time. On the first count, they slow down normal musical rates of change and rescale musical events; the smallest change or gesture now appears huge and dramatic, whilst the scale of musical becoming that is so important to noise is multi-levelled in a new way, apparent both in tiny gestures and in larger contrasts between such gestures and the resonating chamber of the backdrop. On the second count, they use drawn-out sounds of different kinds – stochastically repeating, monolithically configured static and crunch or wet and warm low-end drones and pads – to create an affective experience of architectural and re-shaped space-time, a sonic environment in which listeners immerse and, perhaps, lose themselves. In this latter respect, the wall/atmosphere dialectic I referenced earlier is important. All these musics evoke immersive space with boundaries and atmospheric pressure but they configure this space differently, HNW toggling more to harshness and pushing, death industrial/dark ambient to sepulchral haziness and pulling. Through all this, these musics approach a kind of limit case of perception for the listener, time and space dilated to the point of transcendence or explosion. The (musical, personal) self almost blurs into the slow, spacious sonic objects themselves as close listeners lose their grip on normal time and enter the immersive spaces of the sound, their consciousness and felt experience altering and attuning to the beating alterity of the music.

Of course, as ever, it's possible to hear these musics at a distance, without going as far as I've just gone. Or simply to read them in terms of formal musical qualities. And yet, those formal musical qualities – the stretched and the extreme or dark nature of the sound – very easily slip into symbolism and even affect, as listeners struggle for some cognitive and, finally, subjective mooring in the immersive walls and atmospheric spaces of the music. Such immersion, such blurring of listening self and overwhelming noise sound and idea, is a central theme in our next chapter, which focuses on noise erotics.

8

Noise erotics: Traumatic bodies and desires

In autumn 2013, Margaret Chardiet – noise/power electronics artist Pharmakon – had surgery to remove a benign cyst that had grown so large that it had almost caused organ failure. The experience was such an intense one for Chardiet that she based much of her next album, *Bestial Burden* (Sacred Bones Records, 2014), on it:

> The record is about the disconnect between mind and body, and when I was bedridden for three weeks after my surgery, my mind was in Europe, on tour, doing my music, because that's where I was supposed to be. It took a while for my brain to catch up to the reality of what my body was doing. It created this separation between the two that resulted in me feeling almost as though the body had this separate will from my own – just this vessel I was stuck inside of.
>
> (Cited in Stosuy 2014)

Bestial Burden therefore attempts to evoke claustrophobic body horror and estrangement: the self in pitched battle with the body. From the hyper-ventilating fast breaths of opener 'Vacuum' to the abject screams of 'Body Betrays Itself'; from the power-electronics-vitriol of 'Autoimmune' to the wheezing and coughing of 'Primitive Struggle'; not to mention the stark, death-industrial thwacks, clangs and buzzing feedback found across the album, *Bestial Burden* is sonically run through with Chardiet's (dis)embodied experiences. But it's not just the sounds that anchor and evoke the bodily theme. Equally important are the album's cover, a set of organs overlaid on Chardiet's naked body; the album and track titles; and the narrative of body horror put forward by Chardiet in interviews like the one quoted above. Even if the coruscating sounds of the album play a key role in its effect (and affect), then, the partner role of visual imagery and words is clear. *Bestial Burden* is bodies all the way down. (We'll return to Chardiet and Pharmakon in our final chapter.)

Many other noise artists confront the traumatic (and often grotesque or abject) body – the body as a site of trauma, trauma as a site of the body – in similarly panoramic, often erotically charged ways. Hegarty indeed compares the 'retching' on *Bestial Burden* to similarly charged, though different inflected, retching in Puce Mary's 'The Viewer' (2020, 115–16), from 2014's *Persona* (Posh Isolation). These confrontations are erotic, that is, not just in terms of sexuality and desire in their everyday senses but in the more expansive tradition of de Sade and Georges Bataille. For de Sade, the 'erotic' is about risk, otherness, violence and even depersonalization, the latter both in the sense of desire for 'objects' human and inhuman and in the sense of an erotic, 'plural' body that escapes, in Gaëtan Brulotte's words, the 'imperial supremacy of the self' in emphasizing the hungry, animal body as opposed to the supreme, 'civilized', intellectual self (2000, 52–4). The importance to noise of this liberated, desiring body is emphasized by Guesde and Nadrigny, as I began to note in Chapter 4: 'Far from being the simple physical support of a mind that exercises itself best when it disregards its physical sensations, the body becomes itself a true organ of evaluation' (2018, 71). For his part, extending this point, Bataille very much built on de Sade in framing the erotic as a violent, death-lensed violation of norms and emotional boundaries and even as a potential arena in which transcendence or annihilation of one's intellectual self-concept would be possible (Land 1992; more on this in '**Trauma, disease, and the body**').

Like Chardiet, other noise artists stage complex plays of Bataillean erotic anguish in which body-centred trauma, abuse or disease are confronted and perhaps discharged. In such cases, the erotic, overwhelming charge of noise *sound* is a potent partner and setting for topics concerned with a similarly erotic, overwhelming charge; noise form and content align beautifully in such cases. Again, Guesde and Nadrigny make a connection between noise form – its volume, its overwhelm, its unpredictability – and erotic affect here, emphasizing the point that 'the immersed body' particular to noise listeners no longer sees music 'as a delimited object but as a medium'; rather than being a container for the music, this immersed noise body is actually 'included in it' (2018, 72). In its overwhelming affect, its super-rational and self-transcendent sonic excess, then, noise is inherently erotic. As we'll see throughout the chapter, when this quality is alloyed to extreme, traumatic themes and imagery, powerful moments of catharsis and immersion can arise.

The chapter therefore uses the lens of noise erotics to explore noise artists' confrontations with bodily trauma and the self. The first section provides establishing context on the relationship between music, trauma and affect. The second and third group a series of case studies into two broad and to some extent overlapping categories – sex and death; and trauma, disease and the body – using key artists and albums to explore noise musicians' engagement with such themes. The chapter covers some ground that will be familiar from previous chapters but moves the story of noise erotics forward to the twenty-first century (with the exception of one album) and outward to different artists and styles.

Music, trauma and 'affect'

It's long been acknowledged that music can play a powerful role in helping to heal trauma and disease. Popular psychological books and films tell miraculous stories of dementia patients suddenly 'waking up' upon hearing a familiar piece of music. Scholars have likewise described ways in which forms of creative expression such as music can support healing and resolution of trauma (Johnson 1987; Baleav 2018). Such scholarly studies similarly emphasize the healing power of music in returning patients to themselves by fostering connections and processing traumatic experiences:

> Music can play a role in helping individuals and communities to cope with trauma ... Here we recognize that the perception of a net loss of resources accompanying a traumatic event (objects, personal characteristics, conditions, or energies which have value to us) engender the destabilizing and overwhelming 'black hole of trauma'. This sense of loss needs to be offset by other resources.
> (Garrido et al. 2015)

Outside of strictly therapeutic contexts, many people draw support and solace from music. Sound, often noise, is especially comforting to young babies, for example, mimicking cosy experiences in the womb: 'Terrified babies, stuck in fight-or-flight mode, attach to these familiar noises and slowly calm themselves down' (Greene 2017). But it's not only babies that retain such a primal association between noise or sound and their own wellbeing. Sounds experienced in early traumatic experiences lodge in our limbic system; the focus of music therapy is often on bringing such experiences to the surface by recreating early sensations in a safe, clinical context, where they can be properly processed and integrated.

Coming more directly to the sort of territory explored by the artists in this chapter, Patricia Clough has reflected in this spirit on how writing about, meditating on, and reliving the sound, the vibrations, of her mother's screams – formerly emblems of traumatic early experiences – can shift and transform trauma. In this process, trauma is encountered as a bloc of energy (echoing Deleuze and Guittari's description of art works as 'blocs of sensations'), to which remembered and relived sonic vibrations give access. In re-listening to and processing those sounds anew, Clough can dissociate from their traumatic origins and, in turn, discharge traumatic energy; 'there might well be a shift in the thought of trauma too, from its being conceived as a blocked unconscious repetition to its being engaged as a bloc of energy matter through which a vibrational force forces a new path, allows for a swerve, a difference in rhythm' (2013, 69). Clough's discussion of screaming as both a source of, and potential release from, trauma is especially apposite here given the scream's centrality in noise music (as seen in the Pharmakon example). Picking up on the affective power of the scream and getting us even closer to the way noise often functions for listeners, Marie Thompson has described the scream as 'an exemplary mode of affective communication' (2013, 147). The scream is, in this sense, equal parts 'affection', in its capture and evocation of physical pain or pleasure; 'affective', in how it transforms receivers; and 'affect', as something that exists within but also beyond the sonorous object, an impersonal 'compound of affects' that is 'entwined with – but also distinct from – the affections of expressing and affected bodies' (158).

Like other forms of sonically unpredictable and invasive noise, then, from feedback to scraping or static, screams impact us intensely whilst also containing a great deal of intensive, even metaphysical energy within themselves. Put simply, screams and other noisy sounds are unsettling and powerful; they destabilize us, put us off our game, throw us into uncertainty as we anxiously scramble for familiar emotional or sonic reference points. This can have a negative impact on listeners. But, as well as offering a simple aesthetic pleasure, it can also be a source of aesthetic or psychological release: a way for musicians and listeners to confront difficult experiences or feelings in a safe, controlled context. Creative expression that thematically and musically explores difficult, traumatic experiences or repressed desires through extreme, unsettling sound can in this sense restage and release the anxiety, anger, rage and shame that is invariably wrapped up in those experiences and desires. Dave Philips, picking up on this notion of release through noise, notes how 'powerful' it is 'to put experiences into a body of work', and then, with the release of that work, 'you release all the demons associated with it'; 'it helps you to process, it helps you to heal, it helps you to move on' (Connelly et al. 2022).

Sex and death

In essence, the domain of eroticism is the domain of violence, of violation.

(Bataille 1984, 16)

'Keep going,' I said, and leaned back, offering it all. 'Grab it.' I can't make sense of what I felt. The force and torque, of pain gathered toward a breaking point, a sensation I never imagined was a part of sex. Because submission, I soon learned, was also a kind of power ... To arrive at love, then, is to arrive through obliteration. Eviscerate me, we mean to say, and I'll tell you the truth. Fuck. Me. Up. It felt good to name what was already happening to me all my life. I was being fucked up, at last, by choice.

(Vuong 2019)

There is a lot of sex in noise music. Whether in terms of titles, subject matter, imagery, reference points, sounds or whatever, sex and pornography – often infused with death and violence – are common themes across the genre; look at acts like Contagious Orgasm or series such as Masami Akita's ZSF Produkt *Sexorama* compilations (1984–6). It isn't hard to see why sex has been such a go-to in noise, given the genre's close relationship with transgression and extreme, outré subject matter. Probably in some cases the use of sex and pornography as subject matter therefore arises out of genre habit more than anything else. In other cases, artists drawing on extreme sexual themes may well not have any traumatic relationship to the material. And yet, in many other cases still, noise musicians have deliberately used themes of sex, sexual abuse, pornography, sadism and more to explore trauma and/or extreme states of mind. We'll look at two notable examples of this: Atrax Morgue and Himukalt. We'll return, briefly, to this theme of trauma and abuse in our discussion of Lingua Ignota in Chapter 9.

Atrax Morgue

Atrax Morgue was the alias of Italian noise and power electronics artist and label head, Marco Corbelli. Corbelli was active under the Atrax Morgue name, amongst others, from 1993 until his suicide in 2007. Corbelli released an array of albums on his label Slaughter Productions, which also released notable compilations such as the aforementioned *Death Odors* (1994), and artists such as Subklinik, Taint and Con-Dom. Most of Corbelli's work as Atrax Morgue was themed around sex and death. Album titles such as *In Search of Death* (1993), *Woundfucker* (1994), *Esthetik of a Corpse* (1995), *Cut My Throat* (1996) and *Death-Orgasm Connector* (2003) point to an obsessive focus on sex, sadism and death (all these albums were released on Slaughter). I'll discuss two Atrax Morgue records in more detail – the first reaching back to the 1990s – to give a sense of how this focus plays out in the music.

Corbelli's second album, *Black Slaughter*, was released in a run of thirty-six tapes on Slaughter in 1993. As described in the original insert, Corbelli aimed with this album to 'create sounds associated with a diseased brain, a murderess, a person who has abnormal behavior towards society'. Primarily based on Corbelli's ever-present line-up of analogue synth (a Sequential Circuits Six-Trak), mixer and vocal samples (Corbelli's processed vocals, normally a key touchstone, are absent), the album is indeed heavily themed around death, abuse, serial killers and murder. For example, a sampled Ted Bundy interview is the basis of 'The Mind of a Killer', whilst, as we'll see in more detail below, 'Necrosadism' features lurid descriptions of violent, murderous acts. In a similar vein, 'In Dahmer's Apartment' is inspired by Jeffrey Dahmer. The music on the album is very much in the mould of Corbelli's typically harsh but minimal and drawn-out, death-industrial/power-electronics style. Slowly oscillating, distorted low drones and delicate, atmospheric textural noise appear throughout either as backdrop ('Mind of a Killer') or on centre stage ('Nekroskopik Examination', 'Death for Company'). Structures are almost exclusively repetitive and drone-based, the mix is careful and essentially smooth and the textures are continuous and steady. If it weren't for the titles and the potentially offensive subject matter of the sampled interviews, in fact, the album would provide something of a relaxing – albeit grimy – listen, the usual dialectical tension and intensity of noise flipped into something less confrontational, more enigmatic. Even something like the swirling, flanging screams and scrapes of 'In Dahmer's Apartment' are mixed low and distant, as if heard through a gauze. The music is therefore not *itself* somehow sadistic or sexual; it may be erotic, but its full potential in that arena is unlocked by the themes. And yet, when aligned with the subject matter and narratives presented across the album the sounds take on an unsettling pallor, marshalled into creepy service as willing handmaidens to Corbelli's theatrically murderous obsessions. Strong lyrical and vocal themes of this sort don't have to work very hard to assimilate musical sound to their overriding messages.

The track 'Necrosadism' is an excellent illustration of this marrying of dirty, enigmatic, but gentle sounds with truly horrifying themes. 'Necrosadism' is based on two interviews excerpted from the M. Dixon Causey-directed 1987 Mondo film *True Gore*; the first with a woman with violent dreams and fantasies, often about corpses, and the second with a man who had tortured and murdered women, often mutilating their corpses, before being locked up. These two interviews are played in full across the almost eight-minute track, one after the other. The title itself is therefore a fitting one: defined broadly as the desire to murder someone to have sex with their corpse, it refers more generally to a tendency to derive pleasure from inflicting harm on corpses.

Already disturbing and upsetting, the interviews become only more so when staged within the music. A spray of room static opens things up at the start, giving way to the woman's voice somewhat casually intoning, 'I should like to torture people, even after they are dead.' This line reappears later in that same interview (and track), as a bookend to a series of brutal, horrifying fantasies based around transgressive sex, bestiality, cruelty and death. The second half of the track is more disturbing still, the male interviewee graphically describing his infliction of torture and necrosadism on various unnamed victims. The music scores this dreadful history, with the voices grounded in a sustained, droning sound: a throbbing, low oscillation that's clean and warm on the right of the stereo picture and slightly phased and flanged on the left. The only other sounds we hear on the track are some higher range sine waves and harmonics, which puncture the gory imagery with emphasis and detail at various points. (This contrast between elongated, droning noise sounds and more intermittent, higher-range gestures is a tactic found across Corbelli's work.) For example, some soft, swelling electronic tones in the centre of the picture pierce through around the five-minute mark, as the man describes a particularly graphic act of sadism. Other, more distant high pitches bring out different textural shades in the final minute. Echoing similar juxtapositions of synth pads and tones with disturbing, abusive, murderous content in Whitehouse and Throbbing Gristle, 'Necrosadism' nevertheless represents a style and a voice all Corbelli's own, with its intense, unfiltered and yet sonically moderate and even relatively conventional working through of such appallingly extreme imagery and experiences.

Corbelli's 2000 album, *Paranoia* (Old Europa Café), addresses sado-masochistic sexual themes even more explicitly and consistently than *Black Slaughter* had. It does so by placing Corbelli himself – or, at least, his performing persona – front and centre. Corbelli's distorted, scowling vocals skulk menacingly across tracks like 'Sperm on Red Plastic', 'Plastic Baby, Pleasure Toy', 'Leave Me Alone' and 'Perfect Kill (Your Beauty Is Your Condemnation)', adding noise and growl to the sound. 'Miss Self-Destruct' takes this approach even further, almost totally annihilating words and melody as Corbelli's voice becomes scratchy, distorted noise and feedback; twisted verbal desires made sonic flesh. Meanwhile, the lyrics of these and other tracks fixate on characteristic erotic themes and imagery, on the loss of self amidst consuming, overwhelming desire. This foregrounding of Corbelli's voice, yearning with pain, lust and drive, and the lyrical voicing of what would normally be private desires, fills the album with a sense of extreme diaristic confession.

The musical voice of *Paranoia* is even more refined, more concentrated, than that of *Black Slaughter*. Musical backdrops and textures are pared down to bare minimum, the sonics serving as stark settings for the vocals' unvarnished erotic id. To wit, on 'Leave Me Alone' a held high tone and quiet static beating below it give way periodically to aggressive shards of feedback, as Corbelli begs to be left alone due to being 'disturbed'. 'Sperm on Red Plastic' features Corbelli's heavily compressed, distorted voice prowling around and spitting out different versions of the title. A low, droning electrical hum plays throughout that track (as a similar one does on the aforementioned 'Miss Self-Destruct'), whilst piercing single tones, sometimes on an implied tonic, sometimes a semitone above and sometimes a dominant seventh below, interject noisily after each line reading. By contrast, an unsettling, held high telephone tone (modulated here and there) and particularly aggressive overloaded vocals fill 'Plastic Baby, Pleasure Toy' with a fizzy, shaking density. Finally, 'High Heels inside My Throat' presents desperate, gurning invitations from a goblin, Gollum Corbelli for an unnamed person to 'pusssh down, your high heels inside my throatttt', as he 'licks your heels like ice cream'. This is all as a mid-range hum phases and oscillates throughout (occasionally producing acoustic beating as it modulates).

This quick-fire selection of tracks from across *Paranoia* gives a picture of the thematic concerns and affective space that dominate the album. In most cases, these themes and affects are constructed using abrasive but minimal sounds and unloosed, distorted vocals; as noted, the focus here is less the broiling sonic becoming of harsh noise and other forms and more a kind of twisted, creeping sonic annihilation or abjection realized in the interstices of distortion and buried desires. Though I don't have the space to cover any of Corbelli's other albums in detail, it's worth pointing out that, like *Black Slaughter* and *Paranoia*, they tend to share a similar concentration on somewhat rudimentary but extreme musical material and an obsession with sadomasochistic, death-filled subject matter. In describing a couple of key Corbelli tracks, Drew Daniel indeed gets at the broader, characteristic musical flavour and affective atmosphere of Atrax Morgue:

> Using synthesizers to generate audio icepicks of piercing ultra-high-pitched tones, Atrax Morgue cuts such as 'Nerveshatter 2' [on *L'Ame Electrique Presents Old Europa Café*, L'Ame Electrique, 2002] work the upper reaches of the frequency spectrum in order to deliberately induce pain and distress, while on 'Brainshock' [on *Comptrax Morgue*, Slaughter Productions, 2006] overdriven signal chains sand midrange textural details down into a powdery ash of noise.
>
> (2020)

Reflecting on both my own analytical descriptions and Daniel's points, an obvious way to think about and interpret Corbelli's music is to draw on Bataille, whose work on transgression and, in particular, his image of eroticism-as-death has clear parallels with Corbelli's obsessive fixation on sex and/as death. The most immediate connection between the two can be seen in Bataille texts such as *La pratique de la joie devant la mort* (1986 [1939]) and *L'Erotisme* (1957; subtitled 'Death and Sensuality' in English – see 1984), where eroticism, calling back to the points earlier, is described as an experience in which our sense of a fixed, independent self is transcended. For Bataille, we lose, or perhaps destroy ourselves when we fully enter the erotic space, which is defined by violence and war, boundary-breaking and transgression. As Bataille notes in the first of the six short pieces that make up *La pratique*, 'I abandon myself to peace, to the point of annihilation.' And, in the sixth: 'I imagine myself covered with blood, broken but transfigured and in agreement with the world, both as prey and as a jaw of time which ceaselessly kills and is ceaselessly killed.'

It's not hard to find a similar yearning for transcendence and annihilation or abjection in Corbelli's work. Track after track, album after album, Corbelli fixates on death as release, and sex and erotic fetish as paths to that release. This is both on the level of explicit verbal messaging and on the more indirect level of affective sound, where droning noise atmospheres and cyborg vocals seem to unsettle individual boundaries – both Corbelli's and, if listened to intently, perhaps even listeners' – in their overwhelming insistence and intensity. This kind of effect is perhaps most obvious in tracks like 'High Heels inside My Throat', where the vocal persona seems to shiver hellishly but ecstatically as it role-plays itself into oblivion. It's also present in a more *affective* sense across much of the music discussed above, as for example in the subsumption of Corbelli's voice into noise on 'Miss Self-Destruct', or the intimate considerations of death and torture on 'Necrosadism'. Corbelli's music could be seen in this sense to unleash the same erotic id pointed to in the two quotes that open the section, where violence and violation serve as tools to escape the ego and attain some kind of self-loss and inner release; ecstatic experience defined or attained more through Con-Dom-like abjection than through anything like Ehrenreich's collective joy.

And yet, that kind of transcendent reading notwithstanding, Corbelli's choice of subjects and imagery are not always the easiest to defend. As with Macronympha and other noise artists, defenders of artists' right to confront and play with these murderous, violent ideas must also reckon with the potential damage such choices might have for listeners. In this sort of spirit, as with Bataille it would be easy enough to read Corbelli not in terms of radical transgression but rather in terms of conservative patriarchy. This kind of reading is based in the simple observation that Bataille and Corbelli's work can be seen as merely re-presenting the hierarchical sexual status quo, albeit in more extreme form, where familiar tropes of misogyny and violence (largely) against women are introduced perhaps without challenge. Lisa Downing and Robert Gillett indeed offer precisely this kind of reading of Bataille: 'the whole of his system, including his classifications, his oppositions, his epistemologies and his pornography is bound up with a view of women that, far from being transgressive, is urgently in need of transgression' (2011, 95). Going further down this line, in fact, Kai Heron has suggested that, seen through a Lacanian lens, the pervert (in the sense of someone who violates laws and norms à la Corbelli here) can be seen as a 'paradoxically conservative figure'. Heron argues that 'the pervert's incessant staging of transgressive practices is not the expression of uninhibited *jouissance* (or enjoyment) but of the desire to set limits to their *jouissance* by bringing the law into being'. Heron goes on, 'For Lacan, while it is true that the pervert transgresses social norms, this is not because they are operating beyond the law but because they desire their full integration *into* the law' (2020, 15–16). Corbelli's dangerous desires, in this sense, would simply be a desire for Daddy's desires.

However, three key factors support a different reading of Corbelli's work to the conservative-patriarchal one; and indeed to any other, more condemnatory reading we might put forward. For starters, Corbelli's sheer obscurity suggests that any argument against his music on the basis that it may negatively impact or trigger listeners by giving a platform to murderers and abusers seems like something of a non-starter: it is highly unlikely that anyone not explicitly looking for and therefore aware of the likely content of Corbelli's music would come across it in the first place. Secondly, it's important to acknowledge the extent to which Corbelli so resolutely objectifies himself, so frequently places his 'self' on the line in his music either through the assumption of a 'sub' position in his song-fantasies or by exploring ideas and experiences of self-annihilation and transcendence by subsuming his voice into noise and terrible ecstasy. In the piece quoted from above, Drew Daniel indeed offsets the prevalence of violent fantasies inflicted on others in Corbelli's music with the equivalent prevalence of violent fantasies directed at himself: 'The polarity of force in which Corbelli imagines attacking others is evoked often in the work, but its counterforce is a continuous thread of descriptions of himself as an object to be destroyed, brutalized, degraded, killed' (2020). Given this self-objectification and given the mix of 'sub' and 'Dom' points of view we can find in Corbelli's music, I would suggest that any critique of his work as patriarchal or misogynistic leaves important counterevidence out of the equation. It may also veer into kink shaming, given the work's status as fantasy and as art, not as political statement or criminal act. This line of critique may indeed therefore take on a conservative and puritanical moral stance of its own. Finally, and perhaps most notably for us, the music's *sound* complicated any criticism that would pin a clear political viewpoint on to it. That is, Corbelli's conjuring of quietly overwhelming, even self-transcending affect through piercing high tones, bare but bristling textures, distorted vocals, throbbing hums and unpredictable patterns of feedback and static, renders the music affective – likely to produce vivid emotional reactions of one sort or another – before it's anything else. This places the music, for all its disturbing imagery and creepy, distressing sound, into a space of aesthetic and political complexity where a case for condemnation or cancellation may not be clear cut.

Himukalt

Himukalt is Ester Kärkkäinen, a Nevada-based musician and visual artist active since 2016. Like Corbelli, Kärkkäinen explores extreme, sometimes sexual and/or traumatic themes in her work (Himukalt's name, fittingly, translates as 'lustfully' from the Estonian). Himukalt's music is filled with various forms of real and symbolic violence and sex, though it also betrays a sense of anxiety and claustrophobia that is all Kärkkäinen's own. Kärkkäinen herself describes the project in terms of a 'replication and reproduction of the body through sound via desire, lust, hostility, rage, mania, depression, blood, flesh' (2021a). This point, though not exhaustive of the themes and ideas in Himukalt's work, is borne out across various aspects of that work. For starters, album covers and other Himukalt images on Tumblr and Instagram are usually black and white, grimy, multi-Xeroxed images of the female body. Track titles are in the same vein, as can be seen in tracks like 'Want You to See Me (The Voyeur Tapes #10)', 'I'm Afraid', 'The Gun in Her Mouth' and 'The Drive to Oblivion' (the first two from 2018's *Knife through the Spine* and the second two from 2020's *Septic*, both Malignant Records). Meanwhile, the sound of these and other tracks likewise trucks in the dark and the dank. As with Corbelli, Kärkkäinen makes music that sits broadly within the power-electronics, death-industrial template of throbbing synths, crackling textures, cutting high tones and distorted, flanged, confrontational vocals. In terms of the last of these elements, it's clear that language is important in Himukalt's music even as it is often torn or cut up, subsumed into noise, indistinct. In writing about both the sounds and imagery on Kärkkäinen's tapes, Jack Chuter has indeed pointed to 'the mechanistic grind and distortion that obfuscates her voice, the blurs and smears that drench her multi-xeroxed self-portraits' (2017).

As can be seen, Kärkkäinen's work is shot through with themes of sonic, verbal and visual abjection and eroticism. But the two albums that are most pertinent to this are probably *Sex Worker* (Total Black, 2019) and *Sex Worker II* (Total Black, 2020). As described by Kärkkäinen, these albums are 'homage[s] to sex workers around the globe' (2021b). Each is based at least in part on interviews with sex workers: Kärkkäinen thanks seven different women in the case of *Sex Worker II*, for example, for being willing to lend their 'voices, stories, and presence' to the album (2021b). The interviews with these women are embedded into bristling, industrial noise landscapes across both albums.

Sex Worker is composed of five tracks that run between five and nine minutes each, and three shorter interludes each about a minute long. The album is by turns coruscating and claustrophobic. The remarkable opening track, 'Puncture Punishment', contrasts tearing, unwieldy phrases of punching power-saw noise with silence, or exhalation, or sexual noises, or angry declamation, over a propulsive seven minutes. The track, in this contrast of noise with interjecting not-noise, plays out as a series of gnawing, sawing noise-sentences punctuated by moments of repose, almost as if we're hearing a person aggressively shouting or grunting, pausing for breath and then kicking off again. Interlude 1 follows this opener. It is shorter and more concentrated, a fuzzy, sustained, static tone backing up a matter-of-fact description of how a woman got into sex work.

Later tracks are sometimes less forthright than these opening salvos, though sonic and affective intensity is always high in one way or another. 'Nothing but Contempt for Her' creates internal pressure via distant synth loops, interpolating whip lashes and slowly thickening and rising, off-kilter jerks and spazzes, all as heavily processed vocals circle around the title phrase. Characteristically, the verbal narrative here is largely subsumed into effect. And yet, the atmosphere set up by the preceding track, the vocally cleaner 'Interlude 1', and the odd clear word that slips through (e.g. 'sex', or the title phrase, whose climactic final emergence at 5'20" produces a barrage of fuzzy noise in response), combine with the racketing, rocketing tension of the music to create an unsettling impact, the building, unpredictable noise pushing tensely against our attention. The track, in the end, seems to suggest nothing but contempt for those holding contempt for sex work in the first place, though such a neat interpretative conclusion is likely too pat for this complex, affectively, formally and discursively unresolved music.

The interview samples are clearer in 'Cold and Empty', where a whispered voice (presumably Kärkkäinen) repeating the words 'My bed is cold and empty, but I made it this way' contrasts with a woman's calmly voiced reminiscences about her history in sex work. Dark-ambient pads and loops accompany these voices, arcing out across a distant, echoing sonic space, interrupted only periodically by outbursts of static, buzzing or feedback. As on 'Nothing but Contempt for Her', it's easy to hear the two voices in this track as commenting on each other, the whispered statement perhaps lamenting the decision to engage in sex work. This is just as the dark-toned sounds of the track might be given affective authority over the calm voice, somehow heard as revealing the 'true' emotional reality of the situation. But such takeaways are, again, probably too pat: in the case of 'Cold and Empty', for example, the woman's reminiscences about sex work are more calm and even humorous than they are, say, regretful. It's hard to draw one, clean emotional conclusion from the track, even if the unresolved, tense atmosphere of the music might suggest darkness and despair. The final track on the album, 'No Safe Distance', seems to offer a clearer political statement or view. It calls back to the intensity of the slashing, tearing gestures of the opening track, with a mournful, sweeping synth-bass tattoo and basic drum loop slowly building into a distorted mass of cutting and overloaded vocals. A woman cries and emotes about her experiences whilst Kärkkäinen interjects along the way to suggest that 'there's no safe distance'. But it's never clear exactly what the woman is saying, nor is it clear what the title phrase is getting at. Similarly, again, though the music is intensely drawn it's hard to hear it in singular terms, to identify any clear, likely emotional takeaway for the listener. The album, indeed, is never didactic in conveying any message, leaning instead into suggestive themes and erotic atmospheres: the overriding impression here is of a dark, unresolved, nocturnal affect that's filled with both empathy and ambiguity. It is rare for a piece of music to map neatly onto pre-existing political categories or worldviews. This is the case even on an album like *Sex Worker*, which seems on the surface to take a side but in practice is harder to pin down.

The same is true of *Sex Worker II*, where uneasy feelings and consuming, erotic sound encase similarly drawn personal narratives and reflections from a range of sex workers. Even a gruelling listen like the eleven-minute 'Panic Attack' steers towards ambiguity. The track opens with a woman crying and then moves swiftly to a wall of consuming distortion. An array of crunchy, shrieking sounds are progressively drawn from the distortion as the woman's tears progress into more concrete regrets and memories. Overwhelming noise affect, slowly but unpredictably mutating sound, and characteristic language blurring (both literally and in terms of noise's habitual style-play) muss up any clear statement of purpose. The same could be said of pummelling but carefully drawn tracks such as 'Limitless Series of Natural Disasters' and 'Another Body', where titles and snatched vocal samples might suggest regret or imply condemnation, but unpredictable, overwhelming overlays of thumping drum loops and restlessly bristling voice and crunch push things into murkier, far more ambiguous territory. Noise becoming undermines political becoming on every track.

Kärkkäinen's music swims in dark and familiarly brutal genre waters, then, but is always complex in how it both trucks with but refuses clear biographical or social narrative, and in how it so vividly immerses itself into imaginative will. Noise *feel* overrides any sense of didactic lesson here. This point harks back to the final argument in the Corbelli section, where, despite the potentially misogynistic and/or conservative themes and imagery played with in Atrax Morgue, the music's overwhelming affect and stylistic irresolution were felt to complicate any simple political interpretation we could place on it. That is true here too, though it should also be noted that Kärkkäinen's music seems to be situated in a different place to Corbelli's in one key political respect; its platforming of female-identifying voices and experiences, as opposed to the mostly male-centric fantasies of Atrax Morgue, and its alignment with an emerging sex-worker-positive political perspective. This alignment is testament to the broader shift in noise to more outwardly progressive political positions that I mentioned in the Introduction. We'll encounter more of this in the next section.

Trauma, disease and the body

I examine three artists here: Moonbeam Terror, Puce Mary and Bacillus. The themes of sex and death covered in the previous section are present again in these artists' work, though more obliquely than in Himukalt and Atrax Morgue. Instead, the focus here is on trauma, or disease, and the body. And, in particular, on the way in which noise can be used to purge suppressed memories and traumatic affect and/or can help us confront disease and bodily decay.

Moonbeam Terror

Moonbeam Terror is Anjilla, a Wisconsin-based musician who was one half of Autoerotichrist, before releasing her debut album as Moonbeam Terror, *Comfort Knife*, on Hospital Productions in 2019. Anjilla's work as Moonbeam Terror confronts experiences of abuse and trauma. This comes through to some extent in the music, but it's conveyed primarily through track titles, explicit descriptions in interviews and promotional material. For example, the Hospital Productions press release for *Comfort Knife* describes it as 'a startling and confrontational document of sheer noise textures from the immortal corpse or the corpse you can't get rid of' (2019). Similarly, in an interview on *Noisextra*, Anjilla reflects on her close relationship with the film *The Heart Is Deceitful above All Things*. The film, which includes child abuse, drug-taking and poverty, is described by Anjilla as 'kind of my childhood'. She goes on,

> I feel like I can add lived experience to a lot of the themes people talk about. I've come a really, really long way, with a lot of work and a lot of therapy. But things I had been through in my upbringing made me a bit of a monster. And I don't know a lot of people exploring that and talking about the cyclical nature of things. I've done a lot of things to survive and defend myself that I would hope I would never

do now. But I wanted to confess all of that shit, and explore it ... I'm just kind of there to dissociate and expunge evil.

(Connelly et al. 2019)

These themes are embodied in live shows via Anjilla's use of theatrical costume (e.g. chain mail) and confrontational attitudes and behaviour (such as on-stage urination). They can also be heard explicitly in different ways on *Comfort Knife*. An obvious example comes in the terrible, cathartic screams that are heard on tracks such as 'Reluctant Immortal'. The *most* obvious example, though, is heard on the opening track, 'I Repeat', which indeed acts as a kind of mission statement for the album.

'I Repeat' is based on a series of vocal samples from the 1996 Dario Argento Giallo film, *The Stendhal Syndrome*. The film features a detective, Anna, who, whilst on the trail of a rapist and murderer succumbs to the titular condition, in which individuals enter fugue states when viewing works of art. The murderer exploits this, kidnapping Anna and brutally beating and raping her. Once she escapes, Anna is unable to enter into sexual relations with her new boyfriend, Marie. Anna eventually murders Marie, her colleague Marco, and the psychologist who had been supporting her. Anjilla suggests that *The Stendhal Syndrome*

> really explores kind of what I'm trying to explore with Moonbeam Terror, which is the cycle of abuse. And, abuse begets abuse. She was raped, she was hurt. And she got kind of vicious from it. I related to that. I thought that was a fitting sample.
>
> (Connelly et al. 2019)

As is typical for Anjilla's work, 'I Repeat' plays with these messages to some extent, mulching them into noise and obscuring some of their potential meanings by cutting them up, overlaying them in the mix, and so on. At the start of the track, for example, a heavily compressed vocal from the film, overloaded and sparking with distortion, runs through a couple of phrases in which we can only hear isolated words clearly, for example, 'disgust me' and 'having sex'. Much of the rest of the track is more explicit in its messaging, however; after the opening, the film samples become much cleaner and clearer, and the relationship between the noise and the narrative is more supportive and enhancing than it is complexifying. For example, relatively early in the track, as noise starts to build in the distance on the right of the spectrum, Anna says 'I'm scared ... I'm not your woman any more', and Marie replies, pleadingly, 'I'm sorry, it's been so long since we made love'. The texture thickens, distortion moving into the centre of the picture, and Anna and Marie start to fight. As the fight reaches a climax, we hear the words 'something inside of me, that makes me hurt myself; making me hurt myself', and a wall of popping static pushes and explodes around us. Finally, Anna says 'it makes me feel alive'. The static takes over here, building in volume and density, the right side with constant, thrashing noise and the centre cutting in and out, the texture on all sides thicker and thicker and thicker. Then, the noise peals away, and the voice of Anna's psychologist emerges, saying, 'You have to try to love yourself. Stop despising yourself because you were raped [you aren't responsible for that]. Don't hate yourself because he desires you.' Noise here works almost as a conventional score, accompanying and helping to stage the story.

Aided by noise, the narrative arc of the track is therefore broadly clear, despite the murkiness of the beginning and the messing with linearity and cohesion that happen along the way. It moves, essentially, from traumatic sexual encounter, through a rejection of 'healthy' sexuality and an embrace of violence, to a cathartic release of noise, which finally makes possible the expression of a potentially healing, adult perspective on sexual trauma and shame. This is less the kind of depersonalization of the listener through an immersion into noise we've seen elsewhere as it is a kind of theatricalization of a process of personalization through noise re-traumatization and ultimate catharsis.

Such relative narrative clarity is absent from the rest of the album, however, where clear vocal samples, for example, are dropped in favour of murky, overwhelming noise. Even on a track like 'Cruelty of Care', where the title might seem to give some of the topical game away, much of the thematic work is buried under layers of molten, crumbling, sizzling noise. Built on a martial 1–2 thump, the music sounds like a giant rock monster struggling to climb over an exploding volcano, as showers and spits of water rain down around it. Extra-musical narrative interpretation is difficult for pretty much the whole of the track; that is, until the surprise, brief coda, which consists simply of a modulated voice uttering the sentence 'they tend to stay antisocial and they tend to turn into long-term offenders'. But until then, though the martial noise could be heard as an expression of righteous, repressed anger borne of trauma, the meaning is unclear since that noise could be heard in many ways, its roiling burning and sizzling evoking restless, fervent, unresolved sonic becoming more than anything denotatively clear cut. 'Flesh House into Flesh Home' is similar, in that its chaotic jumble of feedback, distortion and buried churn and crumble *might* be heard as a performance of emotional turmoil or a working through of suppressed trauma or anger. But it might also be heard in other frames. 'Revenant', too, even though the screams and shouts we hear amidst its thundershower hail of mouldering noise perhaps do reveal something of a clearer emotional through line. The more withdrawn, though still packed-full, noisily rickety 'Weakest Link' and 'Abraxas' are more abstract still, with very few verbal or vocal tics to pull us in to any particular, prescribed narrative frame. Concrete interpretation can't really be anything more than impressionistic, speculative, on these tracks; extra-musical narrative cohesion must be borrowed from the opening track and from extra-musical knowledge of artist intent. I mention this as a way of thinking about how trauma and noise catharsis may work through this music.

And yet, these and other tracks have a deeply bodily, non-rational, erotic impact. *Musical* and/or *affective* narrative cohesion is therefore perhaps more direct here; everything broils and flows, without rest, in a state of held-in-tension becoming, and the listening body, à la Guesde and Nadrigny, is immersed into the noisy sound such that its borders start to merge and melt. After all, though musicality is present throughout, musical resolution in the form of a cadence or clear rise-and-fall never quite arrives. The sheer welter of noise chaos on 'Flesh House', for instance, never lets up. In this, the track can't help but overwhelm the listener, robbing them of any clear

Noise Erotics: Traumatic Bodies and Desires 181

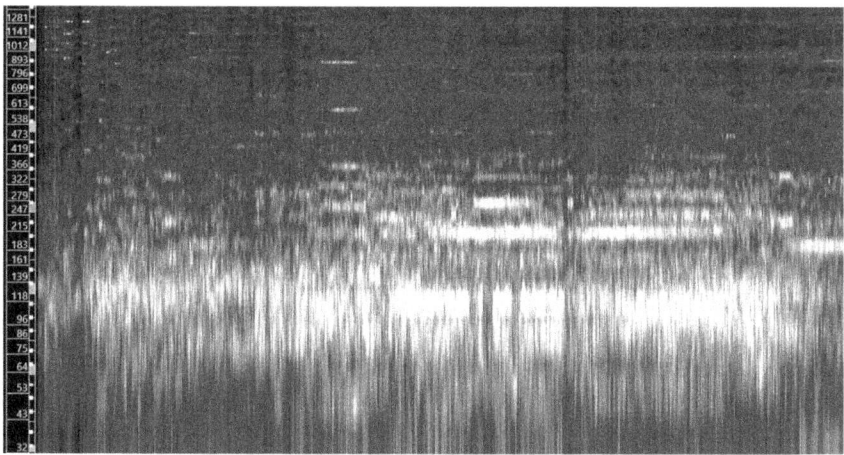

Figure 8.1 Melodic range spectrogram of 'Flesh House' from Moonbeam Terror's *Comfort Knife* (2019).

anchor point. Figure 8.1 gives a good picture of how dense, eventful and unpredictable the track is, with a sustained blast of essentially white noise underlying variegated noise spikes and spears, à la classic harsh noise.

So, despite the evident gap between intent and precise effect here, we can nevertheless see how for some listeners there may be a closer relation of intent and *a*ffect in the work. As Anjilla's crumbling, smouldering blasts of noise push and pull such listeners into transformed emotional states, they might thereby reach catharsis, discharging micro-pockets of tension as past traumas big and small are released. In this, these listeners would align with Anjilla's clearly deeply felt emotional programme of trauma, abuse and release through noise.

Like Anjilla herself, then, it is possible to use music like this to confront violent memories and trauma in a safe, controlled environment. As with Ocean Vuong at the beginning of the last section, noise therefore serves in Moonbeam Terror as a safe room, a place to go down and deep but always with a strong tether back to reality. In this sense, noise resembles forms of trauma-based therapy, such as EMDR and Holotropic Breathwork, where the reliving and processing of traumatic memories within a controlled and supportive environment is a cornerstone of the clinical method. Noise, with its particular capacity for the staging and experiencing of extreme emotional states and memories through overwhelming, unresolved and non-traditional sound, can act as a kind of therapeutic resource in this way.

Puce Mary

Puce Mary is Danish noise musician and sound artist Frederikke Hoffmeier. Hoffmeier has been releasing music on labels like PAN and Posh Isolation since 2010. Hoffmeier combines sounds and techniques from industrial, dark ambient, harsh noise and field recording to create a novel, hybrid noise style filled as much with silence, textural contrast, drones, spoken word and other traditional musical elements, from steady drum patterns to intermittent melody, as it is with more typical noise tropes of sonic harshness, inharmonicity and aperiodicity. As Hegarty says of Puce Mary and also Pharmakon, they 'make harsh soundworlds that rehybridize micro-avant-garde styles and processes' (2020, 110). Similarly, Hoffmeier explores thematic territory and visual imagery that is both noise-familiar in scope and often strikingly new in feel. Albums like *The Spiral* (Posh Isolation, 2016) engage explicitly with sex and violence but do so from new angles. The softening of the rough sexual image on the cover of the album with a soft pink hue is perhaps the most obvious embodiment of this. But equally, the emphasis of the music often feels less on a fantasy infliction *of* violence and more on somehow living in a space of violence. The album's mix of intensities and moods and its variegated use of different vocal styles serve in this way to stage different perspectives on, and realizations of, violence. The work I'll focus on is 2018's *The Drought* (Pan), in which Hoffmeier explores themes of drought and apocalypse (both personal and collective), and trauma and alienation.

The Drought features several carefully hewn instrumental tracks. The looped percussive thwacks, droning cluster chord and gawping growls of opener, 'Dissolve', contrast with the equally sepulchral, but more drawn-out, dark-ambient atmospherics and glinting minor-second synth tones of the next track, 'A Feast Before the Drought', where a version of those earlier percussive thwacks returns in the final minute to increase intensity. The range of these two tracks usefully describes the overarching moods and sounds heard across the album. A number of vocal-led tracks are interspersed amongst the instrumental tracks. 'To Possess Is to Be in Control' builds on some of the musical material of the opening two tracks in creating spacious, penumbral ambience out of intermittent percussive crackles, cutting and buzzing distortion and the ever-present sustained, thin synth tones sounding out diatonic minor motifs with touches of chromaticism adding colour here and there. Breathy spoken word occupies the centre of the track, the lyrics describing a process of losing oneself to another and wanting, instead, to possess that other and regain control. 'Fragments of a Lily', another instrumental, quickly follows, upping the ante established in the thickening climax of 'To Possess' with a steadily thumping, charred percussion loop and slowly arcing and swooping (again) high synth tones. These latter are sine-wave-like in their pure tonality.

This track gives way in turn to what in many ways can be seen as the centrepiece of the album, 'Red Desert', the first single and the place in which many of the thematic threads come together. The lyrics are powerful, describing the passing of time, the decay of nature and trauma: 'I'm an old woman now and I have lost my attraction … Some experience under our skin forever, Like the trauma of child abuse … To watch everything is so deceptive.' The narrator here, calm but close-miked and slightly urgent in the recording, describes a feeling both universal and particular, personal and dream-like, as they contemplate the chronic, prickly nature of trauma as something that lives almost under the skin, alienating one from reality and fellow-feeling. The narrator is abject to themselves, removed from trust as they long for the connection that such trust would both make possible and be based in. The music of the track creates a cavern of sound in which we return again and again to the resonating frequencies of the space. A glistening, tense cloud of chromatically inflected, minor-scale synth tones resolves, around the 75-second mark, into a more musically direct organ part, which moves diatonically around that same minor scale, sonically cleaner than the synth tones from before but more bereft in feeling, suspended, hanging minor sixths and major seconds underscoring the longing for connection of the narrator. Thumping heartbeats, frayed static and rickety field recordings add to the busy but finely woven textures, all of it rising gently towards an unexpected resolution into a deliquescing relative-major tone at the end. This ending serves as if to answer, to embody, both the broader desire for community expressed in the track and the mention of 'deception' in the last line, the resolution therefore ringing both true and false depending on which way you take it.

The other two instrumental tracks extend and enhance the techniques and mood of these earlier tracks. The sustained synth tones of 'Coagulate' echo the *Kosmiche* atmospheres of 'A Feast before the Drought', in particular, whilst the closing 'Slouching Uphill' uses chromatic drone and tense cut-up whistles and vocal sounds to answer and qualify a lot of the earlier material with a sense of unresolved, but at least stilled, quietude. Similarly, the other vocal-led tracks 'The Size of Our Desires' and 'The Transformation' extend and enhance the themes of personal abjection and alienation from earlier. The latter, in particular, with its use of hypnotic, steady percussion loops; distant, arcing drones and chromatic tones; and a reserved, pinched voice, evokes a sense of self-as-abstract, self-as-metaphor, self-as-nightmare, as the narrator suggests 'I freeze and I liquefy ... Your law is in my vellum'. Both these lines, and the closing vocal images of the track, as spectral, pitch-shifted flute flies around the stereo space and then the chromatic drones return, create an eerie sense of present absence, the voice there and not there, the sound both intentional and blank. In this spirit, Hegarty indeed discusses Hoffmeier's vocal and sonic textures in depersonalized terms, as creating a kind of 'merging and indistinction between object and vocal' (2020, 115). All of this achieves an unnerving affect by the time we reach those closing lines, as self and other, object and human, collapse into each other: 'He pulls his hand out of his pocket. But that is not a hand. And that is not a pocket. I pull a hair out of my mouth. But that is not a hair. And that is not my mouth.' Three minutes of winding, thickening, off-kiltering instrumental sound follows.

As we can see, then, *The Drought* deploys clever contrasts between affect-laden but in some ways abstract instrumental tracks on the one hand, and vocal-led tracks where the narrative theme and perhaps message are more obviously direct and accessible, on the other. The vocal tracks indeed use first-person narrative and intimate detail to suggest an aspect of the confessional, of autobiography, even as layers of artifice in the form of impossible details or fantastical metaphors are put into the mix to, perhaps erotically (or at least, abjectly), undermine the self-world division. *The Drought* places us in a space of personal reflection, pain and trauma, all of which nevertheless take place very much within an aesthetic frame in which fantasy and unnerving uncertainty of voice and atmosphere are the overriding messages. Trauma here is therefore less directly voiced than in previous examples, just as the aesthetic frame and style are less extreme. This is noise trauma filtered through the lens of relative musical order and more familiar stylistic tropes, notwithstanding elements of noise disorder in the album's use of feedback and drones. The prevalence of such order and familiarity is indeed reflected in the ordered analytical language that dominated my discussion. And yet, as a strategy for confronting and potentially processing dark sensibilities and traumatic sentiments it is a powerful one nonetheless. It exploits the gap between that musical accessibility on the one hand and both the weird apprehensions described in the lyrics and the stark affect built into the music on the other. Through this, Puce Mary creates musical crucibles for the concentration and discharging of intense, difficult emotions.

Bacillus

A small but important strain (no pun intended) of noise music echoes the fleshy, traumatic, deathly obsessions of the artists looked at so far but focuses these more particularly on the specific area of disease, virulence and microbiology. As with the other artists examined above, it uses the metaphorical sonic gruesomeness and real affective extremity of noise to enhance its themes.

We already explored this type of approach and theme with Body Carve in Chapter 6. Many other examples can be cited. For instance, harsh noise act Sickness (Chris Goudreau) explicitly themes his precise, chiselled music along these lines, following Goudreau's childhood experience of serious illness. Death-industrial group Steel Hook Prostheses explore similarly sickly territory, where crackling, unforgiving noise and/or cold, humming electronics embody forms of disease, decay and phobia, as on albums such as *Light Reflected from a Cold Cutting Table* (Pain Compliance Productions, 2005). An act like Premature Ejaculation, meanwhile, focused on extreme states of pain and discomfort across gruesome live performances and haunting, unconventional, dark-ambient-leaning albums like *Necessary Discomforts* (Cleopatra, 1993). The act I'll focus on, though, is Bacillus (Peter Keller), an Ohio-originating, Seattle-based noise artist active intermittently since 1994. Keller's work concentrates exclusively on disease. The name of the project refers to a genus of bacteria that includes anthracis (which causes Anthrax) and other pathogenic bacteria; Keller often wears Hazmat suits and brandishes biohazard stickers at live shows whilst much of the physical packaging of Bacillus releases is themed around disease in different ways.

Early Bacillus albums give a clue to the conceptual uniformity that would come to define the project. *Pregnant Disease Formation* (1994), *Black Plague* (1995), *Epidemic* (1995) and *Failed Disease Control Effects* (1996; this one came out on Marco Corbelli's Slaughter Productions whereas the other three were released on Keller's own Clotted Meat Portioning) are all explicitly themes around disease, as can be seen from their titles. All of these early albums used a rudimentary set-up of old ghettoblaster for mixing and recording. For sound sources, they drew on decayed tapes and repurposed tape loops, turntables and broken or fabricated records and processed samples from radio and television. This resulted in buzzing, beating noise that was invariably scrappy in source and sound but often thrillingly intense in tone and texture, as walls of static decayed and throbbed unpredictably, and snippets of strange real-world samples bled through layers of tape and deliberately discomposed material. Unlike other noise or noise-adjacent acts that draw on concrete sonic material, where the intention is often a kind of postmodern plunderphonia or recontextualization, Keller's intention in using found and repurposed material was to evoke 'entropy' in sound (Connelly et al. 2019). That is, to use objects in deliberately decayed or decaying ways to enable music to embody the impact of disease on living organisms. This would be such that the weak integrity of a ramshackle tape loop or a brittle, crumbling record made of glue, or, say, the overloading of a source through the extremely 'hot' and unreliable ghetto blaster mic would produce unpredictable patterns of sonic decay in a kind of quasi-stochastic fashion that mirrored the movements of disease.

After going on hiatus from 1996 to 2004, then again to 2010 and again until 2018, Keller had a particularly fertile period from 2018 on. The Covid-19 pandemic proved particularly inspirational, with a series of EPs, 7"s, and albums released over the course of 2020 and 2021 that were all explicitly themed around the pandemic in different ways. The twinned November 2021 releases, *Variants of Concern* and 'Delta' (both on Patient Records), with their talk of the 'decay of social order', 'morgue trucks' and hospitals at capacity, and their pairing of news samples with buzzing, crunching distortion and messy noise, are excellent illustrations of this perhaps predictable Covid productivity (the former's packaging in a medical kit pouch, along with a mask and disinfectant, underlines the point). As with the continuity within the conceptual underpinnings of Bacillus, little had changed in Keller's set-up for these later releases; instead of an old ghetto blaster an XLR mic and mixer was now used, and Keller also made use of a couple of effects pedals (including a pitchshifter). But the set-up was otherwise the same, dominated by degraded tapes, records and cheap mixers. The sound world is therefore largely consistent with the earlier music even as these new tools expand possibilities in some interesting ways.

The 2018 album, *Serial Infector* (Nefarious Activities), offers a good window into Bacillus' thematic preoccupations and musical approach in this later period. Based around the idea of humans who deliberately infect others, the tape was released in a biohazard bag in a limited edition of 100 copies. Each track offers a characteristic wall – or maybe a less chiselled, messier rock pile – of churning, crunchy distortion, beating static and piercing, overloaded highs and throbbing lows. The sonic textures on the album aren't nearly as monolithic as harsh noise wall artists like Vomir: distinct registral contrasts, gestures, concrete sources and even beat patterns emerge regularly here. And yet this is harsh noise very much configured as unpredictable, overwhelming, blasting meteor shower (in the process of forming the aforementioned rock pile, perhaps); moments of silence, clear space and resolution or rest are rare.

The album, equally characteristically, features a series of vividly named tracks that suggest very specific microbial, or real-world viral or viral-related, phenomena. 'Intentional Transmission' and 'Malicious Intent of Diagnostic Needle Punctures' are typical both in what they reference and in what tone they reference it. Despite the specificity of titles like this, many of these tracks sound very similar to each other. 'You Go Under and You Wake Up Hours Later and You Don't Know Who Was Around You' and 'The Deliberate Infection of Over 400 Children With HIV', for example, are both built on hairshirt walls of churning static. Though there are distinct sonic components in each – for instance, the dive-bombing pitch shifts on the right of the picture and the scintilla high tones in the first track, and the more stuttered blasts and Morse-code-like bleeps of the second – they feel made from the same sources, with similar tools, and with the same broad effect and affect resulting; as in other cases we've seen throughout the book, the relationship between the sonic and the verbal here is really only suggestive at best.

All these tracks therefore closely parallel each other in density, frequency range and texture, and in their emphasis on unresolved sonic becoming in their constant undermining of clear musical conclusions or contours, without saying too much specifically or directly about their supposed themes. Of course, as we saw with The Rita, the conceptual underpinning of different projects and, more specifically, the thematic frames put around music by titles, packaging, imagery and commentary nevertheless imbue that music with a narrative force that only serves to enrich and amplify its impact. That is certainly the case with Keller and Bacillus.

Some of the pandemic-era music offers variations on the musical and narrative themes explored on *Serial Infector*, as we started to see above. *Mask It or Casket* (Patient Records, 2021), a CDr release, was housed inside the pocket of a black two-layer cotton washable mask. Its three tracks maintain the spirit of the packaging. 'Anti-Maskers Forced To Dig Graves For COVID-19 Victims' offers 150 seconds of high-gain, blasted noise wall which starts off hot and generally only gets thicker, louder and more brutal as it goes on, even as Keller offers a couple of windows of relative quiet. Figure 8.2 gives a good illustration of the unrelenting ferocity and saturation of the track, where, for example, 0–70Hz is almost completely consumed with churning rumble, and 70–200Hz is intermittently saturated with fried white noise.

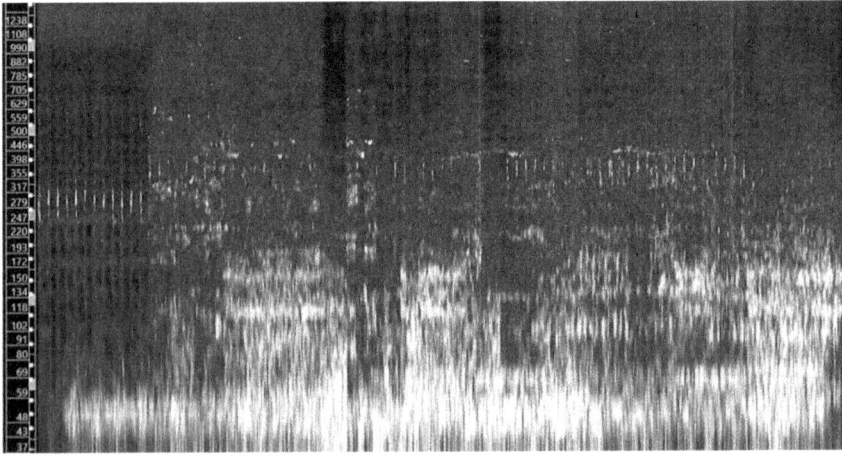

Figure 8.2 Melodic range spectrogram of 'Anti-Maskers Forced to Dig Graves for COVID-19 Victims' from Bacillus' *Mask It or Casket* (2021).

'The Hidden Danger In The Air' is only fifty-nine seconds and is similarly harsh-walled, though as compared to the first track it features a more driving, pulsing static in its lower register and an unexpectedly clean three-second coda. 'Natural Herd Immunity' offers more variety within its wall and is all the heavier for it; the turntable scratches sixty seconds in make way for a pile-driving full-stereo blast. Chopped up vocal samples and an intermittent high tone from 1'30" culminate in ten seconds of cod-Merzbow ('cod' in their endearing cheapness), techno-noise beats. These are pulverizing, heavy tracks, where the noise, despite brief moments of respite or clear musical order, is mostly unrelenting and unsettled.

As can be seen, Keller's music focuses obsessively on themes of disease and death. The erotic intensity and profile of these noise walls, their pulverizing power and slowly mutating textures, can be heard as metaphors for the destructive power and spread of a disease within a body, even if the connection between theme and tone isn't always direct. This is, ultimately and instead, noise that uses the affecting context of disease as an activating backdrop for noise music that tussles between suppressed order and marauding disorder. It evokes disease and the extreme, potentially traumatic associations listeners have with disease in the context of a bristling noise erotics that affords those listeners an opportunity to immerse bodily either into such associations and themes or, failing that, simply into a more generalized, non-signifying depersonalized overwhelm.

Conclusion

Bacillus, then, provides listeners with the opportunity to confront difficult, perhaps repressed aspects of their experiences within a heightened, immersive but controlled setting. Though the music doesn't directly denote disease, by anchoring such themes in the context of overwhelming noise Bacillus' work can discharge trapped associations and repressed affect, bringing listeners into a fuller relationship with their own existence and selves as a result. As we've seen throughout this chapter, artists such as Atrax Morgue, Pharmakon, Moonbeam Terror and Himukalt all similarly exploit noise's ready capacity to embody different forms of repressed trauma, or traumatic desire, through its exploration of themes of extreme sexuality, death and disease, and, in turn, its immersive, unresolved and overwhelming sonic eroticism. These twin elements, the extreme themes and the extreme sounds, give listeners the opportunity to confront and perhaps even discharge negative affects they may formerly have been consumed by.

9

Hybrid noisebloom part one: Noise and …

Like all forms of music, noise has followed a natural lifespan or course. In 'Classification as Culture' (2008; see also Lena 2012), Jennifer Lena and Richard Peterson schematize what such lifespans or courses have looked like, describing four distinct music-genre 'types' – Avant-garde, Scene-based, Industry-based and Traditionalist – and, coming out of these, three characteristic 'trajectories' for those genres. The most common trajectory is 'AgSIT', where a genre starts out as a small, 'frustrated with established styles' avant-garde, grows into a scene, becomes incorporated to the industry and then, eventually, attains a kind of traditional status (2008, 700–1). Noise music has followed a *kind* of AgSIT trajectory. Noise started as an (in all senses) avant-garde practice of a select group of musicians, for example Whitehouse in the UK and Hijokaidan in Japan. It then grew into a scene across the 1980s and 1990s. That scene never quite entered the industry stage, notwithstanding a Merzbow or, as we'll see below, a Wolf Eyes signing to a prominent label. But it did concretize into a set of familiar tropes that ultimately played a traditional function in influencing things like the 'mid-2000s explosion' of noise activity in the United States (Preira 2013). It's therefore clear that, by the twenty-first century, noise music had been established as a recognizable genre in the Lena and Peterson mould.

We grappled with this idea of noise music as a normative practice or genre all the way back in the Introduction. In such normative practices, two mutually reinforcing and interpenetrating processes, the first sociocultural and the second music-stylistic (echoing Lena and Petersen's discussion of the 'two dominant approaches to the study of genre' in music, 698), align to create and stabilize genres *qua* genres. In the case of noise, we've tracked the progress of these sociocultural and music-stylistic processes throughout the book. We saw in different ways across Part One, for instance, how noise stabilized socially in the 1980s and, especially, the 1990s. This was such that well-known musicians, record shops, zines and labels emerged and, in turn, generated a canon of records, a lexicon of symbols, language and behaviour and a cast of characters, all of which came to be recognized as constituting a genre with scale and sustainability. On the other hand, noise music's internal aesthetic push-pull, 'suspended' dialectic or dynamic between musical order or language on the one hand and noise disorder or freedom on the other both crested at various points into locally recognizable noise styles (such as harsh noise, or dark ambient, or harsh noise wall) and constituted a sort of meta-style that governed the vast majority of examples of noise music. Noise music, in summary, stabilized across the 1980s and 1990s in ways both sociological and stylistic.

As a result, the now-stable genre of noise music naturally became visible to, and enmeshed within, broader musical contexts. I have argued before in this spirit that noise music should be recognized as being part of the broader international fringe and underground ecosystem composed also of styles like improv and free music, extreme metal, sound art and, perhaps, modern composition and experimental hip-hop, pop, dance and rock music (Graham 2016; see also 2019). After all, it's very difficult to draw lines around these musics. Twenty-first-century audiences have indeed tended to be omnivorous (to use a well-known phrase from Petersen and Kern 1996). Meanwhile, magazines and sites like *The Wire* and BOMB, radio stations like WFMU or NTS, and festivals like Unsound, Sonar, Le Guess Who, Tusk, Rewire, Sonic Protest, No Fun and so on all tend to the catholic rather than the sectarian, for example including noise as an option within a kind of buffet of experimental, largely extra- or para-high-art music forms. In short, in the twenty-first-century noise music has entered what we might call the experimental or fringe 'canon' or ecosystem. Merzbow does Boiler Room sets; Wolf Eyes appear in the *Guardian* (Lucy Allan 2017); and No Fun Festival gets featured in the *New York Times* (Chinen 2007). This is not to suggest that noise scenes or platforms have become wholly absorbed in these broader contexts. For every multi-genre festival like Birmingham's Supersonic you can find noise-specialist labels, message boards and podcasts, from RRRecords to *Special Interests* and *Noise Receptor* to *Noisextra*. But these noise-specialist entities can't really be fully separated from the broader contexts they exist within and in which listeners both specialist and general often encounter them.

In a 2009 *Pitchfork* piece surveying the 'Decade in Noise', Marc Masters summarized a lot of the points I've just been making, underlining the broader contexts that surround noise music. Masters describes the evolving front of noise music through the 1990s and into the 2000s, and in doing so gathers all sorts of styles under the banner of 'noise':

> It grew from disconnected, homegrown scenes to something more recognized and more diverse, more sophisticated and more direct, more ambitious and more reverent, and more open to new sounds, new approaches, and new venues. Thanks to forward-thinking labels and festivals, the umbrella of what could be called 'noise' widened considerably. Many followers now think of it as not just harsh sonic assaults, but also abstract improvisation, ecstatic free jazz, lo-fi pop, outsider avant-rock, minimalist drone, power electronics, and more ... few would deny that noise has come a long way since the turn of the century.
>
> (2009)

Whilst I'm not working with a definition of noise that could accommodate all these musics, the broader point that Masters makes here and throughout the piece is that, whether through an 'increase in local scenes working cheaply and communally' (Masters cites Providence and Detroit), through 'the Internet helping them grow and connect quickly' or through 'indie rock's mainstream drift driving more adventurous fans to edgier music' (2009), it was clear to him that, by the end of the 2000s, noise had claimed a place in the broader international fringe or experimental music scene. Not only that, but that the parameters of what could be counted as 'noise' had themselves expanded.

We'll see evidence of both these closely related points throughout this and the following chapter, whose collective organizing theme is, accordingly, hybridity, where hybridity should be understood not to indicate a new tendency in noise but an intensification and expansion of a tendency present in noise since the beginning. The current chapter focuses on recent examples of style-hybrid noise or noise-adjacent music; I cover artists who have worked in noise but whose music also spreads into other domains. I do this in order to capture some important satellite or parallel, noise-infused musics alongside my central narrative about noise 'itself'. Each section thematizes different aspects of such noise hybridity; I start with noise and experimental music, then move on to noise and rock, and finish with noise and structure. Following Tim Rutherford-Johnson's work on contemporary classical music (2017), I'll use Nicolas Bourriaud's notion of 'radicant' aesthetics – radicant being a botanical term for plants or organisms with no single root, such as ivy – to characterize both these artists and, by extension, the twenty-first-century noise scene in general. The next chapter picks up the discussion in applying that same lens of hybridity to artists who sit a little more squarely in the noise scene as compared to the 'radicant' artists examined here, but whose work nevertheless likewise sits in a broader music ecosystem and further expresses the hybridity of twenty-first-century noise.

Noise and experimental music

The twenty-first-century relationship between noise and experimental music is rich and porous. Masters' end-of-decade survey of noise in the 2000s barely makes a distinction between the two, as we saw, considering styles as varied as avant-rock, improv, harsh noise and lo-fi pop as being very much in concert with each other. By this point, noise music had both been established as a genre and taken its place in a wider ecology of challenging, exploratory music. Separating 'noise' from specifically 'experimental' music – setting aside the thorny question of how to define experimental music and instead considering it simply as a nebulous but useful catch-all term for a host of adventurous academic, mainstream, underground and fringe musics – is therefore extremely difficult. Accordingly, noise musicians operated within a broader experimental field in this period, performing alongside non-noise musicians at festivals, being listened to by similar audiences, and competing for some of the same grant money. Moreover, many musicians operating within that broader experimental field blur boundaries between styles such that musicians like Bill Nace or Okkyung Lee, for example, might be recognized as making 'noisy' music without ever being described as a noise musician. Looked at from the other side, it's also the case that many musicians get labelled as noise artists but more accurately work across boundaries. To wit, figures like Daniel Menche, or Kevin Drumm, or Fennesz, or Aaron Dilloway, or Maja Ratkje, or Lasse Marhaug, or, as we'll see below, C. Spencer Yeh. For all of these artists, the versatile label of 'experimental musician' is probably more appropriate than anything more pigeonholing such as 'noise' or 'rock' or 'improv'. After all, whether it's Menche's abstracted, atmospheric, droning long tones and hacking beats on albums like *Creatures of Cadence* (Crouton, 2006); Drumm's rip-roaring, metal-aesthetic, improv-inspired noise albums like *Sheer Hellish Miasma* (Mego, 2002); Fennesz's glitchy but gorgeous noise pop compositions on *Endless Summer* (Mego, 2001); Dilloway's loop-focused explorations of harsh but texturally varied noise (*Modern Jester*, Hanson, 2012), or of old films, equipment and song with Lucretia Dalt (*Lucy and Aaron*, Hanson, 2021); or Ratkje and Marhaug's playful, pictorial and often pulverising 'Music For …' series (e.g. *Music for Gardening*, Pica Disk, 2009), the sounding result is often noisy and even harsh but the aesthetic approach is usually broadly experimental in character. So, noise and experimental music are hard to separate on several levels, both expressing their own hybrid and often radicant characters.

Mattin and Burning Star Core/C. Spencer Yeh

Two emblematic figures working in the crossover between noise and experimental music are Basque musician Mattin and Taiwanese-American C. Spenser Yeh. Mattin's work takes in everything from radical-anarchist noise rock group Billy Bao; to anti-statist writings and thinking (*Noise and Politics*, 2009); to concept-driven performance art, installations and improvisation (see Graham 2016, 91 and 146–7 for discussions of Mattin performances). Moreover, Mattin often appears in precisely the kind of broader experimental festivals and magazines and websites that form the wider fringe/experimental ecosystem alluded to above; he is not a specialist by any stretch of the imagination. And yet, Mattin has thought a lot specifically about noise, for example publishing his eleven-part *Theses on Noise* in 2006, where he focuses on noise very much as more than merely music genre or sound, instead highlighting its social and political character too. Mattin therefore engages closely with both the idea and phenomenon of noise. But rather than operating somehow 'within' noise, Mattin instead approaches experimental music as a whole, using sounds, practices and styles/genres such as noise and improv as vectors into a political articulation of current conditions. As Mattin himself has said, whilst 'working with noise and improvisation', his practice fundamentally 'seeks to address the social and economic structures of experimental music production through live performance, recordings and writing' (2012).

The breadth of Mattin's approach is typical in a twenty-first-century experimental context in which blurred boundaries are more common than hard ones. C. Spencer Yeh's noisy, rocky, experimental work provides another excellent illustration of this point. Initially releasing noisy drone and improv music from the late '90s on as Burning Star Core (BxC), a band with a rotating line-up centred around Yeh's violin (and, occasionally, vocals and electronics) and including figures such as Hair Police's Robert Beatty and Trevor Tremaine along the way, Yeh's frame of reference and sphere of activity have expanded as he has gone along. For example, BxC gradually experimented with different styles, as when they made more melodic and groove-orientated post-rock with albums such as 2008's *Challenger* (Hospital Productions). Yeh also started to release solo work around 2005/6, much of which has focused around extended vocal or violin techniques, or some other explicitly experimental modality. Yeh made the decision to retire the BxC name around 2010, concentrating on solo work and collaborations with other musicians under his own name.

As may already be starting to become clear, Yeh provides a useful illustration of the 'noise radicant' concept mentioned above. Indeed, even within the BxC oeuvre Yeh's work ranges across everything from semi-structured noise 'freakouts', to contemplative drone pieces, to the aforementioned musical polish of an album like *Challenger*. Some BxC albums serve as a kind of bestiary of all these different styles. As described by the blog 'Tusk Is Better Than Rumours', the 2005 album, *The Very Heart of the World* (Thin Wrist Recordings), moves across each style:

> This one may be the most representative of bsc, in that its four tracks each take one of yeh's approaches to sound as its starting point. 'benjamin' is an uneasy drone, 'nyarlathotep' is an early experiment in nonsensical mouth noises, 'catapults' is a perfectly cromulent post-rock piece, and 'come back through me' is a noisy improvised freak-out.
>
> (Matthew 2020)

Meanwhile, Yeh's solo work and his collaborations with musicians such as John Weise, Jessica Rylan, John Olson, Lass Marhaug and others run just as wide a gamut, encompassing everything from quasi-IDM (*The RCA Mark II*, Primary Information, 2017), to more straightforward song-based work (*Transitions*, De Stijl, 2012), to noise-based music (*Cincinnati*, Drone Disco, 2009, with Weise). Locating Yeh in one or another stable genre is therefore very difficult. Ed Pinsent in *The Sound Projector* describes him as an 'improvising noisemaker' (2011, 88). A biography on the Foundation for Contemporary Arts site – a source that in itself says something about the wider musical and cultural ecosystem of noise – calls Yeh 'a musician recognized for his interdisciplinary activities and collaborations as an artist, improviser, and composer' (2019). The 2020 'Tusk' blog piece just referenced suggests that Yeh 'operates within noise circles but doesn't make music that you would call Noise with a capital N'; BxC's work is ultimately described as 'too noisy for post-rock, too traditionally musical for noise'; 'they're best listened to as a vehicle for yeh to make statements about concepts that aren't related to genre at all' (Matthew 2020).

Yeh's work therefore spreads across different styles and scenes in a truly 'radicant', hybrid manner. For every *A Brighter Summer Day* (Thin Wrist Recordings, 2002), whose two tracks emphasize noisy static, feedback and clamour – the first loose and clatteringly improvisational and the second droning and staticky, although distinct gestures and periodic rhythms appear in both – there is also a *Solo Voice I-X* (Primary Information, 2015), an album for essentially unprocessed solo voice in which Yeh explores various extended vocal techniques, from rolled 'rrrrrrrrs' ('I') to nasal drones and glitchy spits ('VII'). Though these albums are very different in some obvious respects, they also, typically, both hover on the line between noise disorder and structuring order: the freeform and noisy elements of *A Brighter Summer Day*, for example, ensure that there is some unpredictability and uncertainty to the sound, even as the overall grounding in violin and drone offset that uncertainty. *Solo Voice* is timbrally and sonically much cleaner, but likewise plays with rhythmic profiles and clarity of gesture and voice to introduce both a hybrid feel and a level of tension and uncertainty into the sound.

Whether Yeh (or others, like Mattin) is or is not 'noise', then, is an impossible and perhaps uninteresting question to answer; his leaning towards order and structure would suggest perhaps not, but his taste for noisy sounds and loose, exploratory structures and approaches puts that in doubt. What is clear is that the vital hybridity that a figure like Yeh represents, with his searching work that both exists across and directly draws on noise and experimental music, demonstrates vividly what I earlier called the 'rich and porous' interrelationship between the two.

Noise and rock

Noise rock as a style has had considerable impact since it first emerged in the 1980s (though it reached back and sideways to style such as the no wave of Teenage Jesus and the Jerks, the industrial rock of Einstürzende Neubauten and the experimental rock of a group like The Velvet Underground). This impact can be seen in a general sense in the widespread, mainstream appeal and/or impact of artists like Sonic Youth, Liars and Steve Albini (and associated acts like Big Black), where the emphasis is probably a little more on the 'rock' side of noise rock. But even noisier or more abrasive acts like Melt Banana or Swans have achieved cult status or some level of relative popular impact.

Noise and rock make for a potent mix. This is for obvious reasons: the two forms share some basic DNA, an emphasis on volume, spectacle and overwhelm running through both. This is whether we think of the amplifier slashing, feedback-rich work of early rock acts like the Who and Jimi Hendrix or of the rock-infused noise of seminal Japanese groups like Hijokaidan, Hanatarash and Fushitsusha. Noise and rock go *extremely* well together because in some fundamental way they share a source, each wanting on some deep level to shock, to disturb, to energize and perhaps to transcend, often using very loud, amplified sound to do so. Because of this, noise rock writ large is fecund and widespread. Even focusing on acts closer to noise than to rock throws up a wide range, from Japanese acts like Boredoms, Ruins, Boris and Zeni Geva, to Americans like Harry Pussy, Lightning Bolt, Hair Police and Magik Markers, and to British groups like Guttersnipe or Ashtray Navigations. In the rest of this section I discuss two important acts, Lightning Bolt and Guttersnipe, in order to illustrate some important aspects of noise rock in the current century. My examination of Wolf Eyes in the following section picks up threads from this discussion too.

Lightning Bolt and Guttersnipe

Lightning Bolt hail from the same bustling early 2000s, Providence, Rhode Island noise scene that birthed Black Dice, Kites and others. Lightning Bolt's work is anchored in scuzzy rock aesthetics and tends to be shaped around overloaded sounds. Their music consists of driving, distorted, trebly riffs from Brian Gibson's guitar-like five-string bass; thwacking, thumping drums; and fuzzy, almost wordless vocals from Brian Chippendale. The group's sound is exciting, dynamic and loud. Each track is tightly organized around riffs and steady beats for their habitual three to five minutes of length but likewise loose and bursting at the seams with distortion and energy. These qualities can be heard across notable albums such as 2005's commercial and critical breakthrough, *Hypermagic Mountain* (Load), and the more crisply mixed and mastered, but still pile-driving, *Fantasy Empire* (Thrill Jockey, 2015). Some tracks, like 'Blow to the Head' from 2019's *Sonic Citadel* (Thrill Jockey), emphasize complex polyrhythms amidst typical piledriving intensity. Others work in more straightforward four-to-the-floor rhythms and even clearer melodies and traditional forms (e.g. 'Hüsker Dön't' from that same album), move at a faster, frenetic pace, with hardcore-punk or even grindcore-like energy and scuzz (as with 'Birdy' and 'Mega Ghost' from *Hypermagic Mountain*), or add straight out metal growling and splattering, as is the case on much of 2009's *Earthly Delights* (Load). But a template of driving, distorted beats and bass, with vocals congealed into the fuzz, all of it amped up in energy and forward momentum, runs through Lightning Bolt's seven studio albums.

Since Lightning Bolt's work runs on so tight a formula, the qualities of looseness and bursting-at-the-seams I mentioned earlier are key to its impact. Lightning Bolt's music uses simple rock tools of distortion and volume, riffs and beats, repetition and climax, which are pushed to extremes of intensity and energy, to pummel listeners, overwhelming them with immersive sound and energy as opposed to, say, the unresolving disorder and chaos of harsh noise. These qualities of intensity, energy and immersion are accentuated in live settings, where masks (complete with telephone receiver mic for Chippendale), in-the-round and on-the-ground performance, and heaving, moving audiences arrayed around the band make for joyful collective experiences, à la the participatory communal rituals described by Ehrenreich in the Introduction. The sheer volume, speed and propulsion of the sound, and the almost magnetic attraction between the two musicians at the centre of the room and the febrile crowd around them, pull audiences into an experience of what we might call ecstatic self-loss. Rock-conducted noise here becomes a portal into impersonal ecstasy; where earlier noise examples used abjection or overwhelmed, confused depersonalization to transcend self, the experience here is more roundly a positive one. We don't need to conceptualize it in exactly these terms, of course. But Lightning Bolt's music and, especially, their live shows mine the potential inherent in rock and noise for transcendent, selfless experiences of the crowd and the collective.

Something similar happens with the pulverising distortion and chromatics of UK noise rock group – or, as they memorably describe themselves, 'Xenofeminist crisis energy rock duo' – Guttersnipe, even if the sound and the affect here is more extreme than with Lightning Bolt. Guttersnipe's music, as on tracks such as the scrabbling, screaming no wave of 'Like My Voice Was Holothurin' or the extended, quasi-grindcore frenetic noise explosion of 'God's Will to Gain Access' (both from 2018's *My Mother the Vent*, Upset the Rhythm), has a kind of extreme, abject, jamming feel, as if the music is trying to channel the energy from some terrible guitar-and-drum apocalypse to better ends. Edifices of squalling distortion, clattering and thumping drums and primal screams are built, jabbered and then collapsed. The music always moves, always screams, rarely stops, even as thumping beat and guitar spray give way to brief, swirling synth interludes that seem, if anything, merely to ramp up tension and intent. Ecstatic rock propulsion meets dreadful, terrified noise abandon here, the one driving things forward and the other threatening to blow them apart, both of these forces working somehow together to push us towards some final, transcendent revelation. As Jack Davidson remarks in a review at *NoiseNotMusic*, 'Brutal. There is no other word that more accurately describes *My Mother the Vent*. There are neither brakes nor breaks on this unstoppable train of scalding noise' (2018). An October 2020 live performance for Tusk Virtual (a remote version of the UK festival) picks up the ante from *My Mother* and runs with it, drums thwacking and guitar and voice screaming and scraping, with synths occasionally taking over for more fragmented, blocky, disjointed interludes, for a fierce forty-two minutes of music (Tusk TV). This is noise rock as dread-ecstatic ritual, the primal forces of noise, of rock and of life conjured, and ultimate transcendence offered.

As with other noise rock acts, then, from the overwhelming spectacles of Boredoms to the wild musical gesticulations of Ruins to the thumping din and drill of Einstürzende Neubauten, in Guttersnipe the raw, tensile power running through noise and rock is canalized into something powerful, distinctive, immersive and, perhaps, transcendent. Noise rock, in this sense and at its best, can animate even the staidest and chin-scratchy of experimental audiences on the one hand or grab hold of even the most conservative of pop listeners on the other. Noise rock, in this sense, is neither 'noise' nor 'rock', even as it mines from both. Instead, it is a kind of beautiful synergy in which the buried potential for positive transcendence in each form is realized and released.

Noise and structure

This section expands the story of twenty-first-century noise hybridity covered so far. It uses the lens of 'noise and structure' to do this, by which I mean to address noise music that is based in some way on composed (and, therefore, reproducible) structures, whether songs or less straightforward and predictable forms. The use of different kinds of structure within noise leads to productive creative tensions, given what I see as noise's intrinsic emphasis on loose, open, discursive 'becoming', in which structure and senselessness interpenetrate. A huge array of noise music is based on one or other pre-planned structure; indeed, several such examples have already been mentioned in this chapter. I therefore can't offer a comprehensive account; instead, I focus on two main examples, Wolf Eyes and Jenny Hval, both of whose work has reconciled structure with noise looseness. A final case study on Lingua Ignota rounds things off. The next chapter continues the discussion of noise and structure in its examination of Dominick Fernow/Prurient.

Wolf Eyes

> Dig up descriptions of Michigan trio Wolf Eyes from any time during their 16-year existence, and I doubt you'll see much use of the word 'precision'. But their music has always had this quality – even if it's sometimes been covered in whirring distortion, brittle cacophony, or psychotic howls. Go back as far as 'Half Animal, Half Insane', from 2002's *Dread*, and you can hear them picking and placing their sounds meticulously. Even though the results could feel abrasive or abstract, the attack has never been messy or careless. Most of the time, it's a precise rendering of Wolf Eyes' horror-movie visions and hard-edged sonic obsessions.
>
> (Masters 2013)

Out of all the artists examined in this book, Michigan noise band Wolf Eyes are the only ones that rival – and perhaps even surpass – Merzbow's wider impact beyond the noise scene. Before I get to the question of noise structure explicitly, I'll consider some of this broader context by way of setting the scene for a close reading of the group's musical aesthetic.

Wolf Eyes has included John Olson (saxophone and electronics, mostly) and Nate Young (voice, electronics) as core members since its beginnings in the mid-1990s. This has been alongside founding member Aaron Dilloway (guitar, electronics) from 1998 to 2005, then Mike Connelly (guitar, electronics; latterly of the podcast *Noisextra*, which I've referenced throughout the book) from 2006 to 2012, and finally Jim Baljo (guitar, electronics) from 2012 to present. Wolf Eyes started releasing music in 1998, initially in small runs of CD-Rs on Dilloway's Hanson Records and Olson's American Tapes, and then, particularly after a breakthrough with 2001's *Dread* (Hanson Records, American Tapes), from 2004's *Burned Mind* on at a much larger scale on the leading grunge and indie label, Sub Pop. The latter was formerly home of Nirvana, Soundgarden, Fleet Foxes and many other popular acts. Some later albums (and Olson's 2016 book, *Life Is a Rip-Off*) were released on Jack White's Third Man Records, a similarly prominent indie label. Wolf Eyes' relationships with Sub Pop and Third Man outstrip Merzbow's passing arrangement with Relapse in terms of noise incursions into mainstream spaces. For a period in the 2000s and early 2010s, indeed, Wolf Eyes' level of exposure and impact outside noise inner sanctums was unprecedented, with the group regularly being written about in mainstream publications and appearing at music festivals like South by Southwest. By 2012, Grayson Currin and Marc Masters could refer to Wolf Eyes as 'the most visible band in the international noise scene', and as 'perhaps the face of noise for a generation' (2012). Similarly, in the *Miami New Times* in 2013 Matt Preira described the group as 'one of the most iconic bands from the early to mid-2000s explosion of noise music that reverberated (deafeningly) across North America'.

Of course, as with BxC and many others, the 'noise' status of Wolf Eyes is at least partially open for debate. Writing in the *Guardian* in 2017, Jennifer Lucy Allan suggested that Wolf Eyes 'typically get tagged as noise, and while that was accurate for the sand-blasted sonics of their early 2000s material, it's the wrong peg now'. The 'face of noise' quote above indeed continues in a similar vein: 'they've refused to let that oft-disputed term shackle their search for new sounds. Which means that everything is fair game' (Currin and Masters 2012). Making a broader point that yet speaks to this theme, in 2013 John Olson himself even declared that 'noise is over', 'completely, 100%'. This, Olson argued, was due to the proliferation of many different offshoots and hybrids on the noise scene, which in turn meant that 'all the categories, everything has run its course' (Preira 2013). For Olson, the noise centre could no longer hold. We'll get further into this question of the boundaries of noise music and Wolf Eyes' place within that in discussing two of the group's albums below, *Burned Mind* (Sub Pop, 2004) and *No Answer: Lower Floors* (De Stijl, 2013). As will already be appreciated, though, with Wolf Eyes as much as with BxC, we see noise blending into a broader experimental music ecosystem. Wolf Eyes are in this sense yet more 'noise radicants', hovering in and drawing identity and strength from the noise scene and related musics like noise rock without being confined to either.

By 2004, Wolf Eyes had already made waves on the noise scene and elsewhere, their supporting gigs in the early 2000s with Sonic Youth being just one example of their contact with mainstream audiences. The band were in a curious, though not unprecedented, position: the ears of the indie scene turned towards them and some interest in breaking through but an equal or perhaps greater (trickster) inclination to make abrasive, unfriendly sound that would upset many on that scene. The *Pitchfork* review of *Burned Mind* sums up the conflicted nature of the moment and of *Burned Mind*:

> Wolf Eyes are hyperbole-inducing provocateurs whose scalding compositions never fail to get a rise out of unsuspecting bystanders. And that's part of what makes them so appealing/appalling … This is by far Wolf Eyes' most visceral release to date. The masochistic appeal of stertorous noise and the comely allure of pop music are one in the same: *Burned Mind*, like any pop album worth its salt, conjures a deeper realm of images and moods beyond its surface qualities.
>
> (Ubl 2004)

Though other reviews emphasized the intensity and ugliness of the sound over and above its supposed 'pop' status, most expressed some sense of the relationship of the record to slightly more mainstream forebears and styles such as noise rock and industrial. Edwin Pouncey's *Wire* piece, for example, describes *Burned Mind* as 'a horror show of a record that noisily summons up the kind of nightmare images of such outré horror film makers as Dario Argento and Lucio Fulci … In the same tradition as Throbbing Gristle, Whitehouse, Swans and the original Destroy All Monsters, a genuine sense of danger and trepidation stalks through these tracks' (2004, 63).

It's easy to hear the horror, the nightmare and the noise on *Burned Mind*. Opening track, 'Dead in a Boat', follows forty-six or forty-seven seconds of very distant, quiet sound with the same again in blasted, crunching static and feedback. This is wall churn whose brutality is akin to that of someone like Government Alpha. Next track, 'Stabbed in the Face', picks up at the same level; apart from a very brief interlude at the two-minute mark, the track is a near-four-minute, pounding blast of screaming, thumping and squalling. But it never feels chaotic: underlying the whole thing is a steady two-count ostinato in the form of a repeated bass glissando that hugely throbs through the centre of the track. This creates an anchor, a pulse and a driving forward momentum all at the same time. 'Village Oblivia' is built on the same kind of piledriving noise pulsing; skulking low synth notes and hits stretch and vibe as distorted screams and other sonic detritus spray about. And yet here, as on 'Stabbed', the track is always held in tension and poised, the repeated lower tones and percussion creating a sense of shape and scaffolding for the more chaotic noise blasting through otherwise. This is the order/disorder noise dialectic in perfect microcosm, the music suspended in polarity. Even quieter tracks like the balletic, noise-essay-in-delay-and-fuzz 'Reaper's Gong', or the crackly 'Urine Burn', or the gloomier, cavernous 'Ancient Delay', feel sonically deliberate in this kind of way, each gesture cleverly repeated and varied and carefully placed amidst a flow of repeating, sometimes wild sounds. Album closer, 'Black Vomit', spotlights distorted guitar, feedback, screams and, again, skulking, repeated beats. It stretches these and other sounds out over eight white-knuckle minutes, intensity building slowly and purposively as layers and gestures keep getting added to the repeated, four-beat loop that sits at the heart of the first half of the track. Things explode into a faster, choppier array of beats, tears and fission for the second half, which builds to a climax that is ear-shredding but exultant in its screaming, staticky totalizing intensity.

As can be seen in my discussion of these tracks, even an extreme, scorched-earth work like *Burned Mind* was therefore founded at least in part on deliberate sonic layering and formal iteration; on a dialectical tension between structure and non-structure. After all, for all the aggressive walls of static and shredding noise climaxes on the record, each track is clearly undergirded by structural cohesion either in the form of repeating loops and beat patterns or, more subtly, in the sympathetic or complementary interrelationships of its sounds and motifs. This taste for intensity and wildness rooted ultimately in precision persisted in Wolf Eyes' work. For example and as we've seen, by the time we get to 2013's *No Answer: Lower Floors*, the always outspoken Olson was pushing the idea that noise was apparently 'over', a point that seems absurd but does also support my own broader argument about noise's hybridity in the twenty-first century; its ability, for example, to embrace the wild and the precise together. It's just that I don't see this hybridity signalling the end of noise or even a particularly new chapter of it (though the expanded fringe ecosystem discussed earlier does colour noise hybridity anew), as much as I do as an intensification of tendencies towards innovation and change that were present from the beginning.

Olson, in this vein of constant change, describes embracing 'composition' and 'structure' over and above the focus on 'experimentation' that he felt dominated both

Wolf Eyes' earlier work (even if we heard *Burned Mind* differently) and the approach of many other noise artists:

> We were lost in a field of experimentation trying out a million things. You can only do that for so long. You get stuck in the same rut. But now, Jim, the new guy, he's not a jammer at all. We can make stuff that is riff-based and we can make shorter songs with a lot more parts ... It's very much more about mechanics rather than blasting off to the cosmos and hoping the audience is still with you. We're sticking to the songs and getting into the power of composition and structure and stuff like that.
>
> (Preira 2013)

Olson expands on the point, decrying the 'safety' of avoiding structure in making noise, and even suggesting that a focus on 'texture and adjectives', as opposed to a more traditionally music-theoretical 'vocabulary' and 'discipline', gets in the way of being able to assess whether a piece of noise is 'right' or 'wrong':

> All this freeform stuff, you sort of just speak in some safety language and your vocabulary gets more and more limited. Me and Nate got tired of people just using texture and not having enough composition. How many dudes play noise, and you can say 'Oh, that's wrong' or 'That's right'. When you actually get into scales and the power of notes and actually playing, to go back to vocabulary, you just have a lot more to say. Rather than just being stuck on texture and adjectives.
>
> (Preira 2013)

Setting aside the false binaries Olson erects here between both vocabulary and experimentation or texture, and even between 'good' and 'bad', tracking his statements about structure onto *No Answer* itself makes for an intriguing exercise. Because it *is* possible to hear how important clear, even reproducible structures are on the album. Opener 'Choking Flies', for example, uses structure very precisely, the sonic space carved out clearly by a repeated drum tattoo just to the right of the picture, a central buzz of soft distortion and busy sine waves, and a deeper, attacking and decaying fuzz to the left. And then, eventually, clear but louche, Throbbing Gristle-like vocals at the centre. The placing of the vocals in the middle section of the track creates a distinctive off, on, off structure, whilst the relative softness of the sounds and the clear sonic architecture staged by the mix likewise create structural cohesion even amidst the creeping bristle and smatter of the sounds. Similar deliberation and precision run through tracks like 'Born Liar' and the, again, Gristle-like 'Chattering Lead'. Despite some crunch and distortion in the sound of these tracks, the overall style is less confrontational and wild than it had been on *Burned Mind*. But Wolf Eyes' edge had not simply softened or dulled by 2013. It's more that their taste for detail and sonic flavour had transmuted, now leaning less towards blasting walls and more towards the sonic space, silence and compositional variety of an extended track like 'Confession of the Informer'. This track indeed feels like almost like a wistful, delicate phonographic tribute to some of the subtler qualities of power electronics and death industrial music, those musics refracted through age and distance into something new. Similarly with closer 'Warning Sign'; more outwardly abrasive than the other tracks with its repeated slash of guitar-esque distortion, its initial aggression softens as the main loop repeats, twists, reveals new angles through its intermeshing with other subtle touches of feedback, or scraping, or deep echoing.

Once again, then, order anchors or infuses disorder, structure channels search. Compositional or 'musical' blood, noise heart, perhaps. Both on earlier work like *Burned Mind* and, especially, later albums such as *No Answer: Lower Floors*, characteristic toggling between noise and music, or freedom and structure, is everywhere. As such, Wolf Eyes' music, in the end, probably contains too much precision and predictability for it truly to evoke the kind of overwhelming, never-resolving noise becoming present in more traditional harsh examples. And yet, the same engine of order/disorder that drives harsh noise can be seen to drive Wolf Eyes, even if they go at a slightly different speed and in a different style car to artists like Merzbow and Macronympha.

Jenny Hval

The relationship between noise and song, like the broader one between noise and structure just discussed, is a rich one. Many popular artists have incorporated elements of noise in their work, from the Beatles and 'Revolution No. 9' (EMI, 1968) to the distortion of Nirvana's 'Territorial Pissings' (Sub Pop, 1991). But such examples, for the most part, cover cases where noise is used as an exception or special case in a mainstream artist's music. What I'm interested in exploring here, instead, is the related but distinct case of more marginal, often experimentally driven artists who have sought to reconcile noise with song in some meaningfully sustained way in their work. I cover one main example, the Norwegian Jenny Hval, and finish by addressing Lingua Ignota.

Hval is one of a number of 2010s and 2020s artists working in what has been a productive, hybrid space between popular and experimental music; other notable examples include Julia Holter and Grouper. Not all these artists have interacted with or used noise in their work. But, like Puce Mary in the last chapter, Hval does indeed openly engage with noise both in terms of noisy sound and in terms of the kinds of body-centred themes often found in noise. Hval has even closely collaborated with noise musician Lasse Marhaug. As such, Hval presents a useful case study here.

Early album, *Innocence Is Kinky* (Rune Grammofon, 2013), demonstrates the variety of Hval's palette very well. Tracks like 'Innocence is Kinky' and 'Death of the Author' hew to a more atmospheric, tuneful, experimental-folk-like melding of spoken word and song, with traditional instruments such as guitar and keyboards driving the sound. On the other hand, songs like 'Give Me That Sound', whilst sticking to a concise length and including accessible elements such as spoken word, include both abrasive feedback and distortion and fragmented, discontinuous textures. At this stage, then, Hval's work had settled comfortably across styles. Fellow Norwegian Marhaug came on board as a co-producer for the albums *Apocalypse, Girl* (2015) and *Blood Bitch* (2016), both of which were released via Su Tissue and

Sacred Bones Records (the latter of which, notably, has also been Pharmakon's label). Whilst maintaining Hval's characteristic blend of personal, challenging themes; accessible, elegant, pretty tunes and sounds; and less friendly, more nebulous or abrasive textures and colours, these albums represent a further step forward into the challenging and the strange for Hval.

Miles Raymer's *Pitchfork* review of *Apocalypse, Girl* sums up Hval's progression well (though a return to more straightforward and relatively soft melodicism on 2022's *Classic Objects*, on 4AD, belies this linear 'progress' into noise):

> Musically, *Apocalypse* pushes boundaries that were barely visible on her last album. For all its noisy interludes and sharply angular melodies, a lot of *Innocence Is Kinky* was straightforward, held down by fairly conventional arrangements of guitar, drums, and keys. ... There's a dreamy kind of ambiguity to how the songs are put together: Pop melodies emerge from washes of abstract sound, and sometimes they'll take charge of the song, but sometimes they simply fade back into the churn.
> (2015)

This quote indeed captures the breadth of *Apocalypse, Girl*. Songs drift in and out of textural sound, even noise, as on the soft, vocable-driven, elusive and ambient noise of 'White Underground' or the extended, pent-up, stuttery cyborg surface and drawn-out background of 'Holy Land'. And yet, except for the latter, the tracks stay anchored in concise forms driven by spoken or sung texts. 'Heaven' is a good illustration of how the album reconciles compositional control and structure with more floating, textural sound in this kind of way. Starting out in a distant, ambient seaside, the track moves into darkly coloured, beat-driven electro pop, which climaxes with twinkling harp and strained voice, before the music drifts out on cloudy ambience once again. 'Heaven', in this sense, places noise and pop comfortably together in the same space, the one infusing the other as if it was the most natural thing in the world (as with noise and rock earlier). The comfort of the pairing here brings out new shades in my broader argument about noise; that it is founded on an emergent but never fully realized musicality and language. This point is expressed in different ways across noise but all noise dances to a shared, suspended dialectic in which music and noise are engaged in a perpetual *pas de deux*; even such seemingly structured songs as Hval's.

Blood Bitch evinces similar plays of noise and song or structure, with reviews almost universally grappling in this spirit with Hval's position across popular and experimental music (e.g. Hannah 2016; Presley 2016). Explicitly themed around vampires and blood – the blood of menstruation in particular – '*Blood Bitch*' is, in reality, 'about' a multitude of things, from, as Alex Griffin has it, vampires to capitalism to loneliness to pap smears (Griffin 2016). As Griffin also says, the album is 'thick with meaning', its highly literary, political, even theoretical allusions meshing elusively in turn into nesting layers of structure and noise. Those layers take in vocal and non-vocal sound. For example, spoken and sung vocals manifest a kind of quiet, stuttering, clipped, breathy unease throughout, as on tracks like the scrabbling, Adam Curtissampling 'Untamed Region', or 'In the Red', which is anchored in a looped cloud of panting and breathing. Meanwhile, the instrumental portions stretch widely, taking in low synth bass tones, propulsive beats, dream-pop singing and uncertain noisy effects such as scratching of pen or screaming or gasping; the Julia Holter-like 'Female Vampire' contains many of these elements. Finally, drones and white noise add texture and moments of uncertainty throughout the album; 'The Plague' leans particularly intently on sonic harshness, with effects such as feedback, screaming, burning and dripping tearing through its frenetic, pockmarked and percussive surface. And yet, hooky melodies or riffs or basslines anchor many of the tracks in a sense of regularity and pulse. 'Period Piece', with its steady drum pattern, its simple three-chord bassline and its pretty, layered, echoey vocals is a good example; the fact that its lyrics describe medical procedures doesn't undermine its pop appeal. Hval's vocals take on a Trish Keenan-like innocence and softness on 'The Great Undressing'. 'Conceptual Romance' is perhaps the most accessible of all, with its massed backing vocals and its hummable chorus hook.

Blood Bitch, then, issues with a kind of dualistic force that is typical for Hval's work. Hval habitually uses both noise and heavily personal, directly expressed themes in concert with accessible riffs, repetition and traditionally refined sound and structures. The two – 'experimental' or 'noise' on one side and 'commercial' and 'musical' on the other – mesh without much trouble, creating productive tension and power. As if it needed saying: noise could never be antithetical to musical structure or vice versa. Noise is always, or always has the potential to be, structural. As I started to say before we got to *Blood Bitch*, this is what 'becoming' and 'noise *music*' have been all about. Conversely, music can and often does drift to disorder and noise but invariably pulls away from these. An artist like Hval draws out these dynamics in explicit form, revealing and exploring things that are usually hidden, and in turn revealing new shades in the noise/music dialectic we've spent so much time discussing.

Lingua Ignota

Hval is far from alone in this drawing out of the apparent – but not actual – antinomies of noise and song/structure. Providence artist Christopher Forgues provides a good point of comparison, since his work as Kites featured circuit-bent, freely structured harsh noise rubbing shoulders with more song-based tracks, as on the 2005 album, *Peace Trials* (Load). To take just one final, extremely germane example, Californian musician Kristin Hayter has been releasing albums as Lingua Ignota ('unknown language' – an apt moniker given the themes of this Chapter) since 2017. Hayter's work as Lingua Ignota sits somewhere between torch song, industrial music, noise, extreme metal and contemporary classical. Early albums *Let the Evil of His Own Lips Cover Him* and *All Bitches Die* (both 2017, and both self-released, though the latter was reissued by Profound Lore in 2018) were characteristically themed around domestic abuse and violence (recalling Moonbeam Terror and other artists from Chapter Eight). Each of these early albums blended scorching death-industrial fuzz, scream and echo with chamber pop melodies and arrangements. The two often, though not always, collided within the same delicately constructed track, as for example on the fifteen-minute tour de force 'Woe to All (On the Day of My Wrath)' from *All Bitches Die*. Other tracks are more traditionally conceived both in terms of form (often verse-chorus) and melody and harmony (often conventional), even though subject matter is usually brutal. 'Holy Is the Name (of My Ruthless Axe)', again from *All Bitches Die*, is a good example: it opens with Aileen Wuornos describing how she killed a man who was attacking her, then moves into the main song, which is a piano and vocal ballad that is soft and reverberant in sound, swooping and delicate in melody, and grim but perhaps cathartic in words: 'All my rapists lay beside me.'

Later Ignota albums, *Caligula* (Profound Lore, 2019) and *Sinner Get Ready* (Sargent House, 2021), continued in broadly the same thematic territory as before, focusing as they did on gender-based violence, abuse and survival, albeit lensed through biblical imagery and language in the latter case. Their musical palette, still hybrid and varied, shifted a little from the rougher industrial sounds of the first two albums, moving more directly into acoustic, chamber arrangements aligned to experimental folk and pop music. But that's not to downplay the continued noisiness and aggression of Hayter's sound. For example, the nine-minute *Sinner* opener, 'The Order of Spiritual Virgins', twists and turns throughout. It starts off with a choral and piano-led torch ballad underpinned with quiet bass drone. In its fifth minute, it moves into more fragmented territory, noise-piano clouds and percussive clatters and fuzz interjecting between bare, sung lines and feedback. This toing and froing between noise and song shapes much of the last five minutes of the track. Precision in construction contains and channels internal tension between noise overwhelm and sung meaning here, as objects placed on piano strings and unpredictable silences and shapes vie with, push against, spoken word and restrained sound. Hayter indeed finds creative ways to introduce sonic noise into otherwise fairly clearly wrought structures and songs throughout the record. We can hear this on the buzzing, sawing zither and detuned guitar string backing of 'Many Hands', and on the dread-filled, Galas-like screams and hollers of 'I Who Bend the Tall Grasses'. This is truly hybrid music, then. It is connected in theme, in sound and in its Hvalian dialectical tension between song and noise to both noise and industrial music. But it is likewise anchored nonetheless in deliberate compositional structures and arrangements derived from folk, chamber pop and contemporary classical. It is both, and.

Conclusion

This chapter has argued that twenty-first-century noise music had reached the traditional and, by extension, 'hybrid' stage of its genre trajectory, merging into and establishing itself within broader musical ecosystems. This merging has produced many local noise hybrids. We have used the lenses of experimental music, noise rock and structure – though others are available – to think about the way in which noisy music and musicians have produced 'radicant' hybrid work that seeks to blend noise style with techniques from outside noise (or vice versa). I've argued, further, that noise rock, experimental noise and noisy song all in their own way reveal how porous to more traditional musical approaches noise as a style actually is. Noise and music, unsurprisingly, contain each other all the way down. Harsh noise reveals this point in structural aporia, whilst the hybrid noise of this chapter reveals it in more straightforward style and language dialectics. This point will deepen in our final chapter where, in contrast to the 'radicant', hybrid, noise-allied artists of the current chapter, the focus shifts to more straightforwardly 'noise' artists working in either hybrid contexts or styles.

10

Hybrid noisebloom Part Two: Noise music now

'Noise music now' suggests too grand a target for this single, final chapter. Adapting its subtitle from the title of Part Two, the chapter instead simply rounds off the story of noise music, now, which the book has been telling over its previous four chapters. The chapter adapts the 'hybrid' frame of Chapter 9 but switches focus from that chapter's rootless (or multi-rooted) 'radicants' to noise musicians making hybrid work and/or existing within a broader hybrid ecosystem. It is not structured according to geography – the transcultural point so universal as to have slipped into the background – nor is it structured according to the music-stylistic or thematic lenses of the previous four chapters. The focus is instead on three recent noise artists whose music expresses different aspects of noise style and hybridity: Dominick Fernow's Prurient, Masahiko Okubo's Linekraft and Margaret Chardiet's Pharmakon.

Dominick Fernow – Prurient

More than any other, the previous chapter addressed some big names from the noise scene. This was to be expected, given its hybrid frame and therefore the fact that its scope naturally spread out to 'friendlier' and more commercially appealing areas of music than harsh noise. Like Wolf Eyes, Lightning Bolt and Jenny Hval, Dominick Fernow has had a significant impact on the wider contexts of experimental and even popular music surrounding noise. For example, prominent pieces on Fernow have appeared in everything from *Village Voice* to *Fact* (Weingartern 2006; Sande 2012). A 2018 profile in *Resident Advisor* even described Fernow as 'one of the world's most prominent noise musicians', and his Hospital Productions label as 'a driving force in American underground electronic music for the last two decades' (Ryce). Fernow's largest general impact has probably come through his darkly coloured techno as Vatican Shadow and his 2009–11 membership in electronic group Cold Cave. And yet, it's difficult to wall different parts of Fernow's activities off from each other, given their close alignments of aesthetic and tone. The *Resident Advisor* piece just referenced indeed casually and typically covers all aspects of Fernow's work, from noise to techno. In contrast to similarly impactful, hybrid artists like Hval and Lightning Bolt, however, Fernow has been located absolutely at the centre of the noise scene. This is both via his core practice as Prurient and in his role as label head of Hospital, which has released somewhere in the region of 700 albums since its origins in 1997/8 and whose New

York, East Village shop provided a site of pilgrimage for noise, extreme metal and other fringe music fans from 2006 to 2011.

Fernow is therefore rooted in noise but fundamentally hybrid in orientation. This is as true of Prurient's music as it is of any other part of Fernow's work. That music spreads across traditionally 'harsh', power electronics-indebted screams and screeches; techno beats; dark ambience; and even synth pop. To get at this variety, I'll focus in detail on two releases, *The History of Aids* (Armageddon Label/Hospital Productions, 2002) and *Frozen Niagara Falls* (Profound Lore, 2015), the one traditionally harsh and the other more capacious and varied. I discuss other notable albums along the way.

The History of AIDS is a kind of concept album based on texts drawn from the poet Rumi. Though this text is mangled into distorted screams and burbles throughout, the album nevertheless echoes and honours the emotive nature of its stated subject. Fernow's unloosed, strangulated vocals are a particular source of pathos and turmoil. *The History of AIDS* blends power electronics and harsh noise in a manner familiar to us from late 1980s and early 1990s 'harsh power' acts like Blackhouse. It contrasts short, sub-sixty-second, either thrashy and feedback-heavy, or roomy and phonographic, tracks, with more atmospheric, drawn-out tracks filled with synth bass gurgles, screams and feedback. Across both short and longer tracks, a meshing of harsh, restless, searching sounds with intense emotions dominates. The crackling, oscillating wall drone and engorged screams of opener, 'Precious Love', are a great example of this. The same mesh, the same unsettling but moving affect, is present on short, sharp, aphoristic tracks like 'Surrender' and 'Dizziness', just as it is longer ones like the enigmatic, fragmentary 'Bittersweet' or the near-ten-minute looping staticky beat pattern, now loud and stomping, now quiet and concentrated, of closer 'Secret'. All these tracks grab the lapels, holding you in mid-air as musical resolution or closure is suspended in the face of ever-one-more scream or clump of static.

The album's consistent contrast between shorter and longer tracks may suggest that some grand compositional design or structure underlies *The History of AIDS*. Similarly, the slowly unspooling, often sonically nuanced variations of the central loop in 'Secret'. However, both the loose, restless, unpredictable shape of most of the tracks themselves, and the overall sequencing, where there is no clear carry through across tracks or a legible grand arc – apart from some tailing off in intensity in the last few tracks before 'Secret', a sequence in which field recordings of rain and thunder start to dominate – mean that the album in the end feels more extempore than planned. Brief, loose, harsh flourishes on the one hand, and looser, more drawn out, but still unpredictable and harsh atmospheres on the other, dominate. This is ultimately an album that brings together wild, harsh, Masonna-like lacerations with dark-ambient-esque space and gloom and hints of structure. Ultimately, through all these varying techniques, noise overwhelm, depersonalization and restless unpredictability are its abiding effects.

This emphasis on harshness and unpredictability, often realized via terrible screams and restless, hacking microphone and pedal feedback, persisted through later Prurient albums even as newer sounds entered the picture. This can be seen on 2005's pummelling *Black Vase* (Load) and 2006's more rhythmic but still intense *Pleasure Ground* (Load). However, Fernow's work as Prurient particularly began to take on new colours, new atmospheres, new sounds in the 2010s. Jess Harvell's *Pitchfork* review of Fernow's almost synth-pop 2011 release, *Bermuda Drain* (Hydra Head) – as accessible an album as Fernow has released even to this day and one that had a relatively significant crossover impact at the time – sums up Fernow's progression from noise screech to driving beats and even 'beauty':

> This is not the plug-your-ears Prurient you've come to know and possibly love. In the world of 21st-century harsh noise, Dominick Fernow's one-man recordings have been among the harshest, the most physical, the least compromising ... They felt pained, beyond urgent, the product of some need to loose inner turmoil into the world, coming as much from Fernow's body as his machines. *Bermuda Drain* isn't just pleasant by contrast with Prurient's old unholy racket. It's often actively enjoyable, albeit in a decidedly creepy way, rooted as much in familiar retro-rock moves as formless face-eating noise.... *Bermuda Drain* is full of distortion-free keyboard, perverse disco beats, moments of beauty, even hooks.
>
> (2011)

This move into more accessible sound continued over the next few years. To wit, Fernow followed *Bermuda Drain* with the stylistically similar *Time's Arrow* (also Hydra Head, 2011), which featured synth noise on Side A and harsher dark ambient on Side B. Meanwhile, in 2013 Fernow released a much more techno-focused record, *Through the Window* (Blackest Ever Black). All these records maintained Fernow's dark, sometimes cold colours, gloomy affect and harsh overwhelm, but as noted encased these largely in legible rhythms, accessible sounds and riffs.

Fernow's 2015 double album, *Frozen Niagara Falls*, drew together many of the stylistic interests mentioned above, acting as a kind of grand summation of his near twenty-year career to that point. Like most reviews, Tristan Bath's *Quietus* piece picks up on the summatory aspect of the album:

> The offering of crushing icy synth melodies, crashing beats and even (wait for it) the odd acoustic guitar that pierce their way through Dominick Fernow's widest ever array of noises on *Frozen Niagara Falls*, all feel like the logical conclusion to his nearing 20 year musical journey ... *Frozen Niagara Falls* spends 16 tracks in 90 minutes grasping every tool in his arsenal, utilising them to punt emotions around a gloomy icy cave until, bruised and battered, only the freedom of apathetic resignation remains.
>
> (2015)

Frozen contains a few shorter, more purely noise-orientated tracks – as on the glitchy, scratchy 'Wildflowers', the screaming, staticky sprays of 'Poinsettia Pills', and the strangulated death industrial of 'Falling Mask'. But I'll concentrate on some of the longer tracks on the album to articulate the scope of what Bath's 'every tool in his arsenal' means, and to explore how the album mixes sounds and structural approaches in its powerful hybrid noise style.

Ten-minute opening track, 'Myth of Building Bridges', sums up the almost prog-like noise ambition of the album well. The track starts out delicately, distant pitter-patter and feedback patterns piercing through an array of quiet sine waves. A cold-wave-like synth motif enters after seventy seconds, arcing out little minor-key runs and tattoos as static, sine waves, low tones, sequenced arpeggios and kick-drum hits slowly build density over the next few minutes. This first half of the track, then, uses an array of noisy and more musical sounds to build momentum and energy deliberately, reaching a pitch of activity towards the end of the fifth minute. The texture clears near the beginning of the sixth minute, held sine tones beaming in over each other in relaying tension as the main synth motif transfers to what sounds like mandolin or acoustic guitar. That motif continues through several different timbral iterations over the next few minutes. All the while, the sound becomes more fragmented and pockmarked, with cymbal hits, sine waves and, above all, distorted effects (sometimes voice-based, sometimes more abstracted), pushing things this way and that, unsettling stability and balance. The final two minutes see a retreat into further sonic ice and dirge. The main synth motif, arpeggiated sequence and overlaid sine waves create sheeting cold. At the same time, cymbal hits, low tones and roving distortion and static creating a sense of crud and hobble nonetheless; these final passages draw together much of the range of the earlier track, overlaying typical noise instability and tension on cold, hard resignation. Style across 'Myth of Building Bridges' is therefore varied. Noise elements come together in an almost Hvalian way with more traditional musical techniques derived from Krautrock, cold wave and other genres. Form, meanwhile, is organic and flowing – a quality expressed both in the lack of words and extended length, and in the loose, disordering sprays and hits of noise present throughout – and yet also always anchored by a version of the underlying synth motif. That motif gives the track a sense of grounding and definition all the way through, almost like a kind of variation form or, more precisely, an ostinato. Much of the expressive weight is generated out of a clash between the musically firm, anchoring cycles of that motif and the loose noise and flow of the other sounds.

These qualities of stylistic breadth, control and collision carry through to much of the rest of the album. The most vivid example of this might be the best-known track, the pulverizing 'Dragonflies to Sew You Up'. The lyrics of this track, drenched in distortion and exposed emotion in Fernow's performance, describe a car accident in which the narrator's lover is trapped and seemingly killed: 'Are you going mad in there? Are you rotting in there?' Its sound melds death-industrial screams and thwacking, distorted drums with repetitive, minor-key acoustic guitar fills and synth pads. Once again, 'noise' and 'music' blend and mesh strikingly here, the one creating irresistible dialectical tension with the other as a kind of stylistic theatre allegorizing the track's visceral scene.

The longest track on the album at 11'21", closer 'Christ among the Broken Glass' swims in similar stylistic waters again, though its particular approach is worth discussing in more detail as a final illustration of *Frozen Niagara Falls*' breadth and flavour. A slow, gleaming string motif – zither-like in its trebly purity – starts the track off. Texture builds from there in an almost Pink-Floydian way, as isolated low tones;

'concrete' sound effects such as fire, crowd noise and water; a shaker; and acoustic guitar fills gradually bring us into the track 'proper'. With shaker and acoustic guitar holding a steady downbeat pattern across the fourth minute, we move into even proggier territory (proggy not just in an extended formal sense but also, now, a sonic sense) with the return of the opening string melody across the fifth and sixth minutes. Dirtier sounds start to enter towards the end of the sixth minute, though the shaker holds us steady as we go, before a descending pattern based on the earlier string motif brings us into quasi-sacred topical territory. The different string and guitar motifs and fills change places over the next minute, alternating positions and shape freely. The ninth minute introduces a new, lower range and warmer guitar riff, this providing notable contrast with the trebly, gleaming zithery notes above it. The sound drains out for the final passage in the tenth and eleventh minutes, held synth tones revolving as distant rain patters and a hushed Fernow whispers a narrative from somewhere 'Under skyscrapers, And shopping cart tents, Late in the year, When the temperature drops'.

As before, the form of 'Christ among the Broken Glass' feels carefully weighted and patterned in some respects. And yet, it is also somewhat free and unpredictable in scope. After all, as with more adventurous (actual) prog music, the music finds its own tributaries and shapes here, both in terms of the light noisiness of some of the sound and in terms of the unusual arc of the track. The latter veers quite far from the usual templates of verse, chorus and bridge, even though it never completely eschews the kind of organizing principles they imply, as for example the use of distinct motifs, repetition and variation, and rises and falls of tension, volume and textural weight.

As we near the end, 'God and his Son' appear in the track's closing, whispery narrative, found amidst broken images and broken people in a freezing, desolate New York City. This appearance strikes more of a lamenting, humanistic tone than might be expected in the context of an artist whose work has often been known to lean towards lurid harshness and power-electronics brutality. The pretty, sad, plucked sounds of the music at that point only enhance this impression. But really, that humanistic tone is perfectly in keeping with the accessible sounds and loose but legible structures found across *Frozen*, even as it runs up against and alongside the crunchier, dirtier sounds of some of the other tracks. This is an album, after all, that found Fernow, and noise music in general, in an open, receptive position. It sought, and found, consensus between noise as muddling sonic resource and conceptual inspiration on the one hand and contrasting but complementary, conventional ways of making and organizing sound on the other.

With albums like *Frozen Niagara Falls* and *Bermuda Drain*, then, Fernow convincingly made the case for noise as catholic and capacious. As being perfectly able to withstand, or absorb, or gel with the supposedly foreign influence of other styles and with the supposedly disciplining force of musical structure. Post-*Frozen* Fernow continued in this same hybrid vein. For example, 2017's three-hour environmental drone piece of so-called 'doom electronics', *Rainbow Mirror* (Hospital Productions), swung things somewhat back towards inaccessibility via its length and its soft but brooding atmosphere. 2019's *Garden of the Mutilated Paratroopers* (Profound Lore), for its part, leant on short, sharp, terrible punches of noise and grit. Sonic destruction could be heard on *Garden*, whilst across both, a sense of hybrid freedom and personal obsession can be seen writ large. Finally, 2021's collaboration with Merzbow, *Black Crows Cyborg* (Hospital Productions), sits somewhere between these two records, with its industrial churn and fuzz ultimately being softened by more general ambient drone, blur and haze.

Fernow, alongside compatriots like Kris Lapke/Alberich (see an album like 2019's digital, sheened but noisy *Quantized Angel* in particular; Hospital Productions), emphasizes qualities of hybridity and freedom in his noise-based work. Fernow, Lapke and other similar artists' work ultimately shows how fecund noise has been in a twenty-first century where hybridity and adaptation have been key, but where core, even 'classic' genre tropes have likewise remained important. We'll return to this type of hybridity more directly in our final section, '**Pharmakon**'. The next section, by contrast, turns to Linekraft as an example of a twenty-first-century noise artist whose work largely sticks, within itself, to established tropes even as it nevertheless exists within a broader noise and experimental music ecosystem all the same.

Linekraft

Linekraft, aka Japanese musician Masahiko Okubo, makes music that is aligned closely with the noise tradition. And whilst, as with Prurient, Alberich and, as we'll see, Pharmakon, Okubo exists in the broader hybrid ecosystem surrounding noise, unlike those artists his work does not habitually reach out and across to adjacent styles within that ecosystem. To wit, Linekraft's music echoes industrial, power electronics and harsh noise in its use of junk metal and iron plates, rough beats, aggressive vocals and ear-splitting static and feedback. Linekraft does interesting things with these tropes but doesn't often push them into new territory. Linekraft is far from alone in this. Moral Order's heavy, death-industrial-leaning sounds, as on their 2020 EP, *Examples of Solipsism* (Cloister), and, a little earlier in the century, Immaculate: Grotesque's beautifully realized and overwhelmingly intense harsh noise, as on *Circles* from 2003 (Truculent), could be said to operate in a similar way. That is, to sit inside a musical space constructed by previous artists, exploring new nooks and crannies within it or pushing the walls outwards from inside, without regularly breaking through those walls to let sound in from elsewhere. Exceptions can be found in these and similar artists' work – we'll see a partial exception below – but overall, they have tended largely to work comfortably within noise. It's worth emphasizing in this respect that the 'hybrid noisebloom' of the current and previous chapters is not a totalizing argument, at least at the level of musical style. Where 'hybrid noisebloom' *is* totalizing is in its status as a general diagnosis of the scene, where hybridity – which of course includes traditional as well as novel approaches – is more the order of the day than ever. Okubo reflects this in how his music tows fairly trad lines – even if in sometimes subtle and novel ways – even as he inevitably exists within a music broader musical ecosystem.

Linekraft's early music, from 2008 into the later 2010s, as on albums such as the loose, heavy distortion of *Bouryoku Kikai* (Black Plagve, 2012), leant more towards the junk side of post-industrial noise. Later albums, such as 2019's Khmer Rouge-focused *Subhuman Principle* (Tesco Organisation) – Okubo habitually chooses large themes or topics for each release, using them more as loose evocations of mood or idea rather than any strictly programmatic frame – introduced more rigour and control, thus more directly echoing power-electronics discipline in their sound (in the case of 2020's *Industrialized Criminals History* EP on Hospital Productions, this extended to a kind of quasi-minimalistic, chilly synth-driven sound). As Richard Stevenson stated of *Subhuman Principle* in a *Noise Receptor* review, drawing attention to its mix of loose noise and compositional control:

> There is a strong compositional basis on display here, constructed around shuddering bass, looped conveyer belt rhythms, divebombing atonal synths etc., over which are overlaid more chaotic tonal bursts, shredded processed vocals, documentary samples, and sections of scrap metal abuse.
>
> (2020a)

As a way of deepening this initial picture of Linekraft's traditional but subtly fresh later work, I'll discuss 2021's *Asura* (Tesco Organisation) in detail.

Asura is largely a different beast to the preceding *Industrialized Criminals History* (whose focus on the Tokyo Trials was thematically typical but whose music, as noted, largely veered to an unexpected concentration and minimalism). It's true that its stated theme mirrors that of the EP, since it focuses on a murderous moment in recent Japanese history; specifically, the League of Blood Incident from February to March 1932 in which a group of young nationalists assassinated a prominent politician and a businessman. But the music of *Asura* is something else entirely. It eschews the cold, melodic synths and quiet volumes of the preceding *Industrialized Criminals History* in favour of characteristic industrial vocal samples, thwacking beats and destabilizing, grubby, clanging distortion and feedback.

'The Kill for All Living Things' starts out with a tub-thumping drumbeat, which eventually recedes as an oscillating, throbbing low tone and held high static tone increase tension. These two tones then get cut up for ten seconds or so before the initial beat returns to close the track. The track is brief but resolutely full of event, and it's easy to get lost in its loud, dirty, amorphous sound. 'Namu-Myouhourengekyou' loops a sample of what sounds like Buddhist monks chanting, initially heavily clipped and compressed before a second version of the sample, now much less processed, moves into the centre of the track. This sample acts as monophonic drone throughout, anchoring things firmly. Feedback and static pierce or swoop around as the track thickens from its second minute on, little fireworks or divebombs of noise amidst a strangely danceable sound. The title track is noisier and looser still, a trebly ray-gun effect set against whirring noise lower down opening the track in high dudgeon. A low drone is set off in the second minute, shifting momentum, as filters sweep up and down and standing waves fuzz and shimmer. That crinkly, wobbly low drone anchors the sound as a loud, wave-like siren blares for twenty to thirty seconds. Banging, primitive drums enter and a crinkly pedal drone appears an octave above the low one. The final two minutes see each of these elements – the low drone, wave-siren, primitive drums – criss-cross each other, one receding as the other comes to the fore. New elements are added, and others withdrawn, across the final forty-five seconds or so; the removal of the drums and low drone create a particularly striking transformation in the sound, the bottom falling out as various lines and smears of sonic noise hover and wobble until the final fade. 'Asura', as can be seen, ingeniously blends simple musical elements, both forceful and nebulous, increasing volume slowly, moving through different interactions and densities and, above all, using changes in texture and sonic colour as dramatic events, setting listeners into new scenes. This is loud and often loose, messily restless, even disordered noise or sound. But it is also sound that is based in a nimble and alert musicality and drama.

Other tracks take a similar approach. 'Struggle', for example, adds a quixotic, wonky vocal sample at the start, but is otherwise quite an austere, gloomy ballet of tense repeated low tone; murky and dark spoken vocals; blasting mid-range static; and skidding, whirring high tones. Jumping ahead for a moment, album closer, 'One Kills One', similarly adds a strange, in this case monster-esque vocal sample at its opening but is otherwise a track whose brief length and concentrated sonic assault parallel the same in the opening track. The two work as rhetorical bookends for the album in this sense. 'Kill Political Parties, Financial Cliques, and the Privileged', with its bubbling drone, pots-and-pans percussion and chanting samples, and 'Body Warhead', a throbbing, whirring sculpture of simultaneously static and forward-moving noise, are further extensions of the basic harsh, industrial noise template that runs throughout the album. Finally, 'An Assassination in the Organic Universe' is both the longest (at 6'42") and perhaps the most direct of all *Asura* tracks. It starts out with the didgeridoo-like drones heard earlier on 'Industrialized', glazed high harmonics adding passing colour as the drone oscillates slowly. The track builds slowly via the addition of a chugging noise pattern in the middle range, a held high pedal note and, eventually, a distant but relatively sonically clear vocal sample working through a litany of complaints; now spoken, now screamed, always distressed. These vocals give another anchor in the overwhelming sound, though it's a wild, jabbering anchor. By the time we get to the fifth and sixth minutes, 'An Assassination' has settled into something of a steady, minimalist groove, listeners' stability gaining confidence as it goes. A roving, glassy synth line up in the higher register and a simple, quiet four-beat percussion loop anchor things in order even as that voice continues its mad tirade. So, as with much of the rest of the album, 'An Assassination' offsets noise smears and colour with steadier musical shapes and patterns. Like the other tracks, the affective atmosphere here is tense and prone, the music both anchoring and drifting its listeners in and out of ego. But where the shimmering noise sculptures of other tracks – beat or melody, for example, fully dropped in favour of dancing sonic textures – give listeners space to connect to the flow and get out of their heads, the relatively tighter rhythms and phrasing of tracks like 'An Assassination' perhaps leave less space for such immersion.

Either way, these two divergent but related Linekraft releases – the first, *Industrialised Criminals History*, darkly minimal industrial music, the second, *Asura*, louder, more abrasive, messier and looser harsh industrial – demonstrate the vitality of the traditionally orientated noise that is being made amidst the broader, hybrid twenty-first-century noise scene. Industrial music, power electronics, harsh noise and the other musics Linekraft has clearly been inspired by are deep wells whose supply is a long way from being exhausted and/or absorbed. As we move back, in our final example, to a more 'hybrid' leaning noise artist in Pharmakon, we'll nevertheless see this same point in action; after all, Pharmakon's music honours the same industrial and power electronics lineage that is being extended in Linekraft's work. In a sense, Pharmakon serves a kind of middle point between the broad hybridity of Prurient and the more traditional leanings of Linekraft.

Pharmakon

As we saw in Chapter 8, Pharmakon is Margaret Chardiet's industrial-noise project in which themes of abjection, bodily trauma and distress are explored through intense, jagged beats, static and screams, and aggressive and, in Paul Hegarty's words, 'rigorously embodied' performances (2020, 112). Pharmakon's work expresses hybridity in two important senses: in its characteristic musical blends and in its impact and imbrication in broader experimental and alternative music scenes.

As we saw, Pharmakon's 2014 album, *Bestial Burden* (Sacred Bones Records), illustrates Chardiet's typical musical style and thematic character well, with its focus on bodily abjection and its marrying of industrial and power electronics-derived rhythms, static and howling with relatively clean and clear structures and textures. Other Pharmakon albums follow a similar approach. This can be seen in 2017's *Contact* (Sacred Bones Records), which, for Chardiet at least, further focused on mind/body opposition in exploring the kinds of experiences that are possible 'when our mind uses the body in order to transcend or escape it' (cited in Masters 2017). As with *Bestial Burden*, the music on *Contact* focuses on a push-pull tension between grid-like hammering and clanging from percussion and synthesizers on the one hand and looser sonic and vocal elements on the other. Each element combines to create a nervy, tense, prone atmosphere. The focus of my discussion, however, will be 2019's *Devour* (Sacred Bones Records). This album provides another extrapolation of Chardiet's underlying thematic and musical approach, infusing this with a 'live' feel through its two, long, uninterrupted (or, at least, edited together) performances, which are split into three and two tracks, respectively, on each Side but run into each other fluidly.

Devour features characteristically hybrid blends of structure and noise, and style and other style, as we'll see. In terms of theme, *Devour* shifts Chardiet's focus from a struggle between mind and body to one that uses the idea of a self-cannibalizing 'self-attacking-self' – which could be exemplified, for example, by drug addiction or severe mental illness – to explore a broader conflict between self and the external world. Or, as Sasha Geffen puts it, to explore 'the locus where global horrors register on the individual' (Geffen 2019). In terms of style and sound, *Devour* works in a similar vein to previous albums: drums and synths clatter, pulse and revolve; Chardiet screeches and howls; and feedback and static interject or work as noise-texture interwoven into more traditional musical elements. Lisa Busby's review in *Loud and Quiet* sums up the musical style very well, highlighting the looping continuity of the sound, the importance of vertical space in the arrangements and textures and the intensity and impact of Chardiet's vocal performances.

> Loops have always been central to Chardiet's work, but nowhere else so overtly machine-like in their industrial quality as here. There is an intense dynamic, textural and rhythmic continuity throughout; it's an insistently dense album of whirring, pulsing and rotating where slow shifts grind against searing interjections. In this, notions of space are not lost but the horizontal structure and dynamic of previous work is pitched on its end – the voice often clearly framed by relentless, buzzing bass motifs and drilling high feedback.
>
> (2019)

This quote, as well as the points I just made about the album's themes and sound, sums up the broad strokes of the record very well. I now pivot into an extended close reading of *Devour* that, given the hybrid, harsh character of the music, draws on analytical styles from across the book, blending more removed analytical description with present-tense reflections on listening and moment-to-moment event.

'Homeostasis' starts out with a serrated buzzsaw synth loop. Clumping drums banging out the first two beats of a steady 4/4 add martial tension, holding me in place. A heavily echoing, distorted Chardiet enters, screaming and screeching distress. The words are cloaked by effects, almost inaudible (I'm reminded of Hegarty's point that there is often a 'play of excess around and against the voice, or against the clarity of the voice', in Chardiet's music; 2012, 112), though lines like 'Static complacency, A deafening wall of static' do come through (the full lyrics are available online, but when heard they operate more as noise or sound than words). Drilling and sawing interject between verses, acting as noise hooks or licks almost like guitar fills, as the buzzsaw synth and drums contain and constrain. It's exciting, but also unsettling, to be shackled to so tight, fixed a sound; I wait for something to break me free even as I enjoy the hold. The track ends with about a minute of the relentless loops, now thickened with a slowly oscillating drone, Chardiet's vocals dissolved into whispered harmonics and glossolalia.

(Release never quite came.)

Those same whispers creep into 'Spit it Out', underlying pulse now given by another synth throb, this one a tone up from the previous track and looping every two beats rather than four, short-long again and again and again. At 7'32" in length, the track builds texture slowly, layers of slowly arcing fuzz and distortion revolving over each other, before a now howling, throat-shredded Chardiet enters in the third minute, again in some distress. High-pitched feedback and that arcing, swooping fuzz interject between the disgusted verses. The freedom in this sound, both in itself and for me as a listener, is in how the layers of sound spark off each other, never quite settling, never quite being fully contained by the thudding loops at their base. There is another kind of freedom in Chardiet's vocal performance, of course, even if it is the kind of freedom that usually comes in response to some kind of profound trap, again calling to Hegarty's point about the relation of music to voice here.

The music changes quite remarkably towards the end of the fifth minute of 'Spit it Out'. The synth bass loop almost doubles in speed (i.e. almost halves in note values), textures become much more fragmented, Chardiet's screams become even more intense, and sounds come in and out of definition as feedback cuts about. Chardiet reaches a terrible peak at the end of this passage. Things slow, clean out somewhat, in the seventh minute, as the track buzzes, saws, and throbs to its violent, cymbal-frying end. I spoke about freedom a moment ago. The climax of this slowly built track offers a different version of freedom to its listeners, pulling us along as it fragments and tears down the structures that had held us, launching into a state of scream-driven becoming-chaos. We are free in the total surrender to noise.

'Self-Regulating System' doesn't emerge quite so organically out of 'Spit It Out' as that track had out of the opener, though its stereo-swapping, glitchy noise gestures almost sound like processed samples of the cymbals from the previous track. 'Self-Regulating System' soon settles into a locked groove where triplet drums, repeated bass tone, and careening, drilling glitches derived from the opening create a sense of rocking, tilting spaciousness. A ferocious Chardiet enters in the second minute, reflecting angrily in an extended verse that, 'Caught in the spiral of cause and effect', 'Maybe self-destruction is a viable, Self-regulating system'. It's in lyrics like this that the stated themes of the album – self-cannibalization, self against system – come through perhaps most clearly; although Chardiet's open-wound vocal performances also evoke a general sense of self-in-crisis. And yet, the fact that those lyrics are largely inaudible rather undermines the one-to-one relationship that most reviews identified between the stated themes and the aesthetic content of the work. In any case, 'Self-Regulating System' feels more intent, more hypnotized than the previous tracks. Its form plays a role in this, that long opening verse giving way to a rip-roaring noise climax across the fifth minute especially, sawing, buzzing static consuming the texture into almost total disorder. The underlying loops even give way towards the end of the fifth minute. Instead of then moving back into a second verse, the intensity only increases. Chardiet's voice trips over its own delay-rich screams – 'Maybe self-destruction, The only viable, Self-regulating system' – and the sound dissolves into a chaos of feedback, lacerating static, and textural screaming. Grids and guiderails are now completely dropped in favour of overwhelming becoming-noise. 'Self-Regulating System' makes a mockery of rational detachment both in its own affect field and in the affect conjured in listeners. The music slowly tightened its grip on me, introducing a second presence into the room, the climax ultimately scratching me all over as I grasped for some distance, some logic. Ultimately, it just ends, spent, order never recovered but listeners welcoming, perhaps, the stability that the brief silence at its end (this being the end of Side A) offers. I pause and breath.

'Deprivation' is a little cleaner in sound than the previous track, though its metallic glints and sparks and its low chug of drum and bass contain their own kind of febrile life. The track presents a portentous, intense experience. Its slow wind-up of mood over the first few minutes, and its eventual characteristic climactic dropping of the loop (this time in the fifth minute) in favour of a bristlier, messier noise texture into which Chardiet's abstracted screams wind in and out over the sixth and seventh minutes, serve to twist the knife, our sense of remove and order at risk. At this point, there is a minute or so of searching, overwhelming static and feedback that pushes me back to the immediacy of 'Self-Regulating System', even if things never get quite as unloosed as they had been there; the chaos feels more familiar now.

Stepping back slightly from the sound to get a bearing on the album as a whole, a quieter, throbbing coda leads us into the final track, 'Pristine Panic/Cheek By Jowl', the longest of all at 10'12". Chardiet uses that length to stretch out the form, the first two minutes or so tumbling and teetering back and forth in metallic fuzz and bass as relatively clear vocals spit-whisper about 'Primal and pristine panic, The taste of forbidden fruit, In your mouth and at the tip of your tongue, An instant before the thought becomes clear'. Once again, the lyrics here broadly suggest the stated themes without being tied to them didactically; it's possible, for example, to hear the idea of 'forbidden fruit', and the later talk of 'pit of your stomach' and 'depth of your bowels', as relating to a more general sense of abjection and self-terror than one related directly to some idea of self-against-system. In any case, the tumbling motion steadies just before the end of the second minute into a more familiar, locked loop of two-count held-bass and rocking-synth. A different Chardiet now enters, terrible, shredded screams upsetting the listener's equilibrium. The loop revolves but eventually fades out gradually across the fifth and sixth minutes. A fast stream of susurrating vocals and effects push against the slowing, fading loop, as Chardiet's screams return and continue. Suddenly, at 5'33", the locked loop comes back triumphant and terrible, order restored even as Chardiet's screams and howls ('Being and oblivion, Cheek by jowl'), and the buzzing texture, push against it over the next few minutes. Each, the looped 'being' and the buzzing and screaming 'oblivion', is somehow both prison and prisoner at once (echoing our music and noise dialectic in what is probably a too neat microcosm of the book's argument). The final couple of minutes retain a version of the loop but stretch it a little. A searching synthesizer gets cut up and off by huge shards of feedback and buzz but ultimately continues on its way until a quiet, still close.

This coda is a gift to me and to other frazzled, shaken listeners. I'm grateful to be returning to life after going to a precipice but not quite falling off, the oblivion of noise never quite taking me. It feels good to look over the edge, know that it's there, but to be able to walk away all the same; nothing like death, or noise, to remind one of life.

Conclusion

As with much of the noise we've looked at in both this and the previous chapter, the pendulum swings in Pharmakon to the 'order', or 'music', parts of the disorder/order, noise/music, dialectics that have run through the book. As we've seen, loops and grids organize much of Chardiet's work – until, of course, they don't, as in those characteristic moments mentioned above where they drop out and the texture fragments, breaks, a semi-chaotic exploration of disorder replacing the former tension of loop and noise. Just as with Prurient, and Burning Star Core, and Lightning Bolt, and Jenny Hval, and many others, repetition – often in the form of percussion or bass loops, but sometimes just in verse forms or other structures built on iteration – is, in this sense, vital to how the music creates tension and, ultimately, meaning and emotion.

Chardiet and others' music thrives in the collision of noisy static, buzzing feedback and so on with containing loops and rhythmic grids. The two elements spark off each other beautifully; as with noise and structure in the previous chapter, Pharmakon reminds us that musical order and noisy disorder are often interdependent and even interpenetrating and/or self-similar. After all, the one, noise disorder, naturally falls into or creates strange new, ordered patterns and shapes in listeners' minds. The other, those repeating musical loops and grids we've been discussing, equally easily shade into disorder and illogic as the loop or grid strains amidst layers of noise. We indeed saw this in my narration of my own listening experience with *Devour*, which toggled between personal ego stability and a more hyper-personalized instability, the noise often proving both reassuring and confusing and the loops and grids feeling both anchoring and constraining. Noise disorder can both destabilize *and* set free, just as musical order can both reassure *and* imprison. Noise and music, as we've been saying, are distinct but similar.

Is it *noise music*, though, if the weighting is skewed this much to order? If, in other words, the sound is looped, repeated, ordered, pulsed and shaped to such a degree? Looked at another way, did I lose myself in the same, quasi-ecstatic way in response to Pharmakon or the later Prurient as I did with Merzbow or Government Alpha or even Linekraft and Immaculate: Grotesque? Even if this music is comparatively more ordered, more 'become', than the noise examined in earlier chapters, it still includes enough 'noise' – enough roving static, enough distortion, enough feedback, enough aperiodic, amelodic, inharmonic sound; enough white noise! – for it to evoke a characteristic sense of 'becoming'. And therefore, to feel in a state of dialectical formation as a language and signifying system. The examples considered in this chapter, most of which lean towards order in their hybrid forms and yet retain a significant amount of (literal or dialectical) noise as they do, therefore deserve the noise music label as much as more straightforwardly noisy and disordered music does. Much of the hybrid noise music examined here and in the previous chapter in this sense moves the dial further towards 'music' in its use of repetition, steady pulse and even hooks or riffs. But it doesn't dial things so far that the noise/music dialectic is resolved, or so that we lose the tension between noise and music that so readily engages – and estranges – listeners. And that so clearly, for me, in the end defines noise music as a style and genre.

Conclusion

Becoming Noise Music has told a story about the first forty to fifty years of noise music; primarily through its sounds and aesthetics but also in terms of social and cultural contexts and musical history. The story has been partial and particular but nevertheless filled with a diverse range of practices and practitioners, sounds and styles, all of which have been organized around a shared, largely transcultural musical tradition and aesthetic approach. Where that story goes from here is unclear. Our later examples, where styles like harsh noise and more hybrid admixtures are embedded within a broader fringe musical ecosystem – the 'global periphery' referenced especially in Chapter 5 – seem to point in a particular direction, where core substyles such as harsh noise remain vital but where the hybrid, enmeshed approach becomes more and more the focus. The apparent ongoing decline in the cultural presence and policy support around traditional 'high art' supports this. This is because our perennial appetite for challenging, exploratory music has to go somewhere, and with access to such highly developed and cultivated traditions as art music are restricted, broader forms of non-traditional, fringe, DIY music – of which noise and related styles are key examples – seem likely to persist and even grow.

We have used the idea of 'becoming' to organize our story. This has been both in terms of the becoming of the genre itself just alluded to and in terms of the stylistic-aesthetic and psychological becoming I read in and out of noise music. Although we've explored an overarching idea of aesthetic becoming based on a dialectical suspension or interpenetration of order and disorder, 'musical' and 'non-musical' sounds, we've seen through the detailed close readings in each chapter that different examples of noise music 'become' in different ways. So, the murky textures and assaultive overwhelm and subjects of power electronics (and anti-music, to a lesser extent) create disturbing, unsettling, often abject experiences, as do the transitional crud and uncertainty of harsh power. The blitzkrieg static and churn, and the inharmonicity, aperiodicism, amelodicism and aformalism of harsh noise are often overwhelming and unsettling; difficult to orientate within and deconstruct. The walls of HNW and the chambers of dark ambient and death industrial are overwhelming and enveloping, forms in which Guesde and Nadrigny's 'immersed noise body' is made most explicit. We found similar in the erotic charge of the bodies, traumas and diseases of the musics in Chapter 8, though often with more dread and abjection than the walls and chambers. Finally, the variously musical or noisy grids, loops and aporia of the hybrid musics of the final two chapters go in several directions: transcending ecstasy in noise rock; overload in harsh noise like Government Alpha; and ballets of order and disorder, music and noise, in examples like Jenny Hval, Prurient, Pharmakon and Lingua Ignota. All this noise is suspended in one or other version of becoming; some examples veer more to disorder and confusion, some to pleasurable immersion and some to order and structure. But meta-stylistic or aesthetic – and, depending on where those musics veer, psychological – becoming is paramount. This is powerful for several reasons, as we've seen. But, given how much of the book is based around becoming I want to step back and consider the point from as wide a perspective as possible in closing.

Part of the appeal of art has always been its ability to present solvable or unsolvable puzzles to audiences, who immerse themselves in those puzzles, often affirming, augmenting or transcending their 'selves' as a result. More broadly, it is powerful because it connects to and perhaps answers a broader, almost existential question; the urge to arrive at some ultimate destination, to grow, to become *more*. Krishnamurti, who we've heard from a couple of times throughout the book, puts it like this:

> Mankind has always tried to become something.... In all religions, it has always been that you must become something. You must reach … becoming more and more and more and more. What is the root of all this? It is the principle of becoming better outwardly, moving to the inside.
>
> (Krishnamurti and Bohm 1980, Chapter 1)

So much of our lives is defined by the expectation of becoming more. This can be productive: it drives our attitudes to the world, it drives the aesthetic philosophies of important figures like Deleuze, and it drives any and all innovations, expansions and changes in human culture and society. We need all these things! But it can also be a prison, a never-ending cycle of desire moving to newer and newer goals and objects as the horizon of what we think will finally make us happy shifts once again; as Krishnamurti also says, 'Becoming is the worst' (Krishnamurti and Bohm 1980, Chapter 2).

Noise, by contrast with other resolution or catharsis-based forms, never becomes, never arrives, always holds resolution in abeyance. Unlike the false promise of other musics, then, noise music perhaps offers us a true picture of our existence, a theatricalized arena in which we can come to know and possibly finally accept our selves in our own suspended becoming. Noise might help us traverse the fantasy that a lot of us use to get through our days, showing us that our desire to become is a trap, an illusion, in that it will never actually be realised or resolved in the way suggested by other forms. Noise music, in this sense, temporarily frees us from the pressure to become. Noise breaks the illusion of life; that it resolves and completes. This can be strangely comforting, the walls of illusion falling away if only for a moment, allowing us to peek into an infinite oblivion. Noise, in this sense, might hold the key to a truly present presence, an awareness of the nothing that awaits and underlies us all. To quote from 'Nihilist Assfucks Manifesto' again, 'There is solace in the energy of destruction' …

Pray to the void, your destiny

Bibliography

Adler, Gerhard and Aniela Jaffé, eds. 1992. *C.G. Jung Letters, Volume 1: 1906–1950*. New Jersey: Princeton University Press.
Ahmed, Sarah. 2014. 'Atmospheric Walls'. https://feministkilljoys.com/2014/09/15/atmospheric-walls/. Accessed 6 January 2022.
Akita, Masami. 2005. *Cruelty Free Life*. Tokyo: Ohta Books.
ArtDemolition. n.d. 'Art Demolition 9 – con-dom'. https://www.youtube.com/watch?v=lSwnOVYFN20&t=141s. Accessed 7 January 2022.
Aspa, Mikko. 2016. 'The Rise of Power Electronics in Finland'. In *Fight Your Own War: Power Electronics and Noise Culture*, edited by Jennifer Wallis, Location 403–551. Manchester: Headpress Books. Kindle.
Aspa, Mikko. 2020. 'General Information/History'. https://grunt-finland.tumblr.com/info. Accessed 24 July 2020.
Attinello, Paul. 2019. 'Negotiating with the Archetype: Essentialism versus Heteronormativity'. *Radical Musicology*, 7. http://www.radical-musicology.org.uk/2019/Attinello.htm.
Baleav, Michelle. 2018. 'Trauma Studies'. In *A Companion to Literary Theory*, 1st edition, edited by D.H. Richter, 360–72. Oxford: Wiley Blackwell.
Baron, Zach. 'Burning Star Core - The Very Heart of the World'. *Pitchfork*, 29 January. https://pitchfork.com/reviews/albums/1195-the-very-heart-of-the-world/.
Barron, Michael. 2015. 'C. Spencer Yeh by Michael Barron'. *Bomb*, 1 May 2015. https://bombmagazine.org/articles/c-spencer-yeh/.
Bataille, Georges. 1984. *Death and Sensuality: A Study of Eroticism and the Taboo*. Salem: N.H. Ayer.
Bataille, Georges. 1986 [1939]. *La pratique de la joie devant la mort*. Paris: Mercure De Fran.
Bath, Tristan. 2015. 'Prurient – Frozen Niagara Falls'. *The Quietus*, 4 June. https://thequietus.com/articles/18006-prurient-frozen-niagara-falls.
Becker, Judith. 2004. *Deep Listeners: Music, Emotion, and Trancing*. Bloomington: Indiana University Press.
Benhaïm, Sarah. 2018. 'Aux marges du bruit. Une étude de la musique noise et du Do it Yourself'. PhD diss., Université PSL. http://www.theses.fr/2018PSLEH140.
Benhaïm, Sarah. 2019. 'DIY et hacking dans la musique noise Une expérimentation bricoleuse du dispositif de jeu'. *Volume !* 2019/2, 16 (1): 17–35.
Bennett, William. 2013. 'Personal Statement'. Accessed 7 January 2022. http://williambennett.blogspot.com/2013/03/statement.html.
Blake, David K. 2012. 'Timbre as Differentiation in Indie Music'. *Music Theory Online*, 18 (2). https://mtosmt.org/issues/mto.12.18.2/mto.12.18.2.blake.html.
Blignaut-van Westrhenen, Nadine and Elzette Fritz. 2014. 'Creative Arts Therapy as Treatment for Child Trauma: An Overview'. *The Arts in Psychotherapy*, 41 (5): 527–34.
Body Carve. 2018. 'Guts in Red Plastic Out Now'. http://gutterbloat.blogspot.com/2018/12/guts-in-red-plastic-out-now.html. Accessed 7 January 2022.

Boroson, Martin, Martin Duffy, and Barbara Egan. 1993. 'Healing and Transformation: The Use of Non-Ordinary States of Consciousness'. *Irish Association of Humanistic and Integrative Psychotherapy* (13). https://iahip.org/page-1076525.

Braidotti, Rosi. 1993. 'Discontinuous Becomings. Deleuze on the Becoming-Woman of Philosophy'. *Journal of the British Society for Phenomenology*, 24 (1): 44–55.

Brassier, Ray. 2007. 'The Genre Is Outdated'. *Multitudes*, 28 (1): 167–73.

Brodsky, Seth. 2018. 'Rihm, Tonality, Psychosis, Modernity'. *Twentieth Century Music*, 15: 147–86.

Brown, Timothy. 2004. 'Subcultures, Pop Music and Politics: Skinheads and "Nazi Rock" in England and Germany'. *Journal of Social History*, 38 (1) (Fall): 157–78.

Busby, Lisa. 2019. 'Pharmakon: Devour'. *Loud and Quiet*, 26 August. https://www.loudandquiet.com/reviews/pharmakon-devour/.

Cagney, Liam. 2021. 'Neo Rhythms: Why Techno Music and the Matrix Are in Perfect Harmony'. *The Guardian*, 23 December. https://www.theguardian.com/film/2021/dec/23/why-techno-and-the-matrix-perfect-harmony-resurrections-lana-wachowski.

Campbell, Joseph. 2008. *The Hero with a Thousand Faces*. California: New World Library.

Candey, Scott. 2016. 'Chronicling US Noise and Power Electronics'. In *Fight Your Own War: Power Electronics and Noise Culture*, edited by Jennifer Wallis, Location 763–1157. Manchester: Headpress Books. Kindle.

Cassidy, Aaron and Aaron Einbond, eds. 2013. *Noise in and as Music*. Huddersfield: University of Huddersfield Press.

Chinen, Nate. 2007. 'Tough Territory in the World of Experimental Music'. *New York Times*, 21 May. https://www.nytimes.com/2007/05/21/arts/music/21nois.html.

Chuter, Jack. 2017. 'Himukalt: Interview'. *ATTN Magazine*, 27 February. https://www.attnmagazine.co.uk/features/11416.

Clare, Stacey. 2022. *The Ethical Stripper: Sex, Work and Labour Rights in the Night-time Economy*. London: Unbound.

Clough, Patricia Ticineto. 2013. 'My Mother's Scream'. In *Sound, Music, Affect: Theorising Sonic Experience*, edited by Marie Thompson and Ian Biddle, 65–72. New York/London: Continuum.

Coggins, Owen. 2018. *Mysticism, Ritual and Religion in Drone Metal*. London: Bloomsbury.

Connelly, Tara, Mike Connelly, and Greh Holger. 2019. 'In Conversation with Moonbeam Terror'. *Noisextra* (podcast), 18 December 2019. https://www.noisextra.com/2019/12/18/in-conversation-with-moonbeam-terror/. Accessed 23 February 2021.

Connelly, Tara, Mike Connelly, and Greh Holger. 2020a. 'Fatal Impact – Satan For Ever'. *Noisextra* (podcast), 8 January 2020. https://www.noisextra.com/2020/01/08/fatal-impact-satan-for-ever/. Accessed 25 July 2020.

Connelly, Tara, Mike Connelly, and Greh Holger. 2020b. 'Emil Beaulieau – Anti-Performance (with guest Chris Sienko)'. *Noisextra* (podcast), 11 March 2020. https://www.noisextra.com/2020/03/11/emil-beaulieau-anti-performance/. Accessed 25 July 2020.

Connelly, Tara, Mike Connelly, and Greh Holger. 2020c. 'Bacillus – *Epidemic*'. *Noisextra* (podcast), 8 April 2020. https://www.noisextra.com/2020/04/08/bacillus-epidemic/. Accessed 23 February 2021.

Connelly, Tara, Mike Connelly, and Greh Holger. 2020d. 'In Conversation with Dominick Fernow, part 1'. *Noisextra* (podcast), 16 September 2020. https://www.noisextra.com/2020/09/16/in-conversation-with-dominick-fernow/. Accessed 7 January 2022.

Connelly, Tara, Mike Connelly, and Greh Holger. 2021. 'Noisextra Discuss the New Blockaders'. *Noisextra* (podcast). 10 March 2021. https://www.noisextra.com/2021/03/10/noisextra-discuss-the-new-blockaders/. Accessed 7 January 2022.

Connelly, Tara, Mike Connelly, and Greh Holger. 2022. 'In Conversation with Dave Phillips'. *Noisextra* (podcast), 16 February 2022. https://www.noisextra.com/2022/02/16/in-conversation-with-dave-phillips-schimpfluch-gruppe-fear-of-god-ohne/. Accessed 15 June 2022.

Cox, Christoph and Daniel Warner. 2006. *Audio Culture*. London: Continuum.

Currin, Grayson and Marc Masters. 2012. 'The Wolf Eyes Issue'. *Pitchfork*, 18 May. https://pitchfork.com/features/the-out-door/8841-the-wolf-eyes-issue/.

Daniel, Drew. 2020. 'In Search of Death, or Why Bother Listening to Atrax Morgue?' *Hyped on Melancholy*. https://www.hypedonmelancholy.com/in-search-of-death.

Davidson, Jack. 2018. 'Review: Guttersnipe – *My Mother the Vent*'. *Noisenotmusic*, 2 November. https://noisenotmusic.com/2018/11/02/review-guttersnipe-my-mother-the-vent-upset-the-rhythm-oct-26/.

Discogs. n.d. (a). 'Merzbow'. https://www.discogs.com/artist/12551-Merzbow. Accessed 7 January 2022.

Discogs. n.d. (b). 'The Rita'. https://www.discogs.com/artist/212478-The-Rita. Accessed 8 January 2022.

Discogs. n.d. (c). 'Vomir'. https://www.discogs.com/artist/672102-Vomir. Accessed 8 January 2022.

Deleuze, Gilles and Felix Guattari. 2013. *A Thousand Plateaus*. London, England: Bloomsbury Academic.

DeNora, Tia. 2000. 'Music as a Technology of Self'. In *Music in Everyday Life*, 46–74. Cambridge: Cambridge University Press.

Downing, Lisa and Robert Gillett. 2011. 'Georges Bataille at the Avant-garde of Queer Theory?: Transgression, Perversion and Death Drive'. *Nottingham French Studies*, 50 (3): 88–102.

Eco, Umberto. 1977. *A Theory of Semiotics*. London: Macmillan.

Ellis, C., Adams, T. E., and Bochner, A. P. 2010. 'Autoethnography: An Overview'. *Forum Qualitative Sozialforschung / Forum: Qualitative Social Research*, 12 (1).

Fabbri, Franco. 1982. 'What Kind of Music?', translated by Iain Chambers. *Popular Music* 2, Theory and Method: 131–43.

Falisi, Frank. 2017. 'Pharmakon – Contact'. *Tiny Mix Tapes*. https://www.tinymixtapes.com/music-review/pharmakon-contact.

Feola, Josh. 2019. 'Shanghai Noise Act Torturing Nurse on 15 Years of Hard Wear and Harsh Noise'. *Radii*. 24 June. https://radiichina.com/torturing-nurse-15-years-harsh-noise/.

Foundation for Contemporary Arts. 2019. 'C. Spenser Yeh'. https://www.foundationforcontemporaryarts.org/recipients/c-spencer-yeh/. Accessed 7 January 2022.

Frisch, Walter. 1982. 'Brahms, Developing Variation, and the Schoenberg Critical Tradition'. *19th-Century Music*, 5 (3) (Spring): 215–32.

Garrido, Sandra, Felicity A. Baker, Jane W. Davidson, Grace Moore, and Steve Wasserman. 2015. 'Music and Trauma: The Relationship between Music, Personality, and Coping Style'. *Frontiers in Psychology*, 6: 977. DOI: https://doi.org/10.3389/fpsyg.2015.00977

Geffen, Sasha. 2019. 'Pharmakon: Devour'. *Pitchfork*, 14 September. https://pitchfork.com/reviews/albums/pharmakon-devour/.

Gendron, Bernard. 2002. *Between Montmarte and the Mudd Club*. London and Chicago: Chicago University Press.
Glass, Seymour. 1995. 'Macronympha – Mean Streets'. *Bananafish*, #10.
Glass, Seymour. 2004. 'Burning Star Core'. *Bananafish*, #18: 19–30.
Goddard, Michael, Benjamin Halligan, and Paul Hegarty, eds. 2012. *Reverberations: The Philosophy, Aesthetics and Politics of Noise*. London: Bloomsbury.
Goddard, Michael, Benjamin Halligan, and Nicola Spelman, eds. 2013. *Resonances: Noise and Contemporary Music*. London: Bloomsbury.
Graham, Stephen. 2016. *Sounds of the Underground*. Ann Arbor: University of Michigan Press.
Graham, Stephen. 2019. 'From Microphone to the Wire: Cultural change in 1970s and 1980s Music Writing'. *Twentieth-Century Music*, 16 (3): 531–55.
Greene, Jayson. 2017. 'Can Music Heal Trauma? Exploring the Therapeutic Powers of Sound'. *Pitchfork*, 20 September. https://pitchfork.com/features/overtones/can-music-heal-trauma-exploring-the-therapeutic-powers-of-sound/.
Grof, Stanislav. 1998. *The Transpersonal Vision*. Sounds True. Audiobook.
Guesde, Catherine and Pauline Nadrigny. 2018. *The Most Beautiful Ugly Sound in the World: À l'écoute de la noise*. Editions MF. Kindle.
Hannah, Andrew. 2016. 'Jenny Hval's Blood Bitch Finds Comfort in Failures'. *Line of Best Fit*, 26 September. https://www.thelineofbestfit.com/reviews/albums/jenny-hvals-blood-bitch-finds-comfort-in-failures.
Harvell, Jess. 2011. 'Prurient – Bermuda Drain'. *Pitchfork*, 21 July. https://pitchfork.com/reviews/albums/15651-bermuda-drain/.
Hegarty, Paul. 2007. *Noise/Music: A History*. London: Continuum.
Hegarty, Paul. 2012. 'A Chronic Condition: Noise and Time'. In *Reverberations: The Philosophy, Aesthetics and Politics of Noise*, edited by Michael Goddard, Benjamin Halligan, and Paul Hegarty, 15–25. London: Continuum.
Hegarty, Paul. 2013. 'Brace and Embrace: Masochism in Noise Performance'. In *Sound, Music, Affect: Theorising Sonic Experience*, edited by Marie Thompson and Ian Biddle, 133–46. New York/London: Continuum.
Hegarty, Paul. 2020. *Annihilating Noise*. London: Bloomsbury.
Heron, Kai. 2020. 'Toying with the Law: Deleuze, Lacan and the Promise of Perversion'. *European Journal of Political Theory*, 0 (0): 1–21.
Hopkins, Kato David. 2020. *Rumors of Noizu: Hijokaidan and the Road to 2nd Damascus*. Tokyo: Public Bath Press.
Hospital Productions. 2019. 'Comfort Knife'. https://hospitalproductions.bandcamp.com/album/comfort-knife. Accessed 23 February 2021.
Hospital Productions. 2020. 'Merzbow/ Noisembryo / Noise Matrix 2xcd Pre Order'. https://hospitalproductions.net/products/merzbow-noisembryo-noise-matrix-2xcd-pre-order. Accessed 8 January 2022.
Hunter, Elaine, Jane Charlton, and Anthony S. David. 2017. 'Depersonalisation and Derealisation: Assessment and Management'. *BMJ: British Medical Journal*, 356 (20 March 2017–26 March 2017). DOI: https://doi.org/10.1136/bmj.j745.
Hutson, William. 2015. 'Sonic Affects: Experimental Electronic Music in Sound Art, Cinema, and Performance'. PhD diss., UCLA. https://escholarship.org/content/qt8dj8t9dc/qt8dj8t9dc.pdf.
Hyperreal. n.d. 'Cultural Terrorist Manifesto'. Accessed 8 January 2021. http://media.hyperreal.org/zines/est/articles/ctm.html.

Iles, Anthony and Mattin, eds. 2009. *Noise and Capitalism*. Arteleku Audiolab. http://www.arteleku.net/audiolab/noise_capitalism.pdf.
Indymedia. 2011. 'Pro-Nazi, Pro-Rape, Pro-Pedo Music in London'. 14 June. https://www.indymedia.org.uk/en/2011/06/480820.html?c=on.
Johnson, D.R. 1987. 'The Role of the Creative Arts Therapies in the Diagnosis and Treatment of Psychological Trauma'. *The Arts in Psychotherapy*, 14 (1): 7–13.
Johnson, Richard. 2020. *Grudge for Life – A Book about Ramleh*. Austin, TX: Fourth Dimension Publishing.
Jupitter-Larsen, G.X. 2020. *Digging through Time*. Salt Lake City: Helicopter.
Jupitter-Larsen, G.X. 2010. 'The Haters'. *As Loud as Possible* (1) (Fall): x–x.
Jung, C.G. 1995. *Memories, Dreams, Reflections*, translated by Richard Winston. London: HarperCollins.
Junky. n.d. 'Torturing Nurse – Facebook Page'. https://www.facebook.com/torturingnurseforever/about/?ref=page_internal#_=_. Accessed 8 January 2022.
JunkyChaos. 2012. 'Torturing Nurse@lu xun park,sh2012.12.22'. https://www.youtube.com/watch?v=LMQYaSwrs7s. Accessed 8 January 2022.
Kärkkäinen, Ester. 2021a. Himuklat Bandcamp page. https://himukalt.bandcamp.com/. Accessed 23 February 2021.
Kärkkäinen, Ester. 2021b. 'Sex Worker II'. https://himukalt.bandcamp.com/album/sex-worker-ii. Accessed 23 February 2021.
Kahn, Douglas. 1999. *Noise Water Meat*. Cambridge, MA: MIT Press.
Kahneman, Daniel. 2011. *Thinking, Fast and Slow*. New York: Farrar, Straus and Giroux.
Kalsched, Donald. 2020. 'Wrestling with Our Angels: Inner and Outer Democracy in America under the Shadow of Donald Trump'. In *Cultural Complexes and the Soul of America*, edited by Tom Singer, 53–88. New York: Routledge.
Keenan, David. 2000. 'David Kennan Picks Ten of the Best Merz Moments from Akita's Back Catalogue'. *The Wire*, August 198: 32–3.
Keenan, David. 2009. 'Ramleh'. *The Wire*, 305 (July): 30–5.
Kennett, Chris. 2008. 'A Tribe Called Chris: Pop Music Analysis as Idioethnomusicology'. *The Open Space Magazine* (10): 8–19.
Kerman, Joseph. 1980. 'How We Got into Analysis, and How to Get Out'. *Critical Inquiry*, 7 (2) (Winter): 311–31.
Krishnamurti, Jiddu. 2010. *Freedom from the Known*, edited by Mary Lutyens. London: Rider. Kindle.
Krishnamurti, Jiddu and David Bohm. 1975 [2016]. 'Truth Actuality and the Limits of Thought'. Krishnamurti Foundation Trust Ltd. Audible Audiobook.
Krishnamurti, Jiddu and David Bohm. 1980 [2016]. 'The Ending of Time'. Krishnamurti Foundation Trust Ltd. Audible Audiobook.
Kubíček, Jiří. 2020. 'From Kerman to Merzbow: Notes on the Metamorphoses of Music Analysis at the Turn of the Millennium'. *New Sound: International Journal of Music*, 55 (1): 23–46.
Lacan, Jacques 1977. *Écrits*. London: Tavistock Publications.
Land, Nick. 1992. *The Thirst for Annihilation: Georges Bataille and Virulent Nihilism*. London: Routledge.
Lawrence, T.E. 2008 [1926]. *Seven Pillars of Wisdom*. London: Random House.
Lee, Kayoung. 2013. 'The Reception of Bach's Music in Korea from 1900 to 1945'. *Bach*, 44 (2): 25–51.
Lena, Jennifer C. 2012. *Banding Together: How Communities Create Genres in Popular Music*. New Jersey: Princeton University Press.

Lena, Jennifer C. and Richard A. Peterson. 2008. 'Classification as Culture: Types and Trajectories of Music Genres'. *American Sociological Review*, 73 (5): 697–718.
Leyva, Roman. 2019. 'Richard Ramirez'. *Harsh Truths* (podcast), 1 October 2019. https://harshtruthspodcast.wordpress.com/2019/10/01/episode-11-richard-ramirez/. Accessed 24 July 2020.
'Like Hunting in the Wild. Interview with Yasutoshi Yoshida aka Government Alpha'. *African Paper* (2012), 28 January. http://africanpaper.com/2012/01/28/like-hunting-in-the-wild-interview-with-yasutoshi-yoshida-aka-government-alpha/.
Lucy Allan, Jennifer. 2017. 'Wolf Eyes on Detroit: "You can walk a Block from our Studio and see a War Zone"'. *The Guardian*, 3 April. https://www.theguardian.com/music/2017/apr/03/wolf-eyes-detroit-undertow-life-is-a-rip-off-john-olson.
Masters, Marc. 2009. 'The Decade in Noise'. *Pitchfork*, 14 September. https://pitchfork.com/features/article/7702-the-decade-in-noise/.
Masters, Marc. 2013. 'Wolf Eyes - No Answer: Lower Floors'. *Pitchfork*, 10 April. https://pitchfork.com/reviews/albums/17968-wolf-eyes-no-answer-lower-floors/.
Masters, Marc. 2017. 'Pharmakon – Devour'. *Pitchfork*, 30 March. https://pitchfork.com/reviews/albums/22974-contact/.
Matthew. 2020. 'So You Wanna Get into … C. Spencer yeh'. *Tusk Is Better Than Rumours*, 9 March. https://tuskisbetter.substack.com/p/so-you-wanna-get-into-c-spencer-yeh.
Mattin. 2006. 'Theses on Noise'. *Mattin*, 25 May. http://www.mattin.org/essays/THESES_ON_NOISE.html.
Mattin. 2012. 'Mattin – Unconstituted Praxis'. https://www.gold.ac.uk/calendar/?id=5056. Accessed 8 January 2022.
McKinlay, Sam. 2010. 'The Politics of HNW'. *As Loud as Possible* (1) (Fall): 14–17.
Meyer, Leonard B. 1989. *Style and Music: Theory, History, and Ideology*. Philadelphia: University of Pennsylvania Press.
Miller, Jeffrey. 2004. *The Transcendent Function: Jung's Model of Psychological Growth through Dialogue with the Unconscious*. New York: SUNY Press.
'The New Blockaders – The Pulp Sessions II'. *Menstrual Recordings* (2019). Accessed 8 January 2022. http://www.menstrualrecordings.org/the_new_blockaders_the_pulp_sessions_II.html. Accessed 1 August 2020.
Novak, David. 2013. *Japanoise: Music at the Edge of Circulation*. Durham, NC: Duke University Press.
Odderskov, Per Najbjerg. 2017. 'Origins of Death … and Subklinik'. *The BRVTALIST*, 10 May. https://thebrvtalist.com/subklinik/2017/10/5/origins-of-deathand-subklinik.
Peterson, Richard and Roger Kern. 1996. 'Changing Highbrow Taste: From Snob to Omnivore'. *American Sociological Review*, 61 (5) (October): 900–7.
Philips, Dave. 2022. 'Dave Philips Bandcamp Page'. https://dave-phillips.bandcamp.com/. Accessed 15 June 2022.
Pinsent, Ed. 2011. 'Burning Star Core'. *Sound Projector*, 19: 88–9.
Potter, Keith. 2000. *Four Musical Minimalists: La Monte Young, Terry Riley, Steve Reich, Philip Glass*. Cambridge: Cambridge University Press.
Potts, Adam. 2015. 'The Internal Death of Japanoise'. *Journal for Cultural Research*, 19 (4): 379–92.
Pouncey, Edwin. 2004. 'Burned Mind'. *The Wire*: 63.
Preira, Matt. 2013. 'Wolf Eyes' John Olson Says Noise Music Is Over: "Completely, 100 Percent"'. *Miami New Times*, 4 December. https://www.miaminewtimes.com/music/wolf-eyes-john-olson-says-noise-music-is-over-completely-100-percent-6483837.

Presley, Katie. 2016. 'Review: Jenny Hval, "Blood Bitch"'. *NPR*, 22 September. https://www.npr.org/2016/09/22/494571616/first-listen-jenny-hval-blood-bitch.
RateYourMusic. n.d. 'Torturing Nurse'. https://rateyourmusic.com/artist/torturing_nurse. Accessed 8 January 2022.
Raymer, Miles. 2015. 'Jenny Hval - Apocalypse, Girl'. *Pitchfork*, 9 June. https://pitchfork.com/reviews/albums/20638-apocalypse-girl/.
Reed, Alexander S. 2013. *Assimilate: A Critical History of Industrial Music*. Oxford: Oxford University Press.
ReverseRecords. 2014. 'Interview with Ulex Xane (STREICHER)'. https://recordsreverse.wordpress.com/2014/04/23/interview-with-ulex-xane-streicher/. Accessed 8 January 2022.
Reynolds, Simon. 1998. *Energy Flash: A Journey Through Rave Music and Dance Culture*. London: Faber and Faber.
Rockefeller, Stuart Alexander. 2011. 'Flow'. *Current Anthropology*, 52 (4): 557–78.
Rutherford-Johnson, Tim. 2017. *Music after the Fall: Modern Composition and Culture since 1989*. Oakland: UC Press.
Ryce, Andrew. 2018. 'Dominick Fernow: Myth of Building Bridges'. *Resident Advisor*, 11 January. https://ra.co/features/3125.
Sande, Kiran. 2012. 'Interview with Dominic Fernow'. *Fact*, 1 April. http://www.factmag.com/2012/04/01/prurient-and-still-wanting/.
Savage, Mark. 2016. 'China's Music Listening Habits Revealed'. *BBC*, 2 February. https://www.bbc.co.uk/news/entertainment-arts-35470270.
Sienko, Chris. 2010. 'Zone Nord'. *As Loud as Possible* (1) (Fall): 18–20.
Stevenson, Richard. 2016. 'Questionable Intent: The Meaning and Message of Power Electronics'. In *Fight Your Own War: Power Electronics and Noise Culture*, edited by Jennifer Wallis, Location 3424–583. Manchester: Headpress Books. Kindle.
Stevenson, Richard. 2020a. 'Linekraft – Subhuman Principle'. *Noise Receptor*, 13 May. https://noisereceptor.wordpress.com/2020/05/13/linekraft-subhuman-principle/.
Stevenson, Richard. 2020b. 'Gnawed – Subterranean Rites'. *Noise Receptor*, 7 August. https://noisereceptor.wordpress.com/2020/08/07/gnawed-%E2%80%8E-subterranean-rites/.
Stevenson, Richard. 2020c. 'Linekraft – Industrialized Criminals History'. *Noise Receptor*, 30 September. https://noisereceptor.wordpress.com/2020/09/30/linekraft-industrialized-criminals-history/.
Stevenson, Richard. 2021. 'Linekraft'. *Noise Receptor*, 9: 4–10.
Stosuy, Brandon. 2006. 'Show No Mercy'. *Pitchfork*, 11 October. https://pitchfork.com/features/show-no-mercy/6455-show-no-mercy/.
Stosuy, Brandon. 2014. 'Pharmakon'. *Pitchfork*, 14 August. https://pitchfork.com/features/update/9481-pharmakon/.
Swains, Howard. 2015. 'Depersonalisation Disorder: The Condition You've Never Heard of That Affects Millions'. *The Guardian*, September 4. https://www.theguardian.com/society/2015/sep/04/depersonalisation-disorder-the-condition-youve-never-heard-of-that-affects-millions.
Tagg, Philip. 2012. *Music's Meanings: A Modern Musicology for Non-Musos*. Larchmont, NY: Mass Media's Scholar's Press.
Taylor, Philip. 1992. 'Con-Dom'. *Hyperreal*. Accessed 7 January 2022. http://media.hyperreal.org/zines/est/intervs/con-dom.html.

Taylor, Philip. 2016. 'The Genesis of Power Electronics in the UK'. In *Fight Your Own War: Power Electronics and Noise Culture*, edited by Jennifer Wallis, Location 193–360. Manchester: Headpress Books. Kindle.

Thacker, Eugene. 2015. *Starry Speculative Corpse*. Winchester: O Books.

Thompson, Marie. 2013. 'Three Screams'. In *Sound, Music, Affect: Theorising Sonic Experience*, edited by Marie Thompson and Ian Biddle, 147–62. New York/London: Continuum.

Thompson, Marie. 2017. *Beyond Unwanted Sound: Noise, Affect and Aesthetic Moralism*. London/New York: Bloomsbury.

Thompson, Marie and Ian Biddle, eds. 2013. *Sound, Music, Affect: Theorising Sonic Experience*. New York/London: Continuum.

Thornton, Sarah. 1996. *Club Cultures. Music, Media and Subcultural Capital*. Hanover/London: University Press of New England.

TorturingNurse. 2020. 'Torturing Nurse@yuyintang,sh2020.12.26(part.2)'. https://www.youtube.com/watch?app=desktop&v=bLILdy14HnI. Accessed 8 January 2022.

Turino, Thomas. 2008. *Music as Social Life: The Politics of Participation*. Chicago, IL: University of Chicago Press.

Ubl, Sam. 2004. 'Wolf Eyes – Burned Mind'. *Pitchfork*, 30 September. https://pitchfork.com/reviews/albums/8730-burned-mind/.

Underwood, Steve. 2010. 'Broken Flag'. *As Loud as Possible* (1) (Fall): 78–113.

Vomir (Romain Perrot). 2017. 'Manifeste du Mur Bruitiste' [Wall Noise Manifestor]. http://www.reclusoir.com/vomir-hnw-manifesto/. Accessed 8 January 2022.

Vuong, Ocean. 2019. *On Earth We're Briefly Gorgeous*. New York: Penguin.

Walker, Ryan. 2020. 'Linekraft: Industrialized Criminals History – Album Review'. *Louder Than War*, 5 July. https://louderthanwar.com/linekraft-industrialized-criminals-history-album-review2/.

Wallis, Jennifer. 2016. 'Introduction'. In *Fight Your Own War: Power Electronics and Noise Culture*, edited by Jennifer Wallis, Location 91–189. Manchester: Headpress Books. Kindle.

Watson, Ben. 2004. *Derek Bailey and the Story of Free Improvisation*. London: Verso.

Watts, Alan. 2017. *Just so*. Sounds True (audiobook).

Weinstein, Deena. 2011. 'The Globalization of Metal'. In *Metal Rules the Globe: Heavy Metal Music around the World*, edited by Jeremy Wallach, Harris M. Berger, and Paul D. Greene, 34–61. Durham: Duke University Press.

Westerhoff, Jan Christoph. 2018. '2. Emptiness and svabhāva'. *Stanford Encyclopedia of Philosophy*, 8 June. https://plato.stanford.edu/entries/nagarjuna/#EmptSvab.

Weingarten, Christopher R. 2006. 'Generally Inhospitable Hospital'. *Village Voice*, 18 July. https://www.villagevoice.com/2006/07/18/generally-inhospitable-hospital/.

Weymar, Mathias, Andreas Keil, and Alfons O. Hamm. 2014. 'Timing the Fearful Brain: Unspecific Hypervigilance and Spatial Attention in early Visual Perception'. *Social Cognitive and Affective Neuroscience*, 9 (5) (May): 723–9.

Willcoma. 2005. 'Lightning Bolt - Hypermagic Mountain'. *Tiny Mix Tapes*. https://www.tinymixtapes.com/music-review/lightning-bolt-hypermagic-mountain.

Williams, Russell. 2014. 'Anti-Musicality: An Interview with Romain Perrot Of VOMIR'. *The Quietus*, 20 August. https://thequietus.com/articles/16050-romain-perrot-vomir-interview-harsh-noise-wall.

Wilson, Scott. 2015. *Stop Making Sense: Music from the Perspective of the Real*. London: Routledge.

Xane, Ulex. 2016. 'Order of the Boot: Interdiction by Force: Streicher and the Growth of Power Electronics in Australia'. In *Fight Your Own War: Power Electronics and Noise Culture*, edited by Jennifer Wallis, Location 594–731. Manchester: Headpress Books. Kindle.

Zimmerman, William. 2017. 'Interview – Legendary Noise Artist Hiroshi Hasegawa (CCCC, Astro)'. *The Noise Beneath the Snow*, 9 August. Accessed 15 June 2022. https://thenoisebeneaththesnow.wordpress.com/2017/08/19/interview-legendary-noise-artist-hiroshi-hasegawa-cccc-astro/.

Zylo, Arvo. 2019. 'Interview Series #9: GX Jupitter-Larsen'. http://nopartofit.blogspot.com/2019/11/interview-series-9-gx-jupitter-larsen.html. Accessed 8 January 2022.

Index

abjection 12, 36, 47–8, 143, 173–4, 195, 215
Ahmed, Sara 149–51
Akita, Masami. *See* Merzbow
Alberich 212
Alchemy Records 90
Anenzephalia 72
Anjila. *See* Moonbeam Terror
anti-music 28–31, 49–67
Aspa, Mikko. *See* Grunt
Atrax Morgue 66, 82, 118, 171, 173–5
    Black Slaughter 171–2
    Paranoia 172–3
auto-ethnography 16

Bacillus 184–5
    'Delta' 185
    Mask It or Casket 186–7
    Serial Infector 185–6
    Variants of Concern 185
Bananafish 12, 107
Bataille, Georges 66, 167–8, 173–5
Benhaïm, Sarah 1, 3, 15
Bennett, William. *See* Whitehouse
Best, Philip 31, 38
Bianchi, Maurizio (MB/M.B.) 26–7, 118
Blackhouse 72–3
    Holy War 74–5
    Pro-Life 73–4
Black Leather Jesus 112–13
    A.N.T.I. 114–15
    Torture Machinist 115–17
Blind Date 147
Body Carve 143–4
Bolus, Andy. *See* Evil Moisture
Borbetomagus 5, 94
Brodsky, Seth 7
Broken Flag 30, 37–8, 42, 77–8
Burning Star Core. *See* C. Spencer Yeh

Campbell, Joseph 101–2
Cassidy, Aaron and Aaron Einbond 2
C.C.C.C. 106
Chaos is the Cosmos 5, 17–18
Chardiet, Margaret. *See* Pharmakon
China, 137–8
Clough, Patricia 169
Cold Meat Industry 82, 160
Con-Dom (Mike Dando) 27, 47
    All in Good Faith 45–6
    The Eighth Pillar 43–5
    politics 41–3, 46
Come Org 78
Connelly, Mike. *See* Noisextra
Connelly, Tara. *See* Noisextra
Corbelli, Marco. *See* Atrax Morgue

Dando, Mike. *See* Con-Dom
dark ambient 149–51, 159–60, 162–5, 221
Davis, Chad. *See* Subklinik
de Sade, Marquis 167–8
Dead Body Love 118
death industrial 72, 75–6, 149–51, 159–65, 221
Deleuze, Gilles 6 (+viii)
digital 126
Dilloway, Aaron. 191–2. *See also* Wolf Eyes
Drumm, Kevin 191–2

Ehrenreich, Barbara 11–12
Evil Moisture 121–3
experimental music 191–4

Fennesz 191–2
Fernow, Dominick 207–8. *See also* Prurient
Fluxus 52
free improv 7–8

Genocide Organ 82–5
Gnawed 162
  Subterranean Rites 162–4
Government Alpha 90, 129, 133–4, 199, 222
  Affective Imagery 134–6
Grant, Deb vii
Grunt 85–7
Guttersnipe 195–6

Hainge, Greg vi–ix, 1, 8, 16
harsh noise wall 149–59, 221
The Haters 29, 49, 53, 58–61
  Death-Defying Sickness 64
  Ordinarily Nowhere 64
  In The Shade of Fire 61–4, 67
  Wind Licked Dirt 53
Hayter, Kristin. *See* Lingua Ignota
Hegarty, Paul vi–ix, 1, 3, 13, 36, 95, 98, 182–3, 215
Hijokaidan 90–1
  King of Noise 94–5
  Noise from Trading Cards 95–7
  Romance 95
Himukalt 125, 175–6
  Sex Worker 176–7
  Sex Worker II, 177–8
Hiroshige, Jojo. *See* Hijokaidan
Hoffmeier, Frederikke. *See* Puce Mary
Hopkins, Kato David 13, 90
Hval, Jenny 201–2
  Apocalypse, Girl 202
  Blood Bitch 202–3

Immaculate: Grotesque 212
Incapacitants 91, 94
industrial music 23, 28–31
Intrinsic Action 75–7

Jaffe, Debbie. *See* Master/Slave Relationship.
Johnson, Richard 24
Jung, Carl 11
Junko 94. *See also* Hijokaidan
Junky. *See* Torturing Nurse
Jupiter-Larsen, GX. *See* The Haters

Kahn, Douglas 1
Kärkkäinen, Ester. *See* Himukalt
Karmanik, Roger. *See* Cold Meat Industry
Keller, Peter. *See* Bacillus
Kites 203
Krishnamurti, Jiddu 65, 102, 222
Kubíček, Jiří vii, 3, 18

Ladd, Brian. *See* Blackhouse.
Lapke, Kris. *See* Alberich
Lena, Jennifer 189
Lessard, Ron 29, 53, 71
Lightning Bolt 194–5
Linekraft 93, 212–13
  Asura 213–14
  Industrialized Criminals History 213–14
Lingua Ignota 203–4

Macronympha 107–8
  Pittsburgh, Pennsylvania 108–12
  politics 108–9
Marhaug, Lasse 191–2, 201
Masonna 94
  Filled with Unquestionable Feelings 105
  Spectrum Ripper 102–6
Master/Slave Relationship 71–2
Masters, Marc 190, 197
Mattin 52, 125, 192
Mauthausen Orchestra 27
McKinlay, Sam. *See* The Rita
Menche, Daniel 191–2
Merzbow 6, 92–3, 126, 129–30
  Animal Magnetism 130–1
  Aodron 133
  Bariken 131
  Cuts Open 133
  Noisembryo 97–102
  Pulse Demon 6
  Thirteen Japanese Birds 131–2
  methodology 14–18
Mikawa, Toshiji 91, 94
Moonbeam Terror 178–9
  Comfort Knife 179–81
Moral Order 212

The Most beautiful ugly sound in the world. À l'écoute de la noise (Nadrigny and Guesde) vii–ix, 2–3, 7, 9, 13, 101, 168, 221
MSBR 85, 90
Mundy, Gary. *See* Ramleh
Murder Corporation 118–20
   Disturbance 119
   New Crimes 119
   Victims 119

The New Blockaders 29, 49–52
Noise Receptor 24, 163, 190
Noise rock vi, 190–3, 194
Noisextra vii, 97, 114, 178, 190
Novak, David 1, 15, 91–2

Okubo, Masahiko. *See* Linekraft
Olson, John. *See* Wolf Eyes
OVMN 153–4
   Womblicker 154–5

personalization, depersonalization, hyperpersonalization 9–10
Petersen, Richard 189–90
Pharmakon 12, 215, 218–19
   Bestial Burden 167, 215
   Contact 215
   Devour 215–18
Philips, Dave 10–11, 170
Pitchfork 190, 198, 202
Potts, Adam 93–4
Premature Ejaculation 184
Prurient 208
   Bermuda Drain 209, 211
   Garden of the Mutilated Paratroopers 211–12
   The History of AIDS 208
   Frozen Niagara Falls 209–11
   Rainbow Mirror 211
Puce Mary 167, 181–2
   The Drought 182–4

radicant 191, 193, 198, 204
Ramirez, Richard 112–13. *See also* Black Leather Jesus

Ramleh 24–5, 37–9, 47
   31/5/1962–1982 40
   The Hand of Glory 40–1
   politics 38–9
Ratkje, Maja 191–2
Reed, S. Alexander ix, 4, 16
Richardson, Grant. *See* Gnawed
Rissiek, Kate. *See* Rusalka
The Rita 109, 150, 155–7
   Thousands of Dead Gods 157–9
Roemer, Joseph/Joe. *See* Macronympha and OVMN
Rusalka 145
   Base Waters 146–7
   The Way of All Flesh 145–6

Sickness 184
Sienko, Chris 4, 120
Slaughter Productions 82, 118, 160, 171, 184
Smell and Quim 121
Solotroff, Mark. *See* Intrinsic Action
Special Interests vi, 24, 190
spectrograms 16–18
Stevenson, Richard 25–6, 28, 84, 93, 163, 213
Streicher 77–9
   Annihilism ('Nihilist Assfucks Manifesto') 79–80, 222
   politics 79
   War Without End 80–1
Subklinik 160
   Cremator 161–2
Sutcliffe Jügend 27
   Changez les Blockeurs 53–7
   History of Nothing 56–7

Thompson, Marie 1, 169
Throbbing Gristle 28–9, 133
Torturing Nurse 136–8
   All Bastards+ 142–3
   Eerie 141–2
   NanaNanaNanaNanaNanaNana 138–41

transcultural 14, 69–70, 82–5, 90–4
transnational 90–4
transpersonal psychology 10–11

Vomir 151–2
    Claustration 152–3
    Proanomie 5

Wallis, Jennifer 24–5
Watson, Ben 7
Whitehouse 6, 26, 29, 73
    Great White Death 33–6

politics 36–7
Total Sex 31–3
Wolf Eyes 197–8
    Burned Mind 198–9
    No Answer: Lower Floors 199–201

Xane, Ülex. *See* Streicher

Yeh, C. Spencer 12, 192–4
Young, La Monte 52, 57

Zone Nord 120–1

www.ingramcontent.com/pod-product-compliance
Lightning Source LLC
Chambersburg PA
CBHW062141300426
44115CB00012BA/2002